MARKET CIVILIZATIONS

Market Civilizations:
Neoliberals East and South

EDITED BY

Quinn Slobodian
Dieter Plehwe

ZONE BOOKS
near futures

ZONE BOOKS
633 Vanderbilt Street, Brooklyn, New York 11218

Printed in the United States of America.
Distributed by Princeton University Press,
Princeton, New Jersey, and Woodstock, United Kingdom

Library of Congress Cataloging-in-Publication Data
Names: Slobodian, Quinn, 1978– , editor. | Plehwe, Dieter, editor.
Title: Market civilizations : neoliberals East and South /
    edited by Quinn Slobodian, Dieter Plehwe.
Description: Brooklyn, New York : Zone Books, [2022] | Series: Near futures |
    Includes bibliographical references and index. | Summary: "The first
    comprehensive study of neoliberalism's proselytizers in Eastern Europe
    and the Global South" — Provided by publisher.
Identifiers: LCCN 2021036702 (print) | LCCN 2021036703 (ebook) |
    ISBN 9781942130673 (hardcover) | ISBN 9781942130680 (ebook)
Subjects: LCSH: Neoliberalism — Developing countries. | Neoliberalism —
    Europe, Eastern. | BISAC: POLITICAL SCIENCE / Political Economy |
    PHILOSOPHY / Political
Classification: LCC HB95 .M358 2022 (print) | LCC HB95 (ebook) |
    DDC 320.5109724 — dc23/eng/20211023
LC record available at https://lccn.loc.gov/2021036702
LC ebook record available at https://lccn.loc.gov/2021036703

CONTENTS

Part Three: Radical Outposts

Beyond the Neoliberal Heartlands

Quinn Slobodian & Dieter Plehwe

Let's begin with three anecdotes.

Anecdote 1: In 1979, the economist Hernando de Soto, born in Peru, but raised and educated in Switzerland, hosted the recent grantee of the Nobel Prize in Economic Science, F. A. Hayek, at a workshop in Lima called "Democracy and the Market Economy." Also invited were a group of people with biographies very different from the patrician Viennese professor's: they were what the Nobel laureate poet Mario Vargas Llosa, also in attendance, called "black market entrepreneurs"—unlicensed street hawkers, called in Spanish *ambulantes*.[1] With the help of a textile magnate, de Soto founded a think tank after the meeting—the Institute for Liberty and Development—that framed its project as empowering the denizens of the rapidly swelling slums of Latin America through deregulation, even though, as a journalist noted, the hawkers in attendance expressed preferences for more robust welfare programs and sympathy for the Marxist candidate in the upcoming elections.[2]

De Soto's message was pitched perfectly to the moment. After the publication of two best-selling books, *The Other Path* and *The Mystery of Capital*, he became the best-known advocate for a new development approach at the United States Agency for International Development and the World Bank in the 1990s based on formalizing property rights.[3] In the preface to the reissue of *The Other Path*, with a post-9/11 subtitle, "The Economic Answer to Terrorism," de Soto shared what he believed was the secret of his success: "You cannot sell expanded markets and capitalism to the poor outside the West using Western paradigms.... You have to represent progress to people using case histories that come from their own social environment."[4]

Another co-organizer of the 1979 meeting was the Guatemalan policy entrepreneur Manuel Ayau. At that time, he was working closely with the military government in his own country to establish a university as a neoliberal outpost. To date, its recipients of honorary doctorates include dozens of members of the flagship organization of the neoliberal intellectual movement, the Mont Pelerin Society, including the former Czech prime minister Václav Klaus, controversial social scientist and think tanker Charles Murray, and Hayek himself.[5] When Milton Friedman, another honorary PhD, showed up for an interview with later white nationalist Peter Brimelow in 1992, he wore a baseball cap reading "Ayau Presidente."[6]

Anecdote 2: In 1997, the economist Parth Shah returned to India after finishing a doctorate at Auburn University in Alabama, where he worked with the Ludwig von Mises Institute, the think tank established in 1982 as a more radical alternative to the Cato Institute and the Heritage Foundation. Reflecting on his efforts at "awakening a slumbering elephant," as Shah called his project building a neoliberal think tank on the subcontinent, he said, "It was clear to me that in India the message of liberty would need to be framed differently to how it is framed in the USA—within the historical and cultural context of India."[7] Like de Soto, he worked with street hawkers, declaring that it was "the regulatory burden of government that is the real cause of the general plight of the working poor."[8] He denounced the "license-permit-quota raj," implying that the era of empire had not ended after 1947, when the British departed—it had simply transformed into postcolonial statism. Shah's use of the term harked back to a phrase coined in the 1950s by C. Rajagopalachari, whose chief economic adviser, B. R. Shenoy, was a friend of Friedman and Hayek and who sought to combine traditional and free-market principles with an argument that the *dharma* of traditional Hindu society entailed a "minimum state" and that caste had "advantages of comparative cost and maximum production from a given social complex of human aptitudes and talent."[9]

Presenting alongside Shah at a Mont Pelerin Society meeting in Bali in 1999, the UCLA economist Deepak Lal similarly turned to tradition when he asked: "Is liberty a Western concept?" and answered: No.[10] In 2005, he followed up one book praising empires by publishing another titled *The Hindu Equilibrium*.[11] He developed a theory that the West was degenerating in two ways. First, the "sexual and cultural revolutions" of the 1960s were returning Westerners to the mores of "their hunter-gatherer ancestors." Second, what remained of Christian monotheism had undergone a "secular mutation" into "ecofundamentalism."[12] Meanwhile, he said, "traditional cosmological beliefs" in China and India had endured. "They are modernizing without Westernizing," he wrote.[13] As the "social cement" of the West came unstuck, the East was poised to take its place. As the chapters below show, many free-market intellectuals in Japan and China agreed.

Anecdote 3: In the streets of Brazil in 2015, amid the protests against the president, Dilma Rousseff, a sign appeared reading: "Less Marx, More Mises."[14] Mises Brazil, founded in 2008 by the investment banker Helio Beltrão as a franchise of the Alabama original, played a role in the mobilization.[15] In 2016, the businessman and policy entrepreneur Winston Ling put a politician named Jair Bolsonaro in touch with the University of Chicago–trained economist Paulo Guedes, who would become the future president's minister of the economy.[16] In July 2018, Bolsonaro posed smiling with copies of Mises's books and ushered an economic freedom clause into the constitution.[17] One of Bolsonaro's sons lists the study of Austrian economics at the Mises Institute as "post-graduate study" on his résumé.[18]

The Brazilian front against leftism was hardly seamless. "In order to fight the common enemy," Ling described how he "worked hard to maintain unity between the different factions: conservative Christians, anarcho-capitalists, classical liberals, objectivists, etc."[19] The partners included followers of Olavo de Carvalho, the mystic conspiracist living in rural Virginia, where he spoke to his one million YouTube subscribers about the plots of the globalists. Beltrão boasts that he and Carvalho were among the first to warn of the supposed evils of "cultural Marxism."[20] Brazil's "ultraliberalism," as one chapter in this book calls it, has scrambled the conventional political compass in a way repeated around the world in the early 2020s. Egged on by right-wing media, grassroots antagonism has turned against the supposedly interlocked schemes of global elites to push through climate policy, tax expansion, and capitalist reform at the expense of individual freedoms.

How do these diverse stories of neoliberalism "going local" fit into the histories of neoliberalism we have so far?[21] Not particularly well. As Bob Jessop observed, existing histories tend to work from the "heartlands of neoliberalism" outward and often imply a "core-periphery" relationship with ideas developed in the Global North and West traveling to the Global East and South.[22] At other times, the narrative of neoliberalism can swamp geographical distinctions. In 1995, Stephen Gill wrote an influential article arguing that the world had entered a new historical epoch that he called "market civilization" in which "the structure and language of social relations is now more conditioned by the long-term commodity logic of capital."[23] Gill argued that this universal civilization—what Michael Hardt and Antonio Negri would call a few years later "Empire"—is both anchored and propelled not only by private market actors, but by a set of international actors, including the post–World War II Bretton Woods institutions the World Bank and the International Monetary Fund, created to help rebuild the shattered postwar economy and to promote international economic cooperation, and newly created entities such as the World Trade Organization, the European Union, and the North American Free Trade Agreement, NAFTA.[24] Gill noted that the extension of commodification entailed social disintegration, exclusion, and hierarchy, but that there was also an implication of homogenization—a shared human fate as the planet entered a new paradigm.

The first round of scholarship on neoliberalism in the 1990s relied heavily on a language of "market fundamentalism," with its implication of a single world faith extending its tentacles globally and smothering particularity. In the 2000s, a new wave of scholarship emerged to introduce individuals, names, and faces into historical narratives of "neoliberalization," which in previous accounts had often unfolded in the passive tense or with only the unitary actor of "capital."[25] A new body of work on the neoliberal intellectual movement around the Mont Pelerin Society allowed for closer study of the relationship between ideas, interests, and institutions.[26]

Yet even as this literature brought neoliberalism down to earth, it tended to reproduce a perspective that saw the world from Europe and the United States outward. With the notable exception of Augusto Pinochet's Chile, long seen as a laboratory of neoliberalism, the new literature followed a story of diffusion as ideas migrated outward.[27] Criticizing this tendency in 2014, Raewyn Connell and Nour Dados asked: "Where in the world does neoliberalism come from?" They suggested that the story line of neoliberalism offered by scholars was broadly the same, in both the personalized Mont Pelerin Society version and the more abstract political economy account: "A system of ideas generated in the global North gains political influence in the North and is then imposed on the global South."[28] Neoliberalism, they countered, "is not a projection of Northern ideology or policy, but a reweaving of worldwide economic and social relationships."[29]

It is correct to insist, as Jamie Peck has, that "there is no ground-zero location—at Mont Pelerin, in the White House, or in the Chilean Treasury—from which to evaluate all subsequent 'versions' of neoliberalism. There are only unruly historical geographies of an evolving, interconnected project."[30] Yet writing histories that live up to this standard is easier said than done. Since Connell and Dados's article, more scholars have written situated histories of neoliberalism, especially of Latin America and Eastern Europe.[31] But to write persuasively about the reception of the transnational spread of neoliberal ideas, or the domestic production of ideas independently, requires deep knowledge of local histories, including competency in the language, fluency with the inevitably vast relevant literatures, and enough of an awareness of each place's tangled political and economic pasts to locate neoliberal ideology within them.

"One of the remarkable features of neoliberalism is its ubiquity," Russell Prince writes, but "if neoliberalism is to remain a worthwhile analytical concept, then we need to square claims about its 'everywhereness' with its apparent spatial diversity."[32] This is the goal of the collection of chapters in these pages. We find it helpful to think not of market civilization in the singular, but in the plural. In many cases, this is because neoliberal thinkers themselves contested the idea of a single universal *homo economicus* and advocated for hybrid versions of market rationality and tradition or liberalism and conservatism, in addition to genuinely novel ideas and concepts.

The first section of the book, titled "Greater Cultures," includes three examples of such recombinations of neoliberal thought: case studies of Japan, India, and Turkey. While recent work has emphasized how ideas of racial hierarchy in neoliberal thought projected pejorative traits onto nonwhite races, these chapters show the inverse: a claim of superiority for non-European cultural traditions. The neoliberal intellectuals considered here saw nation and race as assets resistant to emulation and able to be leveraged in market competition, varieties of what one of us has called elsewhere "Volk capital."[33]

Reto Hofmann sheds light on two of the most influential Japanese neoliberals, Nishiyama Chiaki and Kiuchi Nobutane.[34] Nishiyama, a student of Hayek in Chicago, would be the first Japanese president of the Mont Pelerin Society. Focusing on Hayek's philosophical ideas of the purposeless character of free society, Nishiyama emphasized Japan's traditional negation of reason and limitations of intellect. Hofmann explains how Japanese neoliberals such as Kiuchi negotiated the tension between cultural identity and economic globalization. Refuting the calls of American neoliberals for global convergence, Japanese neoliberals advanced their own kind of cultural supremacy, prefiguring contemporary varieties of neonationalism and socially conservative culturalism.

Through his example of India, Aditya Balasubramanian argues that studies of the non-Western world need to tackle the intersection of neoliberal ideology with other ideologies to explain how it becomes palatable in local contexts. While postindependence India was known as a stronghold of socialism, only to change rapidly since the 1990s, Balasubramanian shows there is a secret prehistory to that decade's reforms by examining the figure of B. R. Shenoy, mentioned above. Developing a close friendship with the leading neoliberal development economist Peter Bauer in the UK, Shenoy became a key informant on problems of Indian planning in international conferences. At home, he drafted the "Basic Economic Policy" document, a clear market agenda for the Swatantra Party, founded in 1959, which became the largest opposition to Nehru's Indian National Congress. Swatantra and Shenoy combined reactionary social conservatism and market-liberal ideas, prefiguring the concoction that some hoped would define Narendra Modi's mode of governance in the 2010s.

Turkey has been another fertile site of neoliberal culturalism in recent years. Esra Nartok shows how Turkish intellectuals employed religion in a deliberate effort of building support for a project of economic transformation. The creation and internalization of a neoliberal Islamic civilization was the task set by a small think tank, the Association for Liberal Thinking (ALT). Founded in 1992, ALT gained importance advising Turkey's conservative Justice and Development Party in the 2000s. ALT key figures Atilla Yayla and Mustafa Erdoğan—not to be confused with the Turkish president, Recep Tayyip Erdoğan—developed a dedicated neoliberal Islamic perspective that was juxtaposed both with Turkey's secular tradition of modernization and with competing state-driven Islamic petrostate projects fueled by Saudi Arabia, for example. Their project contributed both to the reconciliation of Turkish-Islamic identities and to the international conversation on the need to reconcile neoliberalism and religion. Yayla's "magic formula" of Muslim democracy in Turkey so far plays a minor role compared with the political Islam of the Justice Party under President Erdoğan, but it offers a repertoire of thought and action from which business elites and opposition forces continue to draw.

The goal of global intellectual history is to study not only how concepts diffuse from point to point, but also how they emerge autochthonously, generated from formally similar structural conditions and conjunctures.[35] The second section of this book, titled "Other Paths," in a nod to Hernando de Soto's famous book, shows examples of this.

In the case of Russia, radical reforms such as price liberalization and privatization under President Boris Yeltsin are frequently attributed to foreign influence, particularly the American-dominated World Bank and International Monetary Fund. Tobias Rupprecht revises this story line through a history of domestic neoliberalism composed of different groups of dissidents and economists in Moscow, Leningrad, and Novosibirsk. These groups formed first with limited access to Western literature. They encountered the neoliberal classics of Hayek and Friedman only later and read them into and alongside local concerns and experiences. Local concerns such as Viktor Sokirko's worries about government benevolence, Yegor Gaidar's concern with bureaucratic resistance, and Vasily Selyunin's negative view of the role of the masses at the same time did resemble concerns voiced by ordoliberals, public-choice pundits, and José Ortega y Gasset, the Spanish participant at the famous birthplace of the neoliberal movement, the Walter Lippmann Colloquium in 1938. But the Russian strain still needs to be recognized as a specific local variety of neoliberalism that only later was connected to global neoliberal debates and groups. The irony and tragedy of Russian neoliberal efforts might primarily be considered in their reliance on certain wings of the *nomenklatura* and the authoritarian state to push reforms through in the transition, only to see market-liberal approaches and themselves dropped by the new regime of oligarchic rule advancing under President Putin.

The origins of neoliberal reforms in China are even more hotly debated than in Russia. Isabella Weber complicates the narrative that portrays the World Bank missions of the 1980s as the key drama in the liberalization of the Chinese economy.[36] She focuses instead on the role played by a selective invocation of West Germany's so-called "economic miracle" (*Wirtschaftswunder*) under the postwar economics minister and chancellor Ludwig Erhard in the discussion about how to combine public ownership and market economy in China's transition. High-ranking delegations from China visited Germany in the late 1970s to inquire about postwar economic policy. During Helmut Schmidt's tenure as head of a German government composed of Social Democrats and the liberal Free Democratic Party, several prominent ordoliberals were dispatched from Germany to discuss a wide range of issues related to the opening of the Chinese economy. Weber uses the backdrop of the German case study to show how the ordoliberal interlocutors carefully selected information and what they left out, for example, the hostile reactions to price liberalization by German trade unions exploding into a general strike in the late 1940s. Chinese realities were measured against German myths.

As with Russia and China, the full-fledged arrival of neoliberalism in South Africa is often seen as a phenomenon of the post–Cold War decade of the 1990s. Antina von Schnitzler challenges this interpretation. According to the dominant narrative, neoliberal ideas were imported from the outside, relying on links created between the global financial institutions and South Africa's economic authorities. Contrary to such an explanation, the author shows how neoliberal ideas had already been a part of the counterinsurgency deliberations following the Soweto uprising in 1976. South African intellectuals developed a domestic brand of neoliberal ideas in an effort to tackle urban problems resulting from the racial concepts of separate development (the segregation of Black homesteads and the exploitation of growing numbers of Black laborers in urban centers on a "temporary" basis). Schnitzler shows how these ideas sought to depoliticize and nominally deracialize Black urban dwelling, drawing on neoliberal notions of market subjects and technical expertise. Racist theories of innate difference were transformed into ideas of the sameness of market subjects, and supposedly eternal concepts of white rule and segregation were discarded in favor of an allegedly transitory exclusion of subjects not yet ready to be fully groomed for the culture of market citizenship. By way of equating apartheid and state planning, ideas of economic freedom appeared to provide legitimacy for a new carrot-and-stick strategy: liberal carrots for those who were willing to submit to the vagaries of economic freedom, and the illiberal stick for the others.

While South Africa raises the issue of neoliberalism in light of labor and land, Australia brings to light the question of what has been called the "fossil capital" of natural resources.[37] Jeremy Walker takes us back to the origins of "fossil neoliberalism" in the 1930s, when links between the Australian economist Torleiv Hytten and the Australian members of the heavily thermoindustrial International Chamber of Commerce were developed. Hytten was invited to the first meeting of the Mont Pelerin Society and became the first Australian member in 1951. He worked closely with the first neoliberal Australian think tank, the Institute of Public Affairs, founded in 1943 to oppose the Labor Party agenda. Another global dimension is uncovered in the history of the Murdoch media empire, which also originated in Australia. Although not in agreement with neoliberal agendas from the beginning, Murdoch developed a close alliance with fossil capital in the 1970s to oppose the resource-nationalist agenda of the short-lived Whitlam Labor government. The extraordinary mobilization of resources to defeat strong ecological and nationalization agendas in the primary sector explains the number of neoliberal business activists, think tanks, and dedicated commer-·cial consultancies organized from the 1970s onward in Australia. A self-described "greenhouse mafia" relies on old think tanks such as the Institute of Public Affairs and on new ones, such as the somewhat more conciliatory Centre for Independent Studies, which emphasizes economic approaches to all policy questions, rather than denying climate change. Walker points to the dramatic increase of Australian vulnerability in the face of climate change–related fires and droughts, which at some point in the future may be considered indicators of the Pyrrhic victories won by fossil neoliberalism in Australia since the 1970s.

As the postcommunist reforms in Eastern Europe and libertarian adventures in "charter cities" and "special economic zones" in the Global South make clear, neoliberalism is often most radical when it travels farthest from the "heartland" of the industrialized North and West.[38] The last section of this book, "Radical Outposts," examines examples of such places. It begins with Jimmy Casas Klausen and Paulo Chamon's chapter on Brazil, which is currently at the bleeding edge of evolutions of neoliberal thought. It is likely that nowhere else has the neoliberal and libertarian intellectual movement enjoyed as much support from young people organized in social-movement fashion and splintered in factions, each more radical than the next, than in Latin America's largest country. The authors show how the ecosystem of new neoliberal movements emerged and grew amid the crisis of Brazil's left-wing party Partido Trabalhadores. Brazilian ultraliberals of the local Ludwig von Mises Institute led by Helio Beltrão managed to exploit popular dissatisfaction with the perceived "progressive neoliberalism" of former presidents Luiz Inácio Lula da Silva and Dilma Rousseff. Brazil may have been the first case in which neoliberalism was advanced via social media, relying on the now defunct social-networking site Orkut in the formative decade of the 2010s and now spreading via the widely used Mises Institute website. Aided by new think tanks such as the Instituto Millenium, founded in 2005, sprawling networks of college students and young professionals imbibed a strong antiestablishment ethos that cast them as a minoritarian opposition in civil society. The chapter tracks and traces the splintering of the movement, which paradoxically did not lead to its erosion, but helped to further dynamize and radicalize neoliberal circles in the country under the wild coalitions supporting the government of Jair Bolsonaro.

The mixture of authoritarianism and liberal market principles was pioneered in Latin America in Chile. A less well-known example is Guatemala, which enjoyed a sunny reputation among neoliberals, even during its decades of military dictatorship.[39] While Manuel Ayau, the first president of the Mont Pelerin Society from Latin America (1978–1980), developed his activities dedicated to elite education because he did not trust repression and violence, the chapter shows how close he and his business allies were to authoritarian regimes at different times. In conjunction with partners such as the Foundation for Economic Education in the United States and partners in Spain and Germany, Guatemalan neoliberals went beyond traditional capacity building through think tanks and set up a major elite university in the country: Francisco Marroquín University. Fischer explains how the local confrontation with liberation theory and progressive movements led to the specific focus on education in economics, law, and theology from the single-minded neoliberal perspective of the Austrian school. Faculty are "free" to teach only neoliberal ideas, and each and every student has to take special classes with core readings from Hayek, Mises, and Murray Rothbard. Beyond academic teaching, the university has served as a human development department for a number of policy think tanks founded to direct Guatemala's neoliberal transformation: privatizing state-owned enterprises in the 1990s, blocking tax reforms in the 2000s, and merging social-conservative and neoliberal values in family politics are important causes of Marroquín spin-off ventures in Guatemalan politics.

Although Ayau was somewhat disappointed in the overall accomplishments of his university, the efforts of his circles set an example of institution building that served as a beacon for similar neoliberal movements and has been copied in several countries. One such case is in the tiny Balkan nation of Montenegro. If asked to list ambitious and comprehensive attempts to turn a socialist country into a neoliberal model state, few would think of the microstate born in the breakup of former Yugoslavia. Mila Jonjić and Nenad Pantelić demonstrate the legitimacy of Montenegro's claim to such a title and showcase the contradictions between neoliberal ideals and the resulting outcomes. The authors trace the diligent work of a group of dedicated neoliberals around Veselin Vukotić, a former government official and university professor. Supported by Yugoslavian intellectuals in exile in the United States, Vukotić started an impressive mission of neoliberal institution building as early as the late 1980s. His project University Tribune was followed in 1992 by a program of postgraduate studies in "Entrepreneurial Economy" at the University of Montenegro that attracted support from several neoliberal scholars abroad, including Leonard P. Liggio of the Atlas Economic Research Foundation (now the Atlas Network) and Steve Pejovich of Texas A&M. A think tank named the Institute for Entrepreneurship and Economic Development followed in 1993, as did the Institute for Strategic Studies and Prognoses set up in 1997–1998, which was instrumental in laying out the major reform agendas of privatization and monetarism. Neoliberal intellectuals in Montenegro were close to the majority of Montenegro's main governing party for decades, the formerly socialist party Democratic Party of Socialists (DPS), and held a solid position in the courtyard of power. The University Tribune neoliberals included a strong cohort of Mont Pelerin Society members who helped Vukotić stage his final prestige project: the University of Donja Gorica. This small private university opened its doors in 2007, built around a faculty of international economics and a faculty of law. Modeled to a certain extent on Francisco Marroquín University in Guatemala, the university faculty includes Mont Pelerin staff members, as well as local corporate and political elites.

The book ends with a country that has merely half the population of Montenegro, but has an outsized role in narratives of hyperglobalization: Iceland, a fishing outpost that became a deregulated financial wonderland. As the global financial crisis unfolded in 2008, the island nation looked like one of its most morbid symptoms. Iceland's financial system collapsed. Journalists and filmmakers put the blame on U.S. economists and venal consultants from abroad. However, missing in that account are some of the key domestic figures involved in redirecting the development of Icelandic capitalism in support of globalized finance. Pride of place in Lars Mjøset's chapter on Icelandic neoliberalism is reserved for Hannes Hólmsteinn Gissurarson, a member of the Mont Pelerin Society since 1984. Gissurarson founded a group of young liberals in the youth association of Iceland's liberal-conservative party, the Independence Party. Named after their journal *Eimreiðin* (Locomotive), published from 1972 to 1975, the group included three later prime ministers: Þorsteinn Pálsson, David Oddsson, and Geir H. Haarde. Another member, Kjartan Gunnarsson, was the party secretary of the Independence Party for twenty-six years (1980–2006). Gissurarson also founded the Jón Þorláksson Institute in 1983, which was closed down in 1990 because the University of Iceland became a venue for meetings, including the 2005 Mont Pelerin Society meeting in Iceland. Gissurarson ran the Libertarian Alliance in Iceland from 1979 to 1989, which arranged the visits by the neoliberal founding fathers in Iceland (Hayek in 1980, James M. Buchanan in 1982, Friedman in 1984). Apart from his writing on neoliberal political philosophy, Gissurarson worked hard to demonize left-wing Icelandic writers such as Halldor Laxness and the alleged Communist influence on the history of the country.

Yet there is a twist in Mjøset's story as the country has moved in some ways closer to the Scandinavian model of welfare-state capitalism. As Mjøset shows, a national pact between labor, capital, and the state to end the cycle of devaluation and inflation existed prior to the neoliberal Oddsson government, major institutions that were developed to protect labor and natural resources (fish stocks) became subject to only moderate neoliberal reforms, and the financial collapse resulted from factors that were hardly influenced by self-declared neoliberal revolutionaries. Ironically, many of the efforts of the Independence

Party leadership to constrain new financial firms were unsuccessful and demonstrate the lack of regulatory state capacity once market forces had been unleashed. The role of the *Eimreiðin* group of Icelandic neoliberals in conjunction with Iceland's fisheries stakeholders and factions of commercial, financial, and media interests thus provides important lessons about the vagaries of neoliberal reformism in general and about the contradictions of neoliberal ideology in theory and neoliberal interest group politics in practice. All the turmoil did not destroy Icelandic neoliberalism, however. Oddsson was called to run the major newspaper *Morgunblaðið* to give the fishermen a voice in opposition to the EU. Lacking a university base, Gissurarson founded the Researach Centre for Innovation and Economic Growth in 2012 to continue his quest for neoliberal revolution.

Since 2016, there has been another round of obituaries for neoliberalism. We have written elsewhere of the "nine lives of neoliberalism," which seem to translate into new variants of market civilization emerging after every systemic crisis.[40] The COVID-19 epidemic of 2020 has generated yet more pronouncements of neoliberalism's demise, including from former cheerleaders of competition such as the World Economic Forum's Klaus Schwab.[41] Yet even public health measures designed to protect populations during the pandemic have produced backlash movements that meld grassroots anger at corporate enrichment with the antisocialism of the right-wing media.[42] The cosmic anarcho-capitalism of Brazil's "ultraliberalism" may be a grim foreshadowing of the hybrids of neoliberal thought that a media landscape, which is simultaneously hypernetworked and ever more siloed, will produce as it absorbs future inevitable Anthropocenic shocks.

1. Mario Vargas Llosa, "In Defense of the Black Market," *New York Times*, February 22, 1987.

2. Catherine M. Conagahan and James Malloy, *Unsettling Statecraft: Democracy and Neoliberalism in the Central Andes* (Pittsburgh: University of Pittsburgh Press, 1995), p. 85; Enrique Zileri Gibson, "Von Hayek and Lima's Vendors," *New York Times*, December 5, 1979, p. 31.

3. Timothy Mitchell, "How Neoliberalism Makes Its World: The Urban Property Rights Project in Peru," in Philip Mirowski and Dieter Plehwe, eds., *The Road from Mont Pèlerin: The Making of the Neoliberal Thought Collective* (Cambridge, MA: Harvard University Press, 2009), pp. 386–90.

4. Hernando de Soto, *The Other Path: The Economic Answer to Terrorism* (New York: Basic Books, 2002), p. xxxviii.

5. See the complete list at Universidad Francisco Marroquín, "Honorary Doctoral Degrees," https://www.ufm.edu/honorary-doctoral-degrees.

6. Peter Brimelow, "An Interview with Milton Friedman," *Forbes*, August 17, 1992, https://vdare.com/articles/an-interview-with-milton-friedman -forbes-august-17-1992.

7. Parth Shah, "Awakening a Slumbering Elephant," in Colleen Dyble, ed., *Freedom Champions: Stories from the Front Lines in the War of Ideas. 30 Case Studies by Intellectual Entrepreneurs Who Champion the Cause of Freedom* (Washington, DC: Atlas Economic Research Foundation, 2011), p. 110, https:// www.atlasnetwork.org/assets/uploads/misc/FreedomChampions.pdf.

8. Priyanka Jain, "Neoliberalizing the Streets of Urban India: Engagements of a Free Market Think Tank in the Politics of Street Hawking," PhD diss., University of Kentucky, 2013; Parth Shah and Naveen Mandava, *Law, Liberty and Livelihood: Making A Living On The Street* (New Delhi: Academic Foundation, 2005), p. 20.

9. Aditya Balasubramanian, "Contesting 'Permit-and-Licence *Raj*': Economic Conservatism and the Idea of Democracy in 1950s India," *Past and Present* 251.1 (2021), pp. 215 and 207.

10. Hoover Institution, Mont Pèlerin Society Papers, box 130, "Bali Meeting, 8–11 Jul 1999" folder.

11. Deepak Lal, *In Praise of Empires: Globalization and Order* (New York: Palgrave Macmillan, 2004); Lal, *The Hindu Equilibrium: India c. 1500 B.C.– 2000 A.D.* (Oxford: Oxford University Press, 2005).

12. Deepak Lal, "Towards a New Paganism: The Family, the West and the Rest," *Biblioteca della libertà*, no. 197 (2010), p. 7.

13. Ibid., p. 3.

14. Taylor Barnes, "Greasing the Path to Dilma's Downfall," *Foreign Policy*, March 16, 2015.

15. Jay Baykal, "Interview with Helio Beltrão," October 9, 2012, The Property and Freedom Society, http://propertyandfreedom.org/2012/10/interview -with-helio-beltrao-pfs-2012.

16. Jim Epstein, "Libertarians Forged an Alliance with Brazilian President Jair Bolsonaro. Was It a Deal with the Devil?," *Reason*, July 2019.

17. Rafael Ribeiro, "Brazil Pivots toward Economic Freedom," *Foundation for Economic Education*, May 10, 2019.

18. "Sobre Mim," https://web.archive.org/web/20191117072342/https:// www.eduardobolsonarosp.com.br/sobre-mim.

19. Alejandro Chafuen, "The New Brazil: Philosophical Divisions Should Not Hinder Bolsonaro's Free Society Agenda," *Forbes*, February 19, 2019, https://www.forbes.com/sites/alejandrochafuen/2019/02/19/the -new-brazil-philosophical-divisions-should-not-hinder-bolsonaros-agenda /?sh=66bd7f2e47ec.

20. João Filho and Alexandre Andrada, "Até anarcocapitalistas ganham espaço no governo Bolsonaro," *The Intercept Brasil*, May 5, 2019, https:// theintercept.com/2019/05/05/anarcocapitalismo-bolsonaro-folha-ancaps.

21. Cornel Ban, *Ruling Ideas: How Global Neoliberalism Goes Local* (Oxford: Oxford University Press, 2016).

22. Bob Jessop, "The Heartlands of Neoliberalism and the Rise of the Austerity State," in Simon Springer, Kean Birch, and Julie MacLeavy, eds., *The Handbook of Neoliberalism* (New York: Routledge, 2016), p. 411.

23. Stephen Gill, "Globalisation, Market Civilisation, and Disciplinary Neoliberalism," *Millennium: Journal of International Studies* 24.3 (1995), p. 399.

24. Ibid., 412.

25. Gérard Duménil and Dominique Lévy, *Capital Resurgent: Roots of the Neoliberal Revolution* (Cambridge, MA: Harvard University Press, 2004).

26. For early examples, see Bernhard Walpen, *Die offenen Feinde und ihre Gesellschaft: Eine hegemonietheoretische Studie zur Mont Pèlerin Society* (Hamburg: VSA, 2004); Dieter Plehwe, Bernhard Walpen, and Gisela Neunhöffer, eds., *Neoliberal Hegemony: A Global Critique* (London: Routledge, 2006); Mirowski and Plehwe, eds., *The Road from Mont Pèlerin*; Jamie Peck, *Constructions of Neoliberal Reason* (Oxford, UK: Oxford University Press, 2010); Daniel Stedman Jones, *Masters of the Universe: Hayek, Friedman, and the Birth of Neoliberal Politics* (Princeton: Princeton University Press, 2012); Serge Audier, *Néolibéralisme(s)* (Paris: Éditions Grasset & Fasquelle, 2012); Michel Foucault, *The Birth of Biopolitics: Lectures at the Collège de France, 1978–79* (New York: Palgrave Macmillan, 2008).

27. Juan Gabriel Valdés, *Pinochet's Economists: The Chicago School in Chile* (New York: Cambridge University Press, 1995).

28. Raewyn Connell and Nour Dados, "Where in the World Does Neoliberalism Come From?," *Theory and Society* 43.2 (2014), p. 119.

29. Ibid., 124.

30. Peck, *Constructions of Neoliberal Reason*, p. 8.

31. Maria Margarita Fajardo, "The Latin American Experience with Development: Social Sciences, Economic Policies, and the Making of a Global Order, 1944–1971," PhD diss., Princeton University, 2015; Amy C. Offner, *Sorting Out the Mixed Economy: The Rise and Fall of Welfare and Developmental States in the Americas* (Princeton: Princeton University Press, 2019); Johanna Bockman, "Democratic Socialism in Chile and Peru: Revisiting the 'Chicago Boys' as the Origin of Neoliberalism," *Comparative Studies in Society and History* 61.3 (2019); Elizabeth Humphrys, *How Labour Built Neoliberalism: Australia's Accord, the Labour Movement and the Neoliberal Project* (Leiden: Brill, 2019); Philipp Ther, *Europe since 1989: A History* (Princeton: Princeton University Press, 2016).

32. Russell Prince, "Neoliberalism Everywhere: Mobile Neoliberal Policy," in *The Handbook of Neoliberalism*, p. 331.

33. See Quinn Slobodian, "Neoliberalism's Populist Bastards," *Public Seminar*, February 15, 2018, https://publicseminar.org/2018/02/neoliberalisms

-populist-bastards. On neoliberalism and race, see Lars Cornelissen, "Neoliberalism and the Racialized Critique of Democracy," *Constellations* 27.3 (2020), pp. 1–13; Jessica Whyte, *The Morals of the Market: Human Rights and the Rise of Neoliberalism* (New York: Verso, 2019); Robbie Shilliam, "Enoch Powell: Britain's First Neoliberal Politician," *New Political Economy* 26.2 (2020), pp. 239–49; Quinn Slobodian, *Globalists: The End of Empire and the Birth of Neoliberalism* (Cambridge, MA: Harvard University Press, 2018), ch. 5, "A World of Races," pp. 146–81; Slobodian, "Anti-68ers and the Racist-Libertarian Alliance: How a Schism among Austrian School Neoliberals Helped Spawn the Alt Right," *Cultural Politics* 15.3 (2019), pp. 372–86.

34. Note: Japanese convention places the family name first and the given name second. We follow this usage here.

35. Samuel Moyn and Andrew Sartori, eds., *Global Intellectual History* (New York: Columbia University Press, 2013).

36. See Julian Gewirtz, *Unlikely Partners: Chinese Reformers, Western Economists, and the Making of Global China* (Cambridge, MA: Harvard University Press, 2017).

37. Andreas Malm, *Fossil Capital: The Rise of Steam Power and the Roots of Global Warming* (New York: Verso, 2017).

38. Hilary Appel and Mitchell A. Orenstein, *From Triumph to Crisis: Neoliberal Economic Reform in Postcommunist Countries* (New York: Cambridge University Press, 2018); Bridget Martin and Beth Geglia, "Korean Tigers in Honduras: Urban Economic Zones as Spatial Ideology in International Policy Transfer Networks," *Political Geography* 74.5 (2019), https://www.sciencedirect.com/science/article/abs/pii/S0962629818303743?via%3Dihub#!; Raymond B. Craib, "Egotopia," *CounterPunch*, August 24, 2018, https://www.counterpunch.org/2018/08/24/egotopia.

39. Quinn Slobodian, "Democracy Doesn't Matter to the Defenders of 'Economic Freedom,'" *Guardian*, November 11, 2019, https://www.theguardian.com/commentisfree/2019/nov/11/democracy-defenders-economic-freedom-neoliberalism.

40. Dieter Plehwe, Quinn Slobodian, and Philip Mirowski, eds., *Nine Lives of Neoliberalism* (New York: Verso, 2020).

41. Klaus Schwab, Marcus Gatzke, and Marlies Uken, "'Der Neoliberalismus hat ausgedient,'" *Die Zeit*, September 21, 2020, https://www.zeit.de
/wirtschaft/2020-09/corona-kapitalismus-rezession-wef-neoliberalismus
-klaus-schwab.

42. Quinn Slobodian, "How the 'Great Reset' of Capitalism Became an
Anti-Lockdown Conspiracy," *Guardian*, December 4, 2020, https://www
.theguardian.com/commentisfree/2020/dec/04/great-reset-capitalism-became
-anti-lockdown-conspiracy.

PART ONE

Greater Cultures

CHAPTER ONE

Japan and Neoliberal Culturalism

Reto Hofmann

The shift to the right in the global economic and political landscape in the 1980s changed the relationship between the various strands of neoliberal thought, including in the Japanese contingent. At the heart of the problem was the question of how to reconcile the spread of globalist policies, which were taking root everywhere, with the rise of neoconservative nationalism. Japanese members of the Neoliberal Thought Collective (NTC) were particularly sensitive to this debate.[1] Japan's stellar rise in the world's economic firmament—its industries expanding globally with increasingly deregulated domestic and international markets—engendered a return to a muscular nationalism to explain Japanese success. At once committed to neoliberal "globalism" and to the nation, the core members of the Japanese NTC—Kiuchi Nobutane (1899-1993) and Nishiyama Chiaki (1924-2017)—launched an effort to update the theory and organization of the movement, producing a distinctive neoliberal self-critique.[2] Countering the mathematical, rational models produced by Western, and especially U.S., thinkers as overly universalizing, they called on neoliberalism to integrate national particularity as a central element to stabilize capitalism.

The result of the Japanese critique was what could be called "neoliberal culturalism." This notion elevated national culture as a fix for the shortcomings of globalism and was premised on the conviction that Japan had proven uniquely able to accommodate growth and social harmony. Rooted in prewar nationalism, it regained vigor as Japan entered two decades of high growth (from the mid-1950s to the early 1970s), peaking in the 1980s "theories about the Japanese" known as *nihonjinron*. The Japanese NTC embraced assumptions about Japanese particularity that were shared more widely, but they stood out for abstracting these theories and projecting them onto the global neoliberal movement. Their response, therefore, cannot be reduced to simple parochialism. It was, rather, an answer from the Right to the disembedding effects of laissez-faire markets that threatened liberalism itself.[3] Japan, they argued, had found a solution to reconcile capitalism and community.

Neoliberal culturalism emerged in a large and diverse discursive space made up of academics, public intellectuals, businessmen, and bankers, as well as bureaucrats. This chapter will focus on the roles played by Kiuchi Nobutane and Nishiyama Chiaki, because they were most directly involved in manufacturing culturalist arguments and spreading them in the wider NTC, both at home and abroad.[4] Kiuchi, ex-banker, bureaucrat, and publicist, enjoyed a vast social network among the Japanese establishment. Nishiyama was Japan's Chicago Boy. Having studied under Friedrich Hayek at the University of Chicago (PhD, 1956), he returned to Japan, where he promoted neoliberal economics in academia, especially at Rikkyo University, and beyond. He maintained a close personal friendship with Hayek and would become the president of the Mont Pelerin Society (MPS) in the 1980s. Despite being outsiders to the mainstream in the bureaucracy, society, and academia, Kiuchi and Nishiyama possessed the social capital and determination to form a tightly knit movement that embarked on neoliberalism's "long march" in Japan and attempted to reform the Mont Pelerin Society.[5]

NATION AND NEOLIBERALISM

The Japanese were not the first to stress the link between culture and neoliberalism, but they went further than others in making the nation the central paradigm of neoliberal cultural power.[6] As recent scholarship has shown, several thinkers included culture as a form of "nonmarket social provision" that would help legitimize the neoliberal project.[7] Culture was central to providing the moral values that ought to structure the market. German ordoliberals were notably concerned with building a legal framework that would underpin the morality of the "social market economy."[8] Human rights constituted another moral companion to the expansion of neoliberal policies, as Jessica Whyte has argued. The reason that Hayek himself was deeply concerned with the "morals of the market" was because neoliberal thinkers aimed to establish a "set of moral values that would secure social integration in a context of market competition."[9] The Japanese contribution to this debate was to make the nation the ultimate repository of this morality. Wilhelm Röpke proposed that the safety of capital necessitated a "moral infrastructure" that some populations possessed while others—mainly nonwhite others—lacked.[10] In the eyes of Japanese thinkers, Japan led the world in this cultural infrastructure. They believed that uniquely Japanese beliefs and norms—the family, notions of hierarchy, community, ethics of hard work—positioned Japan ahead of other nations, both East and West, in the quest for the ideal noneconomic terrain on which neoliberal capitalism would flourish.

What is the significance of the Japanese position? The emphasis on the nation—and nationalism—constitutes a thorny issue in neoliberal theory. As argued by Quinn Slobodian, the founding fathers of neoliberalism, especially Hayek and Ludwig von Mises, were skeptical of the nation. As Central Europeans born before World War I, they held up the Habsburg Empire as a model for a world order that was economically denationalized. Hayek spoke of a "double government" in which cultural and economic government were separated, lest nationality concerns impede on the workings of the market.[11] The Japanese neoliberals flipped that argument on its head. Only a symbiosis between culture and economy would guarantee the ideal conditions for a liberal market economy. But because culture varies depending on each national context, so ran the argument, the nation maintained a core that could not be subjected to the global forces of the market. The nation was the prime unit of the world economy.

The neoliberal culturalists fixated on the nation because of Japan's experience of empire. Empire meant something different in Central Europe than in East Asia. Where the Austrian theorists were heirs to the white elites ruling the patriarchal, multinational Habsburg Empire, the Japanese were the descendants of anticolonial nationalists who fought the encroachment of European and American imperialism in Asia. Western hegemony rested on cultural, as well as economic dominance—slighting Indigenous values while exploiting local markets economically. For this reason, resistance to imperial encroachment in Japan was premised on a "single government," the interlocking association of cultural and economic nationalism. Accordingly, since the Meiji period (1868 to 1911), the Japanese understanding of liberalism was never solely political or economic, but also cultural—and civilizational. Capitalist modernity, considered to be a foreign import, brought about wealth and power but unsettled society, because it spread Western values such as individualism, materialism, and competition.

Reconciling liberal capitalism with Japanese culture became a concern that surfaced in recurrent waves. Fukuzawa Yūkichi, the nineteenth-century liberal educator and thinker, championed Western civilization, but argued that it had to be balanced against local sentiments and customs. "The resources of one's own country must always be consulted," he wrote.[12] In the 1930s and during World War II, intellectuals and policy makers alike increased the stakes with claims that it was necessary to overturn the Western order altogether. Through fascism and empire, Japan strove to construct a new order in Asia that would reflect the region's communitarian spirit—spearheaded by Japan itself—and leave behind the divisive materialism and individualism of Western civilization. The goal was to "overcome modernity" altogether, as it was memorably put in a wartime seminar, in order to usher in a world-historical moment that was premised on values and morality synthesized within Japanese culture.[13] Unlike the Habsburg Empire, which constrained the nation, the Japanese Empire projected nationalism as a unifying force to which even the economy had to bend: the "bloc economy" that the Japanese championed during the war was meant to serve this imaginary new community.

Nishizawa Tamotsu has produced a genealogy of Japanese neoliberalism that clearly shows an ideological development that was both parallel to and in conversation with its Western counterpart.[14] But it is important to point out that even as they were often on the same ideological ground when it came to the state, the same was not the case with regard to the nation. While, as recent scholarship has demonstrated, neoliberals cozied up to the state as a means to safeguard the market, Japanese neoliberals went further by invoking the nation as a space of neoliberal governance.[15] Whether it was as a repository of communitarian values that rejected class conflict in favor of harmony or as a subject to be mobilized for hard work or consumption, the nation was a fundamental neoliberal resource—and Japan could show the world how.

NIHONJINRON AND NEOLIBERALISM

Nationalism and neoliberalism were tightly linked for the core members of the Japanese NTC. The encounter between the group and the leaders of the Mont Pelerin Society, which dated to the early 1960s, overlapped with both Japan's economic high-growth period and the emergence, in the cultural realm, of a discourse about Japanese national particularity known as *nihonjinron*. These developments represented an important turning point in postwar history. The first fifteen years after World War II, which were marked by intense social and political conflicts, gave way to a period of stability in which the ruling classes gradually reasserted order in the factories and universities while presiding over an expansion in Japan's economic output, salaries, and consumption. This outcome, though often achieved through state repression, was ex post facto attributed to the tendency of the Japanese to form a harmonic community ideally suited for capitalist growth. From the perspective of Kiuchi Nobutane, Nishiyama Chiaki, and Tanaka Seigen, a former Communist, self-made businessman, and right-wing fixer nicknamed the "Tiger of Tokyo," the Japanese way and the "road from Mont Pèlerin" formed a natural intersection.[16]

Social order was an obsession for the postwar Japanese elites. The years from 1945 to 1960 marked a dramatic rise in social and political conflict on a scale and intensity not seen in Europe.[17] The democratizing reforms enacted under the U.S. occupation unleashed an array of popular forces. The union movement, civic movements, and left-wing parties were just some of the new actors with which industrialists, bureaucrats, and conservative politicians had to contend. Highly visible, they erupted in the form of strikes as well as iconoclastic artistic movements and militant student groups and threatened the hold on society by the establishment.[18] Their goals were multifaceted, but were fundamentally democratizing reforms, including a degree of control over the running of the postwar economy.[19] The conflicts came to a head in the 1960 protests against the renewal of the U.S.-Japan Security Treaty, but ebbed thereafter, just as Japan entered the era of high growth.[20]

The resulting period of relative stability was largely achieved through the collaboration of state and business. To assert their authority, the ruling classes resorted to both coercion and co-optation. While the police often resorted to violent repression, corporations enacted policies such as lifetime employment, rising salaries, and company welfare to placate the labor movement. The corporation, as espoused by one industrialist, became "a cooperative body giving birth to social value," its ethics extending beyond workplaces. Dedication, meritocracy, and competition, coupled with notions of group spirit and the company as family, were promoted through schools, social policies, and laws.[21] These efforts led to what Andrew Gordon calls the "corporate-centered society" through the embedding of the market in a space controlled by management and the rebuilding of an orderly, hierarchically structured society.[22]

But rather than ascribing this outcome to social management, many contemporary commentators, including Kiuchi, Nishiyama, and Tanaka, contended that it sprang from the reassertion of national culture in economic and political life. *Nihonjinron* arguments dating from these years stressed that the racial and cultural homogeneity (*tan'itsu minzoku*) of Japan accounted for its "unique uniqueness."[23] The particularity of the national spirit, often argued to emanate from the Japanese language and its singular capacity to assimilate foreign influences, structured a community that operated smoothly and efficiently. Defeat and foreign occupation caused a period of turmoil, but starting in the 1960s, the argument went, the Japanese were recuperating their true national identity and with it their capacity to reconcile the foreign and the domestic—which for the NTC meant global neoliberalism and national development.

Much as happened elsewhere, the Japanese collective also arose in interlocking networks made up of academics, public intellectuals, businessmen and bankers, as well as bureaucrats.[24] Its members also were characteristically nationalistic in their belief that Japan held the cultural key to the ideal development of neoliberalism. What emerges in their interactions with the Mont Pelerin Society leadership during the 1960s is an attempt to produce an ontological equivalence between Japanese traditional values and the ideals promoted by the MPS. The connection was made explicit by Nishiyama Chiaki at the 1967 MPS meeting in Tokyo. Nishiyama responded to the paper delivered by his teacher, Hayek, by making an argument about the overlap between Japanese sensibility and Hayek's thought. He praised Hayek's understanding of the limits of rationality, agreeing that a nonrational element is necessary to guarantee the spontaneity of the market. Referring to Hayek's point that the order of a free society is "purposeless" and that its nature is "abstract," Nishiyama claimed that this outlook is natural to Japanese people: "It amounts to the assertion of our traditional negation of reason or of intellect, and of our age-old perception of 'nothingness.'" He added that it was "us, the Asians, who realized first the inescapable limitation of our intellect." The Japanese, he concluded, were in "possession of the golden passports to the world of Professor Hayek."[25]

It was Kiuchi Nobutane, however, who wedded the Japanese neo-liberal faith in the world economy most conspicuously with loyalty to the nation. These two elements were consistent throughout his career, which extended from banking and bureaucracy to journalism. A scion of a powerful industrial family—his mother was the daughter of Iwasaki Yatarō, the founder of Mitsubishi—he enjoyed extensive connections to the political and economic establishment.[26] After graduating from the elite law faculty at Tokyo Imperial University, Kiuchi worked for two decades for the Yokohama Specie Bank (YSB). A semipublic institution, the YSB specialized in financing foreign trade and currency exchange and had branches—typically in consular offices—in China, Europe, and the United States. Between 1930 and 1942, Kiuchi was dispatched to Shanghai, Hamburg, London, and Nanjing. After World War II, he was in charge of the Ministry of Finance bureau that liaised with the U.S. occupation forces and was then chairman of the Foreign Exchange Committee at the Ministry of Finance.

In 1955, Kiuchi founded the Institute for World Economics, which championed liberal economics, a springboard from which he conducted advisory work for bureaucrats and politicians, and spread liberal economic principles in business newspapers and magazines. Combining technocratic expertise with the fervor of a public intellectual and patriotism with a cosmopolitan upbringing (he mastered German, French, and English, and probably had a working knowledge of Chinese), he was an important figure in the Japanese establishment. In a 1962 letter to Hayek, Nishiyama Chiaki described Kiuchi as a mediocre theoretician, but also as "the blue-blood of Japan...with four prime ministers among his uncles." He is "one of the Cabinet makers [and] is also the friend or the acquaintance of almost all the most important persons in Japan."[27]

Kiuchi's ideological development displays a tight interdependence between his neoliberal and nationalistic propensities. As early as 1949, he opposed centralized planning while advocating lower taxes and holding the stimulus-induced inflation responsible for Japan's economic woes. Later, he welcomed the end of the age of empire. Colonies no longer strengthened countries, free trade did. He had already reached that conclusion during the war, when Japan failed to make the yen bloc work. Lessons had to be learned from the way that "small countries" such as the Netherlands or Belgium reconstructed after World War II by dropping their overseas possessions and using foreign currency to build export economies.[28] Whether it was the Netherlands or Japan, the loss of colonies and the embrace of the world market brought high rewards.[29]

But even as he promoted free-market policies, Kiuchi remained a staunch nationalist and an active participant in *nihonjinron* debates. As he wrote in his memoirs, it was his goal to prevent Japan from losing again after its defeat in World War II.[30] To succeed in reaching this goal, economics was not enough. A strong national morality was just as important. He saw this morality as rooted in a country's unique "personality" (*kosei*). Japan had admirably developed its personality from the Meiji era in the mid-nineteenth and twentieth centuries until 1945, when the nation lost confidence: the Japanese had to reconstruct not only economically, but also spiritually, and defeat was weighing them down.[31] By the 1960s, however, Japan was rebounding. The country had found its personality again as it developed economically, and at the same time was revaluing its cultural traditions. In this spirit, Kiuchi dedicated himself to language policies. As head of the Japanese National Language Council (*Kokugo shingi-kai*), he professed that the Japanese writing system, composed of three scripts, was superior to other systems and vehemently opposed the simplification of *kanji*, the Chinese characters used in Japanese writing.[32]

According to him, language was integral to Japanese cultural values and therefore shaped all other activities, even economic ones.

The confluence of national values and global political economy was necessary because nationalism and neoliberalism were mutually rein- forcing. For Kiuchi, nationalism was only natural. Caution had to be exercised not to fall into a form of nationalism that was "narrow" and xenophobic, because that would hinder the world economy. National- ism had to be "sublated" (he used the German *aufheben*).[33] What he meant by that became obvious in the mid-1960s, when his dialogue with the MPS began in earnest. Nationalism helped to mediate neolib- eralism. Countries should liberalize their economies, but each one at its own pace and not "100 percent." Lowering trade tariffs was funda- mentally a good idea, but agriculture had to be defended. He argued that it was part of Swiss identity, for example: their national morality has not allowed traditional agriculture to be swept away. He believed it should be the same for Japan. What kind of a country would it become if all Japanese people lived in places like Kawasaki, a heavily industri- alized outpost of Tokyo? Neoliberal reforms had to be balanced by the "being" (*arikata*) of a country. What neoliberals ought to aim for was a "world order based on countries' personalit[ies]"[34]

In the 1960s, then, Kiuchi believed that he had uncovered a func- tional equivalence between Hayekian economic thought and Japanese cultural traditions. As he saw it, it was a productive encounter. Hayek and his school had pioneered the theory of neoliberalism, but in Japan, many of these principles, being engrained in the national culture, were already in practice. Collaboration seemed natural.

PUSHBACK

The optimistic view that countries such as Japan could be received as equals in the global neoliberal movement with their Indigenous approach intact did not last. By the 1980s, Kiuchi concluded that the world was unwilling to learn from Japan. In fact, the peak of Japanese economic prowess in that decade coincided with a wave of anti-Japanese sentiment, especially in the United States. Thanks to the trade agreements between the two countries, Japanese products poured into the U.S. market, while Japanese corporations purchased ever more American assets. The response from the other side of the Pacific often came in the form of anti-Japanese racism and accusations of unfair conduct.[35] Crucially, these frictions erupted at the same time that neoliberal free-trade policies were being championed in Washington, along with the theories of Friedman and the Virginia school. From the perspective of Kiuchi, then, neoliberalism as a global arrangement was falling back into age-old Western hegemony. Asian countries, and Japan in particular, were not being accorded equal competitive status. Neoliberal globalism had to be fixed in such a way, he believed, that it took the national, non-Western characteristics of capitalism into consideration. Dizzied by the success of the Japanese "model," Kiuchi, aided by Nishiyama, pushed to reform neoliberal theory by foregrounding the nation—and nationalism—as a pivotal paradigm.

While Kiuchi had still spoken of Japanese "culture" in the 1960s and had placed some of its features on par with Hayek's thought, by the 1980s, he was making arguments about civilizational hierarchy. Japan had become conscious of its superiority and now had to show it to the whole world. The lessons from Japan, in other words, were universal. How can such boldness be explained? There was, first of all, Japanese economic power. Japan had turned into the world's third-largest economy, after the United States and the Soviet Union, dominating export markets in the auto and electronics industries. High growth rates had ended with the oil shock in 1973, but the country had rebounded, albeit not to earlier levels of GDP growth. Still, economists agree that the turbulence of the early 1970s affected Japan to a lesser degree than other developed economies. Milton Friedman attributed the success to Japan's adoption of his monetarist policies. In 1986, he stated that in the "quarter of a century since I first had the privilege to visit Japan," it "has seemed to me by far and away the best example of the effective conduct of monetary policy among the major nations."[36]

Kiuchi, however, was convinced that the "secret" of Japan's success lay less in Friedmanite policies than in its peculiar "civilization." In a book written for an American readership, but tellingly never published, he lectured the United States on why it ought to learn from Japan. To avoid an "economic catastrophe," he explained, "nothing short of a radical reorientation in [U.S.] economic thinking was needed." That "mode of thinking" was accustomed to the "economics of numbers," which had led to the stagnation of the 1970s. Japan suffered from none of the problems of the United States, and the reason was that "there is something quite unique about Japanese civilization," namely, that Japan had been able to blend the modern with the traditional. He remained vague about specific lessons, but boasted that "it is sufficient if we merely recognize the existence of an economy that contradicts the system of thoughts—ideas and assumptions—held to be true by most Americans."[37]

The second factor that explains the self-confidence of the Japanese neoliberals was Japan's rise to relative prominence in the global neoliberal movement—itself a reflection of the rise of Japanese economic power. Since the early 1960s, Japan had hosted several MPS gatherings. Exponents of the movement, especially Hayek and Friedman, were regular visitors to the country. By his own count, Hayek visited seven times, and Friedman visited eleven times. While tourism was certainly one aspect—on one occasion, Friedman wanted to go skiing in Hokkaido—both kept busy agendas that included radio and TV interviews, talks at universities, as well as meetings with prime ministers, bureaucrats, and businessmen.[38] The Japanese membership in the MPS expanded, and despite not reaching the numbers of their American and European counterparts, their voices could not be ignored.[39] The peak in Japanese influence was reached with the appointment of Nishiyama Chiaki as president of the MPS (1980 to 1982).

From such internal positions, the Japanese culturalist arguments were disseminated not just to American policymakers, but also to the

American contingent within the MPS. In his 1982 presidential address to the MPS General Meeting in Berlin, Nishiyama outlined what he saw as the grave problem confronting the movement, namely, how to organize individuals in a free society. While he defended the original principles set out by the MPS and recognized its many achievements over the decades, he noted that "near-sightedness" was not only an affliction of "our opponents," but "often common to us as well." The debate over whether government should be big or small, he suggested, was stale and had to be overcome. Of course, small governments were preferable, but that did not in itself address a more important problem of all modern democracies—the distance between a government and the people. In other words, it was necessary to bond the state and the individual within a community.

In his 1982 address, Nishiyama acknowledged the centrality of the individual for the triumph of freedom, but also called for the need to form aggregates of individuals. "The argument for freedom," he explained, implied an "adamant belief...in 'the multitude.'"[40] How, though, could such a form of organization be created? Clearly, not from above (the state), because that would constitute an aberration characteristic of a "despotic government...created by modern democracy." Rather, the challenge was to "let the free individuals interact with each other and spontaneously collaborate with the other individuals in the best way humanly ever possible." The principle was what Hayek called a "spontaneous order" among free individuals, which, however, required "a certain set of values." Here lay the crux of the problem. For Nishiyama, current neoliberal thought was unable to provide these values, because it was bogged down with "so-called positive science," which was supposed to be value-free. The MPS, he said, needed "to examine squarely [its] values for their further development."

Having diagnosed the problem, Nishiyama proposed a solution: a world order in which the traditions of East and West were balanced. He saw it as a way to "go back once again to ancient Greece," where East and West were "very much one and united." Because the West was stuck in scientific rationalism, it was necessary that "some analytical tools" be dug "out of the Eastern thought." He had, in other words, embarked on a Toynbee-style argument about the rise and fall of civilizations. To be sure, it was articulated cautiously, with the clear intent not to antagonize his predominantly Western audience. He also reminded the audience that these were thoughts in progress and that he would "report the results" of his current quest in a future meeting. But for those willing to listen, the conclusion was not too subtle. Western civilization—and the MPS with it—had hit an impasse, unable to overcome the limits posed by its rationalistic belief in the individual. The way forward was through the new Greece, Japan.

The neoliberal culturalist argument, in the making for decades, reached its most complete—and radical—articulation in 1989, at the very peak of the Japanese bubble. In a letter sent by Kiuchi and Nishiyama to the MPS leadership, the pair instigated a head-on confrontation with the exponents of the neoliberal movement. They were writing to follow up on the discussions they had initiated at the MPS General Meeting held in Tokyo the previous year, which they wanted to take further by engaging in a series of "personal debates." Trenchantly, the two expressed their "wish to improve the current state of the Mont Pèlerin Society." The society had outlasted the goals of the founding fathers. It had become too large, and "discussions are made excessively from the economic point of view." Instead, the problem of freedom had to be discussed on a "broader and wider scale," for to keep building an "ideal society," they argued, it was crucial to foreground matters of morality and religion. Moreover, the society perniciously emphasized the "uniformity of individuals rather than their diversity." Diversity affirmed the need to utilize the "individualities of societies and nations" to realize "our 'utopian' society."[41] These principles and goals were, of course, an idée fixe of Kiuchi's since the 1960s, but only now did he project them onto the global movement, arguing that they—and the model of Japan—could rescue the MPS from crude Western materialism.

The response from their colleagues was varied in tone, but was negative overall. George Stigler dismissed the request. He curtly replied that "if the Japanese Group wishes to address Freedom and Individuality...in a continuous and fundamental way, you had better start a new society."[42] James M. Buchanan wrote that he appreciated the Japanese criticisms, because they reflected some of the "tensions" within the society. In particular, he acknowledged that the relationship between economists and philosophers within the movement was important and one that Hayek had also stressed. But he concluded on a noncommittal note, suggesting that perhaps a committee could be charged with examining the problem.[43]

The most damaging response to Kiuchi and Nishiyama came from Friedman—not so much for want of courtesy or engagement, but for his incapacity to understand the Japanese position. Friedman welcomed a broader discussion of freedom advocated by the Japanese, but by specifying that in a recent series of conferences he himself had addressed questions of "political freedom, civil freedom, and economic freedom," he was making it clear that he did not grasp the critics' point about national culture. Indeed, he declared himself a "little puzzled" by Kiuchi and Nishiyama's call for more diversity, because, he was adamant, the free market itself "enables people of all backgrounds, attitudes, religions, beliefs, and so on" to cooperate "without conformity." His generic reassurance that "of course, we want to take advantage of the variety of our members" is indicative that on matters of culture and, more decidedly for the Japanese, national particularity, the two sides were talking past each other.[44]

The exchange reveals that there was a gap between Friedman and the MPS more generally and the Japanese contingent. Both sides saw themselves broadly as completing the work of Hayek, but did not regard each other as partners in the endeavor. The Japanese quoted Hayek in their quest to reform the MPS, arguing that it was the master who had claimed that for a "functioning spontaneous order," it was necessary to have an "internally consistent model."[45] In their view, that model was Japan and the principle of national particularity that it would contribute to neoliberal thought. Friedman, although accepting the call to reform the MPS on Hayekian lines, did not think of Japan as central. In his view, the countries where "the original purpose of the Society" was still "vital" were places such as China, Poland, Russia, Guatemala, El Salvador, Argentina, Brazil, Peru, and India. It was necessary "for a Hayek to arise from one of these countries."[46] As far as he was concerned, the developing and imminently post-Soviet world would give birth to the next prophets from the margins, much as Japan had done in the 1960s.

Sidelined, Kiuchi turned his back on the MPS. In his memoirs, written in 1992, he reassessed his earlier enthusiasm about the society, concluding that he had been naive. He admitted that the encounter had been beneficial from a "thought perspective." It also allowed him to visit several places around the world, and meet many "great people." When all was said and done, however, he was deluded, because the society was trapped in its own tensions. The "foremost" lesson he learned from the MPS, he concluded, was that "even the people from Mont Pèlerin can do nothing about decline of Western civilization." The society itself was nothing but a "miniature" of the West.[47] In failing to integrate cultural particularity by following the lodestar of Japan, globalism sleepwalked into a clash of civilizations.

"UNITY OF THOUGHT"

The fixation of the Japanese NTC on the nation and on order raises the question of the relationship between neoliberalism and neoconservatism. This link has been analyzed, notably in the United States, in studies highlighting the interplay between free marketeers, businessmen, and conservative thinkers.[48] The same was the case in Japan. Kiuchi, in particular, advised multiple prime ministers who were on the right in the spectrum of Japanese conservatism, such as Satō Eisaku and Nakasone Yasuhiro.[49] But Kiuchi did not see the relationship between the free market and conservative politics as simply a domestic issue that called for a functional solution. The arc of his career shows that he was deeply concerned that it was a constitutive problem internal to liberalism and therefore also international. While unable to articulate the problem exactly in these terms, he sensed the weaknesses of liberalism, that it needed something else to survive its contradictions. His involvement in the MPS, then, cannot be separated from the larger goal to contribute to a global conservative movement.

Complimenting neoliberal theory with culturalism was consistent with Kiuchi's goal to create "unity of thought."[50] But this quest was not peculiar to Kiuchi. The interwar Marxist philosopher Tosaka Jun had already singled out this tendency in his critique of liberalism. Tosaka argued that liberalism, unable to solve its own contradictions, turned to an "idealist" solution by invoking "Japanist" principles such as national ethics, spirituality, and religion. Accordingly, liberalism was a hybrid, proclaiming freedom as its principle, on the one hand, and resorting to right-wing values such as nationalism and authoritarianism, on the other.[51]

Tosaka's backdrop was the interwar crisis and the rise of fascism, but his analysis is just as valid to understanding the postwar intellectual rise of neoliberals such as Kiuchi and Nishiyama. The free market was always connected for Kiuchi to right-wing and conservative positions. While in Hamburg in 1934, he served the financial markets, but had also expressed enthusiasm about Hitler and his capacity to restore order to Germany. Compared with Shanghai, he observed, everything was "so neat" and there did not seem to be any "inequality among the working classes."[52] He admired Western liberal thinkers, but also Japanese authoritarians, such as colonel Tsuji Masanobu, imperial mastermind and war criminal.[53] Support for a Japanese free-trade agenda went hand in hand with activities for constitutional revision.

A similar pattern emerges on the international level. Kiuchi's flirtations with the Mont Pelerin Society were accompanied by his growing activism in the Unification Church of Moon Sun Myung, a new religious movement active around the world. In the 1980s, Kiuchi collaborated with the International Union for the Defeat of Communism, a Japan-based right-wing group closely affiliated with the church. He denied that it was a "weird" organization, as it was generally perceived in the Japanese press, stressing instead its noble fight against communism, the "disease of modern civilization."[54] His regard for Moon and his church may seem surprising. Kiuchi was a practicing Buddhist and never converted to Christianity. But religious doctrines were secondary to the capacity of spiritualism to unite. It is likely that Kiuchi saw in Moon, a Korean who had embraced a Western religion, a movement that had succeeded where he had failed, namely, in uniting the thoughts of East and West.

It is difficult to know whether it was through Kiuchi that Hayek became involved in the Unification Church. The timing of his lecture to Moon's International Conference (1985) and his receipt of the movement's Founder Award (1986) coincided with Kiuchi's activism in the church and his efforts to bring Eastern spirituality into the MPS.[55] More important, perhaps, is that Hayek was not immune to the spiritualist tendencies observed by Tosaka among liberal thinkers and that underpinned the confluence of neoliberalism and neoconservatism.

CONCLUSION

Japan had its own members in the "larger neoliberal family of thought."[56] They made sure that the conversation with the MPS was not a monologue, but a dialogue in which multiple sides learned from one another. In the way that Kiuchi and Nishiyama linked neoliberal values to Japanese traditions, we see the domestication of an international movement, a process that characterized the encounter in the early stages. But we also see the attempted globalization of national patterns of neoliberal governance—Kiuchi's conviction that national peculiarities ought to be integral to the workings of world markets. In other words, the exchanges could be mutually reinforcing, but also turn acrimonious, as was the case when Kiuchi and Nishiyama proposed neoliberal culturalism as way to challenge the dominance of Chicago school economics. The neoliberal imaginary was at the same time open and conflicted. The Japanese intervention is a reminder of the capacity of neoliberalism to reform itself, even as there were clear limits to the global neoliberal movement to serve as a universal forum for the organization of capitalism.

Recent scholarship has demonstrated that neoliberalism can work with the state, but this article suggests that the nation, too, figured as an important paradigm of neoliberal thought. The Japanese prophesies of world market rested on the sanctity of the nation. Neoliberal culturalism, with its privileging of the nation, undermines conventional mantras that global markets are antithetical to nationalism—economic or cultural—or that nationalism is merely reactive to malfunctioning markets. From the perspective of the Japanese experience, the reverse was true. Nationalism was seen as a fundamental ingredient for the smooth operation of global capitalism, as a repository for communitarian values undermined by the forces of the market. Notions of national harmony, family, a spirit of sacrifice, and competition displaced from a domestic to an international level—all of these restrained resistance to the social unevenness implicated in the neoliberal project. At the same time, a consensus on the nation alleviated the demand for building a large state. In this way, neoliberalism and neoconservatism are not a marriage of convenience, but bound to each other through the nation.

The conflicts that emerged in the Japanese pushback to the MPS reveal the nation as an underexplored terrain of neoliberal history and theory. Kiuchi and Nishiyama were but the standard-bearers of neoliberal culturalism, and it remains to be explored to what extent fellow travelers in the Japanese movement—the fixer Tanaka Seigen, businessmen such as Kikawada Kazutaka, or politicians such as Matsushita Masatoshi—shared and propagated their views. But this history extends beyond Japan. In Asia and the postcolonial world more generally, nationalism and liberal capitalism established a visibly close bond. In this sense, the current accommodation of nationalism and neoliberalism in China might not be as new a development as it appears at first sight.

NOTES

I would like to thank Quinn Slobodian and Dieter Plehwe for their insightful comments and invaluable suggestions.

1. For the Neoliberal Thought Collective, see Dieter Plehwe and Bernhard Walpen, "Neoliberale Denkkollektive und ihr Denkstil," in Christina Kaindl, et al., eds., *Kapitalismus reloaded: Kontroversen zu Imperialismus, Empire und Hegemonie* (Hamburg: VSA, 2007), pp. 347–71; Philip Mirowski and Dieter Plehwe, eds., *The Road from Mont Pèlerin: The Making of the Neoliberal Thought Collective* (Cambridge, MA: Harvard University Press, 2009).

2. For the term "globalism," see Quinn Slobodian, *Globalists: The End of Empire and the Birth of Neoliberalism* (Cambridge, MA: Harvard University Press, 2018).

3. The notion of "disembedding" is part of Karl Polanyi's argument about capitalism's "double movement." Karl Polanyi, *The Great Transformation: The Political and Economic Origins of Our Time* (Boston: Beacon Press, 2001).

4. Note: Japanese convention places the family name first and the given name second. We follow this usage here.

5. The term "long march" is from David Harvey, *A Brief History of Neoliberalism* (New York: Oxford University Press, 2005), p. 40.

6. Another neoliberal thinker who emphasized culture was Deepak Lal. See Deepak Lal, *The Hindu Equilibrium, Volume I: Cultural Stability and Economic Stagnation—India c. 1500 BC–AD 1980* (Oxford: Clarendon Press, 1989).

7. Ben Jackson, "At the Origins of Neo-Liberalism: The Free Economy and the Strong State, 1930–1947," *Historical Journal* 53.1 (2010), p. 138. Slobodian also stresses the importance of an "extra-economic framework" in neoliberalism; see Slobodian, *Globalists*, p. 16.

8. Ralf Ptak, "Neoliberalism in Germany: Revisiting the Ordoliberal Foundations of the Social Market Economy," in Mirowski and Plehwe, eds., *The Road from Mont Pèlerin*, pp. 100–106 and 123–25.

9. Jessica Whyte, *The Morals of the Market: Human Rights and the Rise of Neoliberalism* (London: Verso, 2019), pp. 8–9.

10. Slobodian, *Globalists*, p. 149.

11. See Slobodian, *Globalists*, ch. 3, "A World of Federations," pp. 91–120, especially p. 105.

12. Fukuzawa Yukichi, *An Outline of a Theory of Civilization*, trans. David A. Dilworth and G. Cameron Hurst, III (New York: Columbia University Press, 2008), pp. 20–21.

13. For a translation of the wartime seminar, see Richard Calichman, *Overcoming Modernity: Cultural Identity in Wartime Japan* (New York: Columbia University Press). See also Harry Harootunian, *Overcome by Modernity: History, Culture, and Community in Interwar Japan* (Princeton: Princeton University Press, 2002).

14. Nishizawa Tamotsu and Ikeda Yukihiro, "From New Liberalism to Neoliberalism: Japanese Economists and the Welfare State before the 1980s," in Roger E. Backhouse, Bradley W. Bateman, Tamotsu Nishizawa, and Dieter Plehwe, *Liberalism and the Welfare State: Economists and Arguments for the Welfare State* (Oxford: Oxford University Press), pp. 75–100. The scholarship on the history of neoliberalism is scant. In Japanese, see Kikuchi Nobuteru, *Nihon-gata shinjiyūshugi to wa nanika: Senryō-ki kaikaku kara abenomikkusu made* (Tokyo: Iwanami, 2016). The literature in anthropology and political science is more substantial. See, for example, Amy Borovoy, "Japan as Mirror: Neoliberalism's Promise and Cost," in Carol J. Greenhouse, ed., *Ethnographies of Neoliberalism* (Philadelphia: University of Pennsylvania Press, 2010), pp. 60–47; Nana Okura Gagné, "Neoliberalism at Work: Corporate Reforms, Subjectivity, and Post-Toyotist Affect in Japan," *Anthropological Theory* 20.4 (2020), pp. 455–83; Takaaki Suzuki "After Embedded Liberalism: The Neo-Liberal Hybridization of Japan's Developmental State," *Critique internationale* 63.2 (2014), pp. 19–39.

15. See Jackson, "At the Origins of Neo-Liberalism."

16. Mirowski and Plehwe, eds., *The Road from Mont Pèlerin*.

17. Andrew Gordon, *The Wages of Affluence: Labor and Management in Postwar Japan* (Cambridge, MA: Harvard University Press, 1998), p. 157.

18. See, for example, William Marotti, *Money, Trains, and Guillotines: Art and Revolution in 1960s Japan* (Durham: Duke University Press, 2013).

19. Laura Hein, *Fueling Growth: The Energy Revolution and Economic Policy in Postwar Japan* (Cambridge, MA: Harvard University Press, 1990), p. 240.

20. Nick Kapur, *Japan at the Crossroads: Conflict and Compromise after Anpo* (Cambridge, MA: Harvard University Press, 2018).

21. Gordon, *The Wages of Affluence*, p. 57.

22. Ibid., p. 184.

23. For an overview of the *nihonjinron* scholarship, see Harumi Befu, *Hegemony of Homogeneity: An Anthropological Analysis of* Nihonjinron (Melbourne: TransPacific Press, 2001). See also Befu, "Nationalism and Nihonjinron," in Harumi Befu, ed., *Cultural Nationalism in East Asia: Representation and Identity* (Berkeley: Institute of East Asian Studies, 1993), pp. 107-38, and Yoshino Kosaku, *Cultural Nationalism in Contemporary Japan: A Sociological Enquiry* (London: Routledge, 1992).

24. Nishizawa and Ikeda, "From New Liberalism to Neoliberalism."

25. Nishiyama Chiaki, "Arguments for the Principles of Liberty and the Philosophy of Science," *Il Politico* 32.2 (1967), p. 338.

26. On the patriotic disposition of Japanese elites, see R. Taggart Murphy, "Privilege Preserved: Crisis and Recovery in Japan," *New Left Review* 121 (2020), pp. 21-52.

27. Nishiyama Chiaki to Friedrich Hayek, September 3, 1962, Hoover Institution, Friedrich Hayek Papers, box 40, folder 14.

28. Kiuchi Nobutane, *Tōrai no sekai chitsujo wo mosaku shite* (Tokyo: Gyonin-sha, 1986), pp. 365-67 and 374-76.

29. National Diet Library, Kensei shiryō-shitsu 1938/7, and Kiuchi Nobutane, *Kokusaku wo kangaeru* (Jiji shinsho, 1964), pp. 80-81.

30. Kiuchi Nobutane, *Boku no jigazō* (Tokyo: Zenpon-sha, 1992), p. 9.

31. Kiuchi Nobutane, *Kuni no kosei: sono hakken no tameni* (Tokyo: Bungei shunjū-sha, 1955), pp. 7-9.

32. Basil Khalifa Cahusac de Caux, "Cultures and Politics of Script Reform in Japan, 1945-1995," PhD diss., Monash University, 2019, p. 110.

33. Kiuchi Nobutane, *Sekai no mikata* (Tokyo: Ronsō shinsho, 1961), pp. 18-19.

34. Kiuchi, *Kokusaku wo kangaeru*, pp. 88-96 and 103.

35. There were also some conspicuous admirers of Japan, such as the Harvard sociologist Ezra Vogel, who elevated Japan as a "mirror to America." He agreed with the neoliberal culturalist argument that Japan successfully "recombine[d] different traditions." Ezra Vogel, *Japan as Number One: Lessons for America* (Cambridge, MA: Cambridge University Press, 1979), p. 6.

36. Letter from Milton Friedman to various Japanese personalities, November 17, 1986, Hoover Institution, Friedrich Hayek Papers, box 197, folder 4.

37. Kiuchi Nobutane, "An Appeal To Americans: Some Suggestions from a Japanese to Avert a Catastrophe in the American Economy," sent to Hayek, July 31, 1981, Hoover Institution, Friedrich Hayek Papers, box 30, folder 30.

38. For example, Hoover Institution, Milton Friedman Papers, box 167 folder 2.

39. Japanese MPS members included the bankers Aoba Fumio (Yasuda), Shimanaka Yūji (Sanwa), Nakayama Sohei (Industrial Bank of Japan), Iwasa Yoshizane (Fuji and Yasuda), and Taya Teizō (Daiwa, Bank of Japan, IMF). There were also entrepreneurs, such as Kikawada Kazutaka (TEPCO), Sakurada Takeshi (Keidanren), and the founder of the Ohara Museum of Art, Ōhara Sōichirō. See National Diet Library, Kensei shiryōshitsu, Kiuchi Nobutane kankei monjo, 1970-72. (Hereafter, NDL, KSS, KNKM.)

40. Nishiyama Chiaki, "Presidential Address for the 1982 General Meeting in Berlin: 'For a Free Society in the Coming Decade,'" Hoover Institution, Mont Pèlerin Society Papers, box 25, folder 1.

41. Circular letter from Kiuchi Nobutane and Nishiyama Chiaki to MPS leadership, August 8, 1989, NDL, KSS, KNKM, 6018-4.

42. George Stigler to Kiuchi Nobutane, September 11, 1989, NDL, KSS, KNKM, 6018-4.

43. James M. Buchanan to Kiuchi Nobutane, September 6, 1989, NDL, KSS, KNKM, 6018-4.

44. Milton Friedman to Kiuchi Nobutane, August 29, 1989, NDL, KSS, KNKM, 6018-4.

45. Circular letter, Kiuchi Nobutane and Nishiyama Chiaki to MPS leadership, August 8, 1989, NDL, KSS, KNKM, 6018-4.

46. Milton Friedman to Kiuchi Nobutane, August 29, 1989, NDL, KSS, KNKM, 6018-4.

47. Kiuchi, *Boku no jigazō*, pp. 91–93.

48. Kim Phillips-Fein, *Invisible Hands: The Making of the Conservative Movement from the New Deal to Reagan* (New York: Norton, 2009).

49. Nishizawa and Ikeda, "From New Liberalism to Neoliberalism," p. 27. See also Kikuchi, *Nihon-gata shinjiyūshugi*, pp. 48–49.

50. Kiuchi, *Boku no jigazō*, p. 84.

51. Tosaka Jun, *Nippon ideorogi ron* (Tokyo: Iwanami, 1977).

52. Kiuchi disagreed with anti-Semitism, but still believed that overall, Hitler was misunderstood in Japan and elsewhere. Kiuchi Nobutane, *Tōrai no sekai chitsujo wo mosaku shite* (Tokyo: Gyōjin-sha, 1986), pp. 356–60. For a study of the reception of Hitler in Japan, see Ricky Law, *Transnational Nazism: Ideology and Culture in German-Japanese Relations, 1919–1936* (Cambridge: Cambridge University Press, 2019).

53. Kiuchi, *Boku no jigazō*, p. 42.

54. Kiuchi Nobutane, "Kokusai shōkyō rengōkai nit suite," NDL, KSS, KNKM, 6095.

55. See Robert Leeson, *Hayek: A Collaborative Biography. Part XI: Orwellian Rectifiers, Mises' 'Evil Seed' of Christianity and the 'Free' Market Welfare State* (Cham: Springer, 2018), p. 467.

56. Ptak, "Neoliberalism in Germany," pp. 98–99.

CHAPTER TWO

(Is) India in the History of Neoliberalism?

Aditya Balasubramanian

Neoliberalism has become a vibrant field of historical study since the global financial crisis of 2008.[1] Yet despite the discipline's global turn and a renewed commitment by historians to decolonize knowledge production, the scholarship has tended to focus geographically on the Americas and Europe.[2] The trend is not surprising. The ideas associated with neoliberalism have a clear Western origin in the ideas of economists like F. A. Hayek and Milton Friedman, and their Mont Pelerin Society. Until the recent rise of China, the deeply integrated United States and European economies dominated the rest of the world.[3] Much scholarship thus far has conformed to what Peter Hall described in his influential study of Keynesianism as an "economist-centered approach."[4] Such research focuses on ideas and how they become accepted by an expanding set of professionals who subsequently win over policymakers and others.[5] A modified version of this approach in the study of neoliberalism has examined "thought collectives," painstakingly unearthing ecumenes such as expert networks in which ideas develop and move. This work privileges the social aspects of the generation of ideas and their links to capitalist strategies of accumulation.[6] Other works have taken what Hall describes as a "state-centered approach" that gives attention to the institutional configuration of the state and national history as important forces shaping the adoption of certain kinds of economic ideas in policy.[7]

Can one extend this blend of approaches to connect existing work

to the history of neoliberalism in other parts of the world without making the latter look like a poor imitation of the Western experience? At
what point do local differences in the non-Western world—both in
terms of ideologies and the initial conditions of states that cannot be
called "welfare states"—become so great that we must cease to speak
of neoliberalism? The great utility of the concept—its ability to conjure
a meaning of something in between a philosophy, a way of theoriz-
ing market society, and a set of economic policy prescriptions—can
also be its Achilles heel.[8] It can shape-shift in different contexts and
accept different definitions. Consider the suggestion of political scientist Cornel Ban in his work on Romania and Spain that neoliberalism "goes local." He proposes that neoliberalism connotes a lowest
common denominator of "institutionalized trade/financial openness,
public finances benchmarked by financial market credibility, and
growth strategies based on the relative competitiveness of the national
economy."[9] "Embedded neoliberalism," in his account, is committed
to moderating its key tenets or embedding itself in a wider set of policy choices, as in Spain, which had more mainstream contacts with
post–World War II interventionist Anglo-American economic policy.
Romania offers a "disembedded" case. The absence of an elite with
neoclassical or Keynesian economic training led to more conformity
with the core tenets of neoliberalism, even their radicalization, especially after loan conditionality defeated the neo-developmentalist policy measures that had older antecedents.

Ban's approach, which focuses on the era of high globalization
of the 1990s and beyond, is sensitive to variation. To achieve this,
though, he employs a rather restricted definition of neoliberalism as a
set of macroeconomic policy directives developed from elsewhere that
can then be mixed and matched with other policies. But it is unclear
whether these are new forms of neoliberalism per se, rather than new
policy regimes informed by a set of neoliberal principles. Is this really
a process of local translation? It is not as if neoliberalism is being
reworded or reinterpreted to make it locally palatable. Rather, certain

structural conditions allow partial uptake. An alternative approach for studies of neoliberalism in the non-Western world might be to tackle its intersection with other ideologies to underscore how it becomes politically palatable in local contexts.[10]

The attempts of South Asianists to overcome the problems of Eurocentrism can shed light on how or how not to approach neoliberalism's history outside the West. In the context of the history of capital, Dipesh Chakrabarty has famously theorized a "History Two" for capital in order to understand historical difference as resistance to its universalizing logic of economic transformation.[11] Unlike capitalism, however, neoliberalism has never been understood as an unfolding logic of society's development or even as a system of political economy. Recent histories of liberalism in South Asia offer other pointers. C. A. Bayly has suggested that imperial liberal ideas and governance imperatives diffused into the colonies, but that this process of contact generated new, creative local variations inflected by daily experience, fused with preexisting forms of thought, and repurposed to new ends.[12] But here, the question became, apart from rhetorical similarities, in what meaningful way were everyone from Hindu revivalists to secular modernizers to be understood as both innovative and liberal?[13] A more recent attempt by Andrew Sartori traced a vernacular genealogy of liberalism in Bengali peasant discourses about custom that resemble Lockean arguments about the labor-constituting value of property.[14] In this model, a kind of conceptual homology was adequate to make something pass for liberalism in a South Asian context, its temporal location fitting within an acceptable band for the global concept history of liberalism.[15]

Neither Ban's approach of a rather restricted definition of neoliberalism nor South Asianists' attempts to overcome the problems of Eurocentrism in the study of liberalism, however, fully escape the risk of narrating a Whiggish history of neoliberalism's inexorable rise, one of diffusion from a core to a periphery. All features of political economy not resembling neoliberalism can be perceived as elements of backwardness or cultural difference. But what of the link between economic practice and culture and the ways in which they co-constitute each other? Reorienting the history of neoliberalism from the perspective of the nation-state in the Global South, one without a clear connection to the interventions of Western experts such as the Chicago economists in Chile, can help disrupt a linear view of the development of neoliberalism.[16]

In this essay, I use the Indian experience to think about what such an alternative history might look like. First, I sketch the conventional wisdom about Indian economic policy, which traces neoliberalism's origins to the economic reforms of 1991 as the result of pressure applied by international institutions and the opportunism of savvy technocrats. I examine the cultural characteristics of economic life today and try to evaluate ways in which one may or may not say neoliberalism has manifested itself distinctively in India. Next, I explore the prehistory of neoliberalism in India extending back to the 1950s, beginning with a group of people tied to, but distinct from the Mont Pelerin Society and culminating in a set of select market reforms in the 1980s. This contextualizes the 1991 reforms and shows that there were both internal constituencies and external pressures leading up to their occurrence, even though more often than not, the internal constituencies could not necessarily be considered neoliberals. Finally, I consider the contemporary manifestation of neoliberalism in India, the search for a history to give it a useable past, and its role in India today.

"THE GOLDEN SUMMER OF 1991"

According to a narrative prominent in the media and among neoclassical economists, the chained Indian economy was unshackled by the liberalization reforms of "the golden summer of 1991." The *Economist* proclaimed that if, unlike the "Asian Tigers," the Indian economy had been caged, now "set free," it "can be as healthy and vigorous as any in Asia."[17] Faced with a dwindling balance of payments and overborrowing with origins in the oil shocks of the 1970s, India sought a loan from the International Monetary Fund. Acceptance of the loan required immediate currency devaluation, the introduction of temporary import controls, deficit reduction, and liberalization of key interest rates.[18] But Finance Minister Manmohan Singh and Prime Minister Narasimha Rao, who took over the Commerce Ministry, moved beyond these measures and reversed a number of other statist characteristics of Indian economic policy. Singh and Rao accomplished the de-restriction of domestic production by a "bonfire of controls," trade liberalization, and tariff reduction, as well as some facilitation of foreign direct investment.[19] Crisis presented the opportunity for a group of technocrats led by Singh to author reforms. Rao's efforts made them politically marketable.[20]

Although the lionizing of Singh and Rao and the characterization of one unprecedented event as the beginning of a great transformation offends the historian's sensibilities, this was indeed a paradigm shift from the dominant policy making of the last five decades in a number of respects. For one thing, postcolonial economic policy had been premised on import-substituting industrialization and a skepticism about the benefits of foreign trade. In addition, a strategic focus on public-sector heavy enterprises, a thicket of government regulations tightly controlling the allocation of scarce resources, and a rhetoric of socialism had governed Indian economic policy since the 1950s.[21] Although India had always been a mixed economy and no more than 12 percent of its GDP had ever been accounted for by government spending, the public sector had been the driving force in industrialization.[22] Third, as a leader in the nonaligned world weary of its colonial-era vulnerability to the vicissitudes of the global economy, India had taken pains to demonstrate its autonomy from international institutions and to insulate itself from massive foreign capital inflows and outflows ("hot money"). Even if the country never quite managed to become as self-sufficient as it had intended, India was less enmeshed in the global economy than other actors across the decolonizing world.[23]

The reforms brought a new orientation toward policy and ushered in a period of service sector–led growth—especially in information technology services—and increased foreign trade.[24] The government reduced its stake in public-sector enterprises, and private capital formation expanded.[25] India's central bank, the Reserve Bank of India, began to adopt more indirect instruments of monetary policy and to conduct government borrowing at market-determined interest rates.[26] Poverty reduction through means targeting the poorest replaced more broadly based welfare schemes.[27] As Niraja Jayal has shown, social and economic citizenship have been expressed in terms of rights for those who cannot consume in a world where personal consumption has displaced production for the nation as the imperative of how to bring economic growth. A new vocabulary of consumers, clients, and users pervades discussion of public services that have become increasingly commodified.[28] The central government began to allocate more revenue to states, and economic policy was decentralized.[29]

For certain classes, usually from upper-caste and middle-caste backgrounds, 1991 indeed marked the beginning of a new economic and social life in India.[30] The consumption of foreign goods and services was one way in which this new life was experienced, a corollary of the increased interrelation between India and the global economy and the spread of technology. An enterprise culture of aspiration can be found in the youth, and vocational skills training has become a major industry.[31] The new culture was captured perhaps most strikingly in cinema. Narratives in film gravitated toward the individualized pursuit of economic gain and even began to celebrate market-based entrepreneurship. In the 2010 film *Band Baaja Baaraat* (Band, musical revelry, wedding procession), which is about a wedding-planner business run by two recent college graduates, Bittoo and Shruti, the "market" is seen to be a great leveler between established businesses—which cut corners and skimp on quality—and the start-up of the protagonists, which gives clients a bespoke experience tailored to their budgets. The film celebrates their work ethic, ability to improvise, and drive to succeed. They win more and more business for larger and larger weddings.[32] At the end, Bittoo and Shruti get married. Consumption and entrepreneurialism have become parts of life for the new middle classes in ways they had not been previously.

So if 1991 did mark a paradigm shift toward neoliberalism, does neoliberalism have distinctive characteristics in India? It has been tempting to label today's ascendant Hindu nationalists and their Bharatiya Janata Party (BJP) as neoliberal, but a neoliberal ethos has appealed across most of the political spectrum, with the exception of the Left. It is true that the commodification of the Hindu religion has accelerated. For example, god-woman Radhe Maa became a celebrity whose likeness was portrayed in the 2012 Hindi film *OMG—Oh My God!* Meanwhile, god-man Baba Ramdev leveraged his public visibility to build the billion-dollar ayurvedic brand Patanjali.[33] This process has more quotidian consequences, as well. Matrimonial websites have created new possibilities for those seeking spouses of the same caste. And although not religious in itself, the wisdom of the ancients is consulted by some as a guide to modern business practices.[34] One can certainly see that the local instantiation of neoliberalism has in some cases taken on religious characteristics and that cultural practices have incorporated the logic of markets into their functioning.

But is today's ascendant Hindu nationalism neoliberal, or has it taken on a neoliberal garb? The early 1990s saw the implementation of quotas for what the government designates as Other Backward Classes in the government and higher-education sectors. This was perceived by the BJP to threaten the solidarity of Hindu society. To help create feelings of unity, the party's senior leader, L. K. Advani, made a *ratha yatra* (chariot journey) to the site where the Hindu god Ram was allegedly born. His ultimate objective was the creation of a temple on the site where the Babri Masjid (mosque) stood.[35] A widespread awareness of this theatrical performance was created, thanks to the proliferation of access to television, and the mosque was demolished by BJP supporters.[36] Recently, construction began on a Ram temple at this site.

While it is difficult to establish a philosophical affinity between neoliberalism and Hindu nationalism, one can say that Hindu nationalism has been successful at exploiting the landscape of a neoliberal India for its rise.

The paradigm shift from the past that occurred with the set of economic policies adopted beginning in 1991 created knock-on effects that changed social and economic lives and discourses in India. But why exactly did India go beyond what was required of stabilization, and what accounts for some kinds of neoliberal policies being embraced to the neglect of others? India is hardly held up as a model of neoliberal policy, and most free-market economists and outlets continue to regard the country as not having gone far enough to make markets work.[37] The prehistory of liberalization helps address this question.

THE PREHISTORY OF LIBERALIZATION

While internal constituencies for economic liberalization date back to the early days of Indian independence after 1947, external pressures intensified from the 1970s onward and combined by the 1980s to set India on a path toward reform. State-led developmentalism was dominant in India and associated with the towering presence of its longest-serving prime minister, Jawaharlal Nehru (in office from 1947 to 1964). India pursued a capital goods–led import substituting industrialization strategy of mixed public- and private-sector ownership.[38] Although "socialism" was the dominant idiom of the time it was never hegemonic. From the 1950s on, there was a serious questioning of the trajectory of Indian economic policy. Finance Minister John Matthai resigned his post almost immediately after Nehru constituted the Planning Commission, proclaiming that it meant the end of federalism.[39] Nehru had been unable to take this measure as long as his more conservative deputy prime minister, Sardar Patel (1875–1950), who was more sympathetic to private business, was alive.[40] With the introduction of commodity controls and the inauguration of an industrial licensing policy to manage foreign exchange and direct resources toward heavy industry, the chorus of voices opposed grew louder.

Discourses of "free economy," as opposed to the nominally socialist planned economy, emerged in the English-language urban print public sphere. Born of anticommunism and aversion to business regulation, this discourse developed in some circles into an explicit embrace of free markets.[41] Contacts made with organizations such as the Foundation for Economic Education and the Mont Pelerin Society, especially through an organization called the Libertarian Social Institute, led to the penetration of neoliberal discourse in early independent India.[42] As a matter of fact, a reprint of Hayek's 1952 "The Rebirth of Liberalism" article from the foundation's *Freeman* magazine, which explicitly mentioned "neoliberalism" as a transatlantic phenomenon and listed its votaries, appeared later that year in Bombay's *Free Economic Review*.[43]

India's closest link to organized neoliberalism in this period was through B. R. Shenoy (1905–1978). Shenoy was a monetary economist who began his university education in India with scholars trained in Austria. He subsequently went to the London School of Economics, where he encountered Hayek delivering the lectures that become *Prices and Production* in the 1930s. At this time, Shenoy also published a couple of articles against Keynes's prescriptions in *A Treatise on Money*. Over the next two decades, Shenoy established himself as a respected monetary economist and reached senior positions in the Reserve Bank of India. Early writings reveal him to be critical of deficit financing and sternly conscious of the perils of inflation. However, he was not well known outside of economist circles in India. Shenoy pivoted toward public-affairs commentary after becoming director of the School of Social Sciences at Gujarat University in the mid-1950s. At this time, his widely disseminated "Note of Dissent on the Memorandum of the Panel of Economists" on the Second Five Year Plan appeared.

Broadly speaking, Shenoy critiqued the plan for running a large deficit, alleging that this would create galloping inflation. This caught the attention of the neoliberal development economist Peter Bauer, then at Cambridge and an early member of the Mont Pelerin Society. He invited Shenoy to the society's 1959 meeting at Oxford, where the latter delivered an impassioned speech on how India needed the philosophy of the society and that economic planning was taking India down the road to serfdom. This won Shenoy membership and the esteem of others in the society, most notably, Milton Friedman and Friedrich Hayek themselves.[44] When the United States was debating whether or not to increase foreign aid to India during the 1960s, and modernization theorists of the Kennedy and Johnson administrations lobbied for a "big push" toward industrial takeoff and economic stability that would contain communism, neoliberals such as Bauer waged an (ultimately unsuccessful) battle against them.[45] As Nicole Sackley has shown, Western neoliberals used Shenoy as a kind of Indian informant and made India a cautionary tale against dirigisme in economic policy.[46]

Shenoy's writings, which typically consisted of diatribes against economic controls and celebrations of free markets, also attracted the founders of the Swatantra ("Freedom") Party. Founded in 1959, Swatantra based its platform on a promarket agenda. Shenoy drafted the party's "Basic Economic Policy" document.[47] The party promised the abolition of the Planning Commission, the defense of private-property rights, deregulation of the economy, and openness to foreign direct investment. Swatantra's critique of Indian political economy was that it was a "permit-and-licence *raj*," an oligarchic coalition between the dominant Congress Party's politicians, government bureaucrats who determined the allocation of industrial permits and licenses for trade, and big business.[48] At one level, the party anticipated the critique leveled by the socialist Vivek Chibber decades later: the hold of big business on the economy arrested industrialization and prevented India from making the policy adjustments necessary for a more broadly based process of capital accumulation.[49] However, it would be a stretch to characterize Swatantra as "neoliberal." For one thing, its founders did not by and large subscribe to the methodological individualism of neoliberals. They did not consider economics to be a science or evince much interest in the use of law to produce ideal market activity. And they did not have a well-articulated policy on free trade.

Swatantra has typically been thought of as a reactionary party of feudal elements and ex-maharajas in North India. In this region, the *zamindari* system of large absentee landlords and intermediate revenue collectors was prominent. But this understanding misses that the party's principal theorists hailed from numerically small, but influential landed and mercantile communities from southern and western India. These regions had traditions of landowning cultivation, or *ryotwari*, and the communities in question were often transitioning to small capitalist enterprise.[50] The social constituency for liberalization policy was thus coming from these elements. After liberalization, it would be members of these communities, such as Tamil Brahmins, Patidars (Patels), Kammas, and Reddys, who thrived.[51] These dominant-caste communities have been at the forefront of such industries as agribusiness and construction. Some of their members have established leading conglomerates. Others have partaken of India's booming information technology sector, making use of their English-language training and education in computer science and engineering to make their fortunes in the diaspora.[52]

Swatantra became the largest opposition party in India by the late 1960s and formed a coalition government in one state. At the time, the 1967 election result was the worst ever for the Congress Party in India's one-party-dominant system. Although Congress won a majority in the lower house of Parliament again, it crucially lost major ground in seven state elections and was defeated in the state of Tamil Nadu. These results helped foment a Congress Party split in 1969; a major segment of Swatantra's supporters flocked to the more conservative wing of the split Congress. As Francine Frankel points out, Swatantra merely mirrored the tendencies of the strong, but suppressed right-wing elements in the coalition of the umbrella Congress Party, elements that had been outmaneuvered after Sardar Patel's death.

By the late 1960s, the curtains fell on import-substituting industrialization. The Indian economy fell into crisis. The period between 1966 and 1969 was declared a plan holiday as the country sought to reevaluate its economic strategy. India began to embrace a modicum of import liberalization and to accept greater loan conditionality from international institutions. Planning became more decentralized. The electoral outcomes of the 1967 elections were in part tied to economic discontent as the country experienced falling growth rates and increasing inflation.[53]

The 1971 elections can be seen as a referendum on Indian development. Indira Gandhi's Congress, which ran on a poverty-alleviation platform, was less than sympathetic toward the market line and won an astonishing victory. Both Swatantra and the old wing of Congress were decimated. This has been characterized as an era of populist socialism led by Indira Gandhi (in office from 1966 to 1977 and 1980 to 1984). It saw the nationalization of banks (starting in 1969) and of insurance and coal companies, the passage of anti-monopoly legislation, and the introduction of measures for the well-being of landless laborers and small producers.[54]

But Srinath Raghavan's forthcoming work challenges this thesis by showing how Gandhi's suspension of democracy and declaration of a state of emergency (1975 to 1977) was accompanied by a redirection of policy toward big business and new dynamics in India's relationship to the world economy after the collapse of the Bretton Woods system.[55] Even when Indira maneuvered to insert "socialist" into the preamble of India's constitution in 1976, the country was simultaneously relying on the expertise of market-sympathetic officials and technocrats to tide over balance-of-payments difficulties that had cropped up during the oil shocks of that decade.[56] These shocks forced India into confrontations with the International Monetary Fund and the World Bank. Under duress, the country began increasingly to accept loan conditionality and temporary trade liberalization schemes. Bureaucrats such as P. N. Dhar and B. K. Nehru were sympathetic to such policies and helped persuade the prime minister to accept their terms.[57] The year after India became constitutionally socialist was also when a private company, Reliance (now owned by India's richest Indian), conducted the first initial public offering.[58] This period was also an economic point of inflection of sorts. With the exception of 1979, the year of the second oil shock, India moved to a higher growth trajectory from the middle of the 1970s.

More broadly, the period from the mid-1960s to about 1980 saw the emergence of new actors in the private sector, aided by the reform of certain intellectual property laws and crackdowns on monopoly practices.[59] A number of these actors had agrarian pasts and benefited from agricultural reforms to increase food production through the embrace of high-yielding varieties of seeds. Capital strengthened its hold over labor during the period. It benefited from the government's imperative of disciplining the economy and putting down strikes that responded to the real wage declines prompted by the increasing inflation from the mid-1960s onward.

From the 1980s on, these probusiness measures contributed to increased growth rates from 3 to about 6 percent of the national product.[60] The country began a slow integration into the global economy. Balance-of-payments problems continued to mean that India would have to embrace piecemeal measures to tap larger and larger IMF loans. Reforms initiated during the 1980s increased the power of new capitalist entrants and created a broader constituency for liberalization. However, international pressures had not consolidated around a kind of agenda for development, as they did later. India's balance-of-payments problems continued, but the need for systemic reform did not quite present itself. Thus, the year 1991 proved to be one of opportunity for these latent forces to find expression. They were aided by the decline of the Soviet Union and the early articulation of the Washington Consensus, the emerging set of economic policy recommendations for developing countries. The events of early the 1990s also indicated that politicians and technocrats had managed to overcome challenges to reform posed by the coalition between big business and the Congress Party, or at least that these latter groups perceived the benefits of openness to outweigh the costs.

Owing to the paucity of historical work on independent India and its economic history, this prehistory of liberalization is necessarily sketchy. Nonetheless, it suggests a few things about neoliberalism or the lack thereof in the Indian context. First, India had contacts with mainstream neoliberalism from the 1950s on, but neoliberalism did not catch on in a meaningful way in terms of influencing policy. To the extent that there was engagement with its ideas, it was through opposition figures. Ultimately, it was pressure from international institutions and technocrats inside the government that shaped the beginnings of economic reform processes that would later be seen as key components of neoliberalism. Second, a crisis in import-substituting industrialization coinciding with the collapse of the Bretton Woods system forced India to refashion its economic policies and slowly open up the economy along certain avenues in what was considered rhetorically to be the heyday of socialism. Finally, despite the facilitation of agrarian capital accumulation, the impetus behind the higher growth trajectory from the late 1970s on was the support of existing large firms, rather than the creation of conditions for the entrance of foreign capital and widespread entrepreneurship. This was probusiness, rather than promarket activity.

At this stage, it is also worth pointing out that with the advent of liberalization reforms, there has also been a small, but prominent group of Indian economists working in leading universities in the United States and United Kingdom who have seen themselves as vindicated. Beginning in the 1970s, they leveled major critiques against Indian trade policy and betrayed a skepticism of the policy-making paradigm at large. Chief among these was Columbia's Jagdish Bhagwati, who along with his wife, economist Padma Desai, skewered Indian trade policy for being too inward looking in their 1970 book, *India: Planning for Industrialization*. Bhagwati and Yale University–based T. N. Srinivasan's *Foreign Trade Regimes and Economic Development: India* (1975) made a similar argument.[61] The Ministry of Finance under Singh commissioned the likes of Bhagwati and Srinivasan to write about the reforms shortly after they were passed and to provide them with a certain intellectual ballast, and these two were consulted in the process of defining them.[62] However, while these were neoclassical economists sympathetic to market reforms, one could hardly call them neoliberal at that stage.

ORGANIZED NEOLIBERALISM IN POSTREFORM INDIA

The neoliberal label fits more appropriately with the recently deceased Deepak Lal (1940–2020). A UCL and then UCLA economist, Lal consulted for a number of international institutions and governments over the course of his career. By the late 1970s and certainly from the 1980s on, when he completed a stint as research director of the World Bank, Lal appears to have been won over to mainstream neoliberalism.[63] He advised Conservative UK governments and would go on to become president of the Mont Pelerin Society from 2008 to 2010.[64] Although hardly a major figure in Indian policy making, he was visible in postreform economic discourse, writing a weekly column in the Indian newspaper the *Business Standard*.[65]

Lal has been celebrated by the New Delhi–based Centre for Civil Society (CCS), which held an event for the economist's 2015 book, *Poverty and Progress*, and interviewed him on various topics.[66] Founded in 1997, the CCS in New Delhi is the standard-bearer for neoliberalism in India. Although the organization refers to itself as a liberal, rather than neoliberal think tank, invoking classical liberalism, their interest has been not so much in laissez-faire as in the design of policies to make the market mechanism work better. In the decade before founding the CCS, its director, Parth Shah, trained in the Austrian tradition at Auburn University and taught at the University of Michigan at Dearborn in the United States.[67] The initial funds for starting the organization came from the Earhart Foundation, which closed in 2016, but funded multiple members in the Atlas Network of free-market think tanks.

In a contribution to an edited volume of stories by Atlas Network members, Shah describes his return to India as one that subjected him to the "dehumanizing effects of government monopolies" in telecoms and electricity that made home life a challenge in the beginning.[68] If politically independent, according to Shah, India was not civically independent and required a civil society to be developed to take care of itself while the state, as he hoped, "withers away." Shah described himself in the process of "developing our own soldiers for battle" and undertaking the "mammoth challenge" of "the indoctrination of the Indian youth, who came from a state-dominated education system." Shah believes that India's major challenge is that even if statism in India with respect to production is gone, it still reigns supreme in the domain of social welfare. He wants the state to withdraw and imagines that one day India can become "a liberal utopia" and win its "second movement for Independence." The CCS's website lists its vision as one of "a world where each individual leads a life of choice in personal, economic and political spheres and every institution is accountable."[69]

The organization's primary work is divided into three projects: the school choice campaign, a project to "eradicate market entry and exit barriers" to street entrepreneurs by campaigning against the requirement for licenses, and policy training. It has also been involved in public-interest litigation in the High Court and Supreme Court and has campaigned for the granting of forest land rights to tribal communities. The activities of the CCS thus address both elite and poor communities, underpinned by a stress on the importance of free markets. Over the last couple of years, the CCS's leaders have also taken stewardship of a new school offering a one-year course in public policy.[70]

The CCS has been invested in recovering an Indian history of what it calls liberalism through an online portal called Indian Liberals. These reproduce writings on dissent about socialism and pamphlets of organizations such as the Bombay-based Forum of Free Enterprise and journals from the 1950s such as *The Indian Libertarian*.[71] In 2018, the organization supervised the turnover of the Swatantra Party's papers to the Nehru Memorial Library, marked by a major day-long conference on the party and its legacies.[72] Shah and R. K. Amin, a former Swatantra member of Parliament and Mont Pelerin Society member, have collected B. R. Shenoy's academic and public writings and refer to him as "The Man Who Saw India's Future."[73] We can see this as an attempt of the Indian neoliberal movement to construct a genealogy for itself and to assert that India has had a "liberal" tradition, long suppressed and now finding vindication in the postliberalization world.

CONCLUSION

BJP leader Narendra Modi's election in 2014 caused great excitement for the neoliberal media and nonresident Indians in the Anglosphere who left India in the pursuit of better economic opportunities.[74] Bhagwati lauded the result, considering it the harbinger of a new era of growth.[75] His protégé, Arvind Panagariya, Columbia's Jagdish N. Bhagwati Professor of Indian Political Economy, went to work at the NITI Aayog, the body constituted for economic advice after the BJP disbanded the Planning Commission.[76] However, what the last six years have shown is that while the BJP has adopted certain kinds of market-sympathetic policies, it is far from a neoliberal party.[77] Despite having climbed the scales of the World Bank's ease of doing business rankings, foreign investment remains capital shy. Ambitious plans for public-sector privatization have recently been outlined, but the state sector remains prominent.[78] Election-time handouts, which expanded the fiscal deficit, would be considered anathema to neoliberals.[79] Measures such as the demonetization of the rupee in 2016 were not market friendly and brought down the growth rate.[80] The procedure was regarded skeptically by most of the economics community. The BJP's economic policy has been a product of competing influences of which neoliberalism is a small and relatively insignificant part.

Neoliberalism has an Indian prehistory and even a present that should be acknowledged to contextualize developments in Indian society and economy. Even where neoliberalism is not hegemonic, neoliberals can contribute to policy discourses. But alone—admittedly, in the rather purist way in which I have considered it—neoliberalism is inadequate as a way of thinking about the guiding wisdom behind Indian economic policy. An agenda for future historical research should look at both the intellectual biography of technocrats and government officials who helped usher in market reforms and, as the sources become available, at how the government redesigned welfare policies and institutions in their aftermath. Here, a study of ideas may work best alongside examination of the relationships between forms of capital and the state that produced enterprises of the mixed economy. Both individually and together, these subverted the easy distinction between "public" and "private" and were products both of the state and the market.[81]

NOTES

1. Angus Burgin, "The Neoliberal Turn." I am grateful to Burgin for sharing his unpublished work and giving me permission to cite it.

2. Sebastian Conrad, *What is Global History?* (Princeton: Princeton University Press, 2017); Conrad, "Decolonizing the AHR," *American Historical Review* 123.1 (2018), pp. xiv–xvii.

3. The sum of European and North American GDP comes to just under half of the world's total, and when considered on a per capita basis, the figures are more striking. World Economic Forum, "The $86 Trillion World Economy—in One Chart," September 2019, https://www.weforum.org/agenda/2019/09/fifteen-countries-represent-three-quarters-total-gdp.

4. Exemplars of the "economist-centered" genre include Quinn Slobodian,

Globalists: The End of Empire and the Origins of Neoliberalism (Cambridge, MA: Harvard University Press, 2018).

5. Peter A. Hall, ed., *The Political Power of Economic Ideas: Keynesianism across Nations* (Princeton, NJ: Princeton University Press, 1989).

6. Examples include Philip Mirowski and Dieter Plehwe, *The Road from Mont Pèlerin: The Making of the Neoliberal Thought Collective* (Cambridge, MA: Harvard University Press, 2009); Janek Wasserman, *The Marginal Revolutionaries: How Austrian Economists Fought the War of Ideas* (New Haven: Yale University Press, 2019); Daniel Stedman Jones, *Masters of the Universe: Hayek, Friedman, and the Birth of Neoliberal Politics* (Princeton: Princeton University Press, 2012).

7. Johanna Bockman, *Markets in the Name of Socialism: The Left-Wing Origins of Neoliberalism* (Stanford: Stanford University Press, 2011).

8. Burgin, "The Neoliberal Turn."

9. Cornel Ban, *Ruling Ideas: How Neoliberalism Goes Local* (Oxford: Oxford University Press, 2016), p. 11.

10. In the American context, see Melinda Cooper, *Family Values: Between Neoliberalism and the New Social Conservatism* (New York: Zone Books, 2017).

11. Dipesh Chakrabarty, *Provincializing Europe: Postcolonial Thought and Historical Difference* (Princeton: Princeton University Press, 2000).

12. C. A. Bayly, *Recovering Liberties: Indian Thought in the Age of Liberalism and Empire* (Cambridge: Cambridge University Press, 2012).

13. Neilesh Bose, "The Cannibalized Career of Liberalism in Colonial India," *Modern Intellectual History* 12.2 (2015), pp. 475–84.

14. Andrew Sartori, *Liberalism in Empire: An Alternative History* (Berkeley: University of California Press, 2014).

15. The approach is articulated most clearly in Andrew Sartori, "The Resonance of 'Culture': Framing a Problem in Global Concept-History,' *Comparative Studies in Society and History* 47.4 (2005), pp. 676–99.

16. Greg Grandin, *Empire's Workshop: Latin America, the United States, and the Rise of the New Imperialism* (New York: Holt, 2006); Naomi Klein, *The Shock Doctrine: The Rise of Disaster Capitalism* (New York: Holt, 2007).

17. "The Tiger Caged: A Survey of India," *Economist*, May 4, 1991, quoted in Sugata Bose, "Instruments and Idioms of Colonial and National Development"

in Frederick Cooper and Randall Packard, eds., *International Development and the Social Sciences: Essays on the History and Politics of Knowledge* (Berkeley: University of California Press, 1998), pp. 45-63. See also Gurcharan Das, *India Unbound* (New York: Alfred A. Knopf, 2001), in which one of the chapter titles is actually "The Golden Summer of 1991"; Dani Rodrik and Arvind Subramanian, "From 'Hindu Growth' to Productivity Surge: The Mystery of the Indian Growth Transition," *IMF Staff Papers* 52.2 (2005).

18. Vijay Joshi and I. M. D. Little, *India's Economic Reforms, 1991-2001* (New Delhi: Oxford University Press, 1996), pp. 14-62.

19. Jagdish Bhagwati and T. N. Srinivasan, *India's Economic Reforms* (New Delhi: Ministry of Finance, 1993).

20. Jairam Ramesh, *To the Brink and Back: India's 1991 Story* (New Delhi: Rupa, 2015); Sanjaya Baru, *1991: How P. V. Narasimha Rao Made History* (New Delhi: Aleph, 2016); Vinay Sitapati, *The Man Who Remade India: A Biography of P. V. Narasimha Rao* (New York: Oxford University Press, 2018).

21. Francine R. Frankel, *India's Political Economy, 1947-2004*, 2nd ed. (New Delhi: Oxford University Press, 2005); Sukhamoy Chakravarty, *Development Planning: The Indian Experience* (Oxford: Clarendon Press, 1987).

22. Sushil Khanna, "State-Owned Enterprises in India: Restructuring and Growth," *Copenhagen Journal of Asian Studies* 30.2 (2012), pp. 5-28; The World Bank, "General Government Final Consumption Expenditure (% of GDP) -India," https://data.worldbank.org/indicator/NE.CON.GOVT.ZS?locations=IN.

23. Vijay Prashad, *The Darker Nations: A People's History of the Third World* (New York: New Press, 2007), pp. 207-24; Margaret Garritsen De Vries, *The IMF in a Changing World, 1945-85* (Washington, DC: International Monetary Fund, 1986), pp. 129-48. Of course, the Indian economy had from the early postcolonial period been heavily dependent on foreign aid, which by the 1960s came with an increasing number of strings attached. David Engerman, *The Price of Aid: The Economic Cold War in India* (Cambridge, MA: Harvard University Press, 2018), pp. 227-346.

24. Bishnupriya Gupta, "Falling Behind and Catching Up: India's Transition from a Colonial Economy," *Economic History Review* 72.3 (2019), pp. 803-27.

25. Santosh Koner and Jaydeb Sarkhel, "Disinvestment of Public Sector in India: Concept and Different Issues," *IOSR Journal of Economics and Finance* 3.6 (2014), pp. 48–52; Khanna, "State-Owned Enterprises in India".

26. Reserve Bank of India, *The Reserve Bank of India,Volume 4: 1981–1997* (New Delhi: Academic Foundation, 2013).

27. Kalyan Sanyal, *Rethinking Capitalist Development: Primitive Accumulation, Governmentality and Post-Colonial Capitalism* (New Delhi: Routledge, 2007).

28. Niraja Jayal, *Citizenship and its Discontents: An Indian History* (Cambridge, MA: Harvard University Press, 2013), pp. 163–99.

29. Louise Tillin, *Indian Federalism* (New Delhi: Oxford University Press, 2019), pp. 104–26.

30. Waquar Ahmed, et al., eds., *India's New Economic Policy: A Critical Analysis* (New York: Routledge, 2010).

31. Nandini Gooptu, ed., *Enterprise Culture in Neoliberal India: Studies in Youth, Class, Work and Media* (London: Routledge, 2013).

32. Purnima Mankekar, "'We Are Like This Only': Aspiration, 'Jugaad,' and Love in Enterprise Culture," in Gooptu, ed., *Enterprise Culture in Neoliberal India*, pp. 27–41.

33. John Zavos, et al., eds., *Public Hinduisms* (New Delhi: Sage, 2012); Kaushik Deka, *The Baba Ramdev Phenomenon: From Moksha to Market* (New Delhi: Rupa, 2017).

34. Ashok R. Garde, *Chanakya on Management* (New Delhi: Jaico, 2013).

35. Sukumar Muralidharan, "Mandal, Mandir, aur Masjid: 'Hindu' Communalism and the Crisis of the State," *Social Scientist* 18.10 (1990), pp. 27–49.

36. Arvind Rajagopal, *Politics after Television: Hindu Nationalism and the Reshaping of the Public in India* (Cambridge: Cambridge University Press, 2001).

37. "India's Government Is Scrambling to Revive the Economy," *Economist*, August 31, 2019, https://www.economist.com/finance-and-economics/2019/08/31/indias-government-is-scrambling-to-revive-the-economy.

38. Chakravarty, *Development Planning*.

39. V. Haridasan, *Dr. John Matthai, 1886–1959: A Biography* (Kottayam: Church Missionary Society Press, 1986), pp. 92 and 94.

40. Ashoka Mehta, *Economic Consequences of Sardar Patel* (Bombay: Socialist Party, 1950); Rajmohan Gandhi, *Patel: A Life* (Ahmedabad: Navjivan, 1990).

41. Aditya Balasubramanian, "Contesting 'Permit-and-Licence *Raj*': Economic Conservatism and the Idea of Democracy in 1950s India," *Past and Present* 251.1 (2021), pp. 189–227.

42. I discuss this fully in Aditya Balasubramanian, "Free Economy and Opposition Politics in India, c. 1940–70," PhD diss., University of Cambridge, 2018.

43. Friedrich Hayek, "A Rebirth of Liberalism," *Freeman*, July 28, 1952, pp. 729–31, reprinted in *Free Economic Review*, October 9, 1952, pp. 9–11.

44. This paragraph follows Balasubramanian, "Alone at Home, among Friends Abroad: B.R. Shenoy from Austrian School Monetary Economist to Cold-War Public Intellectual," in Srinath Raghavan and Nandini Sundar, eds., *A Functioning Anarchy?: Essays for Ramachandra Guha* (New Delhi: Penguin, 2020), pp. 165–79.

45. Peter Bauer, *United States and Indian Economic Development* (Washington, DC: American Enterprise Institute, 1959); K.C. Pearce, *Rostow, Kennedy, and the Rhetoric of Foreign Aid* (East Lansing: Michigan State University Press, 2001).

46. Nicole Sackley, "The Road from Serfdom: Economic Storytelling and Narratives of India in the Rise of Neoliberalism," *History and Technology* 31.4 (2015), pp. 397–419.

47. Balasubramanian, "Free Economy and Opposition Politics," p. 225.

48. See Balasubramanian, "Contesting 'Permit-and-Licence *Raj*.'"

49. Vivek Chibber, *Locked in Place: State-Building and Late Industrialization in India* (Princeton: Princeton University Press, 2003).

50. On the distinction between these forms of revenue settlement, see Sekhar Bandyopadhyay, *From Plassey to Partition: A History of Modern India*, 2nd ed. (New Delhi: Orient Longman, 2006), pp. 8 and 70.

51. Harish Damodaran, *India's New Capitalists: Caste, Business, and Industry in a Modern Nation* (Basingstoke: Palgrave Macmillan, 2008).

52. David Washbrook, "Brain Drain, Exchange and Gain: 'Hi-Skill' Migrants and the Developed Economies," in Joya Chatterji and David Washbrook, eds., *Routledge Handbook of the South Asian Diaspora* (Oxford: Routledge, 2014), pp. 251–60.

53. Francine R. Frankel, *India's Political Economy: 1947–2004* (New Delhi: Oxford University Press, 2005), pp. 246–92.

54. Srinath Raghavan, "Decoding the Emergency," *Seminar* 677 (2016), http://www.india-seminar.com/2016/677/677_srinath_raghavan.htm.

55. A preview of this work appears in Srinath Raghavan, "What Emergency Meant for Big Business in India," *NDTV*, June 25, 2015, https://www.ndtv.com/opinion/how-the-emergency-transformed-indias-economy-774957.

56. Granville Austin, *Working a Democratic Constitution: The Indian Experience* (New Delhi: Oxford University Press, 1999), pp. 293–391.

57. Raghavan, "Decoding the Emergency"; P. N. Dhar, "Evolution of Economic Policy in India," in Dhar, *The Evolution of Economic Policy in India: Selected Essays* (New Delhi: Oxford University Press, 2003), pp. 15–38; B. K. Nehru, *Nice Guys Finish Second* (New Delhi: Viking, 1997).

58. Surajit Mazumdar, "From 'Outsider' to Insider: The Case of Reliance," *South Asia Multidisciplinary Academic Journal* 15 (2017), http://samaj.revues.org/4278.

59. This paragraph follows Chirashree Dasgupta, *State and Capital in Independent India: Institutions and Accumulation* (Cambridge: Cambridge University Press, 2016), pp. 177–217.

60. Rodrik and Subramanian, "From 'Hindu Growth' to Productivity Surge," pp. 193–228

61. Jagdish Bhagwati and Padma Desai, *India: Planning for Industrialization: Industrialization and Trade Policies Since 1951* (London: Oxford University Press, 1970); Jagdish Bhagwati and T. N. Srinivasan, *Foreign Trade Regimes and Economic Development: India* (Cambridge, MA: National Bureau of Economic Research, 1975).

62. Bhagwati and Srinivasan, *India's Economic Reforms.*

63. His CV is available at http://www.econ.ucla.edu/Lal/cv2004.pdf.

64. One of his attacks on dirigisme is Deepak Lal, *The Poverty of "Development Economics"* (London: Institute of Economic Affairs, 1983).

65. Suman Bery, "For a Conservative, Deepak Lal Saw Deep Strengths in India's Civil Society," *Business Standard*, May 1, 2020, https://www.business

-standard.com/article/beyond-business/for-a-conservative-deepak-lal-saw
-deep-strengths-in-india-s-civil-society-120050101027_1.html.

66. The Centre for Civil Society held a book launch for him on May 13, 2015. "Event Report: Book Launch | 'Poverty and Progress,'" https://ccs.in /event-report-book-launch-poverty-and-progress. A video excerpt from the interview, titled "Deepak Lal on FA Hayek and Milton Friedman," is available at https://www.youtube.com/watch?v=VbXXosdTqEk.

67. On the Austrian school and its ties to neoliberalism, see Wasserman, *The Marginal Revolutionarie.*

68. This paragraph follows Parth Shah, "Awakening a Slumbering Elephant," in Colleen Dyble, ed., *Freedom Champions: Stories from the Front Lines in the War of Ideas. 30 Case Studies by Intellectual Entrepreneurs Who Champion the Cause of Freedom* (Washington, DC: Atlas Economic Research Foundation, 2011), pp. 109–20, https://www.atlasnetwork.org/assets/uploads /misc/FreedomChampions.pdf.

69. Centre for Civil Society, "Vision," http://www.ccs.in.

70. Indian School of Public Policy, http://www.ispp.org.in).

71. Indian Liberals, http://indianliberals.in.

72. Centre for Civil Society, "Swatantra Conference: Principles, People, Politics," https://ccsindia.org/swatantra-conference-principles-people-politics -india-education-diary.

73. R. K. Amin and Parth Shah, eds., *Economic Prophecies: B. R. Shenoy* (New Delhi: Centre for Civil Society, 2004), and R. K. Amin and Parth Shah, eds., *Theoretical Vision: B. R. Shenoy* (New Delhi: Centre for Civil Society, 2004).

74. P. S. Palit, "Modi and the Indian Diaspora," *RSIS Commentary*, no. 241, November 28, 2019, https://www.rsis.edu.sg/wp-content/uploads/2019/11 /CO19241.pdf.

75. "Jagdish Bhagwati Lauds PM Narendra Modi for Reforms Initiatives, Compares Him with Obama," *Economic Times*, January 15, 2015, https:// economictimes.indiatimes.com/news/politics-and-nation/jagdish-bhagwati -lauds-pm-narendra-modi-for-reforms-initiatives-compares-him-with-obama /articleshow/45876368.cms.

76. Nikita Doval and Gireesh Chandra Prasad, "Arvind Panagariya: An Early Champion of Narendra Modi," *Livemint*, August 2, 2017, https://www.livemint.com/Politics/GaaQ8L3ysgmGgOkz1xNEDP/Arvind-Panagariya-An-early-champion-of-Narendra-Modi.html.

77. Gautam Mehta, "Hindu Nationalism and the BJP's Economic Record," in Milan Vaishnav, ed., *The BJP in Power: Indian Democracy and Religious Nationalism* (Washington, DC: *Carnegie Endowment for International Peace*, 2019), pp. 63–72; Remya Nair, "Privatisation Gets Mega Push in Budget 2021, Most Ambitious Plan since Vajpayee Era," *ThePrint*, February 1, 2021, https://theprint.in/economy/privatisation-gets-mega-push-in-budget-2021-most-ambitious-plan-since-vajpayee-era/596280.

78. Aparna Iyer, "A Reality Check on India's Ease of Business Rankings," *Livemint*, July 1, 2019, https://www.livemint.com/market/mark-to-market/a-reality-check-on-india-s-ease-of-business-rankings-1561961880722.html.

79. Aftab Ahmed and Krishna N. Das, "Modi's Pre-Election Handouts to Cost India Billions, Breach Fiscal Targets: Sources," *Reuters*, January 18, 2019, https://www.reuters.com/article/us-india-election-budget/modis-pre-election-handouts-to-cost-india-billions-breach-fiscal-targets-sources-idUSKCN1PC0KC.

80. Gabriel Chodorow-Reich, et al., "Cash and the Economy: Evidence from India's Demonetization," *NBER Working Paper* 2570 (2019), https://www.nber.org/system/files/working_papers/w25370/revisions/w25370.rev1.pdf.

81. Amy C. Offner, *Sorting out the Mixed Economy: The Rise and Fall of Welfare and Development States in the Americas* (Princeton: Princeton University Press, 2019).

CHAPTER THREE

Constructing Turkey's "Magic Political Formula": The Association for Liberal Thinking's Neoliberal Intellectual Project

Esra Elif Nartok

This chapter investigates the efforts of the Association for Liberal Thinking (ALT, Liberal Düşünce Topluluğu) to provide an intellectual foundation for neoliberalism in Turkey. Established in Ankara in 1992, the ALT gathered many of Turkey's liberal intellectuals under one roof. From the start, the group announced that they were not chasing "big claims," such as contributing to liberal philosophy in a universal sense. Rather, their goals were local: "To contribute to the development of liberal thought in Turkey," to "introduce and discuss liberalism as a social and political theory," and to "provide solutions to Turkey's main problems from a liberal perspective."[1] Yet the ALT's motivations were not restricted to the Turkish context in its mission and intellectual sources. It took the London-based Institute of Economic Affairs (IEA), founded in 1955, as a model and saw itself as a part of "the chain of liberal institutes" formed in different parts of the world through the efforts of Friedrich Hayek and Antony Fisher.[2] Similar to other links in the chain, the ALT aimed to both organize locally and to contribute to "the liberal international" represented by the Mont Pelerin Society (MPS).[3]

Investigating the ALT's project sheds light on the intellectual and ideological underpinnings of Turkey's road to neoliberalism. Three notes should be made at the outset to put the Turkish case in global context. First, Turkey's neoliberal transformation resembles that of some Latin American countries such as Chile, where change happened through force (that is, coups d'état), rather than through smooth or gradual processes of reform.[4] The coercive start in the 1980s made the process of manufacturing consent especially important. The ALT emerged as the main liberal intellectual group during the neoliberal restructuring of the economy and society in the 1990s. It participated actively in the neoliberal transformation of the country by disseminating concepts such as "free-market economy" and "rule of law" in Turkey's intellectual and political circles and localizing them. In the early 2000s, it also consulted with the Justice and Development Party (JDP), which has been the country's leading neoliberal party for almost two decades now.

Second, Turkey's neoliberal transformation started with the direct involvement of the Bretton Woods institutions similar to that of many Global South countries. This included the application of multiple successive structural adjustment programs to integrate Turkey's economy with the rest of the world through export-oriented development strategies. The manufacturing of consent for neoliberal economic policies happened through the effective deployment of religion in the neoliberal hegemonic project on the sociopolitical level through a so-called Turkish-Islamic synthesis. Turkey's neoliberal transformation shows significant parallels with that of India in terms of the use of religion, specifically, the religion of the majority—Islam in Turkey and Hinduism in India (compare Balasubramanian, "[Is] India in the History of Neoliberalism?" in this volume)—in the neoliberal project to stabilize social forces in times of neoliberal change.[5] As the main liberal intellectual grouping, the ALT paid special attention to the topic of religion from the 1990s on.

Third, despite its resemblances to Global South countries, Turkey occupies a relatively unusual place in the wider global political economy. The binary of Global South versus Global North is uneasy for Turkey, because it shares features of both.[6] From its establishment under a modernization agenda in the 1920s until the 2010s, complying with the so-called "civilizational" standards of the West was always on Turkey's agenda.[7] As a Cold War ally of the Western bloc, Turkey has been a member of the North Atlantic Treaty Organization since 1952. Contrary to the dominant impression of Turkey as a country failing by the monolithic standards of neoliberal development for a variety of reasons, ranging from religious populism and authoritarianism to economic instability, a number of economic reforms in the 1980s did insert key elements of neoliberal economic governance in the country.

Turkey registered significant economic growth rates with neoliberalization, particularly in the 2000s, when its European Union (EU) membership was in process. Although the country has been commonly placed within the geographical category of the Middle East in the last decade due to the shift in its foreign policy, its regional identity is generally borderline (East and West, South and North) reflecting its geopolitical location, history, and developmental strategies. Turkey's intellectual life also developed in relation to the West's impact. While supporting the military coup that led the country's neoliberal transformation in the 1980s, the liberal circle from which the ALT stemmed, Yeni Forum (New Forum), argued for "the creation and internalisation of a Turkish-Islamic-Western civilisation."[8]

With this global context in mind, this chapter focuses on the ALT's Mont Pelerin Society–inspired and locally motivated intellectual project and in particular how the ALT made neoliberalism Turkey's own through its specific engagement with religion. After a brief account of the Turkish road to neoliberalism, it turns to the ALT's intellectual project by focusing on its reconceptualization of Islam alongside free-market ideology. Finding Islam's particular place in Turkish neoliberalism reflects the ALT's intellectual project in its early years, broadly covering the period between its establishment (1992) and its consultation with the JDP (2004). This chapter reveals that the ALT's construction of Islam as "compatible" with neoliberalism and as "embedded" in Turkish society played a key part in making sense of neoliberalism in

Turkey. The ALT did not simply pay intellectual heed to Islam; instead, it used and reinterpreted Islam with a purpose—to reinforce the acceptance and localization of neoliberal ideas in the Turkish context.

TURKEY'S ROAD TO NEOLIBERALISM

Following a balance-of-payments crisis in the late 1970s, Turkey's neoliberal transition occurred with the January 24, 1980 Economic Stability Program prepared by the U.S.-educated Turkish technocrat Turgut Özal, the undersecretary of the Prime Ministry at the time, who had previously served as a consultant at the World Bank. The program was presented as a remedy for the economic crisis and macroeconomic instabilities that Turkey had been facing for some time. Linking these problems to the development strategy based on import-substitution industrialization that Turkey had adopted systematically since the mid-1950s, the program required a reorientation of the Turkish economy toward a low-wage, export-oriented development strategy while making the International Monetary Fund (IMF) and the World Bank "integral constituents of policymaking process" in the economy.[9] However, this was a difficult task under the existing 1961 constitution, which had given the working class the right to "establish their own economic and political organisations, albeit within certain limitations," along with other important social and economic rights in tandem with strong trade union activity.[10] The political atmosphere of the country had also been marked by class-based politics and a political polarization between the Right and the Left.

Under these circumstances, a natural evolution of the Turkish economy would have taken a long time; instead, the structure necessary for neoliberal transition was provided by the coup d'état on September 12, 1980. The military authorities explained the coup as necessary to end the chaos resulting from political polarization having adverse effects on the economy. The coup paved the way for the January 24 program. Özal, who prepared the neoliberal program, became the interim military regime's (1980 to 1983) deputy prime minister in charge of the economy. He then became prime minister after his Motherland Party (MP)—a right-wing conservative party—won the next elections. A key part of Özal's discourse in this period was *alternatifimiz yoktur*, a direct translation of the Thatcherite slogan "There Is No Alternative," introducing neoliberalism as the only option for the country. Drawing inspiration from Reaganism and Thatcherism, Özal stood for "an economically liberal and socio–politically nationalist and conservative stance."[11]

Özal's stance was underpinned by the Turkish–Islamic synthesis, which had been initiated by the right–wing intellectuals of the 1970s (specifically Aydınlar Ocağı) and which was supported by the coup generals.[12] The reconstruction of the Turkish economy was combined with a reconstruction of Turkish politics, giving rise to a redefinition of national identity along religious lines. The main components of the Turkish-Islamic synthesis were a cultural code favoring Sunni-Muslim identity as one of the key components of Turkish nation, conservatism, and a defensive stance on both domestic and foreign policy matters.[13] Given Turkey's strong commitment to secularism since its establishment, the implementation of the Turkish-Islamic synthesis was not done to encourage the Islamization of Turkey; instead, it was to control social opposition, render the leftist movements prior to the 1980s (with their organic ties to the working class) socially ineffective, and transfer their support bases to conservative parties, making use of popular religion's important place in common sense.[14] Turkey's class-based politics were replaced by identity politics in which Islam (Muslimhood, Sunni-Muslim identity, and so on) gained more prominence.[15]

The prominent liberal circle at the time—the Yeni Forum—in which the ALT's members were raised supported both the military coup of 1980 and the particular understanding of national identity crystallized in the Turkish-Islamic synthesis. The Yeni Forum and its most prominent member, Aydın Yalçın—a professor of economics at

Ankara University—advocated a center-right political position with a blend of liberal, conservative, and nationalist elements in Turkish politics, which was clearly in line with Özal's program.[16] Yalçın stood for the internalization of a Turkish-Islamic-Western civilization, an agenda that corresponded to that of the Yeni Forum's intellectual sources, which included Western liberal thinkers such as Karl Popper, Isaiah Berlin, Ayn Rand, Hayek, and many others.

The Yeni Forum's support for the coup and its support for liberalism require a note about the "liberal ambivalence" that marked the liberal tradition in Turkey, which, as Simten Coşar puts it rightly, "almost turns the liberal stance into a preference for capitalism, devoid of a systematic liberal political content."[17] Both the Yeni Forum and the liberal circles prior to it defined their liberalism within the context of Turkey's strong state tradition. Given the fact that Turkey had implemented etatism as its main economic policy since the 1930s, the state's dominance in Turkish economic life was one of the main targets of criticism for various strands of liberal thought. However, this did not lead to rejecting state intervention as such. These strands of thoughts constantly defined their approaches to individual liberties and liberal democracy with respect to the common good defined by the state.[18]

The ALT signified a break in Turkey's liberal tradition. Although benefiting from the intellectual sources of the Yeni Forum, the ALT prioritized Hayek's thought. Its most prominent founding figures were Atilla Yayla, an academic who received his degree in economics at Ankara University and was a student of Yalçın, and Mustafa Erdoğan, another academic who received his degree in law at the same university. They established relations with the Mont Pelerin Society and the IEA prior to the establishment of the ALT, and Yayla became a member of the MPS in the late 1990s.[19] Therefore, the group who founded the ALT were raised in the Yeni Forum, but were Turkey's first neoliberals.

For the ALT, the free-market economy was an end in itself, and all other things (that is, democracy, individual liberties) were indexed to it, not to the state or to the common good defined by it. As Coşar observes, this was the first time in the Turkish liberal tradition that the individual was conceptualized as "an independent category" and "the decisive actor in determining the common good."[20] While shifting the emphasis in political economy and embracing methodological individualism, the ALT also signaled continuity with its predecessor in its commitment to the Turkish-Islamic synthesis. This can be seen in the "magic political formula of Turkey," suggested by Yayla. The formula brought together Islamic conservative values with free-market principles while putting the latter at the center.[21]

Before dealing with the ALT's particular engagement with Islam, some notes should be made on the 1990s conjuncture into which the ALT was born. On the economic level, the 1990s were the decade of fiscal imbalances in Turkey and successive economic crises.[22] The country's neoliberal transformation came with problems adjusting to international financial flows and repeated standby agreements with the IMF to achieve economic stability. On the sociopolitical level, although the neoliberal hegemonic project initially employed religion as the basis of controlling social opposition, this had unexpected consequences in Turkey. First, neoliberalization prioritized improving economic relations with the West; however, opening up the economy to international finance capital paved the way for the participation of Islamic financial institutions from the Gulf region in Turkey's economy, as well as the participation of Western institutions. The involvement of the Islamic institutions was particularly significant in the banking sector, with their interest-free participatory finance mechanisms. This accelerated the integration of political Islamist groups in the new finance-based economic setting, improving their economic conditions and making them significant actors in Turkish political economy from the 1990s onward.

Second, the 1990s were marked by the rise of political Islam in Turkey, crystalized with the political Islamist Welfare Party's (WP) solidifying popular support. This created tensions between the state, which included the military forces, and the political Islamist groups, due to the military's perception of Islamists as a threat to Turkish democracy and its principle of secularism. The WP came from the National Vision Movement (NVM) of the 1970s, which not only understood Islam as a key constituent of the Turkish nation, but also advocated the redesign of the nation along Islamic lines. It stood for both an anti-Western and an anti-EU ideology, suggesting collaboration with Islamic, rather than Western countries. This was different than the Turkish-Islamic synthesis's conservative interpretation and instrumental application of religion in Turkish society, which would remain under the control of the state and military forces.

However, once Islam was deployed as a key element of the Turkish nation in the post-1980s conjuncture, political Islamist groups also benefited from Islam's growing importance, as well as from neoliberal economic policies. For that reason, religion in general was a hot topic on the political agenda around issues ranging from the problem of wearing head scarves in public institutions, including educational institutions, political Islamist groups' religious and business activities, the military intervention with the WP, and the Islamist intellectuals' participation in academic debates and media. In the midst of this agenda, the ALT, which did not have any organic intellectual relationship with (political) Islamism and its associated groups, set out to conceptualize Islam in a neoliberal way, as well as to combine neoliberalism with Islam.

MAKING NEOLIBERALISM TURKEY'S OWN: THE ALT ON RELIGION

In his first article in the ALT's journal *Liberal düşünce* (Liberal thought) in 1996, Yayla wrote that Hayek started an "intellectual struggle" against socialism, totalitarianism, and other forms of collectivist ideology by writing *The Road to Serfdom*.[23] With reference to the IEA and the way it affected the Thatcherite reforms in the UK with its consultation on neoliberal policies, Yayla declared that the ALT sought to provide a similar kind of consultation by producing ideas, allegedly without getting involved in politics.[24] In a volume compiled in 2011 by the Atlas Network that brought together "freedom champions" from different parts of the world who occupied "the front lines in the war of ideas," Yayla spoke from his almost twenty years of experience in the ALT to repeat that the ALT did not refer to a political movement, nor were its members practitioners; rather, the ALT was an "opinion movement," and its members were "the transmitters of ideas" who *have to* influence the politicians, bureaucrats and intellectuals."[25]

In reality, however, ideas work in more complex ways, because their intellectual organization is engendered by the particularity of those who produce them, which gives ideas their shape and class character. In that respect, similar to the case of the IEA or the MPS as a whole, the social purpose of the ALT, and its precise focus on consulting with the policy makers, was to "reeducate the capitalists"[26] and "organize individualism" in Turkey.[27] Despite drawing a clear line between purely educational efforts and more straightforward political ones, much like its role models, the ALT necessarily and frequently crossed this line.

In the early 1990s, the ALT's efforts were to "introduce" neoliberal concepts and sources to the Turkish audience. For the ALT, on the one hand, Turkey had gone through a positive change with Özal's neoliberal reforms, but they were applied without much intellectual foundation.[28] On the other hand, for them, the Cold War was over with the "defeat" of socialism, but they felt that Turkey's intellectual circles were still dominated by socialists and Kemalists.[29] It is worth mentioning here that the ALT put Kemalists in line with socialists because of their etatist stances, which advocated the state's involvement in the economy and state-led industrialization. For Kazım Berzeg, another leading founder of the ALT, who as a veteran lawyer contributed to the Yeni Forum, Turkey's liberals at the time were "a small, beleaguered minority"—a phrase borrowed from Milton Friedman in his self-description in *Capitalism and Freedom*.[30]

The ALT attempted to begin to change the situation and deploy liberal thought in Turkey without explicitly connecting their efforts to Turkey's liberal tradition. Rather, they presented their efforts as almost new and unique in the sense of acknowledging the "true" sources of liberalism (that is, Hayek) by prioritizing their linkage with the MPS and its liberal international.[31] Acknowledging the liberal ambivalence mentioned previously, for the ALT, Turkey's liberal tradition had grown within a context that valorized a strong state, but the ALT's aim was to "instrumentalize the state and humanize political power."[32]

With these motivations, in the early 1990s, the ALT started translating the works of neoliberal thinkers (that is, Hayek and Mises) and discussing their ideas in terms of their necessity for and relevance to Turkey. Much consideration was paid to explaining generic concepts such as a free-market economy, the minimal state, the rule of law, individual liberty, and so on with reference to the neoliberal thinkers without much addition. However, there was one topic discussed in relation to these concepts with important additions with regard to the Turkish context, namely, religion, and specifically Islam. As Yayla reminded his audience in his opening speech of the MPS's special meeting in Istanbul in 2011, the ALT was ultimately founded three months after Yayla's participation in the MPS General Meeting in 1992 in Toronto, and "it was first of [the MPS] kind in the Islamic world."[33]

Seen in the context provided in the previous section, the ALT's thought was in line with Özal's neoliberalism, which combined a free-market economy with a clear focus on Islamic values as a part of a Turkish nation. However, the ALT considered the rise of the WP's political Islam worrisome, because the WP put Islam at the center of its political project, instead of the free-market economy. For the ALT, the WP's commitment to neoliberalism was questionable for two reasons. First, the WP's political Islam was considered a collectivist ideology similar to those prior to the 1980s, even similar to socialism, with their focus on the "just order" and Islamic forms of socioeconomic solidarity. Second, it was ambiguous about the state's regulatory role, which still sounded determinant in the economy.[34]

The ALT nevertheless gave conditional support to the WP in the context of the right to freedom of expression and religion and criticized the state's measures against it. Since religion was the popular topic of the political agenda, and the ALT was dissatisfied with political Islamist understandings of religion, they embarked upon an intellectual journey to reconceptualize Islam in line with neoliberalism, particularly its free-market logic. This was crucial for the "magic political formula of Turkey" formulated by Yayla, because it was a search for a way to maintain Islam and neoliberalism together while putting the latter at the center.

This issue was mainly handled by Yayla, Mustafa Erdoğan (not to be confused with the president),[35] and Ahmet Arslan—a philosopher at Ege University—in the 1990s, with occasional contributions by other Turkish intellectuals, as well as those from the liberal institutes linked to the MPS. In the main cadre working on religion, only Arslan specialized in Islam (its philosophy), whereas others specialized in economics (Yayla), law (M. Erdoğan) and public administration (both). There were two main questions around the issue: "Whether Islam is compatible with liberal democracy and market economy?"[36] and "What is Islam's place in a liberal-democratic sociopolitical system?"[37]

THE SEARCH FOR THE IMPLICATIONS OF NEOLIBERAL CONCEPTS IN ISLAM

The ALT's discussion of religion started with a reference to the ongoing debate in the 1990s over Islam's compatibility with liberalism. For M. Erdoğan, Turkey's intellectuals were divided between those who rejected any sort of compatibility and those who argued for it.[38] For Yayla, this division also corresponded to those who "reject[ed] the notion of democracy and market economy" and those who did not *categorically* reject them.[39] For both, the first group mainly referred to political Islamists who stood for a total reorientation of state *and* society along Islamic lines. For this group, liberal democracy and a market economy were understood as part of the "West" and its value systems, and thus not suitable for Turkey, the majority of whose population was Muslim.

For Yayla and M. Erdoğan, this group also included Kemalists (and socialists, as well), due to their "radical secularism," which was pro-Western, but saw religion as a competitive, reactionary ideology to be controlled by the state. The second group, however, included some Islamist intellectuals who "attempt[ed] to discover the roots of democracy and market economy in Islamic sources and [the] history of Islam"[40] and liberals, that is, the ALT members, who saw "such an effort as valuable and useful" for "the prospects of deploying a liberal and pluralist sociopolitical system in *Muslim Turkey*."[41]

The ALT contributed to the 1990s debate about religion by adopting "a traditional definition of religion"[42] that understood Islam as "a worldview, a cosmologic and moral reference framework," not an ideology that claimed a monopoly over religion, as seen in political Islam.[43] With such a definition, M. Erdoğan stated that Islam did not necessarily compete with or contradict liberalism and its market economy.[44] Arslan meanwhile suggested making a separation between Islamic doctrine (present in the holy Quran and the hadiths, that is, the words of the prophet) and Islamic societies' historical practices.[45] Agreeing with that, M. Erdoğan searched for "whether it is possible to have a liberal interpretation of Islam" by working on Islamic doctrine.[46]

For M. Erdoğan, Islam had many elements which were "sympathetic" to liberalism. He listed his points in an article in 1996: Islam has pluralism with its different sects, which have no monopoly over one another. It addresses individuals. It is not in contradiction with human rights. There is no basis for the state's dominance over the market in Islam; therefore, it is compatible with a market economy. Trade has a prestigious place within Islam, and the prophet was a merchant. Islam acknowledges property and inheritance rights. Social solidarity is not an obligation, but is ultimately left to the will of individuals. Finally, Islam respects the rule of law, and independent Muslim scholars, not politicians, are responsible for the law-making processes. In that sense, M. Erdoğan wrote, "lawmaking in Islam is a result of a discovery process in a Hayekian sense."[47] Yayla repeated similar topics in 1997 and contended that "one can find some elements in Islamic sources that seem to have the capacity to support a free-market economy and democracy."[48]

All authors who addressed this question stressed that these points neither made Islam and liberalism identical, nor did they free them from tensions. However, the tensions were generally understood as *exceptions*, as can be seen in the discussions of interest and zakat, to offer two examples. Like other Islamist authors at the time, the ALT's members argued that the Quran did not forbid interest, but only usury.[49] Zakat is an order in the Quran that makes it compulsory for believers to give a certain amount of their income to the poor, and it implies individual social solidarity as an obligation. Turkish neoliberal intellectuals preferred to see this as some sort of tax and a communitarian value that also keeps the state at bay.[50] Meanwhile, they found the current state of Islam (in Islamic societies, referring to the Middle East) at odds with liberalism, but they thought this was related to Islam's historical practice, not its doctrine.[51] This had occurred because Islam had become a part of the state (that is, part of Islamic states) or because of the state's control over Islam (that is, Turkey's radical secularism), as well as because of Islam being under the influence of collectivist ideologies (that is, political Islam).[52] Therefore, for Turkish neoliberals, when the state factor was minimized, Islam's capacity to reconcile with liberal democracy would become easier.

The ALT collaborated with intellectuals from other neoliberal institutes on the topic of religion in the late 1990s. Norman Barry and Chandran Kukathas from the IEA and Detmar Doering from the Friedrich Naumann Foundation contributed to a volume titled *Islam, Civil Society and Market Economy* edited by Yayla and published in 1999. While finding Hayekian understandings in Islam (particularly Islamic lawmaking as "an exploration of cases and customary practices") similar to that of the ALT members,[53] these intellectuals highlighted the importance of promoting civil society and its elements (that is, Islam in Turkey) against the state. In this volume, Yayla argued that promoting civil society was contingent upon promoting market economy, because "there [could] be no civil society in the absence of a market economy."[54] Based on a solid union of purpose between civil society and the market economy and a clear separation between these two and the state, a "reciprocal" relationship between religion—as an element of civil society—and market economy could be derived.

What this reciprocal relationship suggests is, as Kukathas explains, that a market economy brings an enriched civil society, creating more space for religion and religious individuals to express themselves, which in turn benefits the market economy.[55] Barry explains how: "The market is morally validated *only when* it is embedded in institutions which have ethical justification independent of pure choice. In this context, religion is very important for civil society since it provides just that framework of morality which binds individuals to one another by methods other than market exchange."[56] These words make clear that the relationship between religion and the market economy does not merely refer to a reciprocity; rather, it is a *necessity* for promoting market economy, because the latter is unable to promote itself with its own means.

Once Islam is defined as compatible with liberalism and the market economy, as shown above, there is no reason for Islam—as a religion, a worldview, and a set of beliefs and morals—to be excluded from the function of morally validating the market. While institutions such as law and justice provide individuals with a rational ground for their actions, this might not be enough for the market's validation. Then Islam, just like any other religion, offers them as believers "a divine ground" that complements the workings of other institutions[57] and reduces transaction costs in the market economy.[58]

As the above examples show, in the 1990s, the ways in which the ALT members argued for the compatibility of Islam and liberalism offered a specific social purpose for Islam, namely, validating the market economy. Such an approach can be found in other MPS-associated efforts toward other (either Abrahamic or non-Abrahamic) religions. Specific examples include the work of Murray Rothbard, Bruno Leoni, and Deepak Lal. Rothbard, for instance, has used the Jesuit School of Salamanca to derive Christianity's compatibility with neoliberalism by partly solving the tensions between the two with regard to both interest and usury.[59] Similarly, Leoni expressed his interest in Confucianism in terms of its compatibility with modern liberal theory at a special meeting of the MPS in Tokyo in 1966, even stating that "Confucius could be fully eligible as a member of the Mont Pèlerin Society if he lived in our days."[60]

While these were certainly Eurocentric perspectives that took the virtues of the West for granted and searched for them in other cultural contexts to reconcile neoliberalism with these contexts, Lal's work on culture and capitalism moved beyond Eurocentric explanations of economic development. Thus, the contributions coming from these different contexts (such as the ALT's correspondence of Islam and capitalism and Lal's "The Hindu Equilibrium" in the Indian case), but within their MPS network, particularly mattered for the neoliberal project. As Barry argued, "Western liberal writers would certainly benefit from knowing that certain crucially important features of Islam are perfectly consistent with their own doctrines."[61]

The ALT's case also reveals how sets of ideas other than market-related ones, including religion and religious ideas, are employed in advocating the neoliberal transformation of Turkey. This sheds light on neoliberalism's variegated nature and different manifestations in and across different times, scales, and geographies. This variegation manifests itself not only in neoliberalism's policy applications, but also in ideas underpinning neoliberalism.[62] For that reason, far from being a monolith, neoliberalism "needs to be thought of as plural in terms of both political philosophy and political practice."[63] This is true for its intellectual sources (that is, different strands of neoliberal thought), as well as ideas through which neoliberal hegemonic projects are filtered (that is, elements of common sense; culture, religion, ethnicity, and so on). In Turkey, the neoliberal project was filtered through Islam on the sociopolitical level, and the ALT contributed to it, exemplifying a cultural variety within neoliberalism.

The examples presented in this section also show that the ALT's separation of Islam's historical practice from its doctrine results in a transhistorical definition of Islam. However, the social purpose of Islam envisioned by the ALT, that is, validating market-economy social relations, was specific to a particular juncture of neoliberal transformation of Turkey that started in the 1980s and to the rise of political Islam in the 1990s. It was to support the acceptance of the neoliberal ideas by linking them to one of the significant elements of common sense in Turkey, Islam as popular religion. In that sense, the first moment of the ALT's discussion of religion was also the first component of the effort to make sense of neoliberalism in the Turkish context not as an "import," but as something that is compatible with and even rooted in Turkey's values and belief systems. Another component of it in this context is supporting this understanding with a particular understanding of Turkey and Turkishness, which will be elaborated in the following section.

REINTERPRETING ISLAM'S PLACE IN TURKEY

The ALT's construction of Islam as compatible with neoliberalism in the 1990s accompanied the construction of Turkey as a Muslim country. The ALT aimed to diagnose Turkey's problems and provide solutions to them from a neoliberal perspective. In that context, M. Erdoğan depicted a "paradigm error" in handling the issue of religion in Turkey's political and intellectual circles in the late 1990s. His discussion covered the reactions to the military intervention against the political Islamist WP on February 28, 1997, which ended with the party's closure by the Constitutional Court a year after. He reevaluated Islam's place in Turkish politics and contended that "the advance of Islam in Turkey has been considered an accidental, even pathological, phenomenon.... Islam, however, is a formative component of Turkey's social and cultural fabric. Historically and culturally, Turkey is a Muslim country."[64] This quote makes clear that the ALT's definition of religion was not limited to a worldview or a set of beliefs and morals, but it also connoted "a socio-political entity" in the Turkish context.[65]

This entity is closely linked with Turkishness. As M. Erdoğan explained, "Islam has penetrated Turkish social fabric deeply, has shaped interpersonal relations and individuals' conduct, and has remained the main reference for Turks in terms of the meaning of life.... Not only as a religious faith, but also as a code of conduct for individual and public concerns, Islam is *embedded* in Turkish society."[66] Although Islam's definition broadened when placed in the Turkish context, its transhistorical quality remained. Delinking Islam from its (controversial and incoherent) historical meanings and roles, Yayla also stated around the same time that "Islam is not a phenomenon of today or yesterday in Turkey. It has been a part of Turkey's sociological reality. There is nothing unusual or frightening in this."[67]

Such discussions making Islam a "constituent" part of Turkish society were, first, related to the Turkish-Islamic synthesis and its particular blend of conservatism, nationalism, and liberalism. Second, they were rooted in the ALT's particular reading of Turkish history, based on the center-periphery framework in which there is a tension between the center (the Kemalist elites as the founders of the strong-military-state tradition) and the periphery (the Turkish society and people).[68] For the ALT, throughout history, the people's will lined up with conservative political parties supporting liberal economic reforms, but most of them were surpassed by the strong-state tradition (that is, military coups and interventions).

Yayla's reference points here were the center-right parties in Turkish history—the Democratic Party (DP) of the 1950s, the Justice Party

(JP) of the 1960s and 1970s, and Özal's MP of the 1980s, all of which advocated market liberalism and Turkey's integration into the global political economy, with the latter playing a crucial role in Turkey's neo-liberal transformation. Moreover, all of them were known for their populism, whose crucial element was religion as one of the key constituents of the Turkish nation, and for their mass political support. The DP was opposed to etatism and foregrounded themes including "respect for indigenous culture and freedom for businesses and religious activity."[69] The DP's government was overthrown by the military coup of May 27, 1960, citing DP's misuse of power, its endangering of the principle of secularism, and its inability to solve Turkey's economic problems. The JP was considered a continuation of the DP in the 1960s and 1970s, but it was also closed by the coup of 1980, along with other political parties.

Against such a background, Yayla argued that civil society in Turkey could not grow properly because the Kemalist elites' radical secularism was opposed to Islam, and their etatism was opposed to liberalism.[70] In this sense, Islam and liberalism were partners in destiny, in that the establishment of liberalism in Turkey depended on the liberal understanding of Islam, as well as the acceptance of liberalism by Islam.[71] For that reason, the ALT advocated, the state should "come to terms with 'Muslim reality' in Turkey to set the grounds of 'Muslim democracy.'"[72]

What Yayla conceptualized as "the magic political formula of Turkey" was rooted in this partnership between Islam and liberalism. Although Yayla enunciated it in the late 2010s, it retrospectively explains the ALT's efforts in the 1990s to conceptualize religion alongside the free-market economy, reevaluating its role in Turkish society. The formula is a general one and suggests that what works for Turkey is the meeting of liberal ideas with conservative political movements, particularly their conservative leaders.[73] Yayla validates this formula through a particular reading of Turkish history and the examples of the DP, the JP, and especially the MP.[74] It is worth noting that the WP is not in Yayla's list of validators of the formula, again due to the party's ambiguous support for the free-market economy. For Yayla, what Turkey needs is a conservative government that embraces Turkey's morals, that is, Islam as a part of Turkishness, that has popular acceptance, and is strongly committed to the free-market economy. And the ALT's mission in such a formula is to consult with this conservative government, supplying it with neoliberal ideas. The validator of this formula from the 2000s on was the JDP for Yayla, and the ALT was ready to provide advice to the party.

The JDP came to the stage in 2002 with a full commitment to neoliberalism, although its founding cadres were raised in the political Islamist NVM, and in the WP. The NVM faced an internal cleavage in the late 1990s between the traditionalists, who accepted the NVM as it was (anti-Western, anti-EU, welcoming trade and investment only from Islamic countries, and so on) and renovators, who sought changes within the movement (a younger leader and greater integration with the global political economy, including the EU).[75]

It was the renovators who initiated the JDP, which differentiated itself from the NVM and its ambivalence in committing to neoliberalism. Although Islam was still central to the JDP's political project, and it was critical of the state's measures against it, the party treated it in a more moderate manner in its early years, referring to Muslim identity as in the Turkish-Islamic synthesis, rather than referring to a whole system designed along the lines of political Islam. In response to the instabilities of the Turkish economy throughout the 1990s and the devastating social effects of the 2001 economic crisis, the JDP embraced the center–right and won the 2002 general elections with an absolute majority. The JDP's center–right profile welcomed political Islamists (both from the NVM tradition and others), but obtained a far more variegated support base, including business groups and ethnic groups, as well as liberal circles in Turkey.

For Yayla, this was how the JDP validated the "magic political formula of Turkey," with its full commitment to a free-market economy, management of the reconciliation between the political Islamist groups and neoliberalism's Western elements, conservatism built upon a Muslim identity, and popular acceptance.[76] From the early 2000s on, the ALT's collaboration with the JDP crystallized under the concept of "conservative democracy." The concept did not exist in the social science literature until it was formally launched in the International Symposium on Conservatism and Democracy, which was organized by the JDP with organizational and intellectual support from the ALT in 2004. It was reminiscent of currents of thought such as liberal conservatism or concepts such as Christian democracy, however, it was announced as the specific political identity of the JDP. Members of the ALT who attended this conference with their collaborators such as Barry[77] contributed to the JDP's political identity in the early 2000s. This contribution included their conceptualization of the role of religion, based on the reconciliation of Islam and neoliberalism, but this time highlighting it as both liberal and conservative, in line with the formula advocated by Yayla.

The ALT put Islam, as an element of Turkish cultural identity, in a neoliberal context with the purpose of validating the market as a way of making sense of neoliberalism in Turkey. It also linked the future of neoliberalism in Turkey to Islam. However, Islam is more embedded in the neoliberal hegemonic project in Turkey than it is in Turkish society. It is true that Islam is an important element of the common culture in Turkey but, as mentioned previously, the religious element was used in a transhistorical fashion in the ALT's project, free from its incoherent and conflicting meanings. Religion is a "collective noun"[78] that joins socioeconomic and sociohistorical processes of transformation and that "takes on different roles, functions and meanings at specific historical moments."[79] At that specific historical moment, religion, specifically Islam, mediated Turkey's neoliberal transformation on the sociopolitical level with the particular functions of controlling social opposition and assuring liberal-conservative value sets, and it thus helped to establish neoliberal ideas in the local context. The

ALT's "magic political formula" best expressed its collaboration with the JDP and served to reinforce these functions.

CONCLUSION

This chapter has investigated the ALT's intellectual project as it revolved around its discussions of religion, mainly in the 1990s. It explained how the ALT's ideas about Islam were linked to the neoliberal hegemonic project in Turkey that was put in place in the 1980s and that has been led by the JDP from the 2000s on. Along with other countries outside the Western neoliberal sphere, Turkey offers an example of how neoliberalism is culturally variegated, in this case, with Islam mediating the neoliberal project. In its neoliberal intellectual project, the ALT has made neoliberalism Turkey's own by linking it to Islam as one of the most prominent elements common in Turkish culture.

Although the rise of religious politics in Turkey is commonly identified with the JDP and its neoliberalism, this chapter has shed light on the period before the JDP, the start of the neoliberal transformation in the 1980s, and has shown the ALT to have been one of the intellectual forces behind the continuation of this process in the 1990s. Political Islamist groups' reconciliation with neoliberalism was consolidated with the JDP. Subsequent periods witnessed the party's mainstreaming of Islam along political Islamist lines and setting out on an authoritarian path of governance in the country (mainly in the 2010s) while maintaining its commitment to neoliberalism and its relations with the international finance institutions.

As long as free-market logic was at the center of the neoliberal hegemonic project (as it was in the JDP), political Islam was not a problem for the ALT, nor was authoritarianism. Although the ALT was skeptical about political Islam because it conflicted with liberalism in its early years, the last two decades have witnessed the ALT collaborating with various political Islamist groups that support the JDP and contributing to their tabloids. The ALT's interaction with the JDP in the 2000s was a win-win situation for Yayla in which the JDP benefitted from the ALT's ideas, and the ALT benefitted from the JDP's social acceptance, all of which worked toward reaching neoliberalism's objectives in Turkey.[80]

Yet the ALT's engagement with the JDP and its support for the party resulted in a split within the ALT in the first half of the 2010s. Some of its members believed that the ALT had failed to criticize the JDP's authoritarian tendencies and that it supported the party at the expense of liberalism.[81] It lost some of its influential members, including M. Erdoğan, who was an advocate of a Muslim democracy, but who is now describing the current stage of what the so-called conservative democracy has become as a "presidential autocracy."[82] However, with Yayla's significant presence, the ALT has remained as one of the main supporters of the JDP after the split within the ALT.

The neoliberal conception of Islam that was prepared by the ALT and that contributed to the JDP's political identity in the early 2000s is moderate, compared with the political Islamist framework employed by the JDP from the 2010s on. Nevertheless, both are organically connected to and legitimators of the Turkish-Islamic synthesis of the 1980s that accompanied Turkey's neoliberal transformation. Moreover, the ALT (a Mont Pelerin Society–inspired project in the Islamic world, as Yayla saw it) contributed to this process. Joining the debates about Islam in the late 1990s, when religion was a critical issue in Turkey's political agenda, and collaborating with the JDP in the 2000s, the ALT, with its conceptualization of Islam in a neoliberal way and reinterpretation of Islam as embedded in Turkish society, contributed to constructing an intellectual means for reaching the objectives of neoliberalism in Turkey.

NOTES

1. Liberal Düşünce, "Takdim," *Liberal düşünce* 1.1 (1996), p. 1.

2. Atilla Yayla, "Pratikteki açmazlarıyla liberalizm ve liberal düşünce topluluğu," *Liberal Düşünce* 1.1 (1996), pp. 9-10 and 13.

3. Yayla, "Pratikteki açmazlarıyla liberalizm ve liberal düşünce topluluğu," p. 10.

4. For Turkey's comparison with Latin American countries, see Meltem Yılmaz Şener, "The Relationship between Neoliberalism and Authoritarian States: The Case of Turkey," *Robinson Rojas Archive* (2004), http://www.rrojasdatabank.info/neolibstate/meltemyilmazsener.pdf.

5. For Turkey's comparison with India in terms of religion's place in neoliberalism, see Esra Elif Nartok, "Rethinking Religion's Interaction with Neoliberal Ideology: A Comparison between India and Turkey," PhD diss., University of Manchester, 2019.

6. Poland shows this tendency, too, with a different historical background. See Stuart Shields, "The Paradoxes of Necessity: Fail Forwards Neoliberalism, Social Reproduction, Recombinant Populism and Poland's 500Plus Policy," *Capital & Class* 43.4 (2019), https://journals.sagepub.com/doi/10.1177/0309816819880798.

7. From the 2010s on, neo-Ottomanism became the main tendency in Turkey's foreign policy, which prioritized relations with the Middle Eastern countries, claiming some sort of leadership role in regional politics.

8. Aydın Yalçın, quoted in Simten Coşar, "Liberal Thought and Democracy in Turkey," *Journal of Political Ideologies* 9.1 (2004), p. 85.

9. Galip L. Yalman, "The Neoliberal Transformation of State and Market in Turkey: An Overview of Financial Developments from 1980 to 2000," in Galip L. Yalman, Thomas Mauris, and Ali Rıza Güngen, eds., *The Political Economy of Financial Transformation in Turkey* (Oxford: Routledge, 2019), p. 51.

10. Galip L. Yalman, "The Turkish State and Bourgeoisie in Historical Perspective: A Relativist Paradigm or a Panoply of Hegemonic Strategies?," in Neşecan Balkan and Sungur Savran, eds., *The Politics of Permanent Crisis: Class, Ideology and State in Turkey* (New York: Nova, 2002), p. 34.

11. Coşar, "Liberal Thought and Democracy in Turkey," pp. 79 and 85.

12. Ibid., p. 85.

13. Simten Coşar, "Türk-İslam sentezinden Müslüman türklüğün kur(t) uluş mitine: AKP'nin Bitmeyen Dansı," *Ayrıntı Dergi*, January 20, 2018, https://ayrintidergi.com.tr/turk-islam-sentezinden-musluman-turklugun -kurtulus-mitine-akpnin-bitmeyen-dansi.

14. Sungur Savran, "İslamcılık, AKP ve burjuvazinin iç savaşı," in Neşecan Balkan, Erol Balkan, and Ahmet Öncü, eds., *Neoliberalizm, islamcı sermayenin yükselişi ve AKP* (Istanbul: Yordam, 2013), p. 78.

15. Galip Yalman, "Politics and Discourse under the AKP's Rule: The Marginalisation of Class-Based Politics, Erdoğanisation, and Post-Secularism," in Simten Coşar and Gamze Yücesan-Özdemir, eds., *Silent Violence: Neoliberalism, Islamist Politics and the AKP Years in Turkey* (Ottawa: Red Quill Books, 2012), pp. 21–42.

16. Coşar, "Liberal Thought and Democracy in Turkey," p. 85.

17. Ibid., p. 78.

18. Ibid.

19. The ALT also developed relationships with and received help from some of the liberal institutes, such as the Friedrich Naumann Foundation (FNF) and the Atlas Economic Research Foundation, which is currently known as the Atlas Network. Former MPS presidents James M. Buchanan and Gary Becker were on the ALT journal's advisory board, and members of the liberal institutes such as the IEA and FNF participated in many of the ALT's events and contributed to its publications. For the ALT's relations with the MPS, see Atilla Yayla, "Changing the Climate of Opinion in Turkey," in Colleen Dyble, ed., *Freedom Champions: Stories from the Front Lines in the War of Ideas. 30 Case Studies by Intellectual Entrepreneurs Who Champion the Cause of Freedom* (Washington, DC: Atlas Economic Research Foundation, 2011), p. 181, https:// www.atlasnetwork.org/assets/uploads/misc/FreedomChampions.pdf, and Atilla Yayla, "27 yaşında bir fidan: Liberal düşünce topluluğu," *Hür Fikirler*, December 26, 2019, http://www.hurfikirler.com/27-yasinda-bir-fidan-liberal -dusunce-toplulugu.

20. Coşar, "Liberal Thought and Democracy in Turkey," p. 87.

21. Halime Atalay, "Prof. Dr. Atilla Yayla ile mülakat," *Hür Fikirler,* May 6, 2019, http://www.hurfikirler.com/halime-atalay-prof-dr-atilla-yayla-ile-mulakat.

22. Yalman, "The Neoliberal Transformation of State and Market in Turkey," p. 75.

23. Yayla, "Pratikteki açmazlarıyla liberalizm ve liberal düşünce topluluğu," p. 8.

24. Ibid., pp. 9–10.

25. Yayla, "Changing the Climate of Opinion in Turkey," pp. 181 and 184–85, emphasis added.

26. Dieter Plehwe, introduction to Philip Mirowski and Dieter Plehwe, eds., *The Road from Mont Pèlerin: The Making of the Neoliberal Thought Collective* (Cambridge, MA: Harvard University Press, 2009), p. 7. For Yayla's specific focus on "reeducation," see Yayla, "Pratikteki açmazlarıyla liberalizm ve liberal düşünce topluluğu," p. 9.

27. John Zmirak, quoted in Plehwe, introduction to *The Road from Mont Pèlerin,* p. 15.

28. Yayla, "Pratikteki açmazlarıyla liberalizm ve liberal düşünce topluluğu," p. 12.

29. Ibid.

30. Kazım Berzeg, "Neden liberalizm," *Liberal Düşünce* 1.1 (1996), p. 15.

31. Simten Coşar, "Türk liberalliği üzerine," *Birikim,* no. 110 (1998), https://www.birikimdergisi.com/dergiler/birikim/1/sayi-110-haziran-1998/2305/turk-liberalligi-uzerine/3835.

32. Mustafa Erdoğan, "Niçin liberalizm?," *Liberal düşünce* 1.1 (1996), p. 28, http://www.libertedownload.com/LD/arsiv/01/04-mustafa-erdogan-nicin-liberalizm.pdf.

33. Atilla Yayla, "Opening Speech of the Mont Pelerin Society İstanbul Special Meeting," *Liberal Düşünce Topluluğu,* September 30, 2011, http://www.liberal.org.tr/sayfa/opening-speech-of-the-mont-pelerin-society-istanbul-special-meeting-atilla-yayla,238.php.

34. Ahmet Arslan, "İslam, adalet ve Refah Partisi üzerine," *Liberal Düşünce* 1.1 (1996), p. 8.

35. I refer to Mustafa Erdoğan as M. Erdoğan in this chapter to avoid

confusion with the president, Recep Tayyip Erdoğan, to whom I did not specifically refer in this chapter.

36. Atilla Yayla, "Prospects for Democracy and Market Economy in Turkey," *Liberal Düşünce* 2.8 (1997), p. 136.

37. Mustafa Erdoğan, "İslam ve liberalizm: Kısa bir bakış," *Liberal Düşünce* 1.4 (1996), p. 7.

38. Ibid., pp. 7–8.

39. Yayla, "Prospects for Democracy and Market Economy in Turkey," p. 136.

40. Ibid.

41. Erdoğan, "İslam ve liberalizm: Kısa bir bakış," p. 7, emphasis added.

42. Yayla, "Prospects for Democracy and Market Economy in Turkey," p. 137.

43. Erdoğan, "İslam ve liberalizm: Kısa bir bakış," p. 11.

44. Ibid., p. 9.

45. Ahmet Arslan, "İnsan hakları ve İslam," *Liberal Düşünce* 2.5 (1997), p. 41.

46. Erdoğan, "İslam ve liberalizm: Kısa bir bakış," p. 8.

47. Ibid., pp. 11–17.

48. Yayla, "Prospects for Democracy and Market Economy in Turkey," p. 137.

49. Ibid.

50. Erdoğan, "İslam ve liberalizm: Kısa bir bakış," p. 16.

51. Arslan, "İnsan hakları ve İslam," p. 40.

52. Erdoğan, "İslam ve liberalizm: Kısa bir bakış," pp. 18–19.

53. Norman Barry, "Civil Society, Religion and Islam," in Atilla Yayla, ed., *Islam, Civil Society and Market Economy* (Ankara: Liberte, 1999), p. 14.

54. Atilla Yayla, "Introduction: Islam or Democracy," in Yayla, ed., *Islam, Civil Society and Market Economy*, p. xxii.

55. Chandran Kukathas, "Islam, Democracy and Civil Society," in Yayla, ed., *Islam, Civil Society and Market Economy*, p. 39.

56. Barry, "Civil Society, Religion and Islam," p. 1, emphasis added.

57. Arslan, "İslam, adalet ve Refah Partisi üzerine," p. 5.

58. Ömer Demir, "Piyasa ekonomisinde işlem maliyetini düşüren kurumlar olarak hukuk, ahlak ve din," *Liberal Düşünce* 3.10–11 (1998), pp. 103–104.

59. On the School of Salamanca, see "The True Founders of Economics: The School of Salamanca," Mises Wire, https://mises.org/wire/true-founders -economics-school-salamanca.

60. Bruno Leoni, "Two Views of Liberty, Occidental and Oriental (?)," Mises Institute, *Libertarian Papers* 1.15 (2009), p. 7, https://mises.org/library /two-views-liberty-occidental-and-oriental.

61. Barry, "Civil Society, Religion and Islam," p. 20.

62. On how neoliberalism is linked with other sets of ideas other than market, see Ian Bruff, "Overcoming the Allure of Neoliberalism's Market Myth," *South Atlantic Quarterly* 118.2 (2019), pp. 363–79.

63. Plehwe, introduction to *The Road from Mont Pèlerin*, p. 3.

64. Mustafa Erdoğan, "Islam in Turkish Politics: Turkey's Quest for Democracy without Islam," *Liberal Düşünce* 4.14 (1999), pp. 102 and 104.

65. Coşar, "Liberal Thought and Democracy in Turkey," p. 86.

66. Erdoğan, "Islam in in Turkish Politics," p. 114, emphasis added.

67. Yayla, "Prospects for Democracy and Market Economy in Turkey," p. 137.

68. Ibid.

69. Sencer Ayata, "Patronage, Party, and State: The Politicization of Islam in Turkey," *Middle East Journal* 50.1 (1996), p. 43.

70. Atilla Yayla and Mehmet Seyitdanlıoğlu, "Türkiye'de liberalizm," *Liberal Düşünce* 3.10–11 (1998), pp. 55–57.

71. Mustafa Erdoğan, *İslam ve liberalizm: Bir deneme* (Ankara: Liberte, 1999), p. 36.

72. Coşar, "Liberal Thought and Democracy in Turkey," p. 86.

73. Atalay, "Prof. Dr. Atilla Yayla ile mülakat."

74. Atilla Yayla, "AK Parti'nin liberallerle zor ama zorunlu ilişkisi," Liberal Düşünce Topluluğu, March 9, 2008, http://www.liberal.org.tr/sayfa /ak-partinin-liberallerle-zor-ama-zorunlu-iliskisi-atilla-yayla,340.php.

75. Burak Gürel, "İslamcılık: Uluslararası bir ufuk taraması," in Balkan et al., *Neoliberalizm, İslamcı sermayenin yükselişi ve AKP*, p. 45.

76. Yayla, "AK Parti'nin liberallerle zor ama zorunlu ilişkisi."

77. See their discussions in AK Parti, *Uluslararası muhafazakarlık ve demokrasi Sempozyumu* (Istanbul: AK Parti Yayınları, 2004).

78. Antonio Gramsci, *Selections from the Prison Notebooks*, ed. and trans. Quentin Hoare and Geoffrey Nowell Smith (London: Lawrence and Wishart, 1971), pp. 323–25.

79. Philip Roberts, "Passive Revolution in Brazil: Struggles over Hegemony, Religion and Development, 1964–2007," *Third World Quarterly* 36.9 (2015), p. 1664.

80. Yayla, "AK Parti'nin liberallerle zor ama zorunlu ilişkisi."

81. For an insider perspective on the clashes within the ALT, see Tanel Demirel, "Yılında Liberal düşünce topluluğu: Eleştirel bir değerlendirme," *Liberal Düşünce* 23.89 (2018), pp. 25–48.

82. Mustafa Erdoğan, "28 Şubat süreci'nden reisçi otokrasiye," March 2, 2020, http://erdoganmustafa.org/28-subat-surecinden-reisci-otokrasiye.

PART TWO

Other Paths

CHAPTER FOUR

The Road from Snake Hill:
The Genesis of Russian Neoliberalism

Tobias Rupprecht

In contemporary Russia, *neoliberalizm* has become a popular slur for free markets and for the dominance of economics over politics. Commentators from both sides of the political spectrum have used it to criticize what they see as Western-inspired reforms under President Boris Yeltsin in the 1990s. The Left has also attached the label to the ensuing governments, claiming that "neoliberalism has been and remains an organic part of the Putin regime."[1] Anti-Western nationalists, by contrast, have triumphantly declared it a thing of the past: "The neoliberal paradigm was exhausted by the 2008 crisis and never recovered," repeatedly proclaimed Vladimir Yakunin, a longtime associate of President Vladimir Putin.[2] Dirigiste economists, influential once again, have been praising the success of gradual state-led reforms in Deng Xiaoping's China, as opposed to the neoliberalism allegedly imposed on Russia by the International Monetary Fund (IMF).[3]

This antineoliberal rhetoric is in line with notions around the world that reject what is seen as Anglo-American-imposed antistatism and laissez-faire capitalism. "When the Berlin Wall came down in 1989," goes a fairly representative view of contemporary observers and early academic assessments, "there was an army of committed, international economic liberals reared in the Hayekian tradition, armed with clipboards and portable phones, waiting to move in to Eastern Europe and the disintegrating Soviet Union to convert their ailing economies."[4] Such notions of neoliberalism as an anti-state dogma have been questioned in recent years by intellectual historians and economic sociologists. Neoliberal ideas, they claim, are better explained by emphasizing their notions of using a strong state and sometimes international governance, as well as legal and monetary arrangements, to create and defend free markets and liberal institutions from potentially anti-liberal national democratic majorities.[5] But, as the editors of this volume state, even in the most innovative work, the history of neoliberalism is still told as one emanating from the West.

A closer look at the historical evidence suggests that neoliberalism in Russia was not an alien concept imported from abroad in the 1990s. Much less was it a set of economic policies imposed by the West on Russia during a period of weakness, as defenders of Putin's neoauthoritarianism like to portray it. If defined as reflections on how to create and protect free markets and liberal institutions with the help of a strong state, ideas deserving the label "neoliberal"—while not referred to as such—can be discerned among Soviet intellectual elites long before the fall of the Soviet Union and the arrival of Western advisors. These ideas did not necessarily come from abroad. A framing of the history of non-Western neoliberalism, as has been suggested, as one of an active participation of local allies in the process of global neoliberal concepts going local would cover only part of the history of Russian neoliberals.[6] These were not only translators of foreign ideas, but originators of a specific Russian variety of neoliberalism that was created locally before they connected to global neoliberal debates and networks.

Russian neoliberalism, like Russian liberalism more broadly, is better understood as a home-grown phenomenon with multiple intellectual roots,[7] rather than as a distorted copy imported from the West or the local manifestation of a hegemonic global "governmentality."[8] Liberal free-market ideas had always existed in modern Russia, and debates in the final years of the Soviet Union about how to create and protect these markets with the help of a strong state reached back to these intellectual traditions. Some networks and contacts with Western neoclassical economists had been maintained through-out much of the Soviet era,[9] but more crucially, Russian neoliberalism grew out of an intellectual engagement with Soviet economic and political conditions. Small groups of economists and social scientists at leading Soviet research institutions, who were initially rather isolated not only from the West, but often also from each other, combined their insights from the inner workings of the Soviet political economy with Russian intellectual trajectories.

The less repressive environment of Glasnost (transparency) from the mid-1980s on allowed these scholars to communicate more openly. Informal groups of promarket academics, which had independently formed in the major cities of the Soviet Union, now met semiclandestinely. They shared their knowledge of Soviet economic realities and of economic policies in Eastern Europe, the West, and the Global South, and exchanged views on possible economic reforms. A 1986 seminar in the woods north of Leningrad, at a resort called Snake Hill, was the foundational meeting for a group of young Soviet promarketeers. Some of them developed visions on how to implement their economic ideas that could reasonably be called "neoliberal," and several of them would become economic advisors to the post-Soviet Russian governments. Yet notions that a neoliberal antistate fervor wreaked havoc on the Russian economy and society in the 1990s[10] are misled. The Russian neoliberals, whose impact on policy making always remained limited, instead strove for a strengthening of state capacity in order to implement their ideas in times of political turmoil, economic decline, and social upheaval.

THE SOVIET HOTBEDS OF RUSSIAN NEOLIBERALISM

Scholars of global neoliberalism often identify the Mont Pelerin Society or the University of Chicago as cradles of neoliberal thought and international institutions such as the International Monetary Fund as their carriers around the world.[11] Yet to understand the genesis of the

Russian variant of neoliberalism, it is more helpful to look at academic research centers in the Soviet Union. A strong academic tradition of economics in Imperial Russia had initially survived the October Revolution. Russian economists had contributed to international debates on the Austrian School in the 1920s, and until the end of the decade, work could be published on business cycles and even on the impossibility of fixed prices and a nonmonetary economy.[12] The mass exodus of the Russian intelligentsia and then the mass murder of economists in the Stalinist purges from the 1930s to the 1950s nearly finished this tradition, but the study of economics made a spectacular revival after Stalin's death.

Against the backdrop of continuous attempts at economic reform in the 1960s and the need for economic expertise among political decision makers, numerous new economic research centers were created. New branches of the Soviet Academy of Sciences in Moscow, Leningrad, and Novosibirsk provided excellent working conditions, particularly the Moscow Tsentralnyj Ekonomiko-Matematicheskij Institut (TsEMI, the Central Economic-Mathematical Institute). Most research at these institutes was conducted with a view to optimizing the Soviet planned economy with the help of mathematical economics and cybernetic modeling, drawing heavily on the work of the corecipient of the 1975 Nobel Prize in Economics, Leonid Kantorovich.[13]

The accumulated knowledge at the leading Soviet economic research institutes led some scholars to the realization that their elaborate plans did not usually translate into efficient economic practices. Yet in a time of an increasing political reluctance about economic reform under General Secretary Leonid Brezhnev, they failed to get their voices heard. In the mid-1970s, the economist Nikolaj Shmelev wrote a series of internal memos at the Academy of Sciences that criticized Soviet economic policy, demanding that the state monopoly on foreign trade be given up, that joint ventures be encouraged, that the currency be made convertible, and that the USSR join international economic and financial institutions. The documents never made it beyond the desks of his superiors.[14] Another set of suggestions about how to create markets in the Soviet Union was developed in 1981 by Vitaly Nayshul, a young mathematical economist at the economic research center of the chief state-planning institution Gosplan, noting that the Soviet economy was headed for disaster. It was similarly blocked from reaching political decision makers.[15]

Barred from access to politics, some critical economists sought to reach a public audience, instead. Nayshul illegally self-published his ideas for a radical privatization of the Soviet economy. In *Drugaja zhizn* (Another life), he explained for a nonexpert readership what steps would be necessary to turn the Soviet Union into a consumer-oriented market economy. His manuscript circulated in so-called *samizdat* (self-publishing) alongside a small number of other publications that since the early 1970s had pilloried not only the inefficiency of the planned economy, but also the inertia of Soviet intellectuals in standing up against it and their wrong-headed notions of government benevolence. "To demand a high standard of living from the state," Viktor Sokirko told his fellow dissidents in 1979, meant "to contradict the protection of fundamental human rights and freedoms."[16] In his own illegal journal, he demanded "above all the soonest renouncing of the lethal idea of all-encompassing planning [and] the fast legalization of social regulation based on markets."[17]

Another scathing critique of the Soviet economy and of the moderate proposals for reform within the existing system was eventually published in the West. Based on sociological and medical data from the Soviet countryside, the economist Lev Timofeyev argued in 1982 that the whole Soviet economy was in essence a "colossal black market." This not only meant a ridiculously inefficient distribution of resources, but had political implications: it was "an instrument of the party bureaucracy, i.e., a means of preserving the existing order," and "consequently, all discussions of market socialism are an empty pastime."[18] Both Sokirko and Timofeyev, who developed their ideas independently of the future Snake Hill group members, spent several years in prison for their transgressions when the KGB identified them.[19]

There is no indication that these radical antiplanning, antibureaucracy, and promarket ideas emerging from Soviet research institutions and a small group of *samizdat* authors were influenced by Western neoliberal thought. Senior academics at the Academy of Sciences did have access to foreign economic journals and books, including the neoliberal standard references in their original languages, but in their memoirs and recollections, Russian economists mostly recall reading Western econometrics and management literature, and the writings of U.S. Sovietologists, not Western neoliberals.[20] Dissidents kept themselves informed about the West through smuggled copies of Russian émigré literature, not the writings of the Chicago school or the Virginia school of economics. Nayshul remembered knowing no more than gossip about them throughout the 1980s.[21]

One of the very few Soviet economists who knew of the writings of Friedrich Hayek and Milton Friedman from early on was Vasily Selyunin. The prominent journalist, not part of the Snake Hill group, either, had access to Western neoliberal literature in the library of his magazine.[22] But the few others who read it found the insights of promarket economists from other socialist countries more instructional: "Yes, I read Friedman's book with interest, and also Hayek," recalled Yegor Gaidar, a central figure of the Snake Hill collective, and "they were very authoritative for us, but all the same far away from our domestic realities." For more concrete questions of what kind of reforms would be necessary in a socialist planned economy, the work of the Hungarian economist János Kornai was "the Bible."[23]

THE GATHERING OF RUSSIAN LIBERALS IN THE COUNTRYSIDE

In the final years of Brezhnev's rule, a new cohort of well-trained young economists began their careers at Soviet research institutes. They inherited from their teachers knowledge about the workings and the fundamental weaknesses of the Soviet economy. Their teachers "did not rescue [the economy]," one of them remembered, "but the schooling was good."[24] But many of them also increasingly distanced themselves from older academics and developed a rather cynical stance toward the utopias of mathematical optimization and, more broadly, the socialist idealism of the 1960s generation. At the end of the 1970s, recalled Grigorij Glazkov, at the time a student of economics in Leningrad, "there was complete disbelief, a complete disappointment with the existing Soviet system. Anybody with brains was very disillusioned and very unhappy with the system."[25] His colleague and peer Anatoly Chubais concurred: "I felt that official economic scholars were absolutely impotent in the face of the imminent economic disaster. The house was on fire, but they were discussing changing the paint color."[26]

Against the backdrop of yet another aborted economic reform under Soviet premier Alexey Kosygin, these young researchers started debating why the planned economy did not produce the desired results. During their summer work in a remote village in 1979, Glazkov and Chubais picked potatoes and eventually became friends with Yuri Yarmagaev, a mathematical economist who confided his radical anti-Communist sentiments. The group decided to look for like-minded people around the Soviet Union. Over the course of the following years, they connected to a group of thinkers around Yegor Gaidar in Moscow, who were their age mates, but already well-established economists. Together, they organized informal meetings and exchanged their scattered knowledge and views, often sticking cautiously to venues in the countryside. As Mikhail Gorbachev's policy of Glasnost allowed for some more room to maneuver, beginning in 1985, informal groups formed at several institutions, including TsEMI. But their most open discussions still took place during camping trips and meetings in rural small towns, where they avoided an unwanted audience.[27]

The Moscow-Leningrad group of young promarket economists soon found out that an analogous group existed at the Novosibirsk State University. Independently of each other, they had come to very similar conclusions about the Soviet economy, those in the European part of the Soviet Union from the historical study of earlier Soviet economic reforms and from learning from market-socialist reforms in Eastern Europe, and those in Siberia from ethnographic studies of agriculture in the Altai region. The Snake Hill meeting in 1986 brought the groups together. In the secure reclusion of the woods north of Leningrad, about fifty young promarket economists and social scientists between the age of twenty-five and thirty-two from Moscow, Leningrad, and Novosibirsk met, made friends, shared their observations on the state of the Soviet economy, and debated their ideas on how to fix it. Being sons and daughters of the Russian intelligentsia, they also recited poems and sang the songs of the Soviet bards to the strumming of guitars.[28] But their Romanticism did not extend to their economic views.

Yarmagaev presented his ideas for a reintroduction of markets along the lines of the New Economic Policy of the 1920s.[29] Gaidar, who had lived in Yugoslavia in the 1970s and spoke Serbo-Croatian, and experts on Poland and Czechoslovakia discussed Eastern European variants of market socialism, both ongoing and aborted. As opposed to the elder generation of Soviet elite economists such as Abel Aganbegyan or Oleg Bogomolov, who at the time were drafting reform proposals for Gorbachev's Perestroika, the Snake Hill group also openly debated the faults of Eastern European reform socialism: its inefficiency, its amassing of foreign debt, and in the case of Yugoslavia, its high rates of unemployment. But for the time being, their consensus was that reforms of this kind were the maximum possibly achievable under the current political framework. China, again in contrast to the focus of Gorbachev's more senior advisors,[30] was completely absent from their debates. Most attention was given to Hungary. Positive remarks about Kornai's books, which were detailed and deeply critical assessments of Eastern Europe's planned economies, had indeed become a shibboleth for the promarketeers. "János Kornai was for us what Mao Zedong was for Chinese Communists," remembered one.[31]

While Kornai, a globally very well-connected member of the Hungarian Academy of Sciences, had provided at least an indirect intellectual link to the West for the Moscow-Leningrad group, the group from Siberia had developed their radical critique of economic planning exclusively from local sources. A devastating 1983 "Novosibirsk report" on the economic and social malaise in Soviet agriculture had triggered sociological research in the Altai region. At Snake Hill, Petr Aven, Viacheslav Shironin, and Simon Kordonskij, who had joined the expeditions of the economic sociologist Tatyana Zaslavaskaya, reported their experience of "planning in practice": the plans, theories, and mathematical models hatched out in Moscow, they told their new peers, had basically no effect on economic reality on the ground. Rather than executing orders from the state capital, local administrators from different levels regularly got together in the provincial capital to negotiate locally created prices, production output, and investments. All these economic actors did their best to appear (not necessarily to be) productive, because their salary, their decorative orders, and their freedom depended on it. This was no planned economy, the young economists concluded; this was a distorted and inefficient administrative market.[32]

A year after the Snake Hill meeting, in 1987, a similar get-together of young economists took place in Losevo, a remote rural community between Vyborg and Lake Ladoga. This time, Nayshul, the former researcher from Gosplan, joined them. From his firsthand experience in the center of economic planning, he had independently come to conclusions very similar to those of Timofeyev and the Novosibirsk economists: what kept the Soviet economy running was not planning, but a gigantic administrative market. "We had working contact with people running the economy," he recalled later, "when I first started hearing their stories, that made up 80 percent of my economic thinking. It was stories, anecdotes, almost an art form, lasting as long as a cigarette." The bureaucrats were not following a structure of command and obey, Nayshul concluded. They negotiated and traded, even if they were in relationships between bosses and subordinates.[33]

In his presentation at Losevo, Nayshul also suggested the substitution of commodity and financial markets for the administrative market. In order to break the power of the bureaucrats, price controls needed to be lifted and assets needed to be privatized comprehensively. This monetization and privatization should be undertaken by handing out equal and tradable vouchers to every adult Soviet citizen. His proposal, eventually implemented in the 1990s, was rejected as entirely unrealistic by most discussants at Losevo. Some in the audience even wondered whether Nayshul was in fact a KGB agent who was sent to provoke the group with such radical proposals.[34]

The countryside gatherings of the young Soviet promarket economists happened against the backdrop of Gorbachev's attempts to save socialism by making it more democratic and efficient. The palpable idealism behind Perestroika had its roots in the 1960s, when both Gorbachev and his key advisers had begun their professional careers. Many of their visions for a reformed and democratic Soviet Union were based on an idealization of the early Soviet years and of reform socialism of the Prague Spring kind. The political leaders still hailed Lenin and even defended the collectivization of the Soviet agriculture and the party-led industrialization of the 1930s;[35] the economic advisors were still shaped by the cybernetic planning ideas of their youth and skeptical of abandoning state ownership.[36] Instead, they praised Eastern European and Chinese market reforms under the guidance of the Communist Party.[37]

The younger generation of economists, in their late twenties or early thirties when they got together in their semiclandestine seminars, were increasingly skeptical of any kind of economic planning and mathematical optimization of central control.[38] Similar to the Central European neoliberals of the 1930s, but without direct influence from them, young Soviet economists turned against such "high modernist" thinking and the "hubris of knowledge" that dominated in their profession. And just like the Westerners in the interwar period, many of them had turned from cautious supporters into fundamental critics of any kind of socialism. Initially optimistic about Gorbachev's reforms as steps in the right direction, most of the young promarket reformers by the end of the 1980s saw them as too slow and eventually doomed. Some never had much hope for them: for Nayshul and several of his old colleagues from Gosplan, the economic reform attempts of Perestroika were "just bullshit."[39]

LIBERAL FEARS: THE IGNORANT MASSES, THE WEAK STATE

Promarket views had survived among marginal groups of Soviet dissidents, and quite radical notions of the necessity of competition and private enterprise developed among some of the younger Soviet academic economists in the 1980s. What justifies adding the prefix "neo" to the worldview of some of these liberals is that they combined their strong belief in free markets with reflections on how politically to create and if necessary defend them. Having experienced political persecution or cautiously hiding their discussions from secret services and the public eye in their countryside retreats, they knew too well about the resistance they would face for their reform plans from entrenched political and bureaucratic elites, but also from large parts of the population. This integral component of neoliberal thought was similar to the predicaments that Western neoliberals discussed in the 1930s and 1940s. The Soviet economists needed no inspiration from the West, however. Their intellectual trajectory was the Russian intelligentsia's historically grounded fear of ignorant masses and unhinged democracy in populist or socialist form.[40]

References to the defeat of the weak liberal government after the February Revolution of 1917 were rife in the debates of the 1980s, as were recollections of the repression of the Russian intelligentsia by the Bolsheviks. Émigrés and dissidents remembered those prerevolutionary liberals who, during the momentous *Vekhi* (Landmarks) debate, had argued for law and order and an end to Marxist and populist anti-Tsarist radicalism because "we ought to fear the people...and bless this government which alone, with its prisons and bayonets, still protects us from the people's fury."[41] Like the Russian liberals of the early twentieth century and occasionally referring to them explicitly, some dissidents and some members of the Snake Hill group displayed little enthusiasm about unhinged popular sovereignty. What they saw as the plebeian basis of Stalinism led them to a skeptical stance toward the idea of basing an antitotalitarian movement on mass democracy.[42] "The workers are always the pillar of communism or fascism," as the exiled dissident Vadim Belotserkovskij paraphrased this view of many of his colleagues within the Soviet Union in 1985. "In the future Russia...let them have television and other blessings, but keep them down below."[43]

Aware of being a miniscule minority, the Soviet liberals pondered how to overcome the expected resistance to their ideas from above and below. Their attempts to influence policies usually met with little success. In the summer of 1986, Gaidar gave Aganbegyan a letter in which he elaborated his vision for radical economic reforms, but Aganbegyan did not dare to pass it on.[44] And even as late as 1990, a proposal by promarket economists for a gradual transition to a market economy in 500 days was eventually rejected by Gorbachev, who moved to more conservative positions in his final two years in office. At the same time, the free marketeers feared the mentality of a large part of the Soviet population, who expected the state to provide for them and who had been educated to see entrepreneurial activity as theft and exploitation. As soon as Glasnost allowed for such voices to be published, a debate began in the key Soviet intellectual magazines *Literaturnaya Gazeta* and *Novy Mir* about how to fix the ailing Soviet economy and how to raise the productivity of the toiling masses while maintaining public order. The two most influential pieces, which beyond the normal print run circulated to the tune of an estimated fifteen to seventeen million photocopies around the whole country, were written by Shmelev and Selyunin.[45]

Shmelev, in his 1987 article, suggested creating economic initiative through free commerce and free prices and workers' discipline through deregulated labor markets.[46] And Selyunin, a year later, delivered the first account in a Soviet publication that dared to present Stalinist terror as growing from Leninist economic policies. With reference to his own near starvation during his peasant childhood, Selyunin castigated Lenin for creating a system that punished the economically successful, and he concluded that economic freedom is the basis for political freedoms and human rights. Populist promises of social equality, to the contrary, could result in totalitarian rule: "Give me a free apartment, give me cheap butter, give this, give that," as Selyunin graphically portrayed the attitude of ordinary Russians as Lenin's economic system created them, "and then take away from my sight this neighbor who decided to subsist from his own means and now lives, this son of a bitch, better than me."[47] If Selyunin's earlier reading of Hayek and Friedman impinged on his views, he did not seem to consider it relevant—the only contemporary Western author that he quoted in his detailed account of Russian and European political economy from Morus to Robespierre and Bukharin was the U.S. anti-Communist Sovietologist Richard Pipes.[48]

The "irrational demands" of the hoi polloi were even more explicitly problematized by Selyunin's former students Larisa Piyasheva and Boris Pinsker. Three trajectories informed their economic thought before they discovered Hayek and Friedman in the 1980s. First, they harked back to the contributions of Russian economists to the socialist calculation debate of the 1920s, such as the writings of Ber Brutskus, an advisor of the pre-Bolshevik liberal Russian government who had postulated the impossibility of socialist economics before his expulsion from the Soviet Union. Second, they had studied contemporary West European social democracy, which they associated with inflation, high welfare costs, and declining growth rates and competitiveness. Third, they pointed to the economic success of market-oriented authoritarian regimes of the Third Word.[49]

Under a pseudonym, Piyasheva published a radical critique of market socialism in 1987. Combining socialism with markets, she argued, was like becoming a bit pregnant. "Where are the pierogies puffier?" she asked her readers in the title and answered: where there are freer markets.[50] The twentieth century, she concluded with a Hayekian argument, was so bloody because free enterprise was stifled by utopianism and by the remnants of feudalism. This "blasphemy"[51] was heavily criticized by Perestroika-friendly economists, who not unreasonably feared that following her advice would bring back capitalism to the country,[52] but also by some of the Snake Hill group who shared Piyasheva's views, but due to their fear of hostile public opinion thought it was more politically prudent not to publicize them.[53]

Unimpressed by this headwind, in 1988 and 1989, Piyasheva and Pinsker published what were probably the first Soviet articles that introduced their readers to the economics of U.S. neoconservatism[54] and to Hayek's criticism of central planning and the pretension of knowledge.[55] Relying on an ostensibly almighty science, they argued, the Soviet leaders had neglected traditional experience and traditions in the name of social-economic utopias, which eventually led to fatal attempts at a total control of nature and society. Based on this recognition of the cul-de-sac of planning, Piyasheva and Pinsker called for individual humility and for cutting and limiting the activities of governments and their unfulfillable promises to the population. The "alliance between the nomenklatura and the industrial working class," Pinsker argued, "is cemented by the common pot of a welfare state" and needed to be broken to that end. Vitally important for him was the constitutional limitation of the state, and "not by parliaments or peoples, since those and others are often subject to illusions and blind fears. The state must be subordinated to the principles of liberalism, and to the highest degree possible limit its role to the supervision and execution of the law."[56]

Among the Snake Hill group, of which Pinsker was not a part, Western neoliberals and U.S. neoconservatives enjoyed some popularity during the final years of Perestroika, but they were not the main source of the group's worldview. As the debates of the 1970s and 1980s testify, these foreign thinkers only lent legitimacy to a historically locally grown attitude of parts of the liberal intelligentsia, who could now justify their elitism with reference to respected intellectuals from the West. In July 1990, *Novy Mir* finally printed parts of Hayek's 1944 book *The Road to Serfdom*,[57] but while it provided an elaborate confirmation for the existing skepticism about mass democracy among the reformers, it offered no advice on how actually to overcome socialist planning and how to transition to a free-market economy.

A debate about more concrete transition models, however, had already begun in 1988. Political scientists and area studies experts, who up to this point had hardly communicated with economists within the vast network of the Academy of Sciences, agreed with many of the Snake Hill group that the philosophies and political economies of the West provided only limited guidance. Development dictatorships in Asia and Latin America were more instructive. Southeast Asia experts suggested that a strong state, as in military-ruled South Korea, could provide the political stability necessary to conduct marketization in hostile environments,[58] and they discussed the "new authoritarianism," the Chinese modernization model along the lines followed by Singapore and Taiwan, developed by Liu Donghua and Bao Tong, which would be rejected by the Chinese Communist Party with the beginning of the student protests in 1989.[59]

"We talk a lot about democracy nowadays, but not a word on how to achieve it," remarked the political scientist Igor Klyamkin in a much-debated interview in 1989.

> We talk a lot about the market, but remain silent about ways of achieving the transition from a noncommodity to a commodity economy.... Such a transition can be achieved only in a structural way.... The masses of the population do not understand this.... There is thinking of the kind that "in the West everything is fine," and we should try to be like the West. But Western democracy was formed over centuries.... I am absolutely

convinced that the transition to democracy can only be achieved [via authoritarianism].[60]

His colleague Andranik Migranjan concurred in the same interview. "We don't have a so-called civil society," he said. "Democracy is opposed to Perestroika." And again Klyamkin: "I completely agree, nowhere and never was the transition from a precommodity economy to the market achieved in parallel with democratization. Political changes were always preceded by longer or shorter periods of authoritarianism. The whole experience from world history from the seventeenth to the twentieth century confirms this."[61]

Some of the young market economists agreed, too. Contrary to notions of an ostensible neoliberal antistate fervor or "market bolshevism,"[62] they had come to the conclusion that not only were popular demands for redistribution to be overcome, but that the Soviet state was too weak to implement the reforms they had in mind. From his observations of the administrative market, Nayshul not only deduced that this was an extraordinarily inefficient economic system, but also that the state organs of central planning lacked the power to actually implement the orders from Moscow.[63] Selyunin, too, in 1988, feared not the state, but its weakness: "We lost control over the events. Today, the American economy is more centrally controlled than ours."[64] The first Snake Hill group members predicted the implosion of the Soviet state in 1988,[65] but this was not seen as a positive development. Some basic legal structures for a market economy had been created during Perestroika, but state capacity needed to be strengthened to be able to actually guarantee the implementation of the law. By 1990, the Snake Hill group realized that they "had to work in a power vacuum."[66]

The transition to a market economy was thus seen as a political problem, not an economic one. It required "political leadership rather than technical expertise to resolve," recalled Gaidar later.[67] At the time, inspiration for how to overcome this problem did not come from the West,[68] but from authoritarian reform in the Soviet past and in the Third World present. Selyunin pointed to the social order and strengthening the rule of law that the combination of free markets and authoritarianism had provided during the New Economic Policy in the 1920s: "It proves the possibility of revolutionary change from above literally within the space of months."[69] And Nayshul led a group of like-minded reformers on a pilgrimage to visit Augusto Pinochet in Santiago de Chile, which catalyzed an enormous fascination among the Russian intelligentsia with a military dictator who fifteen years earlier had violently finished off a socialist government and transferred his country to a liberal market economy.[70] "Liberalism is a very powerful means of implementing social control," Nayshul later recalled. "This is how Pinochet thought about it."[71] As the collapse of the Soviet state and economy became ever more obvious in 1990, a group of anonymous economists from Leningrad, in a rare embrace of the term "neoliberalism" by its proponents, publicly demanded: "We must be prepared for a quick institutionalization of the neoliberal economic-political ideology…a sweeping, logical reform, any unpopular measures notwithstanding."[72]

THE LIMITATIONS OF ACTUALLY EXISTING NEOLIBERALISM

The Soviet promarket reformers—the liberal dissidents, the Snake Hill group of young economists, and the social scientists in the Academy of Sciences—did not usually think of themselves or their reform plans as "neoliberal." The West for them always was an important foil for comparison with life in the Soviet Union, but they embraced Western neoliberal thinkers only briefly before the disintegration of the USSR. Friedman and Hayek became popular readings during the transition period not because they delivered concrete advice for possible reforms, but largely because they lent legitimacy to ideas of political economy that the Russian promarketeers already had developed in engagement with Soviet economic and political realities and with local intellectual traditions. There is some justification to call some of them "neoliberals" nonetheless: their rejection of cybernetic planning, their strong predilection for free markets, and their preference for a strong state that limits popular sovereignty to create and defend them were indeed similar to ideas that West European neoliberals had developed earlier.

These similarities allowed some of the Russian market reformers to integrate easily into global neoliberal networks and think tanks from the late 1980s on. Aven established contacts with Western and Eastern European (neo)liberals while working at the Vienna International Institute for Applied Systems Analysis, beginning in 1987; Chubais and Shironin got in touch with the British Institute of Economic Affairs in Hungary in 1988.[73] After the disintegration of the Soviet Union in late 1991, Nayshul was a popular guest at Mont Pelerin Society meetings. Pinsker founded the publishing house Catallaxy, taking its name from a Hayekian term for economic order, and translated Western neoliberal literature for a Russian readership. Several (neo) liberal institutions set up shop in Moscow with Western assistance: the Moscow International Center for Research into Economic Transformation was led by Gaidar, and later by Vladimir Mau, one of two known Russian Mont Pelerin members. The Heritage Society opened an office and assisted in the creation of a self-professed "neoliberal" Hayek Society in Moscow, but only as late as 2002.[74] The impact of Western neoliberalism in post-Soviet Russia in the 1990s should not be overestimated, however: after their first encounters with their Russians counterparts, members of international neoliberal think tanks often conceded that they had nothing to teach them and much to learn from them.[75]

For some participants in the countryside seminars of the 1980s, the road from Snake Hill eventually led to the Kremlin. The aborted August 1991 putsch against Gorbachev by conservative Communists had further weakened the already destabilized Soviet state organs. Emerging as the new strongman in Moscow, the president of the Russian Socialist Republic, Boris Yeltsin, sought to transform the institutions and bureaucracies of the Soviet Union into Russian authorities under his command. Wresting control over the Soviet economy from the hands of the planning bureaucrats was part of his political strategy to make this transition of power irreversible. "A transition to a market economy," he had already declared in *Izvestia* a year earlier, "would make the entire administrative-command system redundant, and it would effectively wither away."[76] His confidant Gennady Burbulis connected him with some of the Snake Hill group, whose young age appealed to Yeltsin: "I purposely selected those with a minimum of Soviet-time experience. People without mental, ideological blinkers," he said.[77] Gaidar and Chubais would both at various times become ministers of finance, of the economy, and vice premiers in the early 1990s.

It has often been argued that ideological laissez-faire fervor drove Gaidar's team during that period.[78] But it seems that during a time of an already ongoing collapse of state organs and public order, what underpinned their policies was not antistatism, but the desperate attempt, with the help of the state, to establish irreversibly a new social and economic order. It was their notion of low state capacity, developed from observing the limits of central control in the planned economy, and their fear of resistance from entrenched bureaucratic elites and ignorant popular majorities that made them reject any further suggestions of state-led gradual transitions or mixed economies. "This was utter chaos," Gaidar later recalled of the situation in late 1991. "Only clinical idiots could at this point speak of a Chinese-Hungarian gradual type of reform."[79]

Actually existing neoliberalism in post-Soviet Russia thus meant a quick transition to a deregulated market economy, but the transformation of neoliberal ideas into politics had its limitations. First, in the young reformers' own view, accurate or not, the central state was never powerful enough to actually implement sophisticated reform plans, and they thus considered it necessary to accommodate powerful interest groups. Their longing for a strong executive clearly indicates that they bemoaned not the state, but its weakness. Second, the promarketeers always depended on the goodwill of the political leadership, who concurred with them only as long it served their own agenda and who could dismiss them and their economic advice at any time.[80]

Gaidar's most contested measure, only a couple of weeks after taking over as minister of finance, was to end price controls in January 1992. Attempts of the Soviet government throughout the year before to stabilize the economy with administratively raised prices and the annulment of private savings had not only ruined many Soviet citizens, it also had failed to curb excess demand, because the government had given in to popular pressure to raise wages. Continuously very low dictated prices for foodstuffs put a heavy burden on the state budget, hampered production, and nurtured an ever-expanding black market. While Western emergency food help began toward the end of 1991, some regions smuggled their grain abroad to get hard currency.[81] By the end of the year, before Gaidar entered office, the official supply system had collapsed. Initially, Gaidar exempted essential food, housing, energy, transport, communications, and medicine from price liberalization, but soon after, he had to allow the regions to abolish most controls, because there was no more money in the budgets to finance the high subsidies.[82] Inflation spiraled in the aftermath of price liberalization, not only because it had been suppressed, but also because the young reformers failed to gain control over the Central Bank and break up the ruble zone, which prevented them from halting monetary emissions.[83]

The inspiration for this "shock therapy" came from Eastern Europe and from historical role models. References to the West German currency reform after World War II were legion among Russian promarket economists.[84] Some also pointed to the maintenance of price controls by the prerevolutionary liberal government, which had led to food shortages, inflation, labor unrest, and eventually to workers' support for the Bolsheviks.[85] And in 1990, several delegations of Soviet economists had gone to Poland to learn from its ongoing economic deregulation under IMF guidance. Their key takeaway was that price liberalization was the most important first step toward a market economy, in order to create the financial stability necessary for the following mass privatizations. The "neoliberalized" IMF is sometimes blamed for pushing the Russian government toward such radical steps, too,[86] but such an influence happened only indirectly, via the emulation of the Polish transition, not due to any pressure applied from without. By the time Russia joined the IMF and the first advisors flocked to Moscow, decisions had long been made, and the IMF would have little effect on Russian political decision making throughout the 1990s. Its advice was often ignored, and it was involved in neither price reforms nor the privatizations that followed.[87]

This transition of the enormous assets of the Soviet industry and service sector into private hands was another contested measure of the economic reforms of the early 1990s. Here, too, a common reproach is that laissez-faire ideology led to an overhasty radicalism: the neoliberals allegedly did not care who owned the assets, as long it was not the state, which led to short-term profiteering, mass deindustrialization, and economic decline.[88] Some home-grown neoliberal ideas were indeed implemented after the breakup of the Soviet Union. Nayshul's initially contested voucher privatization, designed to turn the whole population into shareholders and to thus overcome popular skepticism about marketization, was undertaken in 1992, after a similar scheme appeared to have worked successfully in Czechoslovakia. Piyasheva, Pinsker, and Selyunin had written a similar privatization plan in 1990, but had suggested handing over small businesses to their staff for free. They found sympathetic ears in the Moscow city government in late 1991, which, after long debates, followed some of their instructions and gave away shops and restaurants, which then often ended up in the hands of shady entrepreneurs.[89]

Yet as in the case of price liberalization, it seems that behind the rapid privatization was not so much ideological neoliberal fervor, but the market reformers' recognition of the limitations of their own power and influence. Allowing well-connected old Communist elites to profit disproportionately from privatization was the reformers' way of gaining necessary support for their project of marketization. Most Soviet citizens had no understanding of a shareholder economy; they cheaply sold their vouchers to the managers of their companies or invested them in one of the many firms that soon went bankrupt. The ensuing concentration of capital was reinforced by a second wave of privatizations through a rigged program of "loans for shares" in the mid-1990s. Oligarchs were given control over much of the profitable assets of the Russian economy; in exchange, they would give their support for Yeltsin's reelection.

This was not laissez-faire economics, but clinging to a strong executive to create and defend markets and to stave off a clear democratic majority of Russians who would by now have voted for radical nationalist and Communist parties.[90] Nayshul pinned his hopes for a Russian Pinochet on the presidential candidate and popular ex-general Alexander Lebed, to whom he—eventually unsuccessfully—offered an economic reform plan in the run-up to the 1996 presidential elections. Most other market reformers continued their support for an increasingly authoritarian Yeltsin: they had cheered when he put down a violent rebellion by the Soviet-era Parliament by shelling its building.[91] They grudgingly supported Yeltsin in his reelection campaign in 1996; Chubais even participated as a key strategist. And some of them initially welcomed the Yeltsin-appointed successor as president, who seemed to be continuing the course of a strong executive defending free markets.[92]

Until Putin's return as president in 2012, the top economic posts were given to free-market economists. While "managed democracy" neutralized any meaningful opposition, they maintained or introduced low tariffs, a flat tax, a convertible currency, and free capital flows.[93] The Russian economy was Westernized at the company level, with Western consulting firms rejiggering the business culture. The Russian state, however, did not become (neo)liberal. Authoritarian rule was always the norm in Russia and needed no inspiration from neoliberals. That Putin insists on fiscal discipline, or "austerity," has less to do with neoliberal advice and more with the multiple times he witnessed the effect of a financial crisis on state power: in the late Soviet Union, in a German Democratic Republic that could no longer service its foreign debts, and in the recent financial crisis in Russia in 1998. Under Putin's rule, the Russian state has no property rights worth the name, and it uses economic policies for geopolitical means. The remaining ministers and advisors from the group of the young reformers have successively been replaced by army and secret service personnel and lately by Putin's friends.[94] While some of them still consider Putin the lesser evil, compared with unhinged populism, many free-market economists and liberal intellectuals have become open and, often, exiled opponents of the regime.

An ideological veneer of orthodoxy, Eurasianism, and economic nationalism in Russia now covers what is essentially crony capitalism and thus a far cry from *neoliberalizm*. Yet during the transformative years of the 1990s and early 2000s, neoliberal ideas permeated the thinking of parts of the Russian intelligentsia and many economists with access to political power. These ideas, reflections on how to create and protect free markets and liberal institutions with the help of a strong state, had formed in the final decades of the Soviet Union. They were based on observations of the workings of the planned economy and on assumptions about the mentality of ordinary Soviet people, but also on interpretations of global models of modernization, often led by authoritarian regimes. The West was an important point of reference for the Russian neoliberals, and its living standards and, for some, political systems were cherished ideals. Western neoliberalism, however, offered little advice on how to accomplish a transformation to a Western "market society." The books of Friedman and Hayek did become popular readings in the transition period, but largely because they lent legitimacy to ideas of political economy that the Russian promarketeers already had developed in engagement with Soviet economic and political realities, with Russian intellectual traditions, and with their own interpretations of international models of political economy.

I want to thank two colleagues for their very thoughtful comments on an earlier draft of this chapter: Adam Leeds, who has put forward a similar argument about the Gaidar group in his unpublished dissertation (Adam Leeds, "Spectral Liberalism: On the Subjects of Political Economy in Moscow," PhD diss., University of Pennsylvania, 2016) and Chris Miller, who did groundbreaking work on the generation of the group's academic teachers (Chris Miller, *The Struggle to Save the Soviet Economy: Mikhail Gorbachev and the Collapse of the USSR* [Chapel Hill: University of North Carolina Press, 2016]).

1. Ilya Matveev, "Russia, Inc.," *Open Democracy*, March 16, 2016, https://www.opendemocracy.net/en/odr/russia-inc; Boris Kagarlitsky, *Russia Under Yeltsin and Putin: Neo-Liberal Autocracy* (London: Pluto Press, 2002).

2. "Yakunin raskassal o svoej bor'be s 'neoliberal'nym globalizmom': Poka, vrode, nich'ja," *Gazeta Sankt Peterburg*, September 3, 2013. See also Anders Åslund, *Russia's Crony Capitalism: The Path from Market Economy to Kleptocracy* (New Haven: Yale University Press, 2019).

3. Anders Åslund, "Sergey Glazyev and the Revival of Soviet Economics," *Post-Soviet Affairs* 29.5 (2013), pp. 375–86; Sergej Glaz'ev, "Zmeinaja Gorka: Nikto ne dumal, chto razvite strany pojdet tak," *polit.ru*, September 26, 2006.

4. Richard Cockett, *Thinking the Unthinkable: Think-Tanks and the Economic Counter-Revolution, 1931–1983* (London: Harper Collins, 1995), p. 307; Janine Wedel, *Collision and Collusion: The Strange Case of Western Aid to Eastern Europe* (New York: Palgrave, 2001), pp. 121–63.

5. Quinn Slobodian, *Globalists: The End of Empire and the Birth of Neoliberalism* (Cambridge, MA: Harvard University Press, 2018); Thomas Biebricher, *The Political Theory of Neoliberalism* (Stanford: Stanford University Press, 2018); Hagen Schulz-Forberg, "Modern Economic Thought and the 'Good Society,'" in Peter E. Gordon and Warren Breckman, eds., *The Cambridge History of Modern European Thought* (Cambridge: Cambridge University Press, 2019), p. 6.

6. This has been similarly argued by Cornel Ban, *Ruling Ideas: How Global Neoliberalism Goes Local* (Oxford: Oxford University Press, 2016).

7. Elena Chebankova, "Contemporary Russian Liberalism," *Post-Soviet Affairs* 30.5 (2014), pp. 341–69.

8. Stephen Collier, *Post-Soviet Social: Neoliberalism, Social Modernity, Biopolitics* (Princeton: Princeton University Press, 2011).

9. Johanna Bockman, *Markets in the Name of Socialism: The Left-Wing Origins of Neoliberalism* (Stanford: Stanford University Press, 2011).

10. Joseph Stiglitz, *Globalization and Its Discontents* (New York: W. W. Norton, 2003).

11. Philip Mirowski and Dieter Plehwe, eds., *The Road from Mont Pèlerin: The Making of the Neoliberal Thought Collective* (Cambridge, MA: Harvard University Press, 2009); Daniel Stedman Jones, *Masters of the Universe: Hayek, Friedman, and the Birth of Neoliberal Politics* (Princeton: Princeton University Press, 2014).

12. Aleksandr Kovalev, "Idei Avstrijskoj shkoly v sovetskoj ekonomicheskoj literature 1920-kh godov," in Institut im. Fridrikh fon Khajeka, ed., *Kapitalizm i svoboda* (Saint Petersburg: Nestor-istorija, 2014), pp. 88–105.

13. Ivan Boldyrev and Till Düppe, "Programming the USSR: Leonid V. Kantorovich in Context," *British Journal for the History of Science* 53.2 (2020), pp. 255–78.

14. Robert D. English and Ekaterina Svyatets, "Soviet Elites and European Integration: From Stalin to Gorbachev," *European Review of History: Revue européenne d'histoire* 21.2 (2014), pp. 225–26.

15. Vitalij Najshul', "Istorija reform 90-kh i ee uroki: Otkuda sut' poshli reform, *polit.ru*, April 21, 2004.

16. K. Burzhuademov (Viktor Sokirko), "A gde zhe zashchita ekonomicheskoj svobody?," *Za zashchitu ekonomicheskikh svobod*, no. 7 (1979), https:// sokirko.com/victor/ecomomy/Zes7/72.5.htm; Burzhuademov, "Ja—obvinaju: Intelligentov—sluzhashchikh i potrebitelej v protovosostojanim ekonomicheskim svobodam i progressu rodiny," *Za zashchitu ekonomicheskikh svobod*, no. 1 (1978), pp. 36–52; Charles Allen, "Trends in Economic Samizdat," *Fletcher Forum* 4.1 (1980), pp. 93–98.

17. Viktor Sokirko, "Ekonomika 1990-go goda: Chto nas zhdet i est' li vykhod?," *Za zashchitu ekonomicheskikh svobod*, November 30, 1979, http:// www.sokirko.info/Tom10/butyrka/a1-3.htm.

18. Leo Timofeev, "Black Market Technology in the USSR," *Telos*, no. 51 (1982), p. 17.

19. Leeds, "Spectral Liberalism," p. 366.

20. Vjacheslav Shironin, "Zmeinaja Gorka: Eto nikogda ne bylo napisaniem sovetov gospodu bogu," *polit.ru*, October 6, 2006.

21. Vjacheslav Shironin, ed., *VIII Mezhdunarodnaja konferentsija 'Delovaja etika i natsional'nye modeli povedenija': Seminar 'Sostojanie nashevo znanija o Sovetskoj i Postsovetskoj Rossiskoj ekonomicheskoj nauke.' Stenogramma* (Saint Petersburg: Saint Petersburg State University of Economics, 2019), p. 20.

22. Joachim Zweynert, "Economic Ideas and Institutional Change: Evidence from Soviet Economic Discourse," *HWWA Discussion Paper*, no. 324 (2005), p. 24; Katy Young, "Russia's Real Radicals: Creating a Moscow Market," *Reason*, no. 4 (1992), https://reason.com/1992/04/01/russias-real-radicals.

23. Yegor Gaidar, in "Interview: What the Future Holds: The Clandestine Meetings of Soviet Economists," *Commanding Heights*, https://www.pbs.org/wgbh/commandingheights/shared/minitext/int_yegorgaidar.html; Paul Dragoș Aligică and Anthony John Evans, *The Neoliberal Revolution in Eastern Europe: Economic Ideas in the Transition from Communism* (Cheltenham: Edward Elgar, 2009), p 155; Yegor Gaidar, *Dni porazhenij i pobed* (Moscow: Vagrius, 1997).

24. Petr Aven and Alfred Kokh, *Gaidar's Revolution: The Inside Account of the Economic Transformation of Russia* (London: I. B. Tauris, 2013), p. 103.

25. Quoted in David E. Hoffman, *The Oligarchs: Wealth and Power in the New Russia*, rev. ed. (New York: PublicAffairs, 2011), p. 82.

26. Aven and Kokh, *Gaidar's Revolution*, pp. 42–44. These are recollections from the early 2010s, but the tone of contemporary *samizdat* publications around 1980 is congruent. See Allen, "Trends in Economic Samizdat."

27. Grigorij Glazkov, "Zmeinaja Gorka: U El'tsina ne bylo real'nogo vybora," *polit.ru*, September 29, 2006; Irina Evseeva, "Zmeinaja Gorka: Reformatory stali politikami v pravitel'stve," *polit.ru*, November 3, 2006.

28. Oksana Dmitrieva, "Zmeinaja Gorka: Kogda stala blizka vozmozhnost' realizatsii—vse i posypalos,'" *polit.ru*, September 14, 2006.

29. Sergej Vasil'ev, "Zmeinaja Gorka: Chubajs ochen' otpiralsja ot idei idti v politiku," *polit.ru*, October 3, 2006.

30. Miller, *The Struggle to Save the Soviet Economy*.

31. Shironin, "Zmeinaja Gorka"; Leeds, "Spectral Liberalism," p. 391.

32. Shironin, "Zmeinaja Gorka."

33. Najshul', "Istorija reform 90-kh i ee uroki."

34. Shironin, ed., *VIII Mezhdunarodnaja konferentsija 'Delovaja etika i natsional'nye modeli povedenija,'* p. 14.

35. Mikhail Gorbachev, *Perestroika: New Thinking for Our Country and the World* (San Bernardino: Borgo Press, 1988).

36. Patrick Flaherty, "Perestroika and the Neo-Liberal Project," *Socialist Register* 27 (1991), p. 135; Pekka Sutela, "The Economic Views of Gorbachev's Advisers: Leonid Abalkin, Nikolai Petrakov and Stanislav Shatalin," *Communist Economies and Economic Transformation* 3.1 (1991), pp. 106 and 111.

37. Adam Leeds, "Administrative Monsters: Yurii Yaremenko's Critique of the Late Soviet State," *History of Political Economy* 51.1 (2019), pp. 127–51; Miller, *The Struggle to Save the Soviet Economy*; Abel Aganbegyan, *The Economic Challenge of Perestroika* (Bloomington: Indiana University Press, 1988); Oleg Bogomolov, "The Socialist Market," *Moscow News*, no. 30 (1987).

38. Leeds, "Spectral Liberalism," p. 66.

39. Najshul', "Istorija reform 90-kh i ee uroki."

40. Rossen Djagalov, "Volksverächter: Der Antipopulismus der Postsowjetischen Intelligentsia," *Transit: Europäische Revue*, no. 42 (2012), pp. 123–43.

41. The quote is from the liberal philosopher Mikhail Gershenzon. See Leonard Schapiro, "The 'Vekhi' Group and the Mystique of Revolution," *Slavonic and East European Review* 34.82 (1955), p. 63.

42. Flaherty, "Perestroika and the Neo-Liberal Project," p. 132.

43. Vadim Belotserkovskij, *Samoupravlenie* (Munich: Neimanis, 1985), p. 180.

44. Vasil'ev, "Zmeinaja Gorka."

45. Philip Hanson, *The Rise and Fall of the Soviet Economy: An Economic History of the USSR from 1945–1991* (London: Routledge, 2015), p. 92; S. Larin, "Pamjati V. I. Seljunina," *Novyj Mir*, no. 12 (1994), pp. 247–48.

46. Nikolaj Shmelev, "Avansy i dolgi," *Novyj Mir*, no. 6 (1987), pp. 142–57.

47. Vasilij Seljunin, "Istoki," *Novyj Mir*, no. 5 (1988), p. 189.

48. Ibid., p. 184.

49. Larisa Piyasheva, "Parting with Socialism," *XX Century and Peace*, no. 6 (1990), pp. 11–14.

50. A. Popkova (Larisa Piyasheva), "Gde pyshnee pirogi?," *Novyj Mir*, no. 5 (1987), pp. 239–41.

51. Tatiana Valovaya, "Trudnyj put' poznanija: Razmyshlenija nad aktual'noj knigoj i nashumevshej statej," *Ekonomicheskaja Gazeta*, no. 35 (1987), p. 9

52. E. Pozdnjakov, "Mozhno li Vse-Taki 'nemnogo zaberemenet'? (Mnenie dilletanta)," *Mezhdunarodnaja ekonomika i mezhdunarodnye otnoshenija* (1987), pp. 113–17; O. Latsis, "'Zachem zhe pod ruku tolkat?': L. Popkovy, avtoru pis'ma 'Gde pyshnee pirogi?,'" *Novyj Mir*, no. 7 (1987), pp. 266–68.

53. Aven and Kokh, *Gaidar's Revolution*, pp. 44–46.

54. Larisa Piyasheva, "Ekonomicheskaja sushchnost' neokonservatizma," *Rabochij Klass i Sovremennyj Mir*, no. 3 (1988), pp. 78–92.

55. Boris Pinsker, "Bjurokraticheskaja khimera," *Znamja*, no. 11 (1989), pp. 183–202.

56. Ibid., pp. 201–202.

57. Zweynert, *Economic Ideas and Institutional Change*, p. 24.

58. Padma Desai, *Conversations on Russia: Reform from Yeltsin to Putin* (Oxford: Oxford University Press, 2006), p. 228.

59. Richard Sakwa, "The New Authoritarianism," *Détente*, no. 16 (1989), pp. 18–25.

60. "Nuzhna 'zheleznaja ruka'?: Intervju S. I. Kljamkinym i A. Migranjanom," *Literaturnaja Gazeta*, August 16, 1989.

61. Ibid.

62. Peter Reddaway and Dmitri Glinski, *The Tragedy of Russia's Reforms: Market Bolshevism Against Democracy* (Washington, DC: United States Institute of Peace Press, 2001).

63. Najshul', "Istorija reform 90-kh i ee uroki."

64. Seljunin, "Istoki," p. 180.

65. Vasil'ev, "Zmeinaja Gorka."

66. Ibid.

67. Desai, *Conversations on Russia*, p. 102.

68. The notable exception was Spain, which provided a model for champions of authoritarian capitalism (along the lines of Franco's liberal economic policies of the 1960s), for democratic monarchists (along the lines of King Juan Carlos's guided transition to democracy), and for moderate Communists, including Gorbachev himself (along the lines of Spain's "return to Europe" under the socialist prime minister Felipe González). See James Mark, et al., *1989: A Global History of Eastern Europe* (Cambridge: Cambridge University Press, 2019), pp. 81–82.

69. Seljunin, "Istoki," p. 171.

70. Tobias Rupprecht, "Formula Pinochet: Chilean Lessons for Russian Liberal Reformers During the Soviet Collapse, 1970–2000," *Journal of Contemporary History* 51.1 (2016), pp. 165–86.

71. Najshul', "Istorija reform 90-kh i ee uroki."

72. "'Zhestkim kursom...' Analiticheskaja zapiska Leningradskoj Assotsiatsii Sotsial'no-Ekonomicheskikh Nauk," *Vek XX i Mir*, no. 6 (1990), pp. 14–19.

73. Shironin, "Zmeinaja Gorka."

74. Boris Pinsker, http://www.libertarium.ru/pinsker; The Gaidar Institute for Economic Policy, https://www.iep.ru/en/e-t-gaydar; The Friedrich von Hayek Foundation, http://hayek.ru. The other known Russian Mont Pelerin Society member is Maxim Boycko.

75. Antonio Martino, opening speech at the 1990 Mont Pèlerin Society meeting in Munich. Liberaal Archief, Ghent, Mont Pèlerin Society BE/173723 /29; Interviews with Carlos Cáceres and Cristián Larroulet in Santiago de Chile, April 2016.

76. Boris Yeltsin, *The Struggle for Russia* (New York: Belka, 1994), pp. 145–78, excerpt in *Izvestia*, May 27, 1990.

77. Desai, *Conversations on Russia*, p. 81.

78. Bruce Kogut and Andrew Spicer, "Capital Market Development and Mass Privatization Are Logical Contradictions: Lessons from Russia and the Czech Republic," *Industrial and Corporate Change* 11.1 (2002); Grigory Yavlinsky and Serguey Braguinsky, "The Inefficiency of Laissez-Faire in Russia: Hysteresis Effects and the Need for Policy-Led Transformation," *Journal of Comparative Economics* 19.1 (1994), pp. 88–116.

79. "Otkuda Poshli Reformatory," *polit.ru*, September 6, 2006.

80. Najshul', "Istorija reform 90-kh i ee uroki."

81. David Lipton and Jeffrey Sachs, "Prospects for Russia's Economic Reforms," *Brookings Papers on Economic Activity*, no. 2 (1992), p. 228.

82. Vincent Koen and Steven Phillips, *Price Liberalization in Russia: Behavior of Prices, Household Incomes, and Consumption During the First Year* (Washington, DC: IMF Working Papers, 1993), p. 4.

83. Åslund, *Russia's Crony Capitalism*, p. 253.

84. Young, "Russia's Real Radicals."

85. Lipton and Sachs, "Prospects for Russia's Economic Reforms," p. 229.

86. Stiglitz, *Globalization and Its Discontents*.

87. Lipton and Sachs, "Prospects for Russia's Economic Reforms," p. 229; Peter Rutland, "Neoliberalism and the Russian Transition," *Review of International Political Economy* 20.2 (2013), p. 344.

88. Kogut and Spicer, "Capital Market Development and Mass Privatization Are Logical Contradictions," p. 19; Yavlinsky and Braguinsky, "The Inefficiency of Laissez-Faire in Russia," p. 105.

89. Evgenij Jasin, *Rossiskaja ekonomika: Istoki i panorama pynochnykh reform* (Moscow: Izdatel'skij dom Vysshej Shkoly Ekonomiki, 2019), p. 237.

90. Steven Fish, "The Predicament of Russian Liberalism: Evidence from the 1995 Parliamentary Elections," *Europe-Asia Studies* 49.2 (1997), pp. 191–220.

91. Dmitrij Travin, "Avtoritarnyj tormoz dlja 'krasnogo kolesa,'" *Zvezda*, no. 6 (1994), pp. 125–35.

92. Dmitrij Travin, *Zheleznyj Vinni-Puch i use, vse, vse: Liberalizm i liberaly v rossijskikh reformakh* (Saint Petersburg: Delo, 2004), pp. 436–41.

93. Chris Miller, *Putinomics: Power and Money in Resurgent Russia* (Chapel Hill: University of North Carolina Press, 2018).

94. Åslund, "Sergey Glazyev and the Revival of Soviet Economics."

CHAPTER FIVE

Shooting for an Economic "Miracle": German Post-War Neoliberal Thought in China's Market Reform Debate

Isabella M. Weber

The tide of neoliberalism that swept the globe under the aegis of the Bretton Woods institutions from the late 1970s onward transformed planned and mixed economies profoundly. The quintessentially neoliberal shock therapy of this period, however, has an antecedent a generation earlier: in the postwar West German price and currency reform of 1948. Indeed, 1948 should be seen as the true origin of the shock therapy doctrine. Although postwar West Germany may be associated with the "social market economy," the qualification "social" is commonly misunderstood as denoting an interventionist, welfare-oriented form of capitalism. Yet as scholars have shown, the social market economy finds its intellectual foundations in ordoliberalism and constitutes a precursor to the rise of neoliberalism as a global policy paradigm at a time when most capitalist economies were organized along Keynesian lines.[1]

In this chapter, I explore the case of China's market reform under Deng Xiaoping and show that the so-called West German "economic miracle" was mobilized as an archetype to promote the neoliberal policy of wholesale price liberalization, the sine qua non of shock therapy. As I argue elsewhere, China ultimately escaped shock therapy and has only partially assimilated itself to global neoliberalism.[2] Yet the Chinese market-reform debate reveals a previously underappreciated thread in the origins of the policy central to the global neoliberal turn.

The revival of market mechanisms was fundamental to the creation of new economic orders after World War II and under socialist reforms such as those in China after 1978. Both periods of transformation began against a backdrop of comprehensive economic controls. Each engendered bitter debates around the question of whether markets require universally free prices and the relevance of price controls for the gradual introduction of a constrained market mechanism. Neoliberal and ordoliberal visions of a free market encapsulated in the free movement of prices to be achieved by rapid liberalization at all costs competed with more pragmatic liberal and socialist outlooks that saw a positive role for price regulation and proposed a gradual transition.[3]

The postwar transition to a peacetime economy presented economists and social theorists with distinct choices about how to construct a market order. Great Britain and West Germany came to represent two alternatives: gradual liberalization under an interventionist state[4] or overnight ordoliberal liberalization to create a social market economy.[5] The West German postwar economic boom eventually overshadowed the grave economic difficulties and deep social tensions that followed on the heels of the 1948 currency and price reform.

Ordoliberals were quick to attribute the boom to Ludwig Erhard. The wholesale price liberalization that had, in fact, unleashed a general strike and that drove the young German Federal Republic into a profound political crisis was refashioned as the "Erhard Miracle." Disputes over the nature of the postwar German reforms were invoked in later theoretical debates over how to transition from a mixed or planned economy, and their example as an apparent success was mobilized in favor of radical price reform by Milton Friedman, among others.

The West German postwar experience was of great relevance to China's political leadership and reform intellectuals after the Cultural Revolution. It was understood as an exemplary transition to a new market-economic order. In what follows, I examine the role that the so-called Erhard Miracle played in China's price-reform debate in the first decade of economic system reform, 1978 to 1988. I show that the West German postwar reforms were schematically presented as the deed of one man and mystified as a policy that generated immediate and automatic economic prosperity. As such, the Erhard Miracle (艾哈德奇迹) developed into a powerful metonym for a radical form of price liberalization akin to what came to be known as the "big bang" when later imposed on Russia.[6] (See Tobias Rupprecht's contribution, "The Road from Snake Hill: The Genesis of Russian Neoliberalism," in this volume). I trace the contributions by prominent German ordoliberals such as Wolfram Engels and Armin Gutowski, as well as Milton Friedman, during their travels to China, and analyze the subsequent instrumentalization of the metaphor of the Erhard Miracle by prominent Chinese free-market reformers such as Wu Jinglian.

The chapter contributes to a growing body of work in global intellectual history that studies the dissemination of ideas.[7] Rather than conceptualizing China's reform debates as isolated by foregrounding its purported "Chinese characteristics," this chapter demonstrates that the fierce struggle in China over how to carve a path for economic reform has been fundamentally linked to international debates regarding market orders. This chapter constitutes a first step toward a new historiography of the intellectual foundations of the transition out of centrally planned economies: the question of plan and market under state socialism is reconnected here with debates over the postwar order and therefore indirectly with what is known as the "socialist calculation debate" of the interwar period.

I draw mainly on German-language scholarship to provide a brief overview of the intellectual origins and actual course of the 1948 West German currency and price reforms. Against this backdrop, I explore how ordoliberal and neoliberal economists introduced the Erhard Miracle into the Chinese reform debate, then turn to how these arguments were employed by Chinese economists lobbying for radical price reform in the 1980s. This analysis is based on Chinese primary sources and synthesizes insights from an oral history project for which I have interviewed more than fifty Chinese and international economists who contributed to China's reforms.[8]

THE "ERHARD MIRACLE":
INTELLECTUAL ORIGINS AND POSTWAR REFORMS

In the midst of World War II, economists around the world had already begun to envision a postwar order and to devise methods for a transition to peacetime reconstruction. F. A. Hayek's *The Road to Serfdom* (1944) was perhaps the most significant and powerful statement of this view.[9] In this work, Hayek argued that only two mutually exclusive ways of organizing economy and society are possible: either central planning or a free society of free competition. Not only must central planning necessarily lead to fascism, he argued, but even minimal concessions to it would lead society down this dangerous path.[10] The debate over the postwar order and price liberalization may be considered an extension of the socialist calculation debate (SCD). Hayek's mentor, Ludwig von Mises, had launched the SCD in the 1920s by claiming that rational socialism is impossible because the price problem is unsolvable without markets.[11] As regards postwar price liberalization, Mises argued along similar lines to those of Hayek. He warned that the "middle-of-the-road policy leads to socialism," as one of his titles put it, and that the government control of only a single commodity's price, such as that of milk, would be sufficient to set in train a process of central planning, thereby destroying the conditions of free competition.[12]

The German ordoliberal agenda of a "social market economy," as promoted by Ludwig Erhard, the Freiburg school, and others at the end of the 1940s, could be mistaken for such a "middle-of-the-road policy." Yet the ordoliberals agreed with neoliberals such as Mises and Hayek about the centrality of freely or market-set prices. In terms of plans for practical reform, the "real conflict of opinion was between those who felt that the price mechanism must be reintroduced into Germany as quickly as possible…and those who thought it must be severely limited in its applications so as to fulfil social and economic priorities."[13]

Occupation authorities and the emerging West German political parties considered and vetted a wide variety of proposals for how to reform the German postwar economy.[14] Ordoliberals, who tended to operate in the American zone, argued in favor of rapid and wide-ranging price reforms, while Social Democrats, whose stronghold was in the British zone, favored a gradual release of price controls and continued direct intervention of the state.[15] Currency reform was to be combined with tax reform and entail the introduction of a new currency, while all existing monetary claims and assets would at once be reduced to 10 percent of the prereform value.

The West German currency reform was implemented on June 27, 1948. While the reform is often attributed to Erhard, it was essentially the making of the U.S. military administration, working in concert with its Western allies.[16] By contrast, the decision to impose price liberalization beyond currency reform alone was made by the Economic Council under Erhard's directorship. Its aim was to rationalize not only the price level, but also relative prices. Erhard announced the liberalization of the majority of prices on the day of the currency reform, without the legal approval of the Allied forces or the Länder Council. Only afterward did he secure retroactive authorization from General Clay.[17]

Ordoliberal and neoliberal economists have promoted a mystified conception of the 1948 German currency and price reform by attributing it to the singular figure of Erhard himself. In a 1977 pamphlet advocating the effectiveness of shock treatment for Britain, Milton Friedman saluted the "German Erhard episode in 1948" as a historic breakthrough that demonstrated the effectiveness of this policy. Friedman claimed that Erhard had "terminated *all* wage and price controls over one weekend."[18] In fact, the 1948 German price reform did not liberalize *all* prices, and crucially, it kept control of the prices of essential production and consumption goods. Indeed, essential foodstuffs, raw materials, rents, and traffic charges continued to be subject to price ceilings for several subsequent decades.[19] One scholar estimates that 30 percent of consumer-goods' prices were regulated by the state in the period from 1948 to 1963.[20] Contradicting Friedman's recollection of the Erhard reforms, wages were likewise excluded from liberalization at the moment price controls were selectively scaled back.[21]

In fact, the immediate effect of the Erhard reforms was to provoke social unrest. Despite the congruent currency reform, aggregate excess demand caused prices to rise rapidly.[22] With wages capped and prices rising, workers suddenly faced falling real incomes on top of lost savings, as well as a sharp rise in inequality. Unions challenged the foundations of the new economic order. On November 12, 1948, West German workers launched a general strike, demanding economic planning and renewed price controls.[23] The unions' actions were ineffectual in blocking the impending liberalization, yet the economic fate of West Germany was left undecided until 1950. Only the outbreak of the Korean War finally induced the boom that set the Federal Republic's economy on a path of export competitiveness and surpluses.[24]

In sum, Erhard's price reform was clearly inspired by the ordoliberal vision for a social market economy, but critically, the prices of scarce and indispensable industrial inputs, as well as those of essential consumer goods, were never fully liberalized through Erhard's efforts. Rather, they were controlled at a lower level than what prevailed during the war. This policy, in turn, enabled wage repression. Cheap material and labor inputs were the prerequisites for the development of the German export model, and these inputs were based partially—but nevertheless decisively—on price controls. It was this peculiar feature of the German path to liberalization that came to be seen as instructive for those who studied the "Erhard Miracle" from abroad.

THE "ERHARD MIRACLE" IN CHINA

At the height of the Great Proletarian Cultural Revolution, Mao Zedong rejected both central planning and the market as all-encompassing economic coordinating mechanisms. The rural communes, the ideal of local self-sufficiency, and the placement of revolutionary politics ahead of economics instead formed the guiding principles for organizing society and the economy.[25] Yet the prospect of a new kind of political economy was revived in intellectual circles in the years before Mao's death in 1976. As early as three years before Deng Xiaoping's ascent to power in December 1978—commonly understood as the beginning of reform and opening up—a Fudan University research group compiled a major publication on the economies of capitalist countries in which the West German transition after World War II was subjected to close study.[26]

The Fudan research group's work was not simply an academic account of recent economic history, but bore an important, albeit implicit message regarding the group's view of Chinese history. Although the book labeled West Germany a capitalist and imperialist country, as was customary at the time, the parallels with China were evident to any attentive reader. China had a centrally planned economy within which the chains of command and order had collapsed as a result of the Cultural Revolution, just as Germany's had after World War II. As the Cultural Revolution and the explicit rejection of a national economic coordinating mechanism came to an end, the question presented itself: How was a new economic order to be established? The challenge faced by China from the mid-1970s onward was confronted from a purely economic perspective; at a certain level of abstraction, where the radically different political and ideological contexts could be de-emphasized, China could be seen as comparable to postwar West Germany.

But the West German case was not only of interest to Chinese intellectuals and political leaders due to the resemblance to the challenges Germany had faced. It was particularly worthy of study because of the great economic success of the West German economic recovery, the so-called Erhard Miracle. Approximately contemporary with China's revolution and the birth of the New China, Erhard had implemented his reforms, which were said to have enabled his country to rise like a phoenix from the ashes of World War II. By comparison, the New China had undergone a series of attempts to push ahead to new levels of development, which had succeeded in erasing the worst aspects of poverty, but had fallen short of achieving a hoped-for prosperity.

After a period in which the market was banned as an economic mechanism during the Cultural Revolution, reform-minded economists in the second half of the 1970s set out to revive Chinese debates from the 1950s and 1960s regarding the use of market mechanisms and the law of value.[27] Already in 1979, Deng Xiaoping had described to a foreign journalist the ways in which China could indeed develop a market economy under socialism.[28] In a surprising way, the German ordoliberals and intellectual fathers of the concept of a social market economy were of interest in this regard. Unlike Hayek or Mises, who rejected the compatibility of socialism and the market, Alfred Müller-Armack, who coined the term "social market economy," articulated an instrumentalist argument for how a free-market economy could still be considered socialist. In 1946, he wrote: "It appears to me to be a mere matter of terminology whether one calls a free-market economy socialist or not. The decisive question is what order is expected to solve our social problems. If this order is the free-market economy, one could no doubt see it as a social, or if you like, a socialist instrument."[29]

As China began opening up to the West in the late 1970s, a notable event was the visit of the delegation to West Germany in May 1978, headed by Vice Premier Gu Mu, a veteran of the revolution and a leader of economic reform. Gu's mission was to study what China could learn from Germany's economic development path.[30] His report drew much interest among Chinese leaders and intellectuals in the economics underlying Erhard's postwar reforms. The Third Plenary Session of the Eleventh Central Committee of the Communist Party of China in December 1978 marked both Deng's ascent to power and the official sanctioning of reform and opening up.[31] One of the most pressing questions under the new agenda—that of putting economic development first, instead of revolutionary politics—concerned the rationalization of the price system as a condition for the reintroduction of economic incentives while simultaneously avoiding inflation. In this regard, Erhard's reforms were thought to hold important lessons.

SPREADING THE "ERHARD MIRACLE" IN CHINA: VISITS BY GERMAN ORDOLIBERALS AND MILTON FRIEDMAN

Among the Chinese delegates to West Germany were Vice Premier Fan Yi and Vice Foreign Minister Zhang Wenjin. In an effort to learn from Erhard's postwar reconstruction, both approached the West German ambassador to China, Erwin Wickert, and requested he arrange for them to meet top experts in German economics.[32] Wickert, a member of both the Nazi paramilitary wing, the Sturmabteilung (SA), as well as the NSDAP, the Nazi Party itself, had previously briefly served in Shanghai for Hitler's government. Wickert had found his way back into the diplomatic service after the war, thanks to the backing of other former high-ranking Nazi diplomats.[33] Zhang Wenjin and Wickert had both attended school in Berlin at the same time. It was there that Zhang first became interested in Marxism; later, he studied under Werner Sombart. The two men were friends and openly discussed the question of economic reform during Wickert's tenure in Beijing.[34] Wickert promptly delivered on the request for experts on the postwar transition and invited Wolfram Engels, a descendant of Friedrich Engels's brother, to China as his private guest in March 1979.[35]

Engels was a prominent German ordoliberal professor of economics. Shortly after his visit to China, he founded two research institutes, the Frankfurt Institute (now the Stiftung Marktwirtschaft) and the Kronberger Kreis.[36] The collaboration of these two institutions was vital for preparing the ordoliberal renaissance in Germany after a succession of Social Democratic governments.[37] At the embassy in China, Wickert hosted a talk by Engels for Chinese economists on German reconstruction after World War II. The lecture sparked so much interest from the audience that several other presentations were arranged, and Engels was invited for a private dinner with Vice Premier Gu Mu.[38] Wickert had initiated the exchange with Engels with the support of the Social Democratic chancellor, Helmut Schmidt.[39] On the occasion of Engels's exchange with Gu Mu, Wickert reported in a telegram to the chancellery: "Gu said...that China had to combine the current system with a market economy. The question was only how this could be done. The principle that the means of production were publicly owned, however, was to be adhered to. He asked himself, if the laws of a market economy could work under this condition, to regulate economic activity. Professor Engels affirmed this and gave several examples."[40]

Once the decision to reform China's economy had been reached by the leadership in 1978, the question of *how* a market system could be combined with China's planning system dominated the question of whether to use the market at all.[41] In this regard, the West German reforms could be instructive.

In his presentations, Engels offered one implicit answer to the question. His key message was that the West German Miracle could be replicated in China by implementing policies akin to what he saw as Erhard's reforms: dramatic stabilization policies in the form of austerity and monetary control, combined with radical and universal overnight price reform. Engels told his Chinese audience that while postwar West Germany was experiencing a period of unprecedented prosperity, the real economic miracle had been brief, unforeseen by most, and only induced by the 1948 currency and price reform.

Engels attributed the miracle solely to Erhard. He argued that after the war, the Allied powers had continued to administer the planned economy of the Third Reich. Casting the ordoliberal reforms as antifascist, Engels stressed that putting an end to this system had been decisive for West Germany's subsequent trajectory. The country had lacked a democratic government and had faced powerful political forces in favor of the nationalization of all industries and planning, making Erhard's establishment of a free-market economy all the more spectacular. In his efforts, the liberalization of prices was an absolute necessity. Suppressing the fact of Erhard's real caution regarding essential consumer goods and production inputs, Engels attributed the persistence of limited price controls for essential raw materials such as coal, steel, and iron to orders by the military occupation regime. But, Engels argued, despite these constraints, and in contrast to the mixture of socialist planning and Keynesianism that dominated in the postwar UK and United States, the West German Miracle had helped to spread free-market economics globally.[42]

Shortly after Engels's talk, in July 1979, another German ordoliberal economist, Armin Gutowski, the director of the Hamburgische Welt-Wirtschafts Archiv (HWWA), an institute of international economics, a former member of the German Council of Economic Experts, and a founding member of the Kronberger Kreis, and his wife—an editor at *Der Spiegel*, Renate Merklein—were invited to China.[43] Gutowski extended the line of argument developed by Engels, but was more subtle in adapting his message to the Chinese context and thus was even more warmly appreciated by the Chinese reformers. Gutowski was even made an adviser to the Chinese government and was perhaps the first Western economist to play this role. He returned to China repeatedly and was invited to high-ranking Chinese delegations until his early death in 1987.[44]

In a 1979 speech published in Chinese in the journal World economy (世界经济), Gutowski, like Engels, stressed the critical importance of Erhard's price and currency reforms for the West German economic recovery. He described the immediate postwar German economic challenges in terms that must have sounded familiar to the Chinese audience: There was severe aggregate excess demand, since production had been aimed at supplying material for the war effort, and not consumer goods. With most goods still rationed, money was of limited use outside of black markets. China's socialist planned economy, focused on heavy industry, had produced analogous conditions.

Gutowski conceded that Germany had experienced high inflation in the immediate aftermath of Erhard's reforms, but he omitted the general strike from his discussion altogether. He claimed that the inflationary upswing had precipitated hardly any social disruption, because the population was aware at the time that it was only a transitional phenomenon.[45] The lacunae in Gutowski's report were diplomatically significant. Social unrest was a top concern for Chinese leaders as they contemplated economic reforms.

During a subsequent visit, Gutowski addressed the question of the compatibility of the market with socialism and focused on what China might learn from the German experience.[46] In 1979, he had argued that the success of Erhard's reforms could be attributed to their establishment of an economic order based on the principle of competition. Although some would insist that a market economy entails capitalism, Gutowski argued, German advocates of the social market economy had rejected this connection as unnecessary. The public provision of social welfare under its program was a case in point.[47] In 1981, he elaborated his position regarding the market's relation to socialism. Tactfully, Gutowski sided with Oskar Lange's position in the SCD: "Public ownership can remain unchanged, but there must be competition for economic vitality."[48] For the purposes of fostering competition—in addition to suppressing inflation—price reform was essential, as Erhard's success had shown. It could only follow, then, that the rationalization of the price system would decide the success or failure of China's reforms.[49]

Gutowski's emphasis on the compatibility of competitive prices with socialism resonated with some of China's most prominent economists of the first generation of revolutionaries, such as Xue Muqiao, who had argued since the late 1950s for restoring the law of value under Chinese socialism by increasing the use of competitive prices as a regulating mechanism.[50] Xue and Gutowski were in fact in close contact, and Xue organized some of Gutowski's visits to China, while Gutowski arranged for the German translation of Xue's major contribution to reform thinking.[51] In his German preface to Xue's work, Gutowski stressed that even though Xue had begun from a Marxist outlook, he shared many of the author's conclusions regarding China's reform.[52]

A third important ambassador of the Erhard Miracle in China was Milton Friedman.[53] While Engels and Gutowski had both occasionally advanced some arguments concerning the origins and consequences of the West German currency and price reform that today do not withstand close historical scrutiny, Friedman took the embellishment of Erhard's Miracle and the mythologization of the West German reforms to an even higher level. Before coming to China, Friedman had already invoked the West German postwar recovery as vindication of the shock treatment of rapid liberalization backed by budget cuts, as in Pinochet's Chile and the crisis in the UK of the late 1970s.[54] As part of the Chinese reformers' policy of "opening the minds to the outside world," Milton and Rose Friedman were invited to China in 1980. During his first visit, Friedman relayed the following anecdote to his audience at the Chinese Academy of Social Sciences: "The so-called economic miracle produced by Ludwig Erhard in 1948 was a very simple thing. He abolished all price and wage controls and allowed the market to operate while at the same time keeping a strict limit on the total quantity of money issued."[55]

Friedman acknowledged some transitional inflation immediately after the 1948 reforms, but as a monetarist, he argued that a relative increase in the quantity of money was the only cause of sustained inflation. As long as the quantity of money was controlled, an increase in the price of one commodity must always be compensated by a relative decrease in other prices and as such was negligible. Friedman ruled out the validity of cost-push inflation theories and did so with reference to Erhard's reforms.[56] Yet Friedman's claim that Erhard had eliminated all price controls was simply false. As we have seen, the prices of essential production inputs as well as of basic consumer goods were not liberalized under Erhard, and neither had wages been liberalized simultaneously, as Friedman contended. These points are especially important, because a source for cost-push inflation would have originated from scarce essential production inputs such as steel and coal, for which demand was inelastic. Similarly, the supply of basic consumer goods was limited, and demand was inelastic, as well, so if these prices and wages had not been controlled, they could have catalyzed a wage-price spiral and sustained inflation.[57] As we will see in the next section, the Chinese anticipated the danger of cost-push inflation and a wage-price spiral and considered these to be significant risks of the mythologized version of Erhard's radical price reform promoted by Friedman.

Unlike the visits by Engels and Gutowski, which were the starting point for repeated exchanges, Friedman's 1980 tour in China elicited no commitments from the Chinese side. Friedman's discussion of the Erhard reforms was innovative in that it was the first to analyze them from a consistent monetarist perspective. In this regard, it was theoretically more sophisticated when compared with the anecdotal contributions of Engels and Gutowski. But Friedman's theoretical erudition was advanced at the cost of historical accuracy. It is likely that Friedman's presentation did not fit with Deng Xiaoping's new paradigm of "seeking truth from facts."[58] Friedman's portrayal of Erhard may have appeared to his Chinese audience to lack sufficient realism.

The Chinese price system had been basically frozen over the course of the Cultural Revolution from 1966 to 1976. In the first years of reform, the price system was adjusted by central command, and the market, as the new regulating mechanism, was introduced at the margins of the system. But a wide-ranging or even universal one-stroke overnight liberalization emulating the mythologized Erhard price reform was not implemented, even though some reform leaders and economists, as well as some World Bank and other foreign advisers, thought that this was the best—indeed, necessary—path for China. Economists such as Wu Jinglian repeatedly invoked the Erhard Miracle metaphor to argue for radical price reform. At the famous 1985 Bashanlun conference co-organized by the World Bank, the former director of the Bundesbank (1976 to 1979), Otmar Emminger, who had helped shape the German monetary policy since 1950, once more advised China to pursue a so-called "big bang," justifying his policy recommendation with reference to the Erhard Miracle.[59] China came close to pursuing shock therapy in 1986 and again in 1988, but ultimately averted this radical policy choice.[60]

CONCLUSION

From the late 1970s on, three distinct dimensions of the so-called Erhard reforms aroused interest among Chinese intellectuals and reform leaders. Each motivated intense exchanges with ordoliberal and neoliberal economists about the nature of price reform. First, the apparently unexpected economic success of West Germany after the destruction of World War II seemed to the Chinese to be the breakthrough that the Great Leap Forward and Big Push Industrialization had intended, but failed to deliver. This misleading representation of spontaneous West German recovery cannot withstand critical scrutiny today, because it is by no means settled whether the cause of success was the leap in the dark or the preexisting industrial foundations, combined with foreign assistance.[61] Nevertheless, Germany's economic boom resonated with the Chinese who were attempting to jump-start rapid economic development at the dawn of the reform era.

The second dimension of the Erhard reforms of special interest to the Chinese was the evident similarity of the two cases in the implementation of price controls. From a technical point of view, the postwar German problem was similar to that of the beginning of Chinese reforms. In both cases, chains of command and order within a centrally planned command economy had collapsed, even if for radically different reasons and in drastically different contexts. Nevertheless, in both cases, the question arose of how to create a new economic order that could allow for a greater role for market mechanisms. Since market competition required some degree of price flexibility, price flexibility quickly became a focus: How was it to be achieved, and to what degree was liberalization necessary? In this regard, the radical West German 1948 price reform was a relevant experience for China.

Third, despite the vastly different ideological contexts of postwar Germany and post–Cultural Revolution China, the ordoliberal vision of a social market economy spoke to China's debate over the compatibility between socialism and the market. The ordoliberals had insisted, rightly or wrongly, that the existence of a market economy did not necessarily entail full-fledged capitalism. As Keith Tribe has observed with regard to the Freiburg school, the ordoliberals had a "conception of economic organization that represents a genuine effort to move beyond the sterile contraposition of market to plan and vice versa."[62] Those ordoliberals who visited China in the 1980s knew how to adapt their vision to the Chinese context by way of economic diplomacy.

This chapter has demonstrated that the German ordoliberals Wolfram Engels and Armin Gutowski, as well as Chicago school economist Milton Friedman, introduced the concept of the so-called Erhard Miracle to China. At the beginning of their efforts, neoliberal overtures mainly took the form of a sugarcoated case study of the postwar West German reforms. Neoliberal advice was solicited by Chinese leaders and economists who thought the German experience held lessons for China, but the West German case was increasingly transformed into a metaphor for the ostensible success of a drastic price liberalization known as the Erhard Miracle. The Erhard Miracle came to play an important role in China's fierce reform debate, mobilized as anecdotal evidence for an essentially magical solution to a complex problem. Over the course of this process, historical details, especially regarding the critical question of the range of the price reform and the continuity in controls of essential consumption goods and industrial inputs, were increasingly disregarded. The Erhard Miracle came to stand for the wonders of overnight and all-encompassing price reform as invoked by Friedman. Such a radical, one-stroke reform was repeatedly prepared, but never implemented in China. From the mid-1980s onward, however, the group of economists who campaigned for radical price liberalization gave the Erhard Miracle a prominent place in their narrative.

As I describe elsewhere, adulation of the Erhard Miracle was once again part of the economic discussion in China in 1988, after an aborted attempt at far-ranging price reforms, when Friedman made his second visit to the country in the hope of assisting the Chinese in their final push toward a "big bang," one component of the "shock therapy" administered to Eastern Europe and Russia.[63] The ordoliberals who contributed to China's search for a market reform approach were not all united in their mystification of the postwar West German experience, however. Wilhelm (Willy) Linder and Hans-Karl Schneider, who had both done extensive research on industrial prices such as energy, approached the question of what China could learn from the West German experience not from the angle of the overall economic order, but from the feasibility of liberalizing specific prices. They warned that essential industrial prices could not be abandoned without risking runaway inflation. Even the leader of the Mont Pelerin Society, Herbert Giersch, cautioned that the institutional reality in China had to be considered carefully before taking a sudden step toward wholesale liberalization.[64] The warnings of prominent ordoliberals resonated with the group of Chinese economists who sought to defend China's experimentalist, gradual reform against shock therapy. Both the proponents of shock therapy and the opponents of this approach to "big bang" marketization based themselves on the West German model. The underlying and competing interpretations of Erhard's reforms of the immediate postwar period thus returned in China's internal debates over the world-making decision to introduce the market into its economy.

NOTES

This is an expanded version of an article previously published as I. M. Weber, "Das Westdeutsche und das Chinesische 'Wirtschaftswunder': Der Wettstreit um die Interpretation von Ludwig Erhards Wirtschaftspolitik in Chinas Preisreformdebatte der 1980er-Jahre," *Jahrbuch für historische Kommunismusforschung* (2020), pp. 55–70. I would like to thank my interviewees, Harald Hagemann, Dieter Plehwe, Peter Nolan, Joshua Rahtz, Gregor Semieniuk, Quinn Slobodian, Wei Zhong, Felix Wemheuer, and the participants of the History of Economic Thought Society's 2018 annual conference and of a workshop at the Bundesstiftung Aufarbeitung for helpful comments. All remaining infelicities are my own.

1. Werner Bonefeld, "Freedom and the Strong State: On German Ordoliberalism," *New Political Economy* 17.5 (2012), pp. 633–56; Dieter Plehwe, "Soziale Marktwirtschaft als Steinbruch?: Zur Neuvermessung der Grezen zwischen Markt und Staat in der aktuellen Debatte über wirtschaftspolitische Leitbilder," in Ariane Berthoin Antal and Sigrid Quack, eds., *Grenzüberschreitungen— Grenzziehungen: Implikationen für Innovation und Identität* (Berlin: edition sigma, 2006); Ralf Ptak, *Vom Ordoliberalismus zur sozialen Marktwirtschaft: Stationen des Neoliberalismus in Deutschland* (Opladen: Leske + Budrich, 2004).

2. On the origins of China's contested relation with neoliberalism, also see Isabella M. Weber, "China and Neoliberalism: Moving Beyond the China Is/ Is Not Neoliberal Dichotomy," in Damien Cahill, Melinda Cooper, Martijn Konings, and David Primrose, eds., *The SAGE Handbook of Neoliberalism* (London: Sage, 2018), pp. 219–33, and Weber, "Origins of China's Contested Relation with Neoliberalism: Economics, the World Bank, and Milton Friedman at the Dawn of Reform," *Global Perspectives* 1.1 (2020), https://online.ucpress.edu/gp /article/1/1/12271/107349/Origins-of-China-s-Contested-Relation-with.

3. David Colander, "Galbraith and the Theory of Price Control," *Journal of Post Keynesian Economics* 7.1 (1984), pp. 30–42; Stephanie Laguerodie and Francisco Vergara, "The Theory of Price Controls: John Kenneth Galbraith's Contribution," *Review of Political Economy* 20.4 (2008), pp. 569–93.

4. Alec Cairncross, *Years of Recovery: British Economic Policy, 1945–51* (London: Methuen & Co., 1985).

5. Werner Abelshauser, *Deutsche Wirtschaftsgeschichte seit 1945* (Munich: C. H. Beck, 2004), pp. 84–106.

6. Anders Åslund, *Post-Communist Economic Revolutions: How Big a Bang?* (Washington, DC: Center for Strategic and International Studies, 1992); János Kornai, *The Road to a Free Economy: Shifting from a Socialist System: The Example of Hungary*, 1st ed. (New York: Norton, 1990); David Lipton and Jeffrey Sachs, "Creating a Market Economy in Eastern Europe: The Case of Poland," *Brookings Papers on Economic Activity* 21.1 (1990), pp. 75–147.

7. Samuel Moyn and Andrew Sartori, eds., *Global Intellectual History* (New York: Columbia University Press, 2013).

8. A more in-depth analysis of this oral history material is available in Isabella M. Weber, *How China Escaped Shock Therapy: The Market Reform Debate* (London: Routledge, 2021).

9. Roger Backhouse, "The Rise of Free Market Economics: Economists and the Role of the State since 1970," *History of Political Economy* 37.5 (2005), p. 368.

10. Friedrich Hayek, *The Road to Serfdom* (London: George Routledge & Sons, 1944), p. 43.

11. Ludwig von Mises, "Die Wirtschaftsrechnung im sozialistischen Gemeinwesen," *Archiv für Sozialwissenschaften* 47 (1920–1921), pp. 86–121.

12. Ludwig von Mises, "Middle-of-the-Road Policy Leads to Socialism," *Commercial and Financial Chronicle*, May 4, 1950.

13. A. J. Nicholls, *Freedom with Responsibility: The Social Market Economy in Germany, 1918–1963* (New York: Oxford University Press, 1994), p. 180.

14. Siegfried Freick, *Die Währungsreform 1948 in Westdeutschland: Weichenstellung für ein halbes Jahrhundert*, 1st ed. (Schkeuditz: Schkeuditzer Buchverlag, 2001), pp. 37–41.

15. Abelshauser, *Deutsche Wirtschaftsgeschichte seit 1945*, pp. 89–94.

16. Ibid., pp. 123–26; Wolfgang Krieger, *General Lucius D. Clay und die Amerikanische Deutschlandpolitik, 1945–1949* (Stuttgart: Klett-Cotta, 1987), pp. 374–81.

17. Ludwig Erhard, *Wohlstand für alle*, 1st. ed. (Düsseldorf: Econ-Verlag, 1957), p. 23; Irmgard Zündorf, "Staatliche Verbraucherpreispolitik und Soziale Marktwirtschaft in Westdeutschland, 1948–1963," in André Steiner, ed.,

Preispolitik und Lebensstandard: Nationalsozialismus, DDR und Bundesrepublik im Vergleich (Cologne: Böhlau, 2006), pp. 134–36.

18. Milton Friedman, *Friedman on Galbraith and on Curing the British Disease* (London: Institute of Economic Affairs, 1977), p. 45, emphasis added.

19. Irmgard Zündorf, *Der Preis der Marktwirtschaft: Staatliche Preispolitik und Lebensstandard in Westdeutschland, 1948 bis 1963* (Stuttgart: Steiner, 2006), pp. 147–57.

20. Ibid., p. 131.

21. Ibid., pp. 61–62.

22. Ibid.

23. Ibid., pp. 62–63.

24. Abelshauser, *Deutsche Wirtschaftsgeschichte seit 1945*, pp. 154–74.

25. Carl Riskin, *China's Political Economy: The Quest for Development since 1949* (Oxford: Oxford University Press, 1987), pp. 163–64.

26. 复旦大学资本主义国家经济研究所《战后西德经济》编写组 (Editorial group for the West German postwar economy at Fudan University's Institute for Research on Capitalist Countries, the West German postwar economy) (Shanghai: Shanghai People's Press, 1975).

27. K. K. Fung, "Editor's Introduction," in K. K. Fung, ed., *Social Needs versus Economic Efficiency in China: Sun Yefang's Critique of Socialist Economics* (Armonk: M. E. Sharpe, 1982), pp. xiii–xxx; Sun Yefang, "The Role of 'Value,'" in ibid., pp. 36–81; Eckard Garms, foreword to Eckard Garms, ed., *Wirtschaftsreform in China: Chinesische Beiträge zur Theoriediskussion von Sun Yefang u.a.* (Hamburg: Institut für Asienkunde, 1980), pp. 7–30; Cyril Chihren Lin, "The Reinstatement of Economics in China Today," *China Quarterly* 85 (1981), pp. 1–48; Liu Guoguang and Zhao Renwei, "Relationship between Planning and the Market Under Socialism," in G. C. Wang, ed., *Economic Reform in the PRC: In Which China's Economists Make Known What Went Wrong, Why, and What Should Be Done About It* (Boulder: Westview Press, 1982), pp. 89–104.

28. Deng Xiaoping, "We Can Develop a Market Economy under Socialism, November 26, 1979," in *Selected Works of Deng Xiaoping, Volume 2 (1975–1982)* (Beijing: Foreign Languages Press, 1984), https://dengxiaopingworks .wordpress.com/2013/02/25/we-can-develop-a-market-economy-under-socialism.

29. Alfred Müller-Armack, *Genealogie der Sozialen Marktwirtschaft: Frühschriften und weiterführende Konzepte* (Bern: Paul Haupt, 1974), p. 30.

30. Martin Albers, *Britain, France, West Germany and the People's Republic of China, 1969–1982: The European Dimension of China's Great Transition* (London: Palgrave Macmillan, 2016), p. 190; Gu Mu, "关于访问欧洲五国的情况报告 (Report about a delegation to five countries in Europe)," in *Documents of the Chinese Communist Party* 1 (2009), pp. 28–36.

31. Susan L. Shirk, *The Political Logic of Economic Reform in China* (Berkeley: University of California Press, 1993), p. 39; Alexander Pantsov and Steven I. Levine, *Deng Xiaoping: A Revolutionary Life* (Oxford: Oxford University Press, 2015), pp. 341–45.

32. Fritjof Meyer, "Fröhlich und ausgeglichen," *Der Spiegel*, April 5, 1982, https://www.spiegel.de/politik/froehlich-und-ausgeglichen-a-d9dce4eb-0002 -0001-0000-000014341642; Ulli Kulke, "Ein undiplomatischer Diplomat und die Freiheitsliebe," *Die Welt*, April 9, 2007, https://www.welt.de/politik /article800571/Ein-undiplomatischer-Diplomat-und-die-Freiheitsliebe.html.

33. Eckart Conze, Norbert Frei, Peter Hayes, and Moshe Zimmermann, *Das Amt und seine Vergangenheit: Deutsche Diplomaten im Dritten Reich und in der Bundesrepublik* (Munich: Karl Blessing, 2010), p. 702.

34. Kulke, "Ein undiplomatischer Diplomat und die Freiheitsliebe."

35. Albers, *Britain, France, West Germany and the People's Republic of China, 1969–1982*, pp. 195, 296; Rudy Maxa, "Gott im Himmel! If Engels Only Knew!," *Washington Post*, October 21, 1979, https://www.washingtonpost.com/archive /lifestyle/magazine/1979/10/21/gott-im-himmel-if-engels-only-knew/2912f92e -6906-44fc-8fe6-f6b557f23cc6.

36. Stephan Pühringer, "Think Tank Networks of German Neoliberalism: Power Structures in Economics and Economic Policies in Post-War Germany," *ICAE Working Paper Series* no. 53 (2016), p. 13.

37. Martin Werding, "Gab es eine neoliberale Wende?: Wirtschaft und Wirtschaftspolitik in der Bundesrepublik Deutschland ab Mitte der 1970er Jahre," *Vierteljahrshefte für Zeitgeschichte* 56.2 (2008), pp. 303–21.

38. Albers, *Britain, France, West Germany and the People's Republic of China, 1969–1982*, p. 195.

39. Ibid., p. 252.

40. Quoted in ibid., p. 195.

41. See Weber, *How China Escaped Shock Therapy.*

42. This section is based on one of Engels's speeches in China on West German economic development that was published upon his return in German in the May 21, 1979 issue of the *Wirtschaftswoche*, the magazine of which Engels was the editor in chief. A Chinese translation came out in the journal *European Research* five years later, when the question of price reform was hotly debated among political leaders and economists. Wolfram Engels, "联邦德国三十年的经济发展 (30 years of economic development in federal Germany)," *European Research* 6 (1984), pp. 37–42.

43. Albers, *Britain, France, West Germany and the People's Republic of China, 1969–1982*, p. 196; Armin Gutowski, "西德经济学家古托夫斯基教授讲演: 战后西德经济的恢复和发展 (West German economist Gutowski's speech: The recovery and development of the postwar West German economy)," *World Economy* 4 (1979), pp. 36–39; Renate Merklein, "China ist derzeit ein grosses Laboratorium," *Der Spiegel*, December 1, 1980, https://www.spiegel.de/wirtschaft/china-ist-derzeit-ein-grosses-laboratorium-a-3ad76b2f-0002-0001-0000-000014332767.

44. Kulke, "Ein undiplomatischer Diplomat und die Freiheitsliebe." The Xue Muqiao chronicle contains detailed information on the dates and procedures of Gutowski's visits to China. Fan Shitao, 薛暮桥年谱 [Xue Muqiao chronicle] (Beijing: n.p., forthcoming).

45. Gutowski, "西德经济学家古托夫斯基教授讲演: 战后西德经济的恢复和发展," p. 38.

46. Armin Gutowski, "西德古托夫斯基教授对我国经济和财政金融问题提出的咨询意见 (West German Gutowski's advice on China's economy and finance)," *Finance Research* 2 (1982), pp. 9–14.

47. Gutowski, "西德经济学家古托夫斯基教授讲演: 战后西德经济的恢复和发展," p. 38.

48. Armin Gutowski, foreword to Armin Gutowski, ed., *Sozialismus in China: Erfolge, Fehlschläge, Reformperspektiven* (Hamburg: Weltarchiv, 1982), p. 14.

49. Ibid., p. 12.

50. Shitao, 薛暮桥年谱.

51. Gutowski, foreword to *Sozialismus in China*, pp. 1–14; Xue Muqiao, *China's Socialist Economy* (Beijing: Foreign Languages Press, 1981).

52. Gutowski, foreword to *Sozialismus in China*, pp 1–14.

53. Milton Friedman, "货币与通货膨胀 (Money and Inflation)," *Comments on International Economics* 1 (1981), pp. 8–23; Friedman, *Friedman in China* (Hong Kong: Chinese University Press, 1990), unpaginated e-book.

54. Freidman, *Friedman on Galbraith and on Curing the British Disease*, p. 529.

55. Freidman, *Friedman in China*.

56. Ibid.

57. Weber, *How China Escaped Shock Therapy*, pp. 212, 217–18, 235.

58. Deng Xiaoping, "Hold High the Banner of Mao Zedong Thought and Adhere to the Principle of Seeking Truth from Facts, September 16, 1978," in *Selected Works of Deng Xiaoping, Volume 2, (1975–1982)* (Beijing: Foreign Languages Press, 1984), pp. 141–44.

59. Otmar Emminger, *D-Mark, Dollar, Währungskrisen: Erinnerungen eines ehemaligen Bundesbankpräsidenten* (Stuttgart: Deutsche Verlagsanstalt, 1986), p. 14.

60. Weber, *How China Escaped Shock Therapy*, pp. 182–258.

61. Abelshauser, *Deutsche Wirtschaftsgeschichte seit 1945*, pp. 67–69; John Kenneth Galbraith, *A Life in Our Times* (Boston: Houghton Mifflin, 1981), pp. 192–206.

62. Keith Tribe, *Strategies of Economic Order: German Economic Discourse, 1750–1950* (Cambridge: Cambridge University Press, 1995), p. 209.

63. Weber, *How China Escaped Shock Therapy*, pp. 131, 188, 195, 219–20, 251–52, 264.

64. Ibid., pp. 185 and 251.

CHAPTER SIX

Disciplining Freedom:
Apartheid, Counterinsurgency, and
the Political Histories of Neoliberalism

Antina von Schnitzler

A dominant narrative of the Left in South Africa has been that the rise of neoliberal reforms in the country were the result of a pact between the higher echelons of the African National Congress (ANC) and the late-apartheid government, an "elite transition"[1] mediated by institutions such as the World Bank and coming into its own with the neoliberal reforms the new government imposed in the mid-1990s. Such narratives of betrayal attributed postapartheid failures and disappointments to an etiologic mix of individual self-interest, a lack of ideological steadfastness, and an external bulldozer of neoliberal policy advice administered by globalized capitalist forces and their proxies.

Integrated in this larger story involving powerful global actors and local moral failings and betrayals, neoliberalism came to be seen as a unitary set of policies developed and imposed wholesale from outside in the 1990s and as something primarily economic. The narrative was strategically effective insofar as it provided the means both to critique the increasing global dominance of neoliberal policy paradigms and to demand accountability from the ANC-led government. Yet it also risked narrowing the terms through which the postapartheid transformation and its discontents could be understood.

In their focus on global institutions and their economic effects, such critiques tend to elide the specific and much earlier historical dynamics through which neoliberal ideas first circulated and became effective in South Africa in the late 1970s. In the process, they risk overwriting the *political* foundation of neoliberal reforms, that is, their deployment not only or even primarily in response to economic concerns, but as solutions to political questions—in this case, to the political crisis of the late-apartheid state.

The following chapter traces the shift in political styles of reasoning and the transformation in governmental techniques introduced, often haphazardly, by these earlier neoliberal reforms. Specifically, I examine the shift away from the blunter techniques and imaginaries of "grand apartheid" toward more oblique micropolitical techniques in the aftermath of the 1976 Soweto uprising. This period produced a series of piecemeal urban interventions, often inspired by neoliberal principles, in which housing and urban services and infrastructures became central. Crucially, the reforms proposed in this period sought to shift some of the most contentious political questions regarding citizenship, political rights, and belonging to an administrative, technical, and increasingly deracialized terrain. As they embarked on the dual task of reforming the apartheid state while holding on to its basic premise of minority rule, reformers pragmatically drew on neoliberal ideas in an effort to depoliticize the resurgent anti-apartheid movement.

This chapter tells a novel story about neoliberalism in South Africa, and in the process, about neoliberalism as a whole. Rather than viewing the Global South primarily as recipients of neoliberal knowledge or as blank slates for neoliberal reforms to take effect, this chapter examines how economists, state officials, and urban reformers translated and appropriated neoliberal ideas in the context of the systemic crises of the late 1970s as a conceptual resource to rethink apartheid modalities of governing urban Black populations. It is this history that fundamentally shaped the terrain of struggle confronted by the anti-apartheid movement in the militant 1980s, and its legacies are alive today as the country has been confronted with waves of protests in townships and informal settlements.[2]

Unearthing this earlier history of neoliberalism in South Africa is important not only to show how neoliberal thought became useful within a larger arsenal of apartheid-era counterinsurgency, but also to enable us to think in more expansive terms about neoliberal reforms and their targets. Importantly, the argument here is not that the voices of neoliberal theorists of the Global South somehow need to be "heard" (a move that has of course been critical for minoritized forms of knowledge)—these figures were by no means marginal in the places in which they wrote. Rather, my point in this chapter is to suggest that colonial and postcolonial contexts provided an epistemological ground for rethinking the neoliberal tradition, in particular in relation to questions of race, but also in the close relation between neoliberal ideas and the decidedly illiberal tools that are often required to bring them to life. Second, in the South African case, neoliberal ideas emerged as a resource to deal with political crisis and, as such, are part of a political, not merely an economic program, one driven as much by forms of resistance as it is by the exigencies of capitalist accumulation.

THE "DISCIPLINE OF FREEDOM"

> Freedom is an artifact of civilization [that] was made possible by the gradual evolution of the discipline of civilization which is at the same time the discipline of freedom.... We owe our freedom to the restraints of freedom. —Friedrich Hayek, 1978

One of the central elements of the neoliberal turn is a critique of rationalism and the promotion of an epistemology based on individual tacit knowledge. Friedrich Hayek, the thinker to whom South African neoliberals often turned, grounded the neoliberal project conceptually in a critique of rationalism. For him, the primary flaw of statist projects is not moral or political, but epistemological. At the heart of the rise of socialism and Keynesianism, he argued, is the rationalist belief in the human capacity for total knowledge and hence for state intervention to effect radical change. Human beings, in this analysis, are not innately rational. Rather, what connects the "natural" field of instinct and the development of reason is culture (in his earlier work referred to as "tradition" or "habit").

As Hayek put it, "Culture is neither natural nor artificial, neither genetically transmitted nor rationally designed. It is a tradition of learnt rules of conduct which have never been 'invented' and whose functions the acting individual does not understand."[3] Culture, conceived as a slowly evolving set of embodied rules, enabled the discipline of instincts and thus governed and enabled the emergence of a "spontaneous order" and the development of the free society. Hence, "what has made men good is neither nature nor reason but tradition."[4] Culture here answers a governmental need and thus paves the way for the evolution toward the Great Society. For Hayek, then, freedom was an "artifact of civilization" that was always dependent on specific forms of discipline. Freedom could emerge only through "the restraints of freedom."[5]

In Hayek's mobilization of the concept, "culture" thus becomes central to a particular political ontology and thus a resource for a particular governmental reason. This conception of culture as an "ordering principle" neatly solves the central neoliberal dilemma of the inherent limits to knowledge and the need for "order." Given that culture is both what makes us reasonable and yet is fundamentally unknowable, Hayek argues that the rationalist faith in state intervention is detrimental. Thus, Hayek's framework is based on a paradoxical attachment to both a conservative account of tradition and to liberal principles of progress and universality articulated in Kantian terms,[6] a tension that provides important clues to the contradictions that would periodically surface as neoliberal reforms were taking shape around the world.

If, in Hayek's formulation, neoliberal ontology assumes preexisting, slowly evolved social institutions with an inevitable bend toward "freedom" and the "market society," how can neoliberalism be relevant to contexts where such institutions take a different form, shaped, for example, by colonial or socialist legacies? New modalities of translation are required in order to make neoliberal thought relevant to contexts not formatted on the model of European social modernity. Because of the often-overlooked neoliberal emphasis on culture, specific and more indirect forms of intervention become central to such reforms—an emphasis on gradualism, rather than radical transformation, and on recoding and incorporating existing contexts in order to redirect them toward a new trajectory.

In the remainder of this chapter, I explore how this conceptual orientation and its paradoxes traveled to late-apartheid South Africa in the 1970s. At the height of the crisis of the 1970s and 1980s, neoliberalism became both a language and an archive for a critique of apartheid and inspired a set of techniques that could be selectively harnessed to a particular counterinsurgency that took a decidedly technopolitical form. Much as liberalism turned pedagogical in the colonial context, in the crisis-ridden moment of late apartheid, neoliberal reformers often opted for selective and frequently illiberal forms of interventionism in the name of safeguarding the "road to freedom."

THE AMBIVALENCES OF APARTHEID LIBERALISM

Liberalism in the colonies often tended to forget its defining ethical and political principles when faced with the exigencies of imperial domination.[7] In the context of colonial and apartheid South Africa, liberal conceptual coherence was stretched to its limits in particularly dramatic ways. While apartheid, as a racist state project reliant on a strongly regulated economy, was an illiberal project par excellence, its origins and initial forms of reasoning were in fact a solution proposed by liberals to the problem of groups outlined by leading liberal intellectual and reformer Alfred Hoernlé in 1939, when he wrote that "the concrete historical setting in which the classical doctrine of liberalism was evolved did not include the setting of a multi-racial society, such as we have here in South Africa, in which, moreover, one racial group, and this one a minority group, is, and is determined to remain, the dominant group." "Liberal ideals," he concluded, "have to be re-examined and rethought in their application to a society of this type."[8]

Throughout South Africa's colonial history, two liberal traditions competed with each other, as they did within the British colonial project as a whole. The first was based on a progressivist-assimilationist project that envisioned that the "civilizing mission" would eventually "uplift natives" toward full membership in colonial society. In South Africa, this strand came to be known as Cape liberalism and was practically materialized in a limited franchise for "civilized natives" and a concomitant rationale for segregation on the basis of civilization.[9] The second tradition, in part a response to the failure of the first, gave up the project of assimilationism in favor of a rule through the establishment of institutional separation, what came to be known, in colonial administrator Frederick Lugard's elaboration, as "indirect rule." This tradition was elaborated in the early Natal colony and involved a more conservative focus on the maintenance of groups on the basis of ethnicity and race.[10]

While South African liberal historiography tended to depict apartheid as the outcome of the crude racism of the Boer republics, its initial conceptual formulation should be seen within the context of the latter liberal tradition in which assimilationism was replaced with a focus on the maintenance of group differentiation. As becomes apparent in the quote above, Hoernlé saw the "multi-racial" nature of South Africa as a problem that ultimately could not be solved through assimilationist strategies.[11] In South Africa, unlike what he depicted as the more homogeneous European context, assimilationism and color blindness inevitably would lead to the domination of one group by the other. It was in response to this liberal problematic that Hoernlé proposed the idea of "total separation," which, he believed, unlike its predecessor of segregation, could be made consistent with liberal principles in that it gave each population group political rights within their "own" societies, thus avoiding the inevitable inequalities associated with assimilationism.

In the 1940s, Hoernlé's suggestions were taken up by more moderate Afrikaner nationalists in an effort to render Afrikaner nationalism compatible with liberal principles. It is in these writings that the term "separate development" first appears with direct reference to Hoernlé. Only much later are the notions of separate development and later "separate freedoms" taken on by the more hard-line, anti-liberal nationalists, such as Hendrik Verwoerd. What made apartheid unfathomable for liberals, then, was initially less the *concept* of "separate development," but rather the ways in which it practically unfolded; that is, on the one hand, its association with race, and on the other, the centrality of the state and state intervention, including the epistemology and associated techniques on which it came to rest.

The global move toward statism beginning in the interwar years, in particular the rise of fascist and socialist state projects, translated in South Africa into a racist state project split into a democratic, welfarist sphere for whites, for Afrikaners, in particular, and a project that envisaged granting "sovereignty" via despotic, "traditional" authorities for the Black majority. This bifurcated state project and the peculiar racial economy it produced—*Volkskapitalisme*, or what Stephen Gelb termed "racial Fordism"[12]—was based on bureaucratic infrastructures that channeled Black laborers via labor bureaus to the farms and mines.

The ideological defense of "separate development" was based in large part on a cultural relativism that argued for the need to "protect" African cultures from the influences of modernity, in particular, "the market" and industrial society. This motif encompassed all areas of life, including, centrally, the economy. As Verwoerd, then still minister of native affairs, put it in defense of the policy of prohibiting private investment in the homelands, "We will not let the wolves in, those people who simply seek where they can make money in order to fill their own pockets."[13] Elsewhere, he more explicitly suggested that "the white man took years to learn how to be a good trader and many

Bantu traders are still deficient as regards capital and knowledge and commercial morality."[14] This suggestion, as many pointed out at the time, was of course ludicrous—most Black workers had been working in industrial conditions for a long time—but it enabled a framing of South Africa's economy as limited to the "white" areas, while migrant labor was externalized on the basis of "national" boundaries, a matter of "international cooperation," rather than a part of one economy. In the urban, now "white" areas, this economic rationale for separate development translated into a stringent set of legislations and regulations instituted throughout the 1950s that severely restricted Black business ownership.

Throughout the 1950s and 1960s, a small number of liberals had protested apartheid and the economics on which it was based. Several economists, such as William H. Hutt, a member of the Mont Pelerin Society from the year after its founding who lived and worked in South Africa, wrote influential neoliberal treatises against apartheid, based in large part on economic arguments positing that "the market is colour-blind" and should be deregulated.[15] And yet, this vocal liberal criticism was always limited, especially during the booming economy of the 1950s and 1960s. Indeed, Hutt himself argued against a universal franchise, opting instead to support voting rights on the basis of wealth to protect the market from majority rule.[16] It was only in the 1970s and 1980s, when the system of racialized Keynesianism began to crumble, and South Africa became locked into what at the time was diagnosed in Gramscian terms as an "organic crisis," that neoliberal critiques of apartheid became more influential.[17]

The crisis was in part global: just as other state projects began to falter in the context of stagflation, the downturn of the economy put severe strains on the viability of the state bureaucracy. However, in South Africa, the crisis was also precipitated by the political developments of the liberation movements that had gathered steam since the early 1970s, the decline of the Portuguese Empire, the coming into power of liberation movements in its northern neighbors, and perhaps most importantly, by the series of protests and mobilizations that began with the Durban strikes in 1973 and the Soweto uprising in 1976.

It is at this moment of crisis that apartheid reformers began to draw on new ideas, and on neoliberal thought in particular, for solutions. As they did so, they grappled with the question of how neoliberalism could be made relevant to South Africa. It is here that Hayek's thought, and in particular, his reliance on the notion of tradition, lent itself to an extension and modification of existing culturalist arguments to justify apartheid. Indeed, it was Hayek's attachment to "culture" and "tradition" and, by extension, to the limits and "discipline of freedom" this entailed, that rendered his thought particularly compelling, because it offered a language with which to articulate the reform of the apartheid state while retaining its basic premise of minority rule. This notion of culture—deployed by Hayek and by his South African readers—ultimately allowed for the deferral of democracy for those not seen as culturally prepared for it and thus for an indefinite extension of apartheid, now justified in liberal terms.

AFTER SOWETO: RETHINKING THE URBAN

In June 1976, hundreds of students were killed during what came to be known as the Soweto uprising. The event of 1976 catapulted South Africa back into international consciousness. The black-and-white image of the dying thirteen-year-old student Hector Pieterson being carried by a teenage boy and accompanied by his anguished sister circulated globally and became iconic of the repressive violence of apartheid. And yet less spectacularly, 1976 also marked a turning point in the apartheid modalities of urban rule. As we will see, while workers had become increasingly militant—with the 1973 Durban strikes as the most visible, forceful sign—the students who rose up in Soweto, many inspired by the Black Consciousness movement, presented as a new kind of political subject to the apartheid state. The immediate response was violent repression, leading to the killing of nearly five hundred students. The Soweto uprising had hit at the core of the grand apartheid strategies and logics of rule.

The aftermath of the Soweto uprising witnessed the emergence of myriad research efforts, conferences, books, and commissions of inquiry that sought to comprehend the subject of the revolt. Motivated by both security and economic concerns, over the ten years following the uprising, the apartheid government contemplated and partially introduced a number of reforms that either by design or in effect moved away from the grand apartheid ideologies and instead drew on neoliberal ideas to reform the apartheid state while holding on to its basic premise of minority rule.

In response to the organic crisis of the 1970s, the South African government embarked on what it called a "total strategy," a counter-insurgency program to protect the white regime from what it claimed was a "total onslaught" from internal and external enemies. First announced by then Defense Minister P. W. Botha in the 1977 White Paper on Defence, total strategy brought security concerns to bear on all aspects of life and entailed the heavy militarization of ever-increasing spheres of society and the state. However, it was also inspired by neoliberal reforms taking place elsewhere. As Michael Mann observed, total strategy was "part of the global anti-statist crusade that has, in the era of Reagan and Thatcher, been described as 'monetarism.'" And yet, Mann continued, this application in South Africa was "contradictory," since it was "applied in the context of a reformist initiative" in which selective state spending to deal with the political crisis ultimately would be central.[18]

Many of the reforms proposed at the time were influenced by neoliberal or monetarist principles, including, for example, a move toward financial liberalization first advocated by the De Kock Commission on monetary policy in 1978. Yet most attention was given to the question of urbanization and specifically to the question of "urban blacks." In the late 1970s, two commissions of inquiry—known as the Riekert and Wiehahn Commissions—were set up in order to devise policies related to labor and the urban Black population. As Adam Ashforth has argued, the Riekert Commission set out to investigate "manpower utilization," envisioning the decentralization, deracialization, and depoliticization of separate development by dissolving the state's bifurcation and instead turning influx control into an administrative matter of the lower tiers of government.[19] Apart from novel dividing strategies and new discourses of security, Riekert also and for the first time introduced "a commitment to 'free enterprise'" for urban township residents that was "seen as a means of deflating the communist 'onslaught.'"[20]

As the Wiehahn Commission put it, "Full involvement, participation and sharing in the system of free enterprise by all population groups with as little government intervention as possible would not only give all groups a stake in the system but would ensure a common loyalty to both the system and the country."[21] In practice, this meant that while migrant labor and persons without Section 10 (urban residence) rights were to be cast out and policed more forcefully, urban residents were promised training, more job security, and mobility within the urban area in the hope they would develop into "labor aristocrats" who would act as a buffer against the rising tides of resistance.[22]

Crucially, the commission also envisaged the establishment of Black local authorities in the townships, which would in turn pave the way for the withdrawal of subsidies from and privatization of housing and infrastructure services. Thus, "the full costs of reproduction were to be imposed directly through rates and taxes levied on consumers, home owners and African businessmen in the townships."[23] Rather than attaching separate development primarily to persons (ethnic and racial identification via passes, labor bureaus, and so forth), which had turned it into a political question of rights, influx control would be shifted "to the non-political sphere of the administration of 'things'—houses and jobs—into which people fit. Control and justification could then be achieved by simple recourse to the 'economic rationality' established and validated through the production and distributions of material things."[24]

Abandoned in such a scheme, at least in theory, was the earlier apartheid state project, with its emphasis on the direct planning of population movements and its faith in centralized state knowledge and intervention. Rather, what emerged in the late 1970s was the ideal of a decentralized, technocratic administration. Apartheid was envisaged as moving toward a more oblique, molecular mode of exerting control. While Riekert's core strategy failed, in part because it ultimately held on to the apartheid fiction of independent Bantustans, the thrust toward a decentralized technopolitics would define South Africa in the years to come.

In the process, "free enterprise" and "economic liberalism" became key words in the larger effort to reform apartheid. While much literature at the time was preoccupied with showing the multiple ways in which the "reforms" fell short, with many suggesting that they were no more than a sham, here, I want to explore and take seriously the modes of reasoning they relied upon, attending in particular to the ways in which neoliberal ideas—and Hayek's, more specifically—were received and repurposed by late-apartheid reformers. It is at this point that the question of culture reemerges, now to justify the deferral of the "free society."

FREEDOM, WELFARE, AND ORDER

> Freedom can only be associated with economic growth and material welfare if the sense of responsibility in the society is of a highly economic kind, i.e. if people are able and willing to read the signs of the market, to make the necessary calculations and to act upon their findings.... "But in fact it is probable that not one tenth of the present populations of the world have the mental and moral faculties, the intelligence and the self-control that are required for it."
>
> —South African economist Jan Lombard, quoting Alfred Marshall, 1978

In 1978, two years after the Soweto uprising, Jan Lombard, one of the most influential South African economists writing at the time and later deputy governor of the South African Reserve Bank, sought to assess the relevance of the Hayekian framework for South Africa. Lombard was a close reader of Hayek's work. In 1979, he was invited by Hayek to join the Mont Pelerin Society.[25] Lombard's account is of interest not only because he was a frequent economic advisor of the National Party (NP) government, but also because he spoke from within an established Afrikaner hegemony, rather than as part of the liberal tradition often associated with the English-speaking business community. As part of a larger critique, Lombard's was a pragmatic search for a way out of the crises of apartheid, rather than a utopian liberal blueprint or radical critique of the apartheid state.

The central question Lombard addressed in two publications—*Freedom, Welfare and Order* (1978) and *On Economic Liberalism in South Africa* (1979)—was the problem of the applicability of "economic liberalism" to South Africa. Arguing that separate development is a "sinking philosophy" whose emphasis on centralized economic control and continual attachment to "race" was responsible for South Africa's "peculiar political problem," Lombard proceeded to outline how "economic liberalism" could provide solutions to South Africa's multiple dilemmas.[26] Structuring his account is the problem of "urbanization" that animated many of the debates in the aftermath of the Soweto uprising. For Lombard, the realization of the failure of the central apartheid strategy of influx control and the grand apartheid plan of instituting Bantustans necessitated a rethinking of received ideas of governance.

The neoliberal framework was attractive to Lombard precisely because neoliberalism (unlike classical liberalism) included a focus on "order" and a gradualist approach to reform. Lombard did not want to abandon "separate development" entirely, but to reinvent its foundations to make it compatible with liberal norms. This proposal for a neoliberal reform of separate development in order to facilitate what

Lombard described in explicitly Hayekian fashion as the "evolutionary progress towards the free society"[27] had several key points, all of which converged on the question of the level of the South African population's readiness for a liberal society.

Drawing on neoliberal theorists, and most centrally on Hayek, Lombard argued that "individual freedom and individual responsibility are two sides of the same coin" and that hence, liberal society could function only in a context where the "sense of responsibility in the society is of a highly economic kind, i.e., if people are able and are willing to read the signs of the market, to make the necessary calculations and to act upon their findings."[28] Crucially, Lombard argued that South Africa was unlike "common societies," due to "differences in the economic rationality and productivity."[29] He elaborated: "The majority of Black and Coloured workers in the urban areas of South Africa lack the ability to use skills and knowledge with the functional competence needed for meeting the requirements of adult living as *responsible* and *free* citizens of a *democratic* society."[30] Interesting here, and defining for the reception of neoliberal ideas in South Africa, is the elision performed by the term "free society": the absence of "economic rationality" entails the absence of "political rationality," that is, in one stroke, economic and democratic reform are collapsed. In *On Economic Liberalism*, Lombard more explicitly elaborated the paradox often at the heart of neoliberal reforms:

> Development economists talk about 'the human factor' in this connection. For a liberal minded person such expression, which makes human beings the input of some total material concept, is almost anathema. In a sense, however, it is true that the liberal order depends for its success upon such human qualities as the will and the ability of the individual members of society to make their own decisions, to calculate the costs and benefits to themselves of alternative behaviour.[31]

Lombard here implicitly articulates a central neoliberal dilemma: the "spontaneous order" advocated by Hayek et al. in fact required specific forms of pedagogy and intervention that would make individuals take on the roles envisaged for them.

Indeed, Lombard's solution to this dilemma was that neoliberalism would need to be preceded by substantial reforms in order to succeed in South Africa. For these reasons, Lombard suggested, a period of "benevolent paternalism" "in preparation for freedom" must necessarily precede the liberal society. In South Africa—"a culturally underdeveloped country"—such paternalism would include a "programme of fundamental cultural reforms."[32] During such reforms—regrettably—"the principle of democracy cannot yet come fully into play" for those "people who are being prepared culturally for their future responsibilities as mature and free men."[33] "Since a liberal order depends wholly upon the consistency and rationality of individual behaviour, the transition from paternalism to liberalism must be determined by circumstances."[34] In other words, the key obstacles to the applicability of neoliberalism—culture, behavioral dispositions—would require reform. Neoliberalism emerges here not only as a critique of apartheid (and the racialized Keynesianism it upheld), but also as a new matrix to rationalize group differentiation as an exceptional, but necessary precursor to economic liberalism.

Importantly, even though the racist, exclusionary character of apartheid is retained throughout, the *logic* of exception, as well as the modality of racist thinking on which it was based, has been transformed. While grand apartheid ideologues viewed "urban blacks" as nonpersons, that is, as persons who in the future would be accommodated in the "traditional homelands," now, "urban blacks" were believed to be in the midst of a transition period, a pedagogical stage toward becoming "free persons." While the ultimate effect remained the same—the Black urban population would continue to be denied political rights, now on the basis of indefinite deferral—the rationality that authorized apartheid had shifted. Simultaneously, the continued denial of political rights could be rationalized as a necessary aspect of the "economic road to democracy," as Lombard called it.

Reforms, Lombard suggested, would include the separation of groups based on economic, rather than racial distinctions while maintaining a territorially based system of differentiation. Thus, he proposed to move from racial "group areas" to (ostensibly) nonracial "depressed areas" and a simultaneous effort toward the decentralization of the state with the aim of depoliticizing local government. Decentralization would "limit the area of politics in social affairs as much as possible"[35] and remove the question of citizenship rights that were at the heart of political struggles.

Lombard's writings enable us to trace the contours of a neoliberal technopolitics by which increasing issues and domains would become subject to administrative-technical, and often indirect or private forms of government. Thus, it was hoped they could be removed from the public domain and by extension from the terrain of nationalist claims by the liberation movement. It is important to note that neoliberal thought was received not as a blueprint here, but reformulated and adapted by practical thinkers such as Lombard. Such neoliberal "moves" became operationalized as a part of a larger program of countering the antiapartheid movement.

Beyond decentralization, a focus on depoliticization could also be observed in other "classically" neoliberal reforms into the 1980s. Thus, for example, while South African proponents of privatization rehearsed many of the arguments concurrent elsewhere in the world that often focused on increased efficiency and fiscal restructuring, they also motivated privatization as an intervention that could depoliticize central areas of persistent struggle, in particular, housing and infrastructure. Throughout such reforms, the focus was on reframing political questions as administrative ones. Despite (or perhaps because of) the ultimate failures of many such reforms, we can here locate some of the conceptual underpinnings for the technopolitical terrain of the antiapartheid struggle during the 1980s that, indeed, continue to resonate in the present.

While Lombard's reflections on the possibilities of "free enterprise" to solve the systemic crisis remained on a largely abstract terrain and were never implemented in the exact way he had suggested, such ideas would soon wield influence in so-called *verligte* or "enlightened," policy circles. At around the same time, throughout the late 1970s, there was an increasingly multidisciplinary effort at understanding what was widely referred to as the problem of "the urban black." Beginning with the Cillié Commission set up to investigate the reasons for the Soweto uprising, there was a sudden interest in the *subjectivity* of the Black urban resident, including his (and sometimes her) attitudes, interests, and values. An edited collection published in 1978 by the School of Business Leadership at the University of South Africa (UNISA), entitled *South Africa's Urban Blacks: Prospects and Challenges,* provides a good sense of the explosion of interest in this subjectivity. Notably, the volume begins with an epigraph from Lombard's *Freedom, Welfare and Order* that encapsulates the larger project: "By the standards of students of the liberal principles, the southern African plural urban society is in need of a great deal of reform before it could be expected to function well."[36]

"Political needs," the editors write, make it imperative that urban Blacks be studied "at the level of the human being in its entirety." Studying the "problem" would be a prerequisite for reform aimed at enabling "the black man to become a city-dweller able to cope with the challenges of the modern city." While the apartheid state throughout the 1950s and 1960s had regarded and treated urban residents as "temporary sojourners" who would eventually find their political homes in the Bantustans, the Soweto uprising had made clear the "permanence of urban blacks."[37] In the book, over a dozen chapters by social scientists, economists, and psychologists cover every aspect of urban Black life, from religious beliefs to basic provisioning, work, education, and political behavior. In many of the essays, the "urban black" emerges as a mysterious creature about whom little is known. And while the theory of urban adaptation so prominent since the colonial period still runs through the collection, with problems of "tribal acculturation" looming latently in the background, the striking feature of the book is the increasing realization that the "urban black" is not only part of South Africa's modernity, but in fact central to solving apartheid's crises.

Lombard's abstract identification of the problem of economic rationality is here (ostensibly) backed up by research and data. Most of the contributions begin with clear racist assumptions and premises, but their starting points—and the *specific logic* of racist reasoning on which they draw—differ from previous understandings in several respects. "Urban blacks," while savvy in many ways, are shown to have a tendency to misread market signals, to consume and spend money irrationally and to "misunderstand" commercial advertising. In the collection, this lack of economic rationality is emphasized in particular in psychological studies pointing to the need for reforms that "emphasize the development of an individual system of values which will motivate each individual to work for the improvement of the community as well as for economic progress." Counteracting the "natural system of African socialism," reforms must "cultivate a desire [in individuals] to advance themselves."[38] One of the most important tasks is the introduction of a discipline attentive to long-term goals, rather than the satisfaction of "immediate needs": "Instead of his behaviour being regulated by custom, his own choice must determine his behavior, a mechanism which has not yet been formed."[39] Another contributor similarly emphasized the need for an "internalisation of business values that will ensure an effective black contribution to the economy of South Africa."[40] In other words, in studies such as these, the Black urban population emerges as deficient, but *potential* economic subjects whose values need to be transformed to enable them to participate fully in the market.

Such studies often had immediate policy implications—indeed, the collection would be cited approvingly by Prime Minister P. W. Botha a year later, and his government increasingly drew on such academic expertise in the formulation of new policy measures, particularly in Soweto.[41] Throughout the 1980s and early 1990s, Lombard himself would be a central advisor to government, often overseeing commissions or the writing of policy documents. While this sudden interest in the subjectivity of the Black population was strongest in the urban areas, it was also extended to "development" efforts in the Bantustans. In 1980, the Department of Co-operation and Development (previously the Department of Bantu Affairs) established a Committee on Motivating Studies staffed by members from the Human Science Research Council (HSRC), the Council for Scientific and Industrial Research (CSIR) and the School of Business Leadership at UNISA, which had produced the collection on "urban blacks" quoted above. The committee was set up with the primary aim "to look intensively and in a co-ordinated way in a national or ethnic context at the psychological make-up of the Black man, his vulnerabilities and susceptibilities, his likes and dislikes and his own particular view of reality," and to "evaluate the place and part of the Black man in the Western capitalist system and the demands it makes on the individual, community and nation." The "exceptional challenge," the report suggested, was to establish "techniques to motivate members of the Black nations or ethnic groups to achieve more in regard to the accelerated economic growth and development." For, the report continued,

> the Black man does not react objectively to facts. He is more likely to react to images of facts which are based on his own specific non-material vision of the reality, which is largely mystical. If it is added that the Black man is still strongly linked to the rhythm of his own culture and that innovations and changes are often seen as a threat to the existing...order, intensive research is warranted.[42]

A 1984 government report entitled "Measures Which Restrict the Functioning of a Free Market Oriented System in South Africa" similarly noted as one obstacle to the free market the "less sophisticated consumer": "Coming from a culture of poverty and underdevelopment, they are often unaware of the elementary principles of personal or domestic budgeting and consequently buy injudiciously.... their predilection for immediate usage is strong and...they are often inclined to build up too much debt.... They often react irrationally to advertisements and allow themselves to be easily misled into ignoring their real needs."[43]

The report, while focusing throughout on the vulnerability of the "less sophisticated consumer," moved away from the Verwoerdian idea of "total protection," suggesting that "overprotection of the consumer limits experience which will enable him ultimately to look after his own interest in the market."[44] Similarly, the focus was no longer explicitly on race, but on culture, and more specifically on a "culture of poverty" and associated behavioral traits. While this still authorized the state's continued racist paternalism, there was increasing agreement that Black residents could and should be exposed to "free-market forces" in the hope that such forces would have a pedagogical effect. The market, previously thought of as a destructive force against which the "traditional homelands" would have to be protected, was now increasingly invested with ordering, pedagogical capacities.

The Black population had of course always been an obsessive concern for government, and a myriad of commissions and research efforts had inquired into "its" behavior and movements. Particularly striking in such documents as the report just quoted, however, is the extent to which research into the subjectivity of the urban Black population was perceived as a radically new approach that would provide a key to the multiple problems faced by the apartheid state.

The Black laborer, previously conceived as an object ("manpower") to be moved around and disposed via labor bureaus, always replaceable by the next laborer to be channeled to the mines, industries, and farms, was suddenly transformed into a subject with differential needs, aspirations, and values. Similarly, urban Black residents, previously viewed as a homogeneous mass in perennial transition toward relocation to their "traditional home" in the Bantustans, were now viewed as potential market participants (consumers, entrepreneurs, and property owners) whose values, dispositions, and internal differentiations mattered. Indeed, Black subjectivity here emerged as the key—both obstacle and promise—for the success of wider "liberal" reforms.

The interest in subjectivity was matched by a new set of techniques that increasingly sought to move away from direct racial discrimination and toward a focus instead on accommodating Black demands in a limited fashion and on the creation of an environment in which Black residents would be exposed to "market forces." Following the Wiehahn and Riekert Commissions' recommendations, many township reforms were directed at improving the living conditions of the urban Black population to ensure security by creating an urban Black middle class that could act as a buffer against the inhabitants of the Bantustans, in particular, against migrant labor.

As part of the effort of dividing urban insiders from rural outsiders, urban areas were also promised upgrades, selective forms of liberalization, and fewer restrictions on mobility. Urban residence, previously tied to passbooks indicating belonging and articulated in racial and ethnic terms, now became intricately tied to material and administrative, officially nonracial categories: to housing and infrastructure, on the one hand, and employment, on the other. Indeed, here, we see the beginning of a conception and deployment of infrastructure and the administrative domain as a field of intervention through which society and its environment could be shaped in a less direct fashion. In this context, neoliberal ideas emphasizing decentralization, privatization, and the removal of overt intervention by the central state could be selectively drawn on to rationalize and operationalize a set of reforms through which apartheid rule could be rethought while holding on to its basic premise of minority rule.

CONCLUSION

Many of the "reforms" envisaged by Lombard and others were never fully implemented or failed in their ultimate objectives. They could not and would not address the question of political rights, and mass-based resistance to apartheid surged in the 1980s. And yet, the political rationalities developed here continued to be of influence in the decades to come. Their practical, if haphazard and often unintended effects produced the political terrain upon which apartheid was contested during the 1980s. What emerged in the late 1970s, then, was a particular, neoliberal mode of rethinking apartheid.

Neoliberal thought provided the conceptual resources both for a pragmatic critique of the grand apartheid forms of rule and for an alternative set of techniques to reform apartheid *gradually* while holding on to white supremacy and minority rule. Here, neoliberalism emerges not as a ready-made project imposed from the outside, but rather as a series of adaptable concepts and techniques that built upon and often worked through preexisting contexts. In post-1976 South Africa, this conceptual tool kit could be flexibly drawn on, upholding certain aspects of "separate development" while transforming others, recoding apartheid modalities of rule, rather than rejecting them outright.

Illuminated here, then, was also the dilemma between a conservative attachment to "tradition" and the normative telos of a "free society" that in the late-apartheid period was solved by a project of reform aimed at the habits and subjectivity of Black urban residents. It is this conceptual dilemma—of both removing state influence and shaping state and society in a "liberal" direction—that became exceptionally visible as it was translated to the fraught late-apartheid moment. More than elucidating neoliberalism's internal paradoxes, however, these contradictions were explicitly articulated by reformers and indeed became an integral aspect of reforms, often authorizing illiberal means to achieve liberal goals.

1. Patrick Bond, *Elite Transition: From Apartheid to Neoliberalism in South Africa* (London: Pluto Press, 2000).

2. This argument is presented more fully in Antina von Schnitzler, *Democracy's Infrastructure: Techno-Politics and Protest after Apartheid* (Princeton: Princeton University Press, 2016).

3. F. A. Hayek, *Law, Legislation and Liberty: A New Statement of the Liberal Principles of Justice and Political Economy* (Chicago: University of Chicago Press, 1978), p. 155.

4. Ibid., p. 160.

5. Ibid., p. 163.

6. John Gray, *Hayek on Liberty* (London: Routledge, 1998), p. 155.

7. See, for example, Uday Singh Mehta, *Liberalism and Empire: A Study in Nineteenth-Century British Liberal Thought* (Chicago: University of Chicago Press, 1999).

8. Reinhold Friedrich Alfred Hoernlé, *South African Native Policy and the Liberal Spirit* (Cape Town: University of Cape Town Press, 1939), p. ix.

9. See Saul Dubow, *Racial Segregation and the Origins of Apartheid in South Africa, 1919–36* (New York: St. Martin's Press, 1989), and Paul B. Rich, *White Power and the Liberal Conscience: Racial Segregation and South African Liberalism, 1921–60* (Manchester: Manchester University Press, 1984).

10. Mahmood Mamdani, *Citizen and Subject: Contemporary Africa and the Legacy of Late Colonialism* (Princeton: Princeton University Press, 1996).

11. See Martin Legassick, "Race, Industrialization and Social Change in South Africa: The Case of R. F. A. Hoernle," *African Affairs* 75.299 (1976), pp. 224–39.

12. Dan O'Meara, *Volkskapitalisme: Class, Capital, and Ideology in the Development of Afrikaner Nationalism, 1934–1948* (Johannesburg: Ravan Press, 1983); Stephen Gelb, *South Africa's Economic Crisis* (Cape Town: D. Philip, 1991).

13. Hendrik Verwoerd, quoted in William H. Hutt, *The Economics of the Colour Bar: A Study of the Economic Origins and Consequences of Racial Segregation in South Africa* (London: Institute of Economic Affairs, 1964), p. 59.

14. Hendrik Frensch Verwoerd, *Separate Development* (Pretoria: Information Service, Department of Native Affairs, 1958), p. 12.

15. Hutt, *Economics of the Colour Bar*, p. 173.

16. See Quinn Slobodian, *Globalists: The End of Empire and the Birth of Neoliberalism* (Cambridge, MA: Harvard University Press, 2018), p. 151.

17. John S. Saul and Stephen Gelb, *The Crisis in South Africa: Class Defense, Class Revolution* (New York: Monthly Review Press, 1981).

18. Michael Mann, "The Giant Stirs: South African Business in the Age of Reform," in Philip Frankel, Noam Pines, and Mark Swilling, eds., *State, Resistance and Change in South Africa* (Johannesburg Southern Book Publishers, 1988), p. 56.

19. Adam Ashforth, *The Politics of Official Discourse in Twentieth-Century South Africa* (New York: Oxford University Press, 1990).

20. Deborah Posel, "Language, Legitimation and Control: The South African State after 1978," *Social Dynamics* 10.1 (1984), pp. 3-4.

21. Republic of South Africa, *Report of the Commission of Inquiry into Legislation Affecting the Utilisation of Manpower* (Pretoria: Government Printer, 1979), par. 1.19.1-1.19.4.

22. Rok Ajulu, *Wiehahn and Riekert: New Mechanism for Control and Oppression of Black Labour and Trade Unions.* (Maseru: National University of Lesotho, Institute of Labour Studies, 1981), p. 22.

23. Doug Hindson, *Pass Controls and the Urban African Proletariat in South Africa* (Johannesburg: Ravan Press, 1987), p. 84.

24. Ashforth, *The Politics of Official Discourse in Twentieth-Century South Africa*, p. 212.

25. Quinn Slobodian, "White Supremacy and the Neoliberals: South Africa as Laboratory and Limit Case," paper prepared for the conference "Global Neoliberalisms," British Academy, London, June 2018.

26. J. A. Lombard, *On Economic Liberalism in South Africa* (Pretoria: University of Pretoria, 1979).

27. Ibid., p. 27.

28. J. A. Lombard, *Freedom, Welfare and Order: Thoughts on the Principles of*

Political Co-operation in the Economy of Southern Africa (Pretoria: BENBO, 1978), p. 69.

29. Ibid., p. 26.

30. Ibid., p. 72, emphasis in the original.

31. Lombard, *On Economic Liberalism in South Africa*, pp. 38–39.

32. Ibid., p. 35.

33. Ibid., p. 39.

34. Ibid., p. 51.

35. Ibid., p. 16.

36. Jan Lombard, quoted in Georg Marais and Robert Van der Kooy, eds., *South Africa's Urban Blacks: Problems and Challenges* (Pretoria: Centre for Management Studies, School of Business Leadership, UNISA, 1978), p. 9.

37. Marais and Van der Kooy, *South Africa's Urban Blacks*, p. 16.

38. Ibid., p. 95.

39. Ibid., p. 90.

40. Ibid., p. 237.

41. Jeremy Seekings, *Why Was Soweto Different?: Urban Development, Township Politics, and the Political Economy of Soweto, 1978–84* (Johannesburg: University of the Witwatersrand, African Studies Institute, 1988), p. 13.

42. Republic of South Africa, *Report of the Department of Co-Operation and Development for the Period 1 April 1980 to 31 March 1981* (Pretoria: Government Printer, 1981), pp. 13–14.

43. Republic of South Africa, *Measures Which Restrict the Functioning of a Free Market Oriented System in South Africa* (Cape Town: Government Printer, 1984), pp. 149–50.

44. Ibid., p. 153.

CHAPTER SEVEN

Freedom to Burn: Mining Propaganda, Fossil Capital, and the Australian Neoliberals

Jeremy Walker

Culturally and politically aligned with the West and the North, while geographically and economically proximate to the East and the South, Australia provides a signal case of the general history of the neoliberal project, which has always been closely integrated with "fossil capital"—from its origins in the resistance of early twentieth-century business chambers to the regulation of capitalism by parliamentary democracy, through to the global coalition of hydrocarbon interests organized since the 1980s to obstruct climate policy.

Reading the history of the neoliberal globalists from the present of the climate emergency requires us to exceed the conventional terms of economic thought and confront the vast conflagration of hydrocarbon fuels foundational to the globalization of the world economy. Until the recent advances of renewable energy, heat from fossil fire was almost unchallengeable as the primary source of industrial power. Climate policy, competition from lower-cost renewables, and financial divestment present existential threats to the business model of coal, oil, and gas corporations, which is to maximize fire and heat: the energy product it sells and the by-product, gases released during hydrocarbon extraction and combustion. Conversely, the organization of fossil capital to prevent decarbonization threatens not only democracy in jurisdictions where it recently seemed secure, but the survival of human civilization and the Earth as we know it.

Around 2019, Australia became the world's largest exporter of both coal and "natural gas" (fossil methane) and thus the third-largest exporter of greenhouse emissions.[1] This chapter offers a historical outline of the Australian roots and branches of what can only incompletely be understood as the "neoliberal *thought* collective." Emphasizing the long-term structural relationship between the geopolitical strategies of extractive multinationals and the political organizations fostered by them to discipline and capture governments, this is less a chapter in the history of ideas than a history of "corporation-sponsored persuasion and propaganda."[2]

AN AUSTRALIAN GEOLOGY OF NEOLIBERALISM

Anthony Bebbington has written of "the relative invisibility of minerals, oil and gas in the canons of political ecology," an observation equally applicable to the analytical approaches that have framed the critical literature on neoliberal thought and thinkers thus far.[3] With Bebbington, I would urge the "importance of turning our attention to the mining, oil and gas sectors…as a problem…at the core of the relationship between development and democracy."[4] Lacking a national framework for emissions control, clean energy transition, or the phaseout of hydrocarbon extraction, Australia presents an informative case study in the geopolitics of neoliberalism.

Scholars have deployed disparate approaches and terminologies to make sense of Australian neoliberalism. Alex Carey identified local business organizations importing techniques developed by the National Association of Manufacturers for the mass propagation of "economic education" as the New Right.[5] Michael Pusey described the rise of what we now recognize as neoliberal doctrines of public management as "economic rationalism."[6] More recently, Damien Cahill and Elizabeth Humphrys have analyzed neoliberalism in terms of class confrontation in histories predominantly concerned with the unraveling from the 1980s of the postfederation "Australian

Settlement" beginning in the 1980s, in which social and economic policy had been underpinned by tariff protection, wage arbitration, and the institutionalized conciliation of labor and capital.[7] For Australian neoliberals such as the public-choice theorist Geoffrey Brennan, a collaborator with fellow Mont Pelerin Society (MPS) member James M. Buchanan in his Koch-funded project to develop permanent constitutional constraints on popular sovereignty, the preferred term for this process was "microeconomic reform."[8]

Undoubtedly, the neutralization of labor unions and parties as a countervailing power to plutocracy is a consistent feature of the neoliberal project. Yet conceiving of neoliberalism as an ideological machinery of class domination does not exhaust its explanation in a world where political and economic power are intimately correlated with control over energy and access to the "mineral estate."

My analysis builds on the approach to neoliberalism pioneered by Bernhard Walpen, Dieter Plehwe, and Philip Mirowski.[9] Rather than attempt to isolate a unified philosophical doctrine, these authors focus on the international networks forged by neoliberal actors, whom they identify with the private membership of Friedrich Hayek's Mont Pelerin Society, established 1947, and the personnel of a proliferating constellation of think tanks coordinated since 1981 by the Atlas Network, the senior staff of which are commonly MPS members. The Mont Pelerin Society remained an almost secret organization until the 1980s, and its Australian membership list was not available until recently.[10] The Australian neoliberals and their organizations have yet to be systematically treated by scholars in dialogue with the growing literature on the transnational history of the MPS.

In a paper delivered to the Atlas-seeded Centre for Independent Studies (CIS) in Sydney, Oliver Hartwich (MPS, 2010) famously declared "neoliberalism" a meaningless term.[11] Hartwich now leads the New Zealand Initiative, an Atlas Network think tank campaigning against the Zero Carbon Act and the moratoriums on hydrocarbon leasing of Jacinda Ardern's Labour government.[12] Denying both the necessity of deep decarbonization and the existence of the network through which he acts for fossil capital, Hartwich is an exemplary neoliberal for the purposes of my argument.

To insist on the integral relationship of neoliberalism to thermoindustrial corporations may seem counterintuitive, given that the material-energetic dimensions of the world economy are infrequently foregrounded in its intellectual canon. Yet the roots of neoliberal organization have been intertwined with fossil fuel corporations from the beginning, and perhaps none more so than with Standard Oil—now ExxonMobil. The prehistory of the Mont Pelerin Society can be traced to the Graduate Institute for International Studies established in Geneva in 1927 by William Rappard, who moved in the circle gathered around Ludwig von Mises—secretary of the Vienna Chamber of Commerce—including Hayek, Gottfried Haberler, and Fritz Machlup. Geneva school neoliberals were engaged in policy diplomacy to petition the League of Nations on behalf of the International Chamber of Commerce (ICC).[13]

Established in 1920, the ICC aimed to reverse the wartime nationalization of industrial planning and restore international laissez-faire. High on the agenda was tariff removal in order to discipline nascent social democratic governments with low-wage competition and capital flight. The ICC was a project of American fossil capitalists, initiated by A. C. Bedford of Standard Oil, Owen Young of General Electric, and Thomas Lamont of J. P. Morgan—a bank still among the largest fossil financiers. Among the early trade objectives secured by the ICC were, for U.S. oil interests, access to the Middle East via the Mandates Commission, and for General Electric, near monopoly control of coal-fired power grids throughout Latin America.[14] Via the Rockefeller Foundation, Standard Oil provided incomes for Hayek, Mises, and other European neoliberals in the 1920s and 1930s. After World War II, the Austrian school would be transplanted firmly to American soil, supported lavishly by oil wealth, most notably, by the fortunes of Charles and David Koch.

While historians of neoliberalism have rarely contemplated the consistent role of fossil capital in funding its various academic strongholds and policy organizations, climate activists and scholars have routinely named ExxonMobil, Koch, and Scaife Foundations among the "dark money" sources for climate obstructionism propagated by a roster of think tanks, although generally without observing their affiliation with the Atlas Network and thus with the MPS.[15] It is only on the transnational scale at which fossil capital's strategies are conducted that the seemingly disparate forces threatening to transform Australian democracy into the coal-and-gas analogue of an authoritarian petrostate can be apprehended.

Australia's role in the world-historical victories of neoliberalism also come into view at this scale. After all, Australia is the original headquarters of Rupert Murdoch's News Corporation—widely recognized as a "propaganda operation masquerading as a news service" and a "grave threat to democracy."[16] Converted to neoliberalism in the the 1975 countermovement that brought down the Whitlam government, a pivotal U.S. media asset of the Reagan revolution from 1983, Murdoch joined the board of the Cato Institute in 1997.[17] Through his numerous holdings in the tabloid press, the *Wall Street Journal* and the *Australian*, and Fox and Sky television, Murdoch is among the most important figures in consolidating the neoliberal counterrevolution in the UK, the United States, and Australia.

MINING PROPAGANDA AND THE MURDOCH PRESS

The history of the Murdoch press in Australia introduces many of the important elements of the coalition backing neoliberal policies in the country to this day. The origins of numerous Australian mining companies can be traced to the corporate empire built by William Ballieu in the early twentieth century: the Collins House group headquartered in Melbourne. Ballieu's interests also included Carlton United Breweries, Dunlop Rubber, Dulux Paint, Associated Pulp and Paper, and the Herald and Weekly Times newsgroup. Alongside Broken Hill Proprietary (BHP), one of the largest mining ventures at Broken Hill was the Collins House company Consolidated Zinc (merged in 1962 with RioTinto). Confronted by a unionized workforce, Ballieu's fixer Gerald Mussen was dispatched in 1918 with a secret mission. Through proxies, he purchased a newspaper in Broken Hill and another in Port Pirie, where Broken Hill Associated Smelters (BHAS) operated a smelting works, notably, at either end of the Collins House supply chain. As a Collins House executive wrote to the director of BHAS, "There is great room for propaganda in Broken Hill and Port Pirie.... Let us try and educate our men, and the public too."[18]

Further newspapers were purchased and held by an Adelaide company registered in 1922 as News Limited. In 1930, News was placed under the direction of the journalist, political insider, and Herald and Weekly Times director Keith Murdoch, who increased his shareholdings until he became its owner. By the late 1930s, Murdoch owned newspapers and radio stations around Australia and was one of the most powerful men in the country. Through them, Murdoch campaigned against the Australian Broadcasting Commission (ABC, established in 1932 and renamed the Australian Broadcasting Corporation in 1983), exerting pressure through high-level connections to thwart the public broadcaster's attempts to run an independent news service.[19] In 1940, Murdoch was appointed by conservative Prime Minister Robert Menzies as director-general for information, responsible for wartime censorship. Widely distrusted and compared to Goebbels by *Time* magazine,[20] Murdoch soon resigned from the post, returning to his media empire to attack the new Labor government of John Curtin, appointed in 1941 following Menzies's loss of parliamentary support.

When Keith Murdoch died in 1952, News was bequeathed to his son Rupert, who built from it a global media monolith spanning the Anglophone world and beyond. The raison d'être of News Corp as a mining propaganda operation holds true a century later. Perhaps no single figure bears more responsibility than Rupert Murdoch for the dissemination of the "Exxon position" to "emphasize the uncertainty in the scientific conclusions regarding the potential enhanced greenhouse effect,"[21] his outlets routinely amplifying the barrage of profossil, counterscience "content" generated by the numerous front groups of the Atlas Network.

HYTTEN AND THE INSTITUTE OF PUBLIC AFFAIRS: PROTONEOLIBERALISM FROM THE DEPRESSION TO POST-WWII

The Murdoch press offers a prominent link between Australian history and the later history of neoliberalism as an international movement. The little-known Australian economist Torleiv Hytten provides another. In 1946, Mises wrote to Hayek recommending he invite Hytten to the inaugural meeting of the MPS.[22] Hytten did not attend in 1947, but in 1951, he became the first Australian MPS member.[23] When Hytten first engaged with the founders of the MPS remains unclear. He was surely familiar with their work by 1935, when he accompanied former prime minister Stanley Bruce as a delegate to the Geneva conference of the League of Nations, where he likely met ICC delegates through business connections.[24]

In 1935, Hytten left the University of Tasmania to work for Sir Alfred Davidson, manager of the Bank of New South Wales. The dominant figure in banking during the Depression and its aftermath, Davidson ran the largest and most conspicuously wealthy of the merchant banks. The Depression affected Australia profoundly, largely due to the interest burden of public debts raised on London bond markets to provide military forces for the Empire in WWI. As unemployment brought hunger in 1930, the Bank of England sent Sir Otto Niemeyer to Australia to secure full payment of her war debts.[25] Niemeyer demanded immediate elimination of commonwealth and state deficits and across-the-board wage cuts of 20 percent, a radically deflationary policy comparable to the IMF's "shock therapy," minus the capital injection.

As economists advised governments in assembling the slightly less austere Premier's Plan, Jack Lang, the fiery Labor premier of New South Wales, announced a temporary default on bond-interest payments in order to finance welfare and public works such as the Sydney Harbour Bridge. Davidson was a member of the quasi-fascist Old Guard, a clandestine organization of military officers, country estate holders, and business executives who planned to launch a coup d'état with the street militia of the New Guard should Lang's supporters call a general strike.[26] In 1932, Sir Phillip Game, the King's appointed governor of New South Wales, invoked constitutionally undefined "reserve powers" to dismiss Lang. It would not be the last time a Labor Parliament was dissolved by the Schmittian exercise of a sovereign decision.

Attempts to alleviate the Depression were confounded by the fact that Australia's international reserves were held principally by private banks, which effectively determined interest rates and the exchange rate of the Australian pound. Responding to widespread criticism of the banks, the conservative prime minister, Joseph Lyons, established the 1935–1937 Royal Commission on Banking and Monetary Reform, to which Hytten gave evidence "tinged with Hayekian overtones."[27] When the Royal Commission called for a public central bank—a policy of the Australian Labor Party (ALP) since its formation amid the bank failures and depressions of the 1890s—the banks organized a Central Propaganda Committee to coordinate a national network of writers promoting "sound finance" in news articles and letters to the editor, pieces unattributed to the banks that paid for them—a project in which Hytten played a key role.[28]

As in Britain, public opinion swung soundly behind the Labor platform of full employment and social security during World War II. The 1943 election resoundingly returned Curtin's Labor government, fragmenting the conservative alliances of the United Australia Party which had run an indecisive, unpopular wartime government under Menzies. It was in this context that the Institute of Public Affairs (IPA) was launched by the Melbourne establishment in early 1943, with a Sydney branch soon following, and others later in other capitals. The IPA "was intended as a research and publicity organization on behalf of […] industry in Australia", and "the business catalyst in the reconstruction of non-Labor political organization."[30] Many of the IPA founders and fundraisers were also involved in forming the Liberal Party of Australia in 1944 under the leadership of Menzies, who cited IPA policy documents in his inaugural speeches.

Given its dominant position in Australian politics, it is curious that "little is known with authority or in detail about the origins of the Liberal Party."[31] Perhaps more would be understood if the politics of fossil/mining capital were considered. The inaugural IPA board included Harold Darling of BHP, Walter Massy-Greene of Collins House, and media baron Keith Murdoch. Through Murdoch's media, the IPA began disseminating "business propaganda" against the Curtin government's postwar reconstruction program. In 1945, Curtin died in office, and Ben Chifley became prime minister. Unable to forgive the banks for the role he believed they played in deepening the Depression, Chifley overreached and legislated for bank nationalization in 1947.

Working with the IPA, Hytten again organized the bankers' well-funded propaganda campaign against Labor's banking agenda.[32] Faced with a formidable challenge from the banks, Chifley was further tested when the Miners' Federation declared a national coal strike in 1949, an election year. Pressed by intelligence officers who claimed the Communist Party of Australia was inciting the miners toward revolution, Chifley passed emergency legislation deploying the army as strikebreakers. Denounced as a socialist enemy by business and as a traitor by unions, Chifley lost the election to Menzies. Federal Labor remained in the wilderness for a generation. Hytten left the Bank of New South Wales to chair the Australian committee of the ICC, calling for the reinstatement of international trade according to free-enterprise principles and tariff removal to drive an expansion of commodity exports—then dominated by gold, wool, and wheat.[33]

Menzies, however, was not persuaded by the globalists, favoring tariff protection for manufacturing and a social policy that Cahill describes as "anti-socialist Keynesianism."

Hytten established a beachhead for the MPS at a time when Australia's subimperial allegiances were shifting from the fading British Empire toward the ascendant United States. It was not until the 1960s that mineral and hydrocarbon exports would transform Australia's position in the world economy.

A CONSTITUTIONAL COUP: FOSSIL CAPITAL AND THE DISMISSAL

The ascent of neoliberalism since the 1970s is insufficiently explained in narrowly economic terms such as the stagflation crisis of international Keynesianism. At a global level, the rise of neoliberalism coincided with the assertion at the United Nations by postcolonial states of permanent sovereignty over their natural resources, manifest in the calls of the G-77 for a New International Economic Order and the arrival of OPEC as a non-Western oil cartel confronting the U.S.-dominated cartel that had controlled the world oil trade until then. The 1970s also witnessed a sobering transformation of the horizons of the oil-based growth paradigm as scientists revealed a deepening crisis of ecological breakdown and global warming.

The rise of the environmental movement—with its calls for international planning to avert a collapse of the Earth's capacity to maintain "ecological equilibrium" and its legislative gains imposing science-based regulation on polluting industries—was a crucial catalyst for the countermobilization of corporations to defend "free enterprise." Along with the restoration of "free trade"—of an international division of labor where the Global South provides unrestricted resource flows to the Global North—an abiding aim of the neoliberals has long been to "strangle the environmental movement," as Ed Crane put it.[34] Crane was a founder of the Charles Koch Foundation (established in 1974 and later renamed the Cato Institute), along with fellow MPS members Murray Rothbard and the eponymous scion of the petro-leum-based Koch conglomerate.

Though less well known than the drama of the New International Economic Order, Australia witnessed a similar confrontation in the 1970s as a social democratic effort to assert national sovereignty over natural resources ran up against a transnationally organized resistance. The stage was set when Australians elected Gough Whitlam's reformist Labor government (1972 to 1975) after two decades of liberal-conservative rule. The Whitlam government's resource nationalism at the dawn of the long mining boom through which Australia became a major hydrocarbon exporter catalyzed a determined reaction from the predominantly foreign-owned extractive sector. It is to this period, as the largest Anglo-American corporations joined with the largest Australian conglomerates to globalize Australian mining operations, that we can date the integration of local business organizations within the transnational neoliberal think-tank network, matched by a surge of Australian membership in the MPS.

Whitlam's short-lived government in the 1970s was a watershed in Australian political history. Whitlam's ambitious reform agenda put him on a collision course with the business establishment and the Nixon administration. Announcing an independent foreign policy, Whitlam recalled soldiers from Vietnam and questioned the role of U.S. military spy bases on Australian territory. Whitlam's economic policy was by turns liberal and Keynesian, social democratic, and nationalist. Faced with rising inflation, Whitlam hired the IMF economist Michael Porter (MPS, 1987) as an advisor, introducing general tariff reductions of 25 percent. On the domestic front, Whitlam legislated away the institutional racism of the White Australia policy, advanced equal rights for women, and universalized access to health care and universities. Along with the Aboriginal Land Rights Act (1976), Whitlam introduced national environmental legislation: the National Parks and Wildlife Conservation Act (1975), the Environmental Protection Act (1975) and the Australian Heritage Commission Act (1975).

These latter impairments of the traditional role of the colonial state as executive facilitator of land appropriations were vigorously opposed by the Australian Mining Industry Council (AMIC), led by Massy-Greene of Collins House and W. R. Morgan of the Western Mining Corporation (WMC—another Collins House company).[35] Whitlam faced bitter resistance from the corporate establishment in Australia, which, as the economist Ronald Walker had observed, "is an interesting case study on the effects of unrestrained monopoly... one of the few industrial countries where a *laissez-faire* policy toward monopolies and restrictive trade practices has survived" and where "the country has never seen sustained effort at protecting the economy from powerful combines."[36]

During Whitlam's term, business activists were drawn into MPS circles, linking the IPA through Anglo-American corporate networks to its transnational membership. A catalyzing event was the April 1975 speaking tour by Milton Friedman organized by the stockbroker Maurice Newman (MPS, 1976), which would be followed in 1976 with a tour by Hayek. Friedman was flown direct from Chile, fresh from advising General Pinochet in the violent program of "shock therapy" that followed Allende's nationalization of U.S.-operated copper mines. Friedman expounded his monetarist analysis of inflation in an implicit critique of Whitlam's policies. The impact of Friedman's tour "was powerful and immediate," in part due to "a generally compliant and uncritical media" that "following his success in Chile... was willing to give much space to his ideas."[37]

In October 1975, the Liberal-Country Party opposition used its Senate majority to block money-supply bills to the government, triggering a constitutional crisis. On November 11, 1975, the governor general, Sir John Kerr, representative of the Queen in Australia's constitutional monarchy, invoked "reserve powers" to dissolve a twice popularly elected government. In many retellings of the Dismissal, what became known as the "Loans Affair" is the signal event that triggered the constitutional crisis. Yet few now recall what these loans were for.

Historians have focused analyses of the crisis on the constitutionality of Kerr's decision, but not on the project of the Whitlam government for which loans were sought or on the role played by the powerful corporations that had most to lose from the project's success, and that have since gained so much by its defeat.

In a 1973 speech marking his first year in office, Whitlam summarized the ALP program: "The two great guiding themes of this Government have been (1) the promotion of equal opportunity for our people and (2) the promotion of Australian ownership and control of our industries and resources."[38] That year, Whitlam's minister for mining and energy, Rex Connor, introduced legislation to establish a Petroleum and Minerals Authority (PMA), which would operate as a national oil and mining company, restoring sovereignty over Australia's geological resources. For Connor, this meant 50 percent Australian ownership of new mining ventures and in the case of hydrocarbons, 100 percent. Passed by the House of Representatives, the legislation was blocked with other key bills by the Liberal-controlled Senate.

In 1974, Whitlam called a double-dissolution election of both houses of Parliament to resolve the impasse. During the election campaign, Connor received a report by Thomas Michael Fitzgerald on the effect of the mining boom on Australia's public finances.[39] With case studies including Pilbara iron, Queensland coal, Gippsland oil, and Mount Isa and Broken Hill mines, the report found that through generous tax concessions, the net "give and take" between the mines and the commonwealth resulted in a significant transfer of public funds to predominantly foreign-owned ventures. Taxpayers were paying foreigners to remove their mineral wealth. Connor seized upon the report to legitimize his project to "buy back the farm." Whitlam won reelection, but did not gain a Senate majority. Through a constitutional provision used only on this occasion, the PMA Act was passed by simple majority in a historic joint sitting of both houses of Parliament, along with other key bills. The conservative governments of Victoria,

New South Wales, Queensland, and Western Australia immediately mounted High Court challenges to the constitutionality of the act.[40]

Anticipating obstruction from economic liberals in the Treasury Department (such as John Stone, federal treasury secretary from 1979 to 1984; MPS, 2008), Connor was authorized by Whitlam's Federal Executive Council to inquire with international banks awash with petrodollars for the sizeable loan required to finance the PMA. Connor received loan offers from Tirath Khemlani, a London-based "commodities dealer" later alleged to have had connections—as Kerr certainly did—to the Anglo-American intelligence agencies that evidence suggests destabilized the Whitlam government.[41] In an early 1974 speech to the Australian Institute of Directors, the U.S. ambassador, Marshall Green, reportedly incited business leaders "to rise against the Australian government," promising them help from the United States "similar to that given to South America."[42] The Chilean coup had taken place months before. As U.S. ambassador to Indonesia in 1965, Green had provided membership lists of the Communist Party of Indonesia to the U.S.-trained military and police officers who arranged the massacre of half a million to one million unarmed "communist sympathizers"— a response to President Sukarno's threat to nationalize U.S. oil concessions that instantiated General Suharto's New Order.[43] In 1973, Green had advised Henry Kissinger (earlier a personal lawyer for Hayek's onetime doctoral student David Rockefeller) that he "would define U.S. interests in Australia as (1) preserving our defense installations; (2) maintaining our investment and trade there."[44]

The press learned of Connor's correspondence with Khemlani and attacked Whitlam for reckless, even criminal financial incompetence, although no loan agreement had been negotiated. Rupert Murdoch, whose papers had supported Whitlam in the 1972 election, confidentially instructed his editors to "kill Whitlam."[45] Confronting the atmosphere of scandal, Whitlam defended the legitimacy of the project in a July 1975 speech to the House of Representatives: "We are determined to exploit Western Australia's enormous natural gas potential—the

North West Shelf belonging to Australia—rather than selling off this vital part of Australia's farm."[46] Whitlam revoked Connor's loan authority and informed Parliament he was no longer communicating with Khemlani. Khemlani subsequently supplied Liberal MPs Phillip Lynch and John Howard with telexes from Connor, evidence he had defied the instruction from Whitlam.[47] This was cited by opposition leader Malcolm Fraser in his decision to block the money-supply bills, culminating in Kerr's dismissal of Whitlam and the appointment of Fraser to lead a caretaker government until an election in which Whitlam was defeated.

John Howard would later serve as prime minister (1996 to 2007), a staunch neoliberal who refused to sign Australia to the Kyoto Protocol. An avowed "climate skeptic," Howard would lecture after his retirement at the Global Warming Policy Foundation—a London-based misinformation unit founded by Nigel Lawson (who privatized the British National Oil Corporation as Thatcher's minister for energy) and upon whose council sat Deepak Lal (MPS, 1986; president, 2008 to 2010). Howard attended the Sydney meeting of the Mont Pelerin Society in 2010 and became a member the following year.

Like the Norwegian Labor governments of the 1970s, Whitlam's ALP strove to establish a national energy company to exploit Australia's resources for the benefit of Australians. Unlike Norway, which has used the income of Statoil (established in 1972, now Equinor) to finance a generous welfare state via the world's largest sovereign wealth fund—a fund now divesting from hydrocarbons and investing in a postcarbon world—Australians were unsuccessful in retaining ownership and control over their mineral "commonwealth," which has been exported since by predominantly foreign consortiums. Standard Oil successors ExxonMobil and Chevron now play dominant roles in the vast North West Shelf gas projects, along with Woodside, an Australian oil company with close connections to the IPA and senior Liberal-National Party politicians such as Alexander Downer (minister for foreign affairs, 1996 to 2007). By revenue, these are three of the largest fossil corporations on a long list that enjoy an effective company tax rate of zero, according to Australian Taxation Office data.[48]

ANTIPODEAN ATLAS

The Whitlam government catalyzed a new intensity in the political organization of fossil/mining corporations. To that time we can trace a surge in both the Australian Mont Pelerin Society membership and in investment by extractive capital in the civil society infrastructures that would become integrated (formally or otherwise) with the Atlas Network.

Many among the neoliberal recruits of this generation came from companies whose tax arrangements were publicly criticized in the Fitzgerald Report. From Mount Isa Mines (MIM), a predominantly U.S.-owned firm, came the mining executive Ron Kitching (MPS, 1983), an organizer of the Australian branch of the Foundation for Economic Education. Kitching collaborated with the finance journalist Roger Randerson (MPS, 1983)—a student of Hayek's at the London School of Economics and a contemporary of Davidson and Hytten at the Bank of New South Wales—in organizing Hayek's 1976 Australian tour. The Pilbara iron range was leased to RioTinto by Lang Hancock, father of iron and coal billionaire Gina Rinehart, a major funder of the IPA. The Gippsland oil shelf was operated by Esso (an Australian subsidiary of Exxon) and BHP. The boom in Queensland coal exports was initiated by Utah Coal (a General Electric subsidiary, later sold to BHP), Thiess (a subsidiary of BHP), Blair Athol (Collins House), and MIM.[49]

To emphasize the consistent role of fossil/mining multinationals in driving the neoliberal counterrevolution is not to deny the diversity of schools, interests, and policy coalitions across the many branches of the "thought collective." To be sure, a portion of the Australian MPS recruits were university academics, including political philosophers such as Geoffrey Brennan, Kenneth Minogue, and Lauchlan Chipman. Yet whatever claims might be made for the intellectual contributions of Australian MPS members, perhaps the more decisive actors sealing the Australian road to serfdom were the think-tank propagandists and the policy-planning business economists such as Maurice Newman, Michael Porter, and Gary Sturgess (MPS, 1996).

Frequently appointed to governmental and advisory roles, these latter MPS figures have been associated with the Centre for Independent Studies, the most important of the Atlas-seeded think tanks. Founded by the schoolteacher Greg Lindsay (MPS, 1982; president, 2006 to 2008) with the assistance of Antony Fisher, the CIS was launched contemporaneously with Hayek's 1976 tour. Along with Hayek, the initial council of MPS advisors to the CIS included Murray Rothbard (Cato), Arthur Shenfield (Federation of British Industries, Institute of Economic Affairs), and local academics Ronald Hartwell (University of New South Wales, later Oxford, Virginia, and Chicago), Naomi Moldofsky (University of Melbourne), Malcolm Fisher (University of New South Wales), Sudha Shenoy (Newcastle), Lauchlan Chipman (Wollongong) and Ross Parish (Monash).[50]

Initially struggling for financial support, Lindsay began meeting with Australian businessmen such as Maurice Newman who wanted to establish an Australian version of the Institute of Economic Affairs. The founding tranche of corporate funding for the CIS was arranged in 1979 by IPA board member Hugh Morgan, who assumed his father's executive roles with Western Mining Corporation and the Australian Mining Industry Council.[51] The money came entirely from fossil/mining capital and its mass-communications arm—the Murdoch press. Pledging donors included Hugh Morgan (WMC), John Macleod (Conzinc-RioTinto), Douglas Hocking (Shell), John Brunner (BHP), and John Bonython of Murdoch's Adelaide Advertiser Group, cofounder of gas giant Santos.[52] The intergenerational links of fossil/mining wealth to the neoliberal project are embodied in the figure of Michael Darling (MPS, 2007), heir to the Darling family's BHP fortune and a current board member of the CIS.

While both the IPA and the CIS were founded by fossil/mining businesses and their dedicated media arm, and while both would work toward financial deregulation, rollback of labor and welfare rights, and the privatization of public administration and infrastructure, it appears that a division of labor emerged between the IPA and the CIS. As public demands for policy responses to global warming mounted, the IPA became increasingly bellicose in its profossil and anti-science propagandizing, coordinating campaigns with U.S.-based Atlas-affiliated think tanks the Heartland Institute and the Competitive Enterprise Institute. By comparison, the CIS adopts a more civil tone in public debate. Associating openly with business—especially the Macquarie Group, a major beneficiary of infrastructure privatizations and a player in North American gas projects—the CIS leaves to the IPA the prosecution of fossil capital's propaganda war against the socialist conspiracies of natural science, renewable energy, human rights, the Australian Broadcasting Corporation, and the United Nations.

The IPA's present vocation for counterscience propaganda was prefigured in Hayek's 1976 lecture to the IPA. Having denounced the environmental futures modeling of the *Limits to Growth* report in his 1974 Nobel speech, Hayek again warned that among the "greatest dangers to our civilisation is what I have called 'the destruction of values by scientific error.'"[53] Citing his 1950 *IPA Review* article on the dangers of democracy and full-employment policy, Hayek confessed he had grown impatient with mere intellectual argument.[54] In another lecture, Hayek prosecuted his critique of "unlimited democracy" in strident terms which, perhaps inadvertently, recalled the ongoing collaboration of the MPS with Pinochet's brutal dictatorship: "What present trends point to is the emergence of ever larger numbers, for whose welfare and status government has assumed responsibility it cannot discharge, and whose revolt when they are not paid enough, or asked to do more work than they like, will have to be subdued with the knout and the machine-gun."[55]

Hayek's tour included a meeting with Prime Minister Malcolm

Fraser, who was reportedly unimpressed by the Austrian's ultraliberalism.[56] Although the remnants of Whitlam's energy program were dismantled by Fraser, and the North West Shelf was secured for joint development by BP, Shell, California-Asiatic (Chevron), Woodside, and BHP, the neoliberals would be deeply disappointed, even further radicalized by him. A "wet" parliamentary liberal aware that Whitlam's electoral mandate was more legitimate than his own, Fraser completed passage of the Aboriginal Land Rights Act and refused the demands of the "drys" for radical deregulation and the repeal of Whitlam's landmark social, civil, and environmental legislation. The fossil–neoliberal coalition still faced considerable resistance in mainstream opinion and the trenches of Australian political struggle. The widespread confirmation of the greenhouse effect in the 1980s and the rise of the parliamentary Greens—whose support has since been crucial to the formation of ALP governments—can be considered an important spur for another wave of radicalization.

THE RISE OF THE GREENHOUSE MAFIA

The first strides toward mainstreaming neoliberal economic policy in Australia were made by the Labor governments of Robert Hawke and Paul Keating (1983 to 1996), which floated the dollar, lowered tariffs, decentralized wage bargaining, promoted privatization, and renounced the resource nationalism of the Whitlam era. Embracing economic growth through globalization, Keating's "ALP neoliberalism" promised rising living standards, with wage restraint compensated for by the "social wage" of quality public services and benefits, and a national narrative promoting land justice for Aboriginal people, environmental protection, and a cosmopolitan embrace of Australia's place in the Asia Pacific.

In 1985, the Atlas Network held a workshop in Sydney where Ed Feulner (MPS, 1972; Heritage Foundation cofounder, 1973) described the methods through which Atlas units set the terms and agenda of public policy. While intellectuals such as Milton Friedman were nec-essary to articulate ideas such as supply-side economics, privatization, and the flat tax, he said, "it takes an institution to propagandize an idea—to market an idea." Feulner's key message was the need for per-manent saturation campaigns with multipronged, long-term strate-gies: "Proctor & Gamble does not sell Crest toothpaste by taking out one newspaper ad or running one television commercial. They sell and re-sell it every day by keeping the product fresh in the consumer's mind. The institutes I have mentioned sell ideas in much the same manner."[57]

Dominic Kelly has documented the important role of three activ-ists central to the subsequent proliferation of Australian think tanks and the rise of an aggressive, reactionary neoliberalism beginning in the 1980s: Hugh Morgan, his speechwriter, ex-mining engineer Ray Evans (MPS, 1988), and John Stone (MPS, 2008). While his account does not foreground the history of the Mont Pelerin Society, Kelly attri-butes to the troika's access to the highest levels of government much of the rightward momentum of public policy (and to a lesser extent public opinion) through the single-issue forums they established to further the agenda of extractive capital: on industrial relations (the H. R. Nicholls Society), Indigenous land rights (the Bennelong Soci-ety), states-rights federalism (the Samuel Griffiths Society), and cli-mate policy (the Lavoisier Group).[58]

From the 1980s on, state governments began privatizing coal-fired electricity grids, thus fortifying the fossil-neoliberal coalition. In New South Wales, Liberal premier Nick Greiner appointed Gary Sturgess to this task, an economist earlier employed by MIM. Along with the National Electricity Market, Sturgess fostered the privatization of pris-ons and public services and the Coasean "new environmentalism" of tradable rights in air pollution, fishing, and water licenses.[59]

In Victoria, privatization was led by Michael Porter who built an academic base for the neoliberals at Monash University with his Cen-tre of Policy Studies (established in 1979). Porter went on to found the

Tasman Institute, a private consultancy whose supporters included Rupert Murdoch, Esso, BP, Shell, MIM, BHP, WMC, and the Macquarie Group. In 1990, Liberal premier Jeff Kennet hired the Tasman Institute and John Roskam (MPS, 2008) of the IPA to coordinate infrastructure privatizations. The introduction of private markets for electricity resulted in the opposite of the price reductions and service improvements promised to consumers.[60] Yet it did achieve its arguably intended aims: an increasingly powerful role for fossil capital in the determination of Australian energy (and thus climate) policy.

With neoliberal economics accepted by the ALP, Liberal prime minister John Howard (1996 to 2007) moved the political "center" further rightward, embracing the more radical ambitions of the think tanks and assiduously cultivating white nationalists and Christian conservatives. During Howard's reign, however, fears of global heating mounted, broadening public support for climate action and the Kyoto Protocol. The Tasman Institute was rebranded in the Howard years as the private consultancy ACIL Tasman, which shared office space with the Australian Industry Greenhouse Network (AIGN), an emissions-intensive industry lobby. Commissioned by coal and gas corporations, ACIL Tasman's brief was to publicize wildly inaccurate "economic analyses" predicting economic catastrophe from even tokenistic emissions-reduction policy proposals.[61] Under Howard, government policy on climate change was directly authored by a group of AIGN lobbyists, News Corp editors, and MPS figures self-described as "the greenhouse mafia."[62] Meanwhile, Howard appointed Janet Albrechtsen (MPS, 2011) and Maurice Newman to the board of the Australian Broadcasting Corporation, which has since provided "balance" by providing a permanent platform for neoliberals promoting counterscience and profossil talking points in "the climate debate."

We should not underestimate the significance of the IPA's role in defeating climate policy in Australia. Despite the fact that the Atlas Network has been the predominant vehicle for fossil capital's global mobilization against climate science and policy,[63] the only mention of climate change on its public website celebrates the IPA's coordination of the massive media campaign to "axe the tax" mounted against Prime Minister Julia Gillard's historic 2011 carbon-pricing and prorenewables legislation, to which is often credited the hegemonic return of a Liberal-National Party government under Tony Abbott in 2013.[64] Keeping its business donors secret, the IPA disseminates a constant stream of "opinion" pieces via News Corp, its star recruits and policy agendas entering Parliament via the Liberal Party. From the mid-1990s on, the director of climate policy at the IPA was Monash graduate Tim Wilson (MPS, 2011), who was elected to Parliament with the incoming Abbot government. Abbot appointed the vocal science denier Maurice Newman to chair the Business Advisory Council tasked with slashing "red and green tape."[65] In 2014, Abbot repealed the Clean Energy Act (2011), which had already succeeded in lowering emissions and triggering a boom in renewable electricity. Since the repeal, emissions have risen steadily, with the North West Shelf gas projects among the largest sources. Yet the renewables revolution continues, despite the multiple attempts of Abbott and his successors Malcolm Turnbull and Scott Morrison to frustrate investors, to immunize the fossil incumbents from market competition, tax obligations, and environmental law, and to finance unbankable fossil projects directly from the public budget. The current director of the IPA, Janet Albrechtsen, was appointed following a career as one of Murdoch's most aggressive "opinion" columnists. Australia's reputation has suffered ever since as its government has aligned with the Trump administration and Saudi Arabia at United Nations Framework Convention on Climate Change conferences to frustrate the consensus votes required for binding agreements to drive the urgent decarbonization of the world economy—surely the darkest victory of the Atlas Network.

Of course, the fossil neoliberals have not been successful everywhere. Witness, for example, the recognition of the climate emergency by the UK's Conservative government. Committed to much of the neoliberal policy repertoire, the Tories have nevertheless presided over a rapid replacement of coal by renewable energy on the National Grid, which serves a much larger population than Australia's with far less sunshine for solar and land for wind farms. The incoming Biden administration has announced an ambitious climate and energy policy that has left Australia diplomatically isolated. The strategic significance of Australia as a politically secure base for the operations of fossil-fuel multinationals is perhaps indicated by the fact that of the fifty-eight nations represented in the 2013 Mont Pelerin Society membership directory, Australia counted 43 active members, second only to the U.S. membership tally of 308.

CONCLUSION

Work on this chapter began amid the catastrophic firestorms of 2019 as Australia was downgraded from an "open" to a "narrowed" democracy by civil rights monitor Civicus, citing the expansion of secrecy and surveillance under far-reaching national-security legislation, crackdowns on freedom of assembly and the right to protest, arrests of Australian Broadcasting Corporation journalists, and the criminalization of public-interest whistleblowers, even in secret trials.[66] These manifestations of the authoritarian trajectories of neoliberalism can be traced to the capture of government by fossil capital and the redefinition of the national interest in terms that protect fossil projects from taxation, scrutiny, and the groundswell of support for a just transition to renewable energy. It was completed as rains and winter temperatures returned—although huge areas of forest remain in the "burns unit," devoid of insects, animals, and birdsong—and as COVID-19 worked its dramatic transformations of the horizons of commerce and everyday life.

Australians have so far been spared the worst health outcomes of the pandemic, because governments have acted on advice from medical experts. Yet Australia's vulnerabilities have been further exposed, its manufacturing capacity eroded by decades of pro-mining policy; its workforce insecure, low paid, and deskilled; its tourism and education export earnings falling; and its fossil assets devalued as coal, gas, and oil prices have fallen, testament to the rise of renewable energy and the retreat of investors from hydrocarbon development. Prime Minister Scott Morrison responded to the pandemic by temporarily suspending parliamentary sittings and appointing a National COVID-19 Coordination Commission whose operations are largely secret. Its membership was dominated by fossil capitalists such as Andrew Liveris, an executive with Dow Dupont, oil and gas consultancy Worley, and the world's largest oil and gas company, Saudi Aramco—companies interested in the unrestricted disinterment of Australia's fossil-methane deposits. Unsurprisingly, the NCCC recommended further rollbacks of environmental law, overturning of state moratoriums on fracking, and massive increases in public financing for fossil corporations to drive a "gas-led recovery." Yet all the weight of evidence suggests that Australia's interests would be best secured by the development of Australia's vast potential as a producer and exporter of clean energy and a rapid transition to a zero-emissions economy.[67]

In no small part due to the fossil-neoliberal coalition, the time remaining to protect our children from the worst-case scenarios of global heating is at best vanishingly short. It is to the clarification of the profound task facing those who care about their future that this essay hopes to contribute.

NOTES

1. Tom Swann, "High Carbon from a Land Down Under: Quantifying CO2 from Australia's Fossil Fuel Mining and Exports," The Australia Institute, July 2019, https://australiainstitute.org.au/wp-content/uploads/2020/12/P667 -High-Carbon-from-a-Land-Down-Under-WEB_0_0.pdf.

2. Alex Carey, "Conspiracy or Groundswell?," in Ken Coghill, ed., The New Right's Australian Fantasy (Fitzroy: Penguin, 1987), p. 3.

3. Although see Dieter Plehwe, "Think-Tank Networks and the Knowledge-Interest Nexus: The Case of Climate Change," *Critical Policy Studies* 8.1 (2014), pp. 101–15.

4. Anthony Bebbington, "Underground Political Ecologies," *Geoforum* 43.6 (2012), pp. 1152–53.

5. Carey, "Conspiracy or Groundswell?," pp. 3–19.

6. Michael Pusey, *Economic Rationalism in Canberra* (Cambridge: Cambridge University Press, 1991).

7. Damien Cahill, "The Contours of Neoliberal Hegemony in Australia," *Rethinking Marxism* 19.2 (2007), pp. 221–33; Elizabeth Humphrys, *How Labour Built Neoliberalism: Australia's Accord, the Labour Movement and the Neoliberal Project* (Leiden: Brill, 2019).

8. Geoffrey Brennan and Jonathan Pincus, "From the Australian Settlement to Microeconomic Reform," Centre for International Economic Studies, Discussion Paper 0123, June 2002.

9. Dieter Plehwe, Bernhard Walpen, and Gisela Nuenhöffer, eds., *Neoliberal Hegemony: A Global Critique* (London: Routledge, 2006). Philip Mirowski and Dieter Plehwe, eds., *The Road from Mont Pèlerin: The Making of the Neoliberal Thought Collective* (Cambridge, MA: Harvard University Press, 2009), p. 4.

10. In identifying MPS members, I rely on an internal membership directory obtained by *DeSmog*, "2013 Mont Pelerin Society Members List," November 29, 2017, https://www.desmog.com/wp-content/uploads/files/MPS-2013-membership-listing_Redacted.pdf. Hereafter, I indicate MPS members in parentheses after their name, with the year in which they were admitted as members if known. There are currently five Australian Atlas–affiliated organizations: the Institute of Public Affairs, the Centre for Independent Studies, the Mannkal Economic Education Foundation, the Australian Institute for Progress, and the Australian Taxpayers Alliance. See Atlas Network, Global Directory, 2021, https://www.atlasnetwork.org/partners/global-directory/australia-and-new-zealand.

11. Oliver Hartwich, "Neoliberalism: The Genesis of a Political Swearword," *CIS Occasional Paper* 114 (2009), https://www.cis.org.au/app/uploads/2015/07/op114.pdf.

12. Oliver Hartwich, "Zero Carbon Bill Fails the Climate," The New Zealand Initiative, November 8, 2019, https://www.nzinitiative.org.nz/reports-and-media/opinion/zero-carbon-bill-fails-the-climate.

13. Quinn Slobodian, *Globalists: The End of Empire and the Birth of Neoliberalism* (Cambridge, MA: Harvard University Press, 2018), pp. 34–47.

14. Shane Tomashot, "Selling Peace: The History of the International Chamber of Commerce, 1919–1925," PhD diss., Georgia State University, 2015.

15. See, for example, Robert J. Brulle, "Institutionalizing Delay: Foundation Funding and the Creation of U.S. Climate Change Counter-movement Organizations," *Climatic Change* 122 (2014), pp. 681–94. The Scaife family fortune includes the Mellon banks, Alcoa Aluminum, and Gulf Oil (which merged with Standard Oil of California in 1984 to become Chevron).

16. Dennis Muller, "Mounting Evidence the Tide Is Turning on News Corp, and Its Owner," *The Conversation*, May 13, 2019, https://theconversation.com/mounting-evidence-the-tide-is-turning-on-news-corp-and-its-owner-116892.

17. Norman Solomon, "Media Moguls on Board: Murdoch, Malone and the Cato Institute," *Fairness and Accuracy in Reporting*, January 1, 1998, https://fair.org/extra/media-moguls-on-board. Robert Parry traces the rapid expansion of right-wing U.S. media to a 1983 arrangement between Reagan and national security staff with Rupert Murdoch and Atlas-fundraiser Richard Mellon Scaife, for privately funded media support for U.S. interventions in Central America and the Third World. Robert Parry, "Murdoch, Scaife and CIA Propaganda," *Consortium News*, December 31, 2014, https://consortiumnews.com/2014/12/31/murdoch-scaife-and-cia-propaganda/

18. Quoted in Sally Young, *Paper Emperors: the Rise of Australia's Newspaper Empires* (Sydney: UNSW Press, 2019), p. 150.

19. In 1946, Chifley's ALP government legislated for an independent ABC news service. ABC News, "How the Newspapers Tried to Kill an Independent ABC News before It Even Began," https://www.abc.net.au/news/2017-06-01/how-the-newspapers-tried-to-kill-abc-news-before-it-even-began/8568482.

20. "Censorship Down Under," *Time*, December 30, 1940, http://content.time.com/time/subscriber/article/0,33009,795134,00.html.

21. James Carlson, "The Greenhouse Effect," Exxon internal memo, August 3, 1988, http://www.climatefiles.com/exxonmobil/566.

22. Jörg Hülsmann, "Ludwig von Mises e as Organizações Libertárias," *MISES: Interdisciplinary Journal of Philosophy, Law and Economics* 4.1 (2016), pp. 161–81.

23. Hytten appears in the 1951 and 1961 member directories. Hoover Institution Library & Archives, Mont Pèlerin Society Papers, box 57, folders 2 and 5.

24. Australian business chambers affiliated with the ICC in the 1920s. Arthur Balfour, "The International Chamber of Commerce," *Annals of the American Academy of Political and Social Science* 134.1 (1927), pp. 124–31.

25. Alex Millmow, "Niemeyer, Scullin and the Australian economists," *Australian Economic History Review* 44.2 (2004), pp. 142–60.

26. Andrew Moore, *The Secret Army and the Premier: Conservative Paramilitary Organisations in New South Wales, 1930-32* (Kensington: New South Wales University Press, 1989).

27. Alex Millmow, *The Power of Economic Ideas: The Origins of Keynesian Macroeconomic Management in Interwar Australia, 1929-1939* (Canberra: ANU E Press, 2010), p. 241.

28. Warwick Eather and Drew Cottle, "Keep Government Out of Business: Bank Nationalisation, Financial Reform and the Private Trading Banks in the 1930s," *Australian Journal of Politics and History* 59.2 (2013), p. 170. Australia lacked a Federal Reserve Bank until 1962.

29. In 1989, the Sydney IPA was rebranded as the Sydney Institute, since led by Gerard Henderson.

30. J. R. Hay, "The Institute of Public Affairs and Social Policy in World War II," *Australian Historical Studies* 20.79 (1982), pp. 198–210.

31. P. G. Tiver, "Political Ideas in the Liberal Party," PhD diss., Australian National University, 1973, p. 52.

32. Warwick Eather and Drew Cottle, "The Mobilisation of Capital behind 'the Battle for Freedom': The Sydney Banks, the Institute of Public Affairs (NSW) and Opposition to the Australian Labor Party, 1944-49," *Labour History*, no. 103 (2012), pp. 170–73.

33. Torleiv Hytten, *Australia and Post-War World Trade* (Sydney: Australian National Committee of the International Chamber of Commerce, 1949).

34. John Andrews, et al., "The Vision Thing: Conservatives Take Aim at the '90s," *Policy Review* 52 (1990), pp. 38–43.

35. In 1974, Labor MP Paul Keating claimed that the AMIC was "85 percent foreign controlled because 69 of the 93 companies in it are foreign owned." House of Representatives, Official Hansard, no. 32, Wednesday, August 7, 1974, p. 144, https://parlinfo.aph.gov.au/parlInfo/download/hansard80 /hansardr80/1974-08-07/toc_pdf/19740807_reps_29_hor89.pdf. A more recent report found that "Australia's mining industry is 86 percent foreign owned." See Hannah Aulby, "Undermining our Democracy: Foreign Corporate Influence through the Australian Mining Lobby," The Australia Institute, September 4, 2017, https://australiainstitute.org.au/report /undermining-our-democracy-foreign-corporate-influence-through-the -australian-mining-lobby. The AMIC was renamed the Minerals Council of Australia in 1995.

36. Quoted in Edward Wheelwright, *Radical Political Economy: Collected Essays* (Sydney: Australian and New Zealand Book Company, 1974), p. 116.

37. Jerry Courvisanos and Alex Millmow, "How Milton Friedman Came to Australia : A Case Study of Class-Based Political Business Cycles," *Journal of Australian Political Economy* 57 (2006), p. 122.

38. Gough Whitlam, "The Connor Legacy," *University of Wollongong Historical Journal* 3.1 (1979), p. 4.

39. T. M. Fitzgerald, *The Contribution of the Mineral Industry to Australian Welfare: Report to the Minister for Minerals and Energy the Hon. R. F. X. Connor M.P.* (Canberra: Australian Government Publishing, 1974).

40. Led by the "radical Tory" chief justice, Sir Garfield Barwick, the High Court declared the PMA Act invalid on procedural grounds. Barwick had consulted with Hytten in the 1940s as the barrister retained by the banks to challenge Labor's banking reforms and advised Kerr in his decision to dismiss Whitlam.

41. While academic histories document the tension between Whitlam's ministry and the Australian security agencies (ASIO, ASIS) working with U.S. intelligence services, especially over CIA agents associated with the secret Pine Gap installation, it has been left largely to independent writers to collect

evidence suggesting systemic U.S. destabilization, and none have focused on the PMA. See, for example, Jenny Hocking, *Gough Whitlam: His Time* (Carlton: Melbourne University Press, 2013); Guy Rundle, "Proving the CIA-Backed Conspiracy That Brought Down Whitlam, *Crikey*, November 25, 2015; Joan Coxsedge, "Nugan Hand: A Tale of Drugs, Dirty Money, the CIA and the Ousting of the Whitlam Government, *Guardian* (Sydney), no. 1765, February 15, 2017, pp. 6–7; William Blum, *Killing Hope: U.S. Military and CIA Interventions since World War II* (London: Zed Books, 2003), pp. 244–48.

42. John Pilger, *A Secret Country* (London: Vintage, 1992), pp. 204–208.

43. Vincent Bevins, *The Jakarta Method: Washington's Anticommunist Crusade and the Mass Murder Program that Shaped Our World* (New York: Hachette, 2020), pp. 140–42.

44. Henry Kissinger, Memorandum of Conversation, PM Whitlam's Coming Visit, July 28, 1973, NSC Files, Nixon Presidential Archive, box 1027. Quoted in Stephen Stockwell, "Beyond Conspiracy Theory: US Presidential Archives on the Australian Press, National Security and the Whitlam Government," Journalism Education Association Conference paper, Griffith University, December 2, 2005.

45. Phillip Dorling, "Murdoch Editors Told to 'Kill Whitlam' in 1975," *Sydney Morning Herald*, June 28, 2014, https://www.smh.com.au/nationa l/murdoch-editors-told-to-kill-whitlam-in-1975-20140627-zson7.html.

46. Gough Whitlam, House of Representatives, Official Hansard, no. 28, Wednesday, July 9, 1975, p. 3599, https://parlinfo.aph.gov.au/parlInfo /download/hansard80/hansardr80/1975-07-09/toc_pdf/19750709_reps_29 _hor95.pdf.

47. Shane Maloney and Chris Grosz, "Rex Connor and Tirath Khemlani," *Monthly*, October 2013, p. 82.

48. Market Forces, "Do You Pay More Tax than the Big Fossil Fuel Companies?," December 12, 2019, https://www.marketforces.org.au/campaigns /subsidies/taxes/taxavoidance/#.

49. Kevin Hince, *Conflict and Coal: A Case Study of Industrial Relations in the Open-Cut Coal Mining Industry of Central Queensland* (Brisbane: University of Queensland Press, 1982), p. 16.

50. F. A. Hayek, *Social Justice, Socialism and Democracy: Three Australian Lectures* (Sydney: Centre for Independent Studies, 1979), p. i.

51. The Western Mining Corporation would later be absorbed by BHP-Billiton.

52. Paul Kelly, *The End of Certainty: Power, Politics and Business in Australia* (Sydney: Allen & Unwin, 1992), p. 47.

53. F. A. Hayek, "Address to the 33rd Annual Conference of the Institute for Public Affairs" and "Socialism and Science," *IPA Review* (October–December, 1976), p. 83.

54. F. A. Hayek, "Full Employment, Planning and Inflation," *IPA Review* (November–December, 1950), pp. 174–84.

55. Hayek, "Socialism and Science," p. 96.

56. In 1980, Fraser would join Hayek and Gottfried Haberler as an advisor to the American Enterprise Institute.

57. Quoted in Carey, "Conspiracy or Groundswell?," p. 14.

58. Dominic Kelly, *Political Troglodytes and Economic Lunatics: The Hard Right in Australia* (Carlton: La Trobe University Press, 2019).

59. Sturgess recently has been an executive with Serco, an operator of Australia's infamous immigration detention centers.

60. Damien Cahill and Sharon Beder, "Neo-liberal Think Tanks and Neo-liberal Restructuring: Learning the Lessons from Project Victoria and the Privatisation of Victoria's Electricity Industry," *Social Alternatives* 24.1 (2005), p. 43.

61. Tristan Edis, "ACIL Tasman—Confessions of an Economic Hit…Sorry, Miss Man," *Australian*, September 17, 2012, https://www.theaustralian.com.au/business/business-spectator/news-story/acil-tasman--confessions-of-an-economic-hitsorry-miss-man/59ff41cf189c56468fcad497076cdf60.

62. Clive Hamilton, "The Dirty Politics of Climate Change," The Australia Institute, February 20, 2006, https://clivehamilton.com/the-dirty-politics-of-climate-change.

63. For example, see the U.S. Atlas units listed in Brulle, "Institutionalizing Delay."

64. Atlas Network, "Institute of Public Affairs' Repeal the Carbon Tax

Finalist for Prestigious Templeton Freedom Award," August 31, 2015, https://www.atlasnetwork.org/news/article/institute-of-public-affairs-repeal-the-carbon-tax-finalist-for-prestigious-.

65. Newman is currently senior advisor to Marsh Global, insurance brokers for Adani's vast Queensland coal project.

66. Marianna Barreto, et al., "People Power under Attack: A Report Based on Data from the Civicus Monitor," Civicus, 2019, https://civicus.contentfiles.net/media/assets/file/GlobalReport2019.pdf.

67. Judith Brett, "The Coal Curse: Resources, Climate and Australia's Future," *Quarterly Essay 78* (2020), pp. 1–81.

PART THREE

Radical Outposts

.

CHAPTER EIGHT

Neoliberalism Out of Place:
The Rise of Brazilian Ultraliberalism

Jimmy Casas Klausen & Paulo Chamon

Far from being reduced to a moribund set of doctrines or restricted to the works of aging notables, ultraliberal arguments have gained an immense following among Brazilians under thirty-five years old. The swelling ranks have not only influenced the direction of political debate, but also have occupied spaces hitherto reserved for "the Left," such as university campuses, alternative sites of knowledge production, widely circulated newspaper columns, and different channels of cultural life. How has this been possible? The victory is certainly not a matter of chance or attributable to some eternal youthful dream of freedom. Rather, the appeal to youth and the related generational shift in the presentation and representation of ultraliberal ideas has been carefully produced, though not, we caution, conspiratorially or always consciously.

The trends that link the Workers' Party (PT, Partido dos Trabalhadores), the street protests in 2013 and 2015, the impeachment/coup of President Dilma Rousseff, and the election of President Jair Bolsonaro are complex. In what follows, we focus on the emergence of ultraliberal figures, groups, and networks that have most advanced the messy story of neoliberalism in Brazil since the 2000s. Taking a cue from the website *Boletim da Liberdade*, which "focus[es] on the defense of liberal ideas and specializ[es] in the country's proliberty ecosystem,"[1] we use the metaphor of an ultraliberal "ecosystem." Compared with a two-dimensional political continuum, the ecosystem metaphor captures more aptly the possibility of adaptation and differentiation in a three-dimensional space. Brazil's rightward turn and the polemics around its previous leftward turn under the PT created a complex space where to be more radical does not always translate into being further "right" on a spectrum, but rather into being more ultraliberal along multiple possible dimensions. Moreover, since Brazilian political taxonomy defies familiar Anglophone categories such as "libertarian," we employ "ultraliberal" as a genus that includes a variety of anti-statist and market-fundamentalist species.[2] Likewise, the ecosystem metaphor allows us to avoid reductively designating positions as either for or against "neoliberalism."

We argue that in the ultraliberal ecosystem that has risen to dominance in Brazil, the adaptation and speciation of groups and positions has been driven by two dynamics: on the one hand, a push for more radicalization, that is, to position oneself as more properly ultraliberal than others, and on the other hand, an incorporation and reconfiguration of left-leaning and youth-cultural sensibilities—including appeals to minority and women's support and pop-cultural aesthetics. Together, the two dynamics have normalized neoliberalism by dispersing and displacing it through the ecosystem. In doing so, they set the conditions for fringe positions to be increasingly centralized, making the genus of ultraliberalism more appealing, expressive of a diverse society, and even cool and sexy.

Longtime Mont Pelerin Society member Murray Rothbard already prefigured this dual dynamic. In *For a New Liberty: The Libertarian Manifesto* (1985), Rothbard took cues from revisionist historians in his presentation of U.S. political development when he criticized imperialist foreign policy, and he adapted arguments circulated in the sexual revolution by developing permissive positions on abortion, birth control, and pornography.[3] Hence, he entertained and reconfigured claims from a countercultural left. Likewise, a more-radical-than-thou dynamic quite clearly drove Rothbard's criticisms of Milton Friedman for being ultimately a statist.[4] There are deeper contextual reasons for the installation of an ultraliberal ecosystem in Brazil, but what looks superficially like Brazilian mimicry of Rothbard actually evinces an important material reality: as journalists have shown, one reason for this similarity between Brazilian and North American ultraliberal advocacy is the financial and organizational support of right-wing think tanks in the United States.[5]

In the following chapter, we first sketch ultraliberalism's lines of descent before describing its "more-radical-than-thou" dynamic. Then we describe the appropriation of youth-cultural aesthetics and finally analyze ultraliberalism's recent prodiversity appeals. Invoking Roberto Schwartz's interpretation of the nonplace of liberalism in nineteenth-century Brazil, we conclude by considering why neoliberalism has been displaced from this story and indeed has found itself (in and) "out of place" in Brazil.

OUT OF WHERE?

The rise of the ultraliberal ecosystem in Brazil was made possible by the emergence of a new space in the political and intellectual scene of the mid-2000s. It is difficult to make sense of the politics and aesthetics that characterize the ultraliberal movements in Brazil beyond the fringe positionalities they affirm and gradually relocate to the center. Often born in the mid-to-late 1980s, the bulk of members of the emerging ecosystem commonly came into politics in the late 1990s or under PT governments (2002 to 2016) and what would come to be marked as the PT's first corruption scandals. Their dissatisfaction ran deeper than institutional politics, however, involving a carefully (if not always intentionally) crafted sense of exclusion in the face of the perceived hegemony of "the Left" in the public sphere. The harnessing and directing of such dissatisfaction made for the emergence of the ultraliberal ecosystem. In what follows, we highlight three lines of descent that can be traced to the 1980s and 1990s and that set the stage for this radical youth activist positionality.[6]

The first and more direct line of descent is the appearance of the first Brazilian liberal institutes in the 1980s and 1990s. Most important here are the only two remaining from the 1980s: the Instituto Liberal (IL), created in 1983 in Rio de Janeiro by Brazilian businessman and member of the Mont Pelerin Society, Donald Steward, Jr., and the Instituto de Estudos Empresariais (IEE), created in 1984 by the Ling family in Rio Grande do Sul. These institutes were financed by the same businessmen whose interest in market reforms was often tempered by a countervailing interest in localized state protectionism.[7] While this first wave waned in the late 1990s, it left two legacies to the ecosystem that would emerge in the mid-2000s: the translation and circulation among businessmen and politicians of neoliberal and libertarian articles and books, most of all by Hayek, Friedman, and Rothbard, and an initial institutionalization through networks of individuals and organizations, both national and international.[8]

Most notable regarding the latter were some early connections to U.S. groups such as the Foundation for Economic Education, as well as the creation of the Fórum da Liberdade, which became the main gathering space of the ultraliberal ecosystem and its sympathizers. Indeed, all the major think tanks and movements have since been launched at the forum, which changes composition according to the internal displacements of the ecosystem. While it included leftist figures until the early 2000s, the forum became an exclusively liberal and conservative gathering place by the mid-2000s and included an array of guests from the Bolsonaro government in 2019.[9] Together, these legacies laid the foundation of transnational material support that the ultraliberal ecosystem has come to mobilize.

Second and less obvious is the challenge to hegemonic loci of authoritative knowledge by two developments in the 1990s and early 2000s. One is expressed in the role of the figure of Olavo de Carvalho, who, despite his association with a particularly aggressive conservatism in Bolsonarismo's culture wars, played a broader role in the emergence of the ultraliberal ecosystem in the late 1990s and early

2000s.[10] At that time, Carvalho helped mainstream the claim that leftist intellectuals had become imbecilic and were spearheading a cultural catastrophe by turning hegemonic and complacent.[11] This both fused "the Left" and "the intellectuals" as one and the same and marked it as a group as both institutionally hegemonic and intellectually and morally decadent. Fundamentally, it located the path to intellectual and political sophistication and irreverence on "the Right"—a muddied neoliberal and/or conservative position. This disposition was key in constructing a fringe positionality from which to claim authoritative knowledge and vocalize intellectual and political claims with a radical, antiestablishment aura.

This development was compounded by the consolidation in the 2000s of the think tank as a site of authoritative knowledge production. The role of think tanks as marginal and focused loci of knowledge production was itself conditioned by the loss of exclusive access to public universities that wealthy young students felt as an effect of the inclusive higher education policies advanced by the PT federal government. This sense of loss led to the establishment of alternative circuits of knowledge diffusion and acquisition, such as foreign college degrees and internationally connected think tanks.[12] Margaret Tse, a Brazilian former member of the Mont Pelerin Society board of directors and its current newsletter editor, reinforces this idea by presenting think tanks as a response, in the form of "precise information, and rigorous and transparent analyses," to a credibility gap between citizens, elected politicians, and knowledge.[13] This (highly contested) claim associates authoritative knowledge with specialized issue areas and the closed circuit of online, openly biased think tanks, prone as they are to creating echo chambers. While Carvalho took part in mainstreaming the position of the right-wing antileftist young intellectual against established knowledge authorities, the rise of think tanks established a site where such people could converge and that they could rely upon for learning, debating, and publishing, reaching an ever broader audience.

Last is the acceptance and spread of Washington Consensus social and economic policies in the 1990s by the Fernando Henrique Cardoso presidency, later compounded by Luiz Inácio Lula da Silva's 2002 "Letter to the Brazilian People," a document stating the PT politician's commitment to continue his predecessor's socioeconomic policies, and the conciliatory politics of Lulism.[14] The "mainstreaming" of neoliberal policies not only lessened the need for liberal institutes—compounding the waning of the first wave—but more importantly contributed to the stage at which the ultraliberal ecosystem emerged by muddying the categories of "neoliberalism," "state intervention," "social democracy," "socialism," and "the Left." Indeed, the proximity between Cardoso and Lula would facilitate their being bundled together as no more than variations upon a theme. Just as many on the Left have criticized the PT for compromising, to the point of labeling its politics a product of "left neoliberalism,"[15] promarket forces could criticize Cardoso's neoliberalism for "not being radical enough," to the point of labeling it a version of "the Left." This configuration instilled the common reading in the ultraliberal ecosystem of the historical nonexistence of liberal ideas or of a liberal government in Brazil.

Indeed, Helio Beltrão—founder of Mises Brazil—retrospectively characterizes the ideological scene by reference to two "middle ground positions": social democracy and neoliberalism. In his view, both tendencies come from the compromising of liberalism by accepting different roles for state social and economic intervention.[16] This configuration of the field allows fringe positions in the ultraliberal ecosystem to migrate to the center by claiming to be more radical than their peers—rhetorically labeled "social democrat" or "neoliberal."

Together, these lines of descent—the preceding liberal institutes, the advent of alternative sites of authoritative knowledge, and the muddying categories of left and right—set the stage for the rebirth of ultraliberal forces. This space, as we will show, works as much by bringing together diverse groups and positions distinguishing themselves in common from external—read "leftist"—forces as by producing internal distinctions by claiming to be more radical than other positions within that ecosystem. This dynamic of internal and external distancing produces the increasingly porous boundaries that have had a fundamental role in shaping the political scene in the twenty-first century.

FROM MARGIN TO CENTER

The first think tank of this new generation was created in 2005: Instituto Millenium (IMIL). Unlike its predecessors, the still-operating IMIL aims to reach not only the world of businessmen and politicians, but also beyond it, the scientific and student communities. However, like the liberal institutes of the 1980s and 1990s, IMIL is closely linked to positions of authority within the business, financial, media, and academic sectors and thus has had substantial support and resources.[17] Among its first founding and council members, one finds Armínio Fraga and Paulo Guedes, economists with close ties to the financial sector. While Fraga was president of the Central Bank (1999 to 2003) under the Cardoso administration and was announced as prospective minister of economy for presidential candidate Aécio Neves (defeated by Rousseff in 2014), Guedes was nominated minister of economy by President Jair Bolsonaro in 2018.

The ranks of early members also included representatives of important industrial holding groups and of the largest media outlets in Brazil—Organizações Globo and Grupo Abril. Furthermore, although IMIL publishes ideas ranging from those of self-proclaimed social democrats to those of liberals and libertarians, its core principles are attuned to a Washington Consensus version of neoliberalism, including an active role for the state—principles that would quickly place it under critical scrutiny.[18] Thus, IMIL maintained an organic relationship with the establishment, keeping to a somewhat riven position that sustained an important role in spreading ultraliberal ideas through its media connections and vast funding, while falling short of the kind of radical fringe position emerging in and through the ecosystem.[19]

Indeed, most of the movements that make up the ultraliberal eco-system were more decentralized and consisted mainly of young college students and professionals. Positioned on the fringes created by their predecessors and informed by a radical antiestablishment ethos, they saw themselves as minoritarian oppositions fighting hegemonic forces in both public discourse and higher education. While the lines of descent presented above set the stage, the emergence of the ultraliberal ecosystem in the mid-2000s took place in a different scene: online groups focused on the discussion of liberalism in the now-extinct social networking site Orkut.[20]

Orkut's system of theme-oriented communities and discussion forums, alongside its widespread dissemination in the country (in 2014, half the total number of users were from Brazil),[21] amplified a mode of engagement that hitherto had been limited to mailing lists and on-and-off internet blogs. As Bernardo Santoro, one of the people brought in to rebrand the Instituto Liberal to conform to the codes of the ultraliberal ecosystem, recounts: "The liberal movement was dead, [but] in 2006 some people decided to start discussing liberalism seriously in Orkut. I was already a liberal, I had read Locke, I had even read some more radical things, but then there was the Orkut group on liberalism; we were discussing and someone quickly noticed that everyone there was too radical, everyone was more libertarian than liberal."[22]

Explicitly citing the effervescence of this moment of emergence, Beltrão would later criticize Livres[23]—a former wing of the Social Liberal Party (PSL) that broke with it over the acceptance of Bolsonaro as presidential candidate and became a cross-party political movement promoting ultraliberal ideas online and in Congress—for its association with figures close to the Cardoso government. He claimed that "the refoundation of true liberalism in Brazil by the generation of... Orkut, with an avant-garde vibe, left those people in a limbo, completely dumbfounded. The new generation is winning the battle of ideas. Neoliberals are incompatible with what we stand for."[24]

These online communities worked simultaneously as spaces for the discussion of ideas, for the translation and circulation of articles and material, and for identity building and organization. The participants would reinforce their alleged minority position, expressed in the running joke that there were not enough of them to fill a Volkswagen bus. Even as social media brought them together, the debates and proximities would also intensify the dynamic of differentiation within the ecosystem, which led to a proliferation of communities of distinct orientations.[25]

The initiative of these communities would slowly spill out toward a broader scene. Such is the case of the attempt to create a libertarian party in Brazil: the Partido Líber, an idea born and developed in the online Orkut scene. Despite its failing to be fully institutionalized, it represented the first experience in off-line political mobilization for many young liberals, as well as an opportunity to connect with like-minded people across the country.[26] Distributing flyers and mobilizing locally and nationally, this experience built an activist political ethos in many young members of the emerging ecosystem—an ethos that would soon pay off.

Other processes achieved more substantial institutionalization, such as the creation and proliferation of ultraliberal think tanks and movements. In 2007, Beltrão, mobilizing his intensive participation in Orkut communities, spearheaded the creation of Mises Brazil, the largest libertarian think tank in the country. Following in the footsteps of the 1990s generation of liberal institutes, Beltrão associates the creation of Mises Brazil with leftist domination of universities and the ensuing consensus in favor of state interventionism.[27] Against this, Mises Brazil is dedicated to the dissemination of the Austrian school of economics—producing texts, podcasts, and videos, translating books and articles, and organizing seminars, online teaching programs, and summer schools—all aimed at attracting and training a younger public. The online and off-line presence of Mises Brazil makes it one of the main references for a generation of young liberals in Brazil—and possibly beyond, because Beltrão is said to have influenced the founding of the Mises Institute of Sweden.[28] The creation of other institutes, think tanks, and groups has since led to ample ultraliberal networks in Brazil.

Nonetheless, Beltrão and Mises Brazil have also been vulnerable to the radicalization dynamics of the ultraliberal ecosystem. In 2015, the brothers Cristiano, Roberto, and Fernando Chiocca broke with Mises Brazil to create the Instituto Rothbard Brasil, harshly criticizing both Beltrão and the direction he was giving to Mises Brazil and causing a major break in the ultraliberal ecosystem in the process. Cristiano Chiocca accused Beltrão not only of misunderstanding basic tenets of libertarian thought, but also of courting recognition from establishment institutions such as academia, the media, and political parties—in short, expressing a proestablishment ethos.[29] Beltrão's response likewise portrayed Chiocca as both irresponsible and not ultraliberal enough.[30] Symptomatically, their "more-radical-than-thou" polemic over the issue of secession during the 2014 presidential election—in which each party accused the other of not taking the ultraliberal argument far enough in favor of separatism—turned a marginal, regionalized discussion into the matter of online debates and speculations.

The centrality of student movements in Brazil's political history and the expansion of access to high school and higher education led the Orkut "Volkswagen bus" also to move toward student movements. Most notable here is Estudantes pela Liberdade (EPL), created in 2012 in the aftermath of an Atlas Network summer seminar. The EPL was, from the onset, associated with Students for Liberty (SFL), the Atlas Network's partner engaging libertarian college youth, and was supported by both institutions through budget lines and training programs. EPL chapters contested university spaces by organizing reading groups, movie clubs, and seminars, electing student organizations, and engaging in campus activism opposing not only the monopoly of leftist ideas on university campuses, but also the residual positions occupied by those with compromising liberal perspectives.[31] As such, the EPL took part in normalizing fringe positions associated variously with liberalism, libertarianism, and anarchocapitalism in the student scene. By 2015, its success was indisputable, being the largest Students for Liberty partner in the world, with more local branches than any U.S. or European partner, despite its shorter lifespan—which translated into a reflux influence of the EPL in Students for Liberty itself.[32]

Accusations of faulty management led in 2016 to the creation of Students for Liberty Brazil (SFLB), the part of the previous movement that remained connected to and funded by Students for Liberty. The messiness of the affair led to multiple accusations, mostly around the charge of "corruption,"[33] which came to carry special weight in the ultraliberal world—and in the political scene it helped shape—in view of the association of corruption with the derailing of fair (read: both efficient and moral) competition.[34] The affair was also taken advantage of by *Gazeta do Povo*, an online newspaper recently turned a voice of conservatism,[35] which denounced the fragmentation by pondering whether "the liberal student movement has been mimicking the Left not only in the broadness of its influence, but also of its internal divisions."[36] In doing so, of course, ironically, the conservative voice took part in that same dynamic.

Since 2017, the SFLB has organized Liberty con Brasil, a gathering of ultraliberal enthusiasts in São Paulo defined by Beltrão as a "diehard" version of Fórum da Liberdade. While the latter encompasses newcomers to the ultraliberal ecosystem, the former is both smaller and more focused on the student/youth already willing to take antistatist and proliberty ideas seriously. The mutual support as well as differences and rifts between Liberty con Brasil and Fórum da Liberdade might well speak to the coming chapters of the internal and external displacements of the ultraliberal ecosystem.

Although the size of the EPL in its heyday of the mid-2010s speaks for itself, its importance is difficult to dissociate from its relation to Movimento Brasil Livre (MBL). According to Juliano Torres, due to its international funding, the EPL could not participate in political activities such as the street protests of June 2013 in Brazil. To circumvent this problem, they created a brand—Movimento Brasil Livre—and a Facebook profile through which to mobilize and participate in the street protests. With the waning of the 2013 protests, the project was abandoned and would be revived in 2014 only when Fábio Ostermann and Torres brought in Renan Santos and Kim Kataguiri to take care of the Facebook profile, raising the MBL to a new level.[37] Indeed, in 2015, the Atlas Network featured a note dedicated to celebrating the involvement of Students for Liberty in the MBL and the participation of its members in Atlas training programs.[38]

The MBL is best known for its leading role in the movements that led to the impeachment/coup against President Dilma Rousseff in 2016. Their claim to radicality began early on: they were the first to call for demonstrations against Rousseff's electoral victory in 2014, antagonizing similar groups, such as Vem Pra Rua, which felt that upholding electoral results was imperative. Instead, the MBL worked to short-circuit mainstream political opposition, explicitly stating they wanted to sideline the main opposition parties and substitute them with the true and largest opposition: the Brazilian people mobilized in the streets.[39] The MBL's edginess would soon be attacked on a number of grounds, from accusations of juvenile ambitions to statist inclinations and leftist inspirations. Behind the undeniable success of the MBL in the ultraliberal ecosystem lies their skillful mediation between "more-radical-than-thou" practices and adaptation of left-associated mechanisms. In this, they express a heightened version of the second dynamic marking the ecosystem. In the next two sections, we further explore this interplay.

SEX APPEAL: YOUTH AESTHETICS

In this section, we present the second dynamic by which an ultraliberal ecosystem has come to install itself in Brazil: namely, that of an appeal to and reconfiguration by prodiversity youth sensibilities. A dual mechanism has constructed ultraliberal ideas to appeal to—to address and to be desirable to—the younger set. This mechanism operates along the two dimensions by which market fundamentalism and antistatism have been renovated and reconfigured: presentation, mainly in terms of the deployment of youth-culture aesthetics, and representation, principally of women and minorities.

The appeal to youth has involved both giving (making ideas and arguments available to youth) and taking (making them desirable by appropriating youth and leftist culture aesthetically). As regards giving, ultraliberal groups have subsidized the not insubstantial labor of translating Austrian economic thinking into Portuguese and making it available either in blogs and online articles or in handsomely designed editions. Though not conspicuously touting a connection to Mises Brazil, LVM Editora makes available in Portuguese translation the collected works of Mises and a number of other classics that inspire antistatist, liberal, and New Right thought. Sharing Ludwig von Mises's initials, LVM actually abbreviates Liberdade/Liberty, Valores/Values and Mercado/Market. Besides Gustave de Molinari's *The Production of Security* and books by Hayek and Rothbard, LVM Editora publishes translations of works by Hans-Hermann Hoppe and Walter Block and, in a gesture of gender and racial inclusion, features in its Brief Lessons series Thomas Sowell and Ayn Rand.

Moreover, sometimes the giving has occurred not on the production end, but in material distributions as donations to youth. In a revealing convergence of promarket voices, the MBL positively endorsed a 2017 announcement by Helio Beltrão that Mises Brazil would donate five thusand print copies of Mises's *As seis lições*, a translation of *Economic Policy: Thoughts for Today and Tomorrow* published by LVM Editora, to São Paulo public schools to answer the challenge made by the city's businessman-mayor João Doria to encourage more private donations.[40] Aside from its presence in public schools, Mises Brazil makes available for free download most of LVM's books, and, despite the Mises/Rothbard split, Instituto Rothbard does the same. Flooding the market with free video lessons on and texts of Austrian economics, the two institutes' broad dissemination of such ideas has helped to transform anarchocapitalism from a fringe into a mainstream position, such that even statist neoliberals of stature—such as those around Michel Temer, who as vice president benefited from the impeachment of Dilma Rousseff and became president upon her removal—have to defend themselves against Austrian economic arguments.

The spread of ultraliberal ideas in Brazil, especially among younger people, owes some of its success to serious efforts by groups to change the stuffy popular image of promarket politics and to rupture the automatic associations of right-leaning politics with dusty conservatism, militarism, bigotry, or the lunatic fringe. Hence, ultraliberal activists have made concerted efforts to disseminate their message by cultivating seductive influencers. In fact, several groups have openly expressed concern about their "sex appeal" deficit. Not letting the Left monopolize "coolness" has been a refrain among the younger, newer antistatist groups, as a Reason TV report on the young activists of the 2015 protests makes clear.[41] However, cultivating coolness generates contortions around style and substance, especially in the MBL, which reputedly balances ultraliberal economics with moral conservatism while capitalizing on youth appeal.

The EPL, the SFLB, the MBL, and Livres have actively courted younger followers through a variety of techniques, from online book clubs, to targeting potential adherents based on their social-network activity, to producing fast-paced video commentary on current political controversies and classic liberal debates intercut with memes and funny low-tech effects. Before donning suits as elected politicians, members of the MBL became famous for their YouTube juvenilia in which they appealed to followers in irreverent broadcasts looking like video game enthusiasts and "indie rockers."[42] Kataguiri actively cultivated the aesthetics of youth culture by sometimes dressing as a ninja and deploying, according to one *Time* reporter, "an anarchic style" to spread antistatist—not anarchist, but market-fundamentalist—ideas.[43]

Livres counts on Mano Ferreira, a cofounder of the SFLB, as director of communications to produce videos daily, including "#PolíticaEm-2Minutos," which digests controversies from homophobia to the toppling of racist monuments into lessons in ultraliberalism.

The appropriation of a youth aesthetic occurs by fairly obvious presentational effects, then. Not only have the MBL and Livres deployed pop-cultural aesthetic styles for communication, but also many of the groups sell T-shirts with clever phrases ("Less Marx, more Mises") and graphic designs meant to replace leftist social justice icons such as Che Guevara. Market-fundamentalist networks such as Rede Liberdade have also "appropriated" pub space by promoting politicized bar nights, such as "Chopp sem Impostos" (Beer without taxes) to celebrate the date in June when Brazilians' annual tax burden is paid off and their earnings are no longer "confiscated" by the state. If the bid for neoliberal hegemony depends on the construction of popular consent, then these productions carry great importance, for they educate viewers' and consumers' "common sense" by distilling ultraliberal arguments in a way that clarifies and stimulates background experiences and affects.[44]

Other appropriations are more subtle, however, and here we must deal briefly with the harrowing question of the Left/Right convergence and split in the 2013/2015 protests and the Left/Right resonances of antistatism. Even if not a conscious appropriation, the MBL fed off the momentum in the 2013 protests of the MPL (Movimento Passe Livre, the Free Fare Movement), an antiauthoritarian, autonomous, apartisan group that advocates for the right to the city and free urban circulation. The protests of 2013 began initially as demonstrations against the public transportation fare hikes in several Brazilian cities, but exploded in size and scope, especially in response to brutal police repression of some protesters. By mid-June 2013, millions of people had marched in the streets, objecting to political corruption—from across the political spectrum—and the dismal contrast between the quality of public services and local, state, and federal investment in facilities for megaevents that Brazil would host, the World Cup (2014) and the Olympic Games (2016).

Although initially the 2013 protesters were progressive leftist critics of the Brazilian government, some of them organized under the banner of the EPL, which, as already noted, incubated the MBL, which in turn took a coordinating role in the demonstrations of the anti-PT, pro-impeachment protests of 2015. While of course no single group owns the 2013 protests, it nonetheless makes sense to speak of an appropriation by the EPL and MBL of the broad-based youthful energy arising from the MPL's initiative. The swapping of initials—MPL→EPL, MPL→MBL—suggests a revaluation of antistatism from autonomist-inspired to anarcho-capitalist. Typically, after parlaying its capture of political energy into success in 2015 and after, the MBL later tried to "unmask" the MPL as bourgeois opportunists capitalizing on contrived sympathy for urban working classes. Obsessed with routing "Communists" at any cost, the MBL courted associations with Bolsonaro in 2018, and consequently some of its members won local, state, and federal elections.

DIVERSITY'S APPEAL

The MBL's successful appropriation of political energy emerging from the Left and of aesthetic presentation and communication practices associated with youth cultures has provoked reactions by other groups, such as Livres. It also seemingly spurred an autocritique: the sexist animus that Kataguiri and others of the MBL managed to whip up against Brazil's first woman president, followed two years later by its participation in a transphobic and homophobic crusade against Queermuseu, an art exhibit celebrating nonnormative gender and sexual expression, created a bad impression that the MBL later attempted to redress. Certainly, the MBL still offends political correctness, but it expressed regret for creating a polarized public sphere and since 2019 has publicly repudiated its association with Bolsonaro.

Dissociating themselves from Bolsonarista intolerance while sharply rejecting leftist identity politics, ultraliberal activists' initiatives on women's and minority issues have become an important field of neoliberal articulation in Brazil that also functions recursively to rearticulate racial, sexual, and gender identity. Rather than diminish such initiatives as only cynical appeals to capture support, it seems to us important to recognize the fact that even in superlatively unequal Brazil, the New Right cannot afford to ignore the shift in mainstream valuations of inclusive diversity. The imperative appeal to diversity in recent neoliberalism contrasts, for example, with Reaganite or Thatcherite neoliberalism and signals real wins by the so-called identitarian Left.

Liberals' active contestation of the perceived leftist hegemony on questions of minority identity have sometimes provoked acrimonious exchanges: the left-leaning presidential hopeful Ciro Gomes ridiculed Fernando Holiday, an openly gay (but sexually abstinent) Afro-Brazilian politician and prominent MBL organizer, as a "bush captain" in a 2018 interview. Holiday sued over the insult, which refers to a (stereotypically light-skinned Afro-Brazilian) hunter of fugitive slaves. However, we think that the incident marks another sort of boorishness on the part of the Left: namely, a tendency to dismiss support of ultraliberal arguments by women, LGBT persons, and people of color as a species of false consciousness, rather than to understand it in terms of new modalities of racialization and gender and sexual identification on the part of the New Right.[45]

With two prominent national organizers (now politicians) from minority racial backgrounds, one of whom is also gay, the MBL has situated itself in the liberal debate on minority questions. Indeed, optics and self-irony play an undeniably important role in spreading the MBL's criticism of the Left's arguments about racial and sexual minorities: Right-leaning critics avoid appearing racist or homophobic when they advance positions already voiced by Holiday, Kataguiri, or their minority proxies. The MBL frequently accuses the Brazilian Left of reveling in a U.S.–exported victim's mentality and ridicules the Left as beholden to political correctness. Defying PC culture, Kataguiri provocatively ironizes his Japanese heritage with stereotypes. In one video that lures his audience into thinking that he will criticize his MBL ally João Doria for a xenophobic social media post that offensively switches the letters "l" and "r" (a common racist trope), Kataguiri ends up instead rejecting leftist criticism of racial-cultural representations, promotes studious, well-mannered Asians as the "model minority," and closes the video schooling Doria on the correct way to mock Japanese.[46]

Holiday's videos, by contrast, deploy less irony, but the indignation remains loud, and his argument that movements for racial equality lost control after the assassination of Martin Luther King, Jr., lacks nuance, moralistically treating the latter iconically.[47] To the MBL, struggles for racial equality must never engage in violence, vandalism, or terrorism, as Malcolm X, Black Lives Matter, and Nelson Mandela purportedly have done.[48] Against a Left that allegedly reverses racism by stoking Black supremacy, the MBL promotes legal equality, individual initiative, and the capitalist market's expansion of opportunities as solutions to racial and other discriminations. Like its counterparts elsewhere, the MBL flirts with Islamophobia when it charges leftists with self-contradiction for criticizing Orientalist costumes at Carnaval, but supposedly refusing to condemn homophobia and sexism in Islamic societies. To the MBL, Israel merits praise, but the Brazilian Left kowtows to Islamist and dictatorial socialist regimes with a history of repressing women or sexual minorities.[49]

The MBL has recently undertaken two initiatives, MBLGBT and MBL Mulher (MBL Woman), to redress its reputation of being dominated by male enfants terribles who protest women presidents and queer art. Already claiming social media presence, the initiatives offer ultraliberal alternatives to leftist "indoctrination" on gender and sexuality and to right-wing sexism and homophobia. Typical for a group claiming liberty as panacea and objecting to "special" (minority) remedies, MBL organizers had to allay supporters' anxiety about whether their initiatives "segregate" women and sexual minorities.[50] One MBL Mulher debate, featuring perhaps the only prominent woman of the 2015 protests, Adelaide Oliveira of Vem Pra Rua, presented various diagnoses for women's lack of participation in politics. While most participants, including Oliveira, identified restrictive stereotypes in childhood and an ongoing lack of encouragement, others, such as Cris Bernart, a prominent aide to Holiday, suggested that women must overcome innate, cerebral propensities that leave them less suited for dominant modes of politics.[51] (Bernart probably summarizes the research of Leonard Sax's bestseller *Why Gender Matters*, the Portuguese translation of which was published by LVM Editora.)

Whereas the MBL created platforms to encourage LGBT and women's participation, Livres has focused on racism as an ultraliberal concern. Against anarcho-capitalist hard-liners, Livres argues that some remedial policies actually promote the exercise of ultraliberal autonomy where generations of intense inequality have distorted market opportunities. Whereas the MBL's Holiday vocally rejects affirmative action and preferential treatment of minorities, yet publicly deploys his minority identities to promote ultraliberal modes of racial and sexual identification, Irapuã Santana of Livres is an increasingly prominent Afro-Brazilian voice for reconciling ultraliberalism with affirmative action. For Santana and Livres, racial quotas, as well as investment in public education and health, remedy unequal starting points and thus are compatible with meritocracy.[52]

Santana coordinates the Livres's Luiz Gama initiative, named for a freeman sold into slavery who fled to freedom after learning to read and understanding the illegality of his situation. Gama subsequently practiced law to free other slaves. The video publicizing the initiative features a statement by Gama that would shock the sensibilities of Livres's ultraliberal peer competitors: "Any slave that kills his master, whatever be the circumstance, kills in legitimate self-defense."[53] The potent quotation underscores the group's interpretation of chattel slavery as the "biggest attack on liberty invented by humanity" and subsequently of corrosive anti-Black racism as deeply rooted in Brazilian culture.[54] Although seeming to converge with some leftist arguments about structural racism, Livres ultimately aims to generate ultraliberal equality of opportunity that stimulates individualism.

Livres, although a self-identified anarcho-capitalist group, has developed a reputation as the most "leftish" presence in the ultraliberal outburst in Brazil. Individual liberty, Livres insists, undermines itself by egocentrism, and therefore necessarily demands defending others' liberty as well. Thus, according to Livres, ultraliberals must tolerate intolerance only up to the point where intolerance manifestly restricts others' liberty and opportunities.[55] Accordingly, Livres, and Santana specifically, show greater support toward #BlackLivesMatter and #VidasNegrasImportam protests than the MBL, which associates them with violence, and Beltrão, who characterizes them as just as ochlocratic and authoritarian as Bolsonarista fanatics.[56]

Whereas the MBL has tried to distinguish itself on gay issues, Livres celebrated Trans Visibility Day by posting an interview with proud trans and intersex affiliates. The video presents personal liberty as crucial for individual projects of aligning bodily comportment with psychic gender. Against such individualizing personal journeys of discovery, it criticizes leftist activists for the "standardization" of identities.[57] Despite noting the positive impact of decriminalizing homophobia and transphobia, Santana nevertheless cautioned that extending anti-racist legislation to cover homophobia and transphobia, as Brazil's Supreme Court did in 2019, must occur by congressional vote, not judicial activism.[58]

The MBL and Livres have gone furthest in presenting analyses and projects specific to Brazil. Nonetheless, Mises Brazil plays a crucial role in translating and disseminating North American libertarian arguments on minority questions. On Mises Brazil's website, one can access, in Portuguese, nearly a dozen articles by Thomas Sowell, the African-American opponent of affirmative action, alongside Walter

Block's infamous defenses of discrimination. Occasionally, the institute finds Brazilians to parrot Block-type arguments, and the MBL's Holiday might not have (hubristically) put himself on a T-shirt next to Sowell and Martin Luther King, Jr., had Mises Brasil not helped spread Sowell's message.[59] Notably, though, the more youth-engaged groups distinguish themselves from the older guard in their willingness to confront bias. In this sense, they confirm ultraliberalism's historic trend: just as Rothbard criticized the U.S. war in Vietnam—a species of anti-imperialism that later fed antiglobalism—and incorporated 1960s countercultural insights in his libertarian manifesto,[60] so have the new ultraliberals felt compelled to formulate prodiversity positions.

CONCLUSION

Researchers of Brazil and South America debate whether the PT years represented a turn *away* from neoliberalism specifically of the Washington Consensus, a *post*neoliberalism that adapted features of neoliberalism,[61] or *left* neoliberalisms.[62] Whichever the case, though, associations with the "Communist" PT or its discredited predecessors taint neoliberalism in the eyes of Brazil's ultraliberals. In their radicalism, they have paradoxically normalized arguments that surpass neoliberalism, marginalizing it as passé. Neoliberalism has thus been out of place in our story, echoing the fate of classical liberalism in Brazil.

In a famous 1977 essay titled "Ideas Out of Place," the Marxist critic Roberto Schwartz explicated nineteenth-century writers' debates about how liberalism was "out of place" in Brazil.[63] A slave society, Brazil lacked free labor, legal equality, and political universalism. In Europe, such bourgeois ideas were of course properly ideological in the Marxist sense, describing the realm of appearances only, since in reality, capital exploited labor. Yet qua *ideology*, liberalism was at home in Europe. In Brazil, however, the rhetoric of liberalism could not even falsify appearances, because it deceived no one. In the face of racial slavery and a clientelism that joined free whites while differentiating them by status, liberalism became merely decorative, a set of ideas one might spout to sound modish—in short, a misplaced, second-degree ideology. However, this was no secondary matter: while liberalism did not falsify appearances, it was through its all too recognizable out-of-placeness that nineteenth-century cultural life took form, argued Schwartz.

Although neoliberalism does not carry the same decorative verve of its nineteenth-century counterpart, neoliberalism's out-of-placeness has had a fundamental role in giving form to twenty-first-century cultural life. Coming *out of Brazil*, neoliberalism has found itself repeatedly out of place not because it is a decorative, second-degree ideology, but because it is a governing rationality overdetermined by the lines of force generated by nineteenth-century legacies of racial slavery, clientelism, heteropatriarchy, and Indigenous genocide, as well as Brazil's location in the Global South. Thus, each construction of neoliberalism—Cardoso's, those of the PT, Temer's—necessitated calibrations of some patterns of inequalities against others. When Brazil's neoliberal constructions serially encountered turbulence from global financial markets, international trade, and crises of political legitimacy, ultraliberals were able to magnetize popular anxieties by representing "leftist hegemony," "state intervention," "market restriction," and paternalistic attitudes generally as causes of dissatisfaction and resentment. Zeal for individualist freedom via competition and self-investment would correct neoliberalism's failures to *truly* remedy inequalities by sustaining growth.

Hence, Brazilian ultraliberals constructed from relatively fringe elements of neoliberal discourse—anarchocapitalism, market fundamentalism, and U.S. libertarianism—*another* (though perhaps not altogether separate) governing rationality to displace Brazil's series of neoliberalisms. From being a non-Brazilian import under Cardoso to compromised chimeras under the PT and a timid platform under Temer, neoliberalism was never properly itself or at home in Brazil, but now would be displaced by an ultraliberal governing rationality.

Caught in the interplay of the lines of force that Schwartz identified and others that he did not, ultraliberals' bid for a more enduring hegemony will depend on how they construct "state" and "market" relations to rearticulate the contradictory affects/effects generated by the legacies of inequality that continue to beset Brazil. Their opponents face the same daunting task.

NOTES

1. "Quem somos," *Boletim da Liberdade,* https://www.boletimdaliberdad .com.br/quemsomos.

2. Camila Rocha, "'Imposto é roubo!': A formação de um contrapúblico ultraliberal e os protestos pró-impeachment de Dilma Rousseff," *Dados* 62.3 (2019), pp. 1–42, https://doi.org/10.1590/001152582019189.

3. Murray N. Rothbard, *For a New Liberty: The Libertarian Manifesto,* rev. ed. (New York: Libertarian Review Foundation, 1985), pp. 105–108 and 270–82.

4. Murray N. Rothbard, "Milton Friedman Unraveled," *Journal of Libertarian Studies* 16.4 (2002), p. 40.

5. Lee Fang, "Sphere of Influence: How American Libertarians Are Remaking Latin American Politics," *The Intercept,* August 9 2017, https://theintercept .com/2017/08/09/atlas-network-alejandro-chafuen-libertarian-think-tank -latin-america-brazil.

6. For a related trend exploring the ascendency of neoliberalism in Brazil, see Hernán Ramírez, "Neoliberalism in Brazil: An Analysis from the Viewpoint of the Current Situation," *PSL Quarterly Review* 72.289 (2019), https:// www.researchgate.net/profile/Hernan-Ramirez-3/publication/335021997 _Neoliberalism_in_Brazil_An_analysis_from_the_viewpoint_of_the_current _situation/links/5d4acda292851cd046a6d848/Neoliberalism-in-Brazil-An -analysis-from-the-viewpoint-of-the-current-situation.pdf.

7. Camila Rocha, "Passando o bastão: A nova geração de liberais brasileiros," *Nuevo Mundo, Mundos Nuevos,* October 2, 2017, http://nuevomundo .revues.org/71327.

8. Camila Rocha, "O papel dos think tanks pró-mercado na difusão do neo-liberalismo no Brasil," *Millcayac— Revista Digital de Ciencias Sociales* 4.7 (2017), pp. 95-120; Rocha, "Passando o bastão."

9. See Camila Vidal, Jahde Lopez, and Luan Brum, "The Power of Ideas: The Fórum da Liberdade, 1988-2018," *Contexto Internacional: Journal of Global Connections* 42.1 (2020), pp. 55-79; Flávio Henrique Calheiros Casimiro, *A tragédia e a farsa: A ascensão das direitas no Brasil contemporâneo* (São Paulo: Expressão Popular / Fundação Rosa Luxemburgo, 2020), pp. 72-81; Rocha, "O papel dos *think tanks* pró-mercado."

10. Coming from different angles, João Cézar de Castro Rocha (a left-leaning literature professor) and Renan Santos (founder of Movimento Brasil Livre) come to this same conclusion in conversation; see Renan Santos and João Cézar de Castro Rocha, "Obra prima: O professor que desvendou os planos de Olavo e Bolsonaro," April 18, 2020, https://www.youtube.com/watch?v =lVZcWxKRC8M. See also Movimento Brasil Livre, *Não vai ter golpe*, September 4, 2019, https://www.facebook.com/mblcordeiro/videos/n%C3%A3o-vai-ter -golpe-document%C3%A1rio/147927323711711/?__so__=permalink&__rv __=related_videos.

11. Olavo de Carvalho, "O imbecil coletivo," in *O imbecil coletivo*, 7th ed. (Rio de Janeiro: Faculdade da Cidade Editora, 1999), pp. 71-78.

12. Maria Caramez Carlotto, "Inevitável e imprevisível, o fortalecimento da direita para além da dicotomia ação e estrutura: O espaço internacional como fonte de legitimação dos think tanks latino-americanos," *PLURAL* 25 (2018), pp. 63-91.

13. Margaret Tse, "A vez dos think tanks," *Instituto Millenium*, March 4, 2020, https://www.institutomillenium.org.br/a-vez-dos-think-tanks.

14. André Singer coined *Lulismo* as the ideology of conciliation across Brazilian society that combined both neoliberal and redistributive policies, attending to the interests of different sectors of capital, labor, and social move-ments. See André Singer, *Os sentidos do Lulismo: Reforma gradual e pacto conservador* (São Paulo: Companhia das Letras, 2012); Giuseppe Cocco and Bruno Cava, *New Neoliberalism and the Other: Biopower, Anthropophagy, and Living Money* (London: Lexington Books, 2018), pp. 50-78.

15. Alfredo Saad-Filho, "Mass Protests under 'Left Neoliberalism': Brazil, June–July 2013," *Critical Sociology* 39.5 (2013), pp. 657–69.

16. Helio Beltrão, "Não deturpem o liberalismo!," *Folha de São Paulo*, July 17, 2019; Beltrão, "Ele não é liberal?," Instituto Mises Brasil, November 11, 2019, https://www.youtube.com/watch?v=y7z0HhP-3-E&feature=share&fbclid=IwA R13Bf52OUuaEASEa_OUz5fbxdtnZQ5YMATs865WdwD6Edan0K9-erJhB20.

17. Luciana Silveira, "Fabricação de ideias, produção de c onsenso: Estudo de caso do Instituto Millenium," master's thesis, UNICAMP, 2013, pp. 62–118.

18. Instituto Millenium, "Missão, visão, valores," https://www.institutomil-lenium.org.br/institucional/missao-visao-valores.

19. Camila Rocha, "O boom das novas direitas brasileiras: financiamento ou militância?," in Esther Solano, ed., *O ódio como política* (São Paulo: Boitempo, 2018), unpaginated.

20. Rocha, "O papel dos *think tanks* pró-mercado"; Rocha, "Imposto é roubo!." The archives of one of the most important Orkut communities (Liberalismo) are available at https://web.archive.org/web/20160807055345/http://orkut.google.com/c63909.html.

21. "Orkut," Wikipedia, https://en.wikipedia.org/wiki/Orkut.

22. Bernardo Santoro, quoted in Rocha, "Passando o bastão," para. 25.

23. Livres, "O que é o Livres?," https://www.eusoulivres.org/sobre-o-livres.

24. Helio Beltrão (@heliobeltrao), "A refundação do verdadeiro liberalismo aqui no Brasil," Twitter, May 2, 2019, https://twitter.com/heliobeltrao/status /1123868045015908358.

25. Filipe Celeti, "A história do movimento libertário brasileiro," Instituto Mercado Popular, February 11, 2014, http://mercadopopular.org/ politica/a-historia-do-movimento-libertario-brasileiro.

26. Rocha, "Imposto é roubo!," p. 13.

27. Helio Beltrão, "A cabeça da direita," interview by João Batista, Jr., *Veja com*, April 26, 2019, https://veja.abril.com.br/politica/a-cabeca-da-direita.

28. Joakim Kampe, "Helio Beltrao and Mises Global," Mises Institute, June 14, 2011, https://mises.org/library/helio-beltrao-and-mises-global.

29. Cristiano Chiocca, "Colocando o IMB de volta nos trilhos—Uma entrevista esclarecedora com o presidente Cristiano Chiocca," Instituto Rothbard

August 31, 2015, http://rothbardbrasil.com/colocando-o-imb-de-volta-nos
-trilhos-uma-entrevista-esclarecedora-com-o-presidente-cristiano-chiocca.

30. Helio Beltrão et al., "Helio Beltrão fala sobre a polêmica envolvendo os irmãos Chiocca," Sentinela da Liberdade, April 2, 2020, https://www.youtube.com/watch?v=FhGoOfiiYig.

31. Juliano Torres, "Saiba quem são e o que defendem os Estudantes pela Liberdade (EPL)," Instituto Millenium, May 6, 2013, https://www.youtube.com/watch?v=3uS6afJGtno.

32. Marina Amaral, "A nova roupa da direita," *Publica*, June 23, 2015, http://apublica.org/2015/06/a-nova-roupa-da-direita.

33. "Gossip Lib," Tumblr, https://gossiplib-blog.tumblr.com.

34. Savio Cavalcante, "Classe média, meritocracia e corrupção," *Crítica Marxista* 46 (2018), pp. 103–25.

35. Rafael Moro Martins, "Como a Gazeta do Povo, do Paraná, deu uma guinada à direita e virou porta-voz do Brasil de Bolsonaro," *The Intercept Brasil*, December 10, 2018, https://theintercept.com/2018/12/09/gazeta-do-povo-guinada-direita-bolsonaro.

36. Bruno Raphael Müller, "Estudantes pela Liberdade desafia hegemonia da esquerda," *Gazeta do Povo*, June 22, 2017, https://www.gazetadopovo.com.br/educacao/estudantes-pela-liberdade-desafia-hegemonia-da-esquerda-9qk7kw1vsghnu6ulrnup1s6kq.

37. Amaral, "A nova roupa da direita."

38. Atlas Network, "Students For Liberty Plays Strong Role in Free Brazil Movement," April 1, 2015, https://www.atlasnetwork.org/news/article/students-for-liberty-plays-strong-role-in-free-brazil-movement.

39. Amaral, "A nova roupa da direita."

40. MBL, "Instituto Mises faz doações de livros para São Paulo," March 31, 2017, https://www.youtube.com/watch?v=vtRAHf9_q2o.

41. Jim Epstein, "How Brazil's Libertarian Movement Helped Bring Down a President," *Reason*, August 3, 2016, https://reason.com/video/how-brazils-libertarian-movement-helped; Livres, "Claudio Manoel: Há 30 anos dando porrado no estado," Facebook, October 1, 2017, https://www.facebook.com/EuSouLivres/posts/1564456110301833.

42. María Martín, "Não é uma banda de indie-rock, é a vanguarda anti-Dilma," *El País*, December 12, 2014, http://brasil.elpais.com/brasil/2014/12/12/politica/1418403638_389650.html.

43. Matt Sandy, "Meet the Teen Spearheading Protests Against Its President," *Time*, October 27, 2015, http://time.com/4088721/kim-kataguiri-brazil-protests.

44. Stuart Hall, "Gramsci's Relevance for the Study of Race and Ethnicity," in David Morley and Kuan-Hsing Chen, eds., *Stuart Hall: Critical Dialogues in Cultural Studies* (London: Routledge, 1996), pp. 431–32.

45. Daniel Martinez HoSang and Joseph E. Lowndes, *Producers, Parasites, Patriots: Race and the New Right-Wing Politics of Precarity* (Minneapolis: University of Minnesota Press, 2019); Melinda Cooper, *Family Values: Between Neoliberalism and the New Social Conservatism* (New York: Zone Books, 2017).

46. MBL, "Kim ataca racismo e xenofobia de Doria contra os japoneses," August 4, 2017, https://www.youtube.com/watch?v=YRXSSA5_MCw.

47. Fernando Holiday, "Protestos violentos nos EUA e a lição de Luther King," June 2, 2020, https://www.youtube.com/watch?v=-N1r1-D1oHs.

48. MBL, "Nelson Mandela: Heroí ou terrorista?," February 21, 2020, https://www.youtube.com/watch?v=hPwcZli3i7c; MBL, "Derrubem as estátuas!," June 21, 2020, https://www.youtube.com/watch?v=omjjG3QZHsM.

49. MBL, "O politicamente correto quer escolher sua fantasia!," February 9, 2018, https://www.youtube.com/watch?v=1bQtCMal_Ns.

50. Fábrica MBL, "MBL está segregando ou agregando?? MBLGBT e MBL Mulher explicados por Renan e Prof. Ricardo Almeida," May 28, 2020, https://www.youtube.com/watch?v=qaJJCRoWXBQ.

51. Fábrica MBL, "A participação da mulher na política: MBL Mulher debate a respeito," June 5, 2020, https://www.youtube.com/watch?v=x-kw9gbLhno.

52. Fábio Zanini, "Cotas raciais e meritocracia podem coexistir, diz líder de grupo negro liberal," *Folha de São Paulo*, June 12, 2020, https://saidapeladireita.blogfolha.uol.com.br/2020/06/12/cotas-raciais-e-meritocracia-podem-coexistir-diz-lider-de-grupo-negro-liberal; Livres, "Perguntas frequentes," https://www.eusoulivres.org/faq.

53. Livres, "Quem foi Luiz Gama?," June 22, 2020, https://www.youtube.com/watch?v=qo6VHRu7yoE.

54. Livres, "Derrubar estátuas é uma boa ideia?," June 9, 2020, https://www.youtube.com/watch?v=kEoGE2LmGAE.

55. Livres, "Devemos tolerar os intolerantes?," June 16, 2020, https://www.youtube.com/watch?v=sonMJEmbAnE.

56. Irapuã Santana, "Os reflexos de George Floyd no Brasil," part 3 of "O caso George Floyd nos EUA e no Brasil," *Estado da Arte*, June 12, 2020, https://estadodaarte.estadao.com.br/george-floyd-brasil-eua; MBL, "A direita é racista?," June 4, 2020, https://www.youtube.com/watch?v=bkg7xTLDT2k; Helio Beltrão, "Trainees de ditadores," *Folha de São Paulo*, June 16, 2020, https://www1.folha.uol.com.br/colunas/helio-beltrao/2020/06/trainees-de-ditadores.shtml.

57. Livres, "Transexualidade e liberalismo," January 29, 2020, https://www.youtube.com/watch?v=Flgoz_mZFZc.

58. Irapuã Santana, "Regras do jogo e o silêncio eloquente," Livres, February 18, 2019, https://www.eusoulivres.org/artigos/regras-do-jogo-e-o-silencio-eloquente-por-irapua-santana.

59. Paulo Kogos, "A esquerda ataca o elo mais fraco novamente," Mises Brasil, January 23, 2013, https://www.mises.org.br/BlogPost.aspx?id=1506; Isabella Ribeiro, "Camiseta do MBL coloca Fernando Holiday ao lado de Martin Luther King," *O Globo*, March 7, 2017, https://blogs.oglobo.globo.com/blog-do-moreno/post/camiseta-do-mbl-coloca-fernando-holiday-ao-lado-de-martin-luther-king.html.

60. Rothbard, *For a New Liberty*, pp. 272–73 and 103–12.

61. Arne Ruckert, Laura Macdonald, and Kristina Proulx, "Post-neoliberalism in Latin America: A Conceptual Overview," *Third World Quarterly* 38.7 (2017), pp. 1583–1602.

62. Alfredo Saad-Filho, "Varieties of Neoliberalism in Brazil (2003–2019)," *Latin American Perspectives* 47.1 (2020), pp. 9–27.

63. Roberto Schwartz, *Ao vencedor as batatas* (1977; São Paulo: Duas Cidades/Editora 34, 2000), pp. 9–31.

CHAPTER NINE

Latin America's Neoliberal Seminary: Francisco Marroquín University in Guatemala

Karin Fischer

"Many a university has become a wasteland, morally and otherwise," lamented William H. Peterson in 1994, a disciple of Ludwig von Mises at New York University. "An exception to the rule lies about a thousand miles south of the Rio Grande."[1] The remarkable exception to which Peterson referred was Francisco Marroquín University in Guatemala City, the first neoliberal institution of higher education in Latin America. The "free-market university" was founded by businessman Manuel Ayau and his friends at the beginning of the 1970s, still a time when neoliberals were "prophets in the wilderness," as the historian Eric Hobsbawm quipped,[2] even in business circles.

Development thinking in Latin America in the postwar decades was dominated by import-substitution industrialization and state-led development. After the Great Depression and World War II, the "comparative advantage" paradigm, based on the exchange of raw materials for manufactured products, was no longer considered useful in peripheral countries. The new strategy relied on an active developmental state that fostered domestic industrial production and social reform. Protectionist policies, restriction on capital mobility, and minimum-wage legislation were important elements of the development model that many hoped would mitigate external dependency.[3]

The 1950s and 1960s were also a period of heightened conflict and political polarization in Latin America, notably in Central America. In

1954, Guatemala was the scene of the CIA's first intervention in America's "backyard." The CIA helped orchestrate a coup against democratically elected president Jacobo Arbenz and installed a right-wing military dictatorship. The North American Congress on Latin America (NACLA) asserted that the military coup sought "to reverse the progressive measures of the Revolutionary governments . . . and establish new institutions designed to meet the needs of the Guatemalan bourgeoisie and foreign investors."[4] What followed throughout the 1960s and 1970s was a low-intensity war against political opponents and their suspected supporters. Guatemala became a laboratory for "dirty war" tactics such as forced disappearances, extrajudicial executions, and death-squad killings conducted by professionalized intelligence agencies, government forces, and U.S.-trained paramilitaries. With the popular movements defeated and electoral political strategies blocked, a more insurgent New Left evolved that adopted the principle of armed struggle.[5]

At the same time, socialist thinking quickly advanced among the poor and middle classes and reached new allies even in traditionally conservative cultural institutions such as the Catholic Church. Liberation theology, in particular, relied on the early Christian community spirit of devotion to the poor and liberation from suppression. A doctrine based on a new reading of the Bible, liberation theology was at the same time a vast social movement. It involved significant sectors of the church, grassroots educational movements, and Christian base communities of workers and peasants, all actively committed to popular struggles. In the face of military dictatorship, a realignment among moderate and armed forces of the opposition created new brands of liberation movements across Latin America, frequently based on both socialist and progressive Catholic ideas.[6]

In the face of the formation of such formidable challenges to authoritarian capitalism, Guatemala's key neoliberal protagonist, Manuel Ayau, was not convinced by the nearly exclusive reliance on physical violence to protect his class from the masses in his country. Ayau took a longer perspective instead and identified higher education as an important battleground for shaping political change. He felt it was the universities that educated the nation's future business elite and the rulers of the country where "socialist ideas" had dominated. Apart from the public universities, the private universities carrying the revolutionary spirit across Latin America were founded by Jesuits. In the case of Guatemala, this was the Universidad Rafael Landívar, established in 1961. Well equipped with his own funds generated by business undertakings, Ayau, along with like-minded wealthy followers and linked to transnational neoliberal networks, set out to pursue his goal to found a university in order to overcome the "intellectual crisis of our time."[7]

Francisco Marroquín University, also known under the pet name "Marro," eventually opened its gates in January 1972, with Manuel Ayau as its first rector. This unique university became a competitive center of higher learning in Guatemala, served as an important node in Latin American intellectual circuits, and bestowed social capital to leading neoliberals by way of honorary doctorates and other academic merits. Marro eventually became a model for other similar undertakings in Chile, Argentina, Montenegro (see "The Mediterranean Tiger: How Montenegro Became a Neoliberal Role Model," by Mila Jonjić and Nenad Pantelić in this volume), and the post-Communist Republic of Georgia.

Around fifteen years after its inception, travel writer Anthony Daniels visited the newly built campus of Marroquín University, located in an upper-class district in Guatemala City. Full of admiration, he described an atmosphere "of calm and unashamed high culture…a relief after the determined barbarism of San Carlos," the public university. "The students are well-dressed, fresh-looking and optimistic, in sharp contrast to those of San Carlos, many of whom already have the deep sorrow of perpetual failure marked on their faces. In Francisco Marroquín, all is order and concentration on the task at hand and there are computers everywhere. On the walls there are no political slogans."[8]

Little wonder, since the university was itself a political statement. Visiting the campus, you would encounter the "well-dressed, fresh-looking and optimistic students" walking along the Avenue Mont Pelerin, collecting books at the Ludwig von Mises Library, attending seminars in the Friedrich Hayek or Milton Friedman Lecture Hall, taking a break at the Rose Friedman Terrace, and assembling in the Leonard R. Read Auditorium.

The following chapter digs deeper into the founding history of Marroquín University (UFM). Reviewing the 1950s enables a better understanding of the roots of neoliberalism in Latin America and various modes of interaction between neoliberals on the periphery with the already better-known circles of neoliberals in the Global North. Although some attention has been paid to the role and relevance of neoliberalism in the Global South early on in the historiography of neoliberalism,[9] it is still common to consider European and American figures at the expense of global and local interaction. This approach reproduces the intellectual and social hierarchies of U.S.-centric and Eurocentric perspectives. When Latin America and other places in the Global South are considered, we still find a prevailing perspective that sees it as a "laboratory" for ideas "imported" from the North. Guatemala's Marroquín University is one of the best places to observe instead the multidirectional process of neoliberal interaction in the Americas and beyond.

The chapter is structured as follows. In the first section, I portray the first neoliberal think tank in the country, which was the stepping-stone to the founding of the university, and examine the personal, financial, and institutional ties behind it. The second part is dedicated to the Marroquín University and its rather unusual principles, characteristics, and functioning. In the last section, I consider Marro's role in the war of ideas, more concretely, its successes and failures in terms of policy interventions and long-term effects.

THE BEGINNINGS: A THINK TANK
AND THE MONT PELERIN SOCIETY AS MIDWIVES

When Manuel Ayau (1925–2010) returned to Guatemala in 1950 with a degree in mechanical engineering from Louisiana State University in his pocket, he felt the strong need to do something against what he called the "socialist avalanche"[10] that had swept over the country and the entire region. Together with his friends, all of them also members of the country's landed and business elite, he founded the Center for Economic and Social Studies (CEES) in 1959. Its theoretical orientation was unclear at first.[11] The primary objective was negative: to counter not only "collectivist ideology" and "Marxist-Leninist subversion," but also the mainstream development thinking of the time, import-substitution industrialization under the guidance of an active developmental state. CEES was in the vanguard of mobilizing against protective tariffs and minimum wages, corporate and income taxes, and exchange controls. This agenda was new and radical among right-wing and business circles; even among the founding members, there were considerable differences over subjects such as taxation or minimum wages. Much of the activity of CEES was therefore dedicated to educating its own (entrepreneurial) base through seminars and writings. Its pamphlets (*Tópicos de Actualidad*) assembled short and readily accessible articles criticizing price controls, minimum wages, or agrarian reform and achieved high circulation in Guatemala and beyond.[12]

Although the (neoliberal) Right frames its political projects as national, "right-wing organizations believed they were confronting an enemy that transcended their national borders" and "consciously sought out like-minded organizations that operated beyond their nation."[13] Ayau was no exception. From the very beginning, he started to look for international support for his endeavors. On a business trip to Mexico, his fellow CEES founder Ernesto Rodríguez met with Agustín Navarro and Gustavo R. Velasco from the Institute of

Economic and Social Research,[14] both disciples of Ludwig von Mises and early members of the Mont Pelerin Society, the international network of organized neoliberalism founded in 1947. Navarro and Velasco brought Ayau and Rodríguez, the Guatemala group, into contact with U.S. business journalist Henry Hazlitt and with Pierre Goodrich, the founder of the Liberty Fund in Indianapolis. Goodrich's *Education in a Free Society* (1973), in which he advocated an educational system based strictly on private institutions, became an important inspiration for the institutional design of Marro.[15] Perhaps most important, Navarro and Velasco recommended the Foundation for Economic Education (FEE) in New York to their Guatemalan fellows. From there, they got the intellectual instruction they were looking for: Leonard Read, the founder of FEE, put them into contact with the Austrian economist Mises and his student, Israel M. Kirzner, and later to other prominent neoliberals active in the United States.

Back in Guatemala, Ayau and Rodriguez started a reading circle with Mises's *Human Action* at the top of the list. The businessmen did not have light fare with Mises, but, according to UFM economics professor Julio H. Cole, the Austrians had a comprehensive view—Mises, Hayek, etc. tackled issues of order, morals, and law, and that was what they were looking for. Furthermore, Mises with his clear anti-Communist, antistate and anti-intervention position was comprehensible also for the uninitiated.[16] What made him so attractive for Ayau was the importance he attributed to the intellectual field in general and in particular to higher education. According to Mises, the "academic Progressives" must be fought on their own terrain, and that meant economic education must "unmask their fallacies." "What matters was not to change the ideology of the masses, but to change first the ideology of the intellectual strata, the 'highbrows,' whose mentality determines the content of the simplifications which are held by the 'lowbrows.' . . . If the right men are lacking in the hour of decision, the fate of our civilization is sealed."[17] Mises's statement became Ayau's mission.

CEES translated *Human Action* and other books into Spanish and organized, with the financial support of FEE, lecture tours of Mises, Henry Hazlitt, William H. Hutt, Hans Sennholz, Friedrich Hayek, Gottfried Haberler, and others to Guatemala.[18] Also, the Liberty Fund and the German Friedrich Naumann Foundation for Freedom financed trips of neoliberal scholars to and from the United States and Germany, among others, the visit of Ludwig Erhard, German minister of economic affairs (later chancellor), organized by CEES in 1968.[19]

According to Leonard P. Liggio, it was particularly Mises and his lectures that convinced Ayau and his fellows "that higher education is the most important contested area for shaping social change—and the area in which the socialists have seized most of the ground."[20] But the Mont Pelerin Society (MPS) of which Liggio himself was a member and president (2002 to 2004) was as important as the personal impression left by Mises. UFM economics professor Fritz Thomas described the MPS as an "organization with tentacles," linking people, institutions, and ideas.[21] The MPS provided the neoliberals from Guatemala with what they needed and many of CEES's founding generation became members of the transnational elite network, such as Hilary Arathoon, Ulysses R. Dent, Félix Montes, and of course Manuel Ayau himself, who later on advanced to be the first MPS president from Latin America (1978 to 1980). "If the Mont Pèlerin Society hadn't existed," Ayau writes in his memoirs,

> it is probable that we would have discarded the idea of founding a university, since there were already four in our country. The contact we had with these people in the academic world made us more aware that the intellectual crisis of our time, principally in the universities, was worldwide. Remember that this was in the '60s. MPS members had taken part in academic activities at prestigious universities such as Stanford, Harvard, and others and had personally witnessed their state of decadence.[22]

THE FOUNDING OF MARROQUÍN AND
THE FREEDOM TO TEACH ONLY NEOLIBERALISM

After a first rejection by the authorities,[23] Universidad Francisco Marroquín opened its doors to the first students in January 1972, at a time when General Carlos Arana Osorio ruled the country and the military had occupied San Carlos University with the accusation that it was a "den of terrorists."[24] Right from the beginning, the new university offered degrees in economic sciences and law. One year later, these two faculties were joined by a new theology department, expressing the particular challenge liberation theology posed to the established order, both political and clerical, in Guatemala and in Central America at large.[25]

The founding group of CEES was the nucleus of the new university. Many of them made up the sponsoring committee that took charge of the necessary financial resources. After approval, the committee became the board of trustees, which is probably the most influential body of the university. It is made up of approximately fifty members. They are considered to be "capable of raising funds from the private sector." The trustees ensure financial solvency and that the objectives for which UFM was founded are carried out. While the board of directors is by law the highest authority of a university, the board of trustees elects six of the nine members, including the treasurer.[26]

Among the financiers of UFM were, for example, Enrique and Estuardo Novella. The Novella family has interests in natural resources (minerals, gas, oil), finance, and construction and owns the country's largest cement plant. Enrique Novella was already a member of the advisory board of CEES and later received an honorary doctorate from UFM. Another early donor was Ramón Campollo, a descendent of a sugar family who was at the head of an agro-industrial business empire, and sugar and coffee baron Rudy Weissenberg. Also the brothers Castillo—in the 1980s, probably the richest family in the country—were among the first donors to UFM. Their conglomerate comprises shopping malls, cemeteries, power plants, banks, and beverage companies, among them, Cervecería Centro Americana, the biggest brewery in Central America.

Another important "business linker" was Fernando Linares Beltranena. A lawyer by profession, he belongs to the family networks of the traditional oligarchic nucleus in Guatemala. The MPS member and CEES manager was close to Ayau from the beginning; he became the first dean of the School of Law at UFM. Among the first board members was also Luis Canella Gutiérrez, head of the Canella group (cars and motorcycles, machinery, iron and steel, agro-industry, banking and finance, real estate, and insurance) and president of the Chamber of Commerce of Guatemala and of Central America. The family names indicate that the ambitious project had full support from the country's traditional landed (agrarian) elite, which had largely transformed itself into an agro-industrialist elite with diversified economic activities ranging from finance and energy to industry and services.[27]

Martín Rodríguez Pellecer reports that entrepreneurs from the CEES and UFM founding generation supported the dictatorship of Efraín Ríos Montt (1982 to 1983) who was later declared guilty of genocide and crimes against humanity. Enrique Matheu, one of the founding fathers of CEES, became minister of the economy. Juan Carlos Simons, a director of CEES (1977 to 1994) and a trustee and professor at UFM (1977 to 1985), was a member of the State Council, where he met Ramiro Castillo. Prominent entrepreneurs from Ayau's circles donated funds for counterinsurgency, and the regime thanked them officially—among them, Mario Granai, an early champion and trustee of UFM, Ernesto Rodríguez, founder of CEES, and Carlos Springmühl, member of Ayau's Mises reading circle, and a cofounder and trustee of UFM.[28]

Already existing or newly established links to neoliberal circles and conservative and Christian universities in the United States provided a continuous inflow of visiting professors. That gave the university prestige. The regional meeting of the Mont Pelerin Society taking place in Guatemala in 1972 brought together Ayau and Alberto Benegas Lynch, Jr., an Argentine economist and MPS member. Benegas Lynch taught at UFM for three years and exported the Marro model to Argentina. With assistance from Ayau, Benegas Lynch founded a graduate school of economics and business administration (ESEADE) in Buenos Aires.[29] Besides the MPS network, George Mason University, the public-choice bastion of deregulatory policy, ensured a constant influx of ideas and people. The cadre of Austrians and doyens of law and economics at George Mason were all awarded with honorary doctorates.[30] The Liberty Fund and the U.S. think tanks Cato, Heritage, and Acton Institutes, the Aspen Institute, and the Templeton Foundation were certainly valuable in personal, institutional, and financial matters. UFM funding was assisted by Foundation Francisco Marroquín in Stuart, Florida (established in 1981), and since 2010, by Friends of Universidad Francisco Marroquín, with addresses in Virginia and Alabama, primarily as a way to channel U.S. tax-deductible funds to Guatemala.[31]

Due to the robust financial situation, the university expanded rapidly. Marro now has twelve faculties and a postgraduate center. It offers more than thirty bachelors programs (*licenciaturas*), twenty-six masters programs (*maestrías*) and ten postgraduate programs. Students from the Americas are solicited with correspondence courses. Entrepreneurship is paramount at Marro. Beyond its own studies, the university runs an MBA program together with the Acton School of Business in Austin, Texas. The Kirzner Entrepreneurship Center and other units "support, promote, and celebrate" entrepreneurs and young professionals, offering a broad range of activities and online education. Together with Tulane University, the UFM business school runs a double-degree study program in economics and finance and a master of public finance for lawyers in Panama City. Marro's endeavors to expand its way of seeing and teaching economics beyond borders also has reached Europe. Beside a double-degree masters in collaboration with the Centro de Estudios Superiores Online de Madrid Manuel

Ayau (OMMA), an affiliate in Madrid has offered courses in business administration and entrepreneurship since 2018. The mover and shaker of the ambitious project was Marro's current rector, Spanish-born Gabriel Calzada. He is a disciple of the Austrian school of economics and an MPS member.[32]

In line with the visionaries of UFM, its School of Economic Sciences is heavy on Austrian economic thinking. But Marroquín University impressively illustrates the varieties of neoliberalism. Chicago school economics and monetarism are as present as rational-choice-based neoinstitutionalism; the same holds for the Bloomington and Virginia schools of political economy. Cuban-born Armando de la Torre started the school of political science and introduced public-choice theory and constitutional economics into the curriculum.[33] The busy columnist and dean of the Graduate School of Social Sciences presides over the Public Choice Center of UFM (the Centro para el Análisis de las Decisiones Públicas, or CADEP). James M. Buchanan personally attended the inauguration in 2001, where he was awarded an honorary doctorate. Catholic neoliberals such as Michael Novak and Robert A. Sirico, the founder of the Acton Institute for the Study of Religion and Liberty, who received honorary doctorates in 1993 and 2001, respectively, are taught alongside Ayn Rand, an avowed atheist. All of these different neoliberal thought collectives find accommodation under the university's wide umbrella.

The Henry Hazlitt Center deserves special mention, because it has a very specific role within UFM. It provides all students, regardless of discipline, be it architecture, psychology, or medical science, with core courses in the economic, legal, and philosophical principles of neoliberal theories. Courses are obligatory and must be paid for separately, in addition to the tuition fees for the studies selected. Course syllabi are dominated by Austrian thinking and the writings of Hayek and Mises, Rothbard and Hazlitt.[34]

Interestingly enough, the exclusive and one-sided orientation toward a neoliberal thought style is sold as academic freedom. The founding document of the university defines academic freedom as "the right of persons or groups of persons to teach any art or science." In a second step, the mission statement clearly defines that UFM "has the right to decide the contents of the courses it offers in view of what it holds to be true, false, useful or irrelevant.... Those professors who agree to teach what the University wishes become members of the faculty." Those who want to present other teachings or content should do that elsewhere: "Universidad Francisco Marroquín recognizes the academic freedom of any faculty member to teach what is contrary to the University's philosophy or its policies, as long as this is done elsewhere and under someone else's auspices."[35] "There's complete freedom—but not to teach nonsense," travel writer Anthony Daniels quoted Ayau as saying. And asked who decides what is nonsense, Ayau replied: "We do, the trustees."[36]

That said, UFM is definitely a teaching university and training institution, rather than a research university. Unlike neoliberal scholars in Chile and Argentina, for example, UFM teachers and graduates do not stand out through their own publications and original theoretical reasoning. Ayau himself wrote a textbook and devoted himself to easily understandable presentations of liberal doctrines and op-ed pieces. "Simplify and reduce" seemed to be his motto when he "translated" liberal orthodoxy into cheap lines: "The rich are not rich because the poor are poor. Rather, the rich are rich because the poor are less poor." Or: "In our imperfect world, not all become equally rich, but the most important thing is to reduce poverty. And because this can only be achieved through inequality, it is very cruel to insist on equality."[37]

Unlike "popularizing" neoliberal institutions such as the Foundation for Economic Education, Marro surely serves more for the diffusion and less for a transfer of neoliberal ideas in both directions. This corresponds to the founding mission of Ayau, which was to educate the country's future economic and political elite. Policy and functions related to the public, or in other words, ways to carry out the war of ideas, appear more important than research and discovery. What follows evaluates how successful Marroquín University has been in this respect.

MARRO AND THE WAR OF IDEAS: SUCCESSES AND FAILURES

Longtime rector of Marroquín University and MPS member Giancarlo Ibárgüen was highly satisfied with the multiplier effects of the university. In an article in 2008, he stated that columns from the "UFM family" appear regularly in the press and that UFM members dominate the sphere of talk radio. The "Explorations of Liberty," the Spanish version of the Liberty Fund colloquia held at UFM, reach new intellectual communities and provide excellent networking opportunities. UFM graduates are able to put abstract ideas into simple language that is understood by all. In Ibárgüen's view, UFM has fostered a critical mass of liberal thinkers who span generations and professions.[38] The success of diffusion and networking is the result of think tanks that were founded by core figures of the "UFM family." Rather than original thinkers, they turned out to be hustling think-tank entrepreneurs.

Foremost here is the Center of National Economic Studies (Centro de Investigaciones Económicas Nacionales, CIEN) founded at the beginning of the 1980s. The timing was no accident. CIEN became directly involved in the structural adjustment programs of the international financial institutions carrying out the so-called Washington Consensus. While CEES is dedicated to "pure doctrine" and keeps distance from day-to-day politics, CIEN is a "do tank." With active support from "Chicago Boys" from Chile, CIEN personnel took up public-policy issues.[39] CIEN is packed with UFM graduates with access to political and media agents; they engage in setting agendas and framing public discourse, present reform proposals, and are directly involved in legislative processes.

Joint successes of CIEN and UFM in terms of concrete policy action relate to monetary and central bank reform, a subject that was pushed by Ayau for decades. In his view, central banks guided by Keynesian economists and the developmentalist ideas of Raúl Prebisch "expropriate the foreign exchange earned by the citizens."[40] In line with the policy prescriptions of the Washington Consensus, interest rates were liberalized in 1989. In 1993, a constitutional reform prohibited the central bank from lending to the government. Finally, in 2000, capital markets were liberalized and the Law of Free Negotiation of Currencies was approved. Bank accounts could now be held in any currency. The same bill legalized the dollar and other currencies for most transactions in the country.[41]

Another important battlefield was the privatization of public services. Major successes were achieved in the second half of the nineties and the years thereafter, when far-reaching waves of privatization were enacted, particularly under the governments of Álvaro Arzú (1996 to 2000) and Óscar Berger (2004 to 2008), both entrepreneurs from upper-class families. Ayau himself exerted a great deal of pressure to proceed with the privatization of the telecommunications and energy sectors. In 1993, Ayau was appointed commissioner of the state's privatization and demonopolization office, but trade unions successfully demanded his removal. A young member of Congress and UFM graduate did better. He lobbied successfully, was appointed head of the state telephone company, and involved—together with UFM rector Ibárgüen—Chicago economist Pablo Spiller, who prepared a legislative proposal. In 1996, Congress eventually passed one of the most liberal telecommunications laws in the world.[42]

Always high on the political agenda of Marro neoliberals was blocking every attempt to reform the tax system in a progressive direction. Since the 1960s, Ayau has denounced taxes as unfair because they "discriminate against those who earn more" and damage economic progress.[43] "No more taxes" ("No más impuestos") is a perennial demand in the political campaigns of CIEN. It is quite successful, as the figures show: in terms of state revenues through taxes, Guatemala is continuously in last place among Latin American countries, with a tax-to-GDP ratio of around 10 percent in 2016. (The Latin American average is 23 percent). The Berger government in which figures from CIEN played a significant role was particularly "successful" in dropping the rate from 12 percent to the current rate.[44] Other political projects met resistance or failed. For example, the plan to introduce a school voucher system, an idea that Ayau adopted from his close friend Milton Friedman, and an extended scope for private education providers was eventually turned down. When a CIEN affiliate became minister of education under Berger, a decentralization of the school system, accompanied by a disempowerment of the teachers' unions, was enacted, but reversed again by the following government.[45]

In 2014, think-tank entrepreneurs from UFM founded the Instituto Fe y Libertad (Belief and Freedom Institute).[46] The central figure in the think tank is the daughter of Manuel Ayau, Inés Ayau, an Orthodox nun with a doctorate in theology from UFM. The leading staff and advisory council is made up of people associated with UFM and CEES (Armando de la Torre and UFM treasurer Ramón Parellada, for example), businessmen, and hard-right religious leaders from different religious communities. On the international board of advisers we find Alejandro Chafuen, longtime president of the Atlas Network and a member of Opus Dei, Robert A. Sirico, Peter J. Boettke, and Samuel Gregg. All of them, including Parellada, are MPS members. Fe y Libertad disseminates theologically inspired political interventions on issues related to the economy and welfare, and details the synergies between entrepreneurial capitalism and Christianity and Judaism. By aligning religious thought with neoliberal principles, it reaches out for a new following that joins forces in service of varieties of capitalism that are characterized by social-conservative and traditional and illiberal aspirations.

Regardless of this impressive record, Marro's founder, Manuel Ayau, was not satisfied with his achievements, as he told his disciples prior to his death.[47] While he acknowledged that UFM contributed to training future managers and entrepreneurs, he had expected greater influence on Guatemalan politics. Also, his own foray into politics had not met with thorough success.

Ayau was a member of Guatemala's most ultraconservative party, the National Liberation Movement (Movimiento de Liberación Nacional, MLN), and part of the government bench of General Carlos Arana Osorio. The MLN and Arana were directly linked to paramilitary death squads. Ayau left the government due to disagreements, but remained in Congress throughout the whole mandate period from 1970 to 1974. In 1990, he ran for president under the banner of the MLN, but withdrew three months before the elections. Pushed by the business elite, he instead sought the vice presidency. He didn't succeed, but made the 1991 run-off election, coming up with a respectable showing at the polls.

During the decade of the 2000s, Ayau and his colleagues from UFM and the Fatherland League (Liga pro Patria) spearheaded an effort to revise the Guatemalan constitution to strengthen property rights and the rule of law. The proposal was very much inspired by Hayek's constitution of liberty and the fiscal constitutionalism of public-choice theory. Among other things, the so-called "ProReforma movement" proposed to introduce a double-chamber system. A newly established Senate, resembling Hayek's "Council of Elders," was designed to consist of experienced men over fifty years of age, elected for fifteen years and entrusted with extended power. A prohibition of affirmative action or redistributive measures was to be enshrined in the constitution. The proposal received the support of seventy thousand signatures, but was not discussed in Congress. The initiative had already lost momentum when Ayau died in 2010.[48]

The story would be incomplete if Ayau's semipublic activities were not mentioned. Ayau and CEES founding member Ernesto Rodríguez were part of the Asociación de Amigos del País (Friends of the Country), a pressure group of businessmen and landowners in the 1980s.[49] The "Amigos" aimed at putting an end to the (international) isolation of the government due to severe human rights violations.[50] They also were the organized Guatemalan group supporting Ronald Reagan for president and collected considerable money among the Guatemalan propertied class, money that was—of course not directly—transmitted to the Republican Party. As Allan Nairn has shown, Ayau was also on the board of the Guatemala Freedom Foundation, an ultraright organization that lobbied for the resumption of military aid to Guatemala.[51]

CONCLUSION

Guatemala had one of the longest-standing and most brutal authoritarian regimes in Latin America, and yet it also enjoyed consistently high ranking on the neoliberal-created Economic Freedom of the World indices. How to explain the puzzle? The military was appreciated by the economic elite as a way to combat armed struggle and (Indigenous) social mobilizations. At a certain point of history, however, the costs of authoritarianism outweighed the risk of elections—not least because the military pushed for tax increases to finance the counterinsurgency war and showed entrepreneurial ambitions. Reacting to the guerrilla uprisings and concerned about interventionist militaries, the core of the private sector saw the urgency of a new way of doing politics to assure the survival of their preferred model of accumulation. It was not only the national political scene, but the global spread of neoliberalism that played a major role in convincing (not only) the Guatemalan economic elite to support a transition to democracy. The elite's commitment to regime change was restricted to a "protected," "controlled," or "limited democracy," however, and to governments that did not threaten their economic interests. The pact of transition was dominated by the elites, and the peace accord, finally enacted in 1996, was signed by a right-wing president, Alvaro Arzú.[52]

Ayau and his circle did not hesitate to support politically and financially far-right and even paramilitary activities and to take up posts in military governments. But Ayau's long-term strategy of creating a university and think tanks proved to be a second important pillar to sustain elite rule. The first phase was informed by an aggressive anticommunism and antidevelopmentalism. Through its intimate connections with the centers of power, UFM became an intellectual and political weapon in times of insurgency and counterinsurgency in Guatemala and in the region. The second phase saw an "ideological roll-out" of neoliberal doctrines. The neoliberal turn in development policies turned Marro and its "do tank" CIEN into key actors in national politics. Their expertise extended the policy prescriptions of the U.S. governments, starting with the Reagan administration, and the international financial institutions such as (nontraditional) export promotion, privatization, and liberalization—in short, the Washington Consensus—into domestic political arenas. The Washington Consensus agenda and free-trade treaties eventually became a more effective means to protect economic interests than the military and a repressive state apparatus.

Because of its pluralism, neoliberalism provides elites with an effective ideology and concrete routes to governance. Organized by a division of labor, Marro and its offspring institutions comprehensively serve this task. UFM is certainly the ideological powerhouse of the Guatemalan bourgeoisie. Although not necessarily a success story in the world of academic research, Marro succeeded in providing a safe haven in higher education for the propertied classes and a seedbed for neoliberal policy efforts. Marro and the think-tank network can be characterized as a "trench" of capital, to paraphrase Antonio Gramsci. Ayau and his community of collective intellectuals have successfully erected well-equipped fortresses to combat adversarial viewpoints—even if it was not possible to infiltrate state structures or fully dominate politics in the way Ayau had hoped. His companion Leonard P. Liggio has consolation for him: Ayau made an "investment in permanent change." "One may need to be more patient for the dividends, but they will be real and permanent."[53] In this light, Marro might be one of the most significant original contributions to the countermovement against those who challenge the principles of a neoliberal order.

1. William H. Peterson, "A Free-Market-University: Universidad Francisco Marroquín Is Shaping Social Change in Guatemala," Foundation for Economic Education, April 1, 1994, https://fee.org/articles/a-free-market-university.

2. Eric Hobsbawm, *The Age of Extremes: A History of the World, 1914–1991* (New York: Vintage Books, 1994), pp. 176–77.

3. Cristóbal Kay, "Development Theory: The Latin American Pivot," in Henry Veltmeyer and Paul Bowles, eds., *The Essential Guide to Critical Development Studies* (London: Routledge, 2018), pp. 73–83.

4. Stephen M. Streeter, *Managing the Counterrevolution: The United States and Guatemala, 1954–1961* (Athens: Ohio University Center for International Studies, 2000), p. 2.

5. Greg Grandin, *The Last Colonial Massacre: Latin America in the Cold War* (Chicago: University of Chicago Press, 2011).

6. Leonardo Boff, *Cry for the Earth, Cry for the Poor* (New York: Orbis Books, 1997).

7. Manuel F. Ayau, *Memoirs and Comments on the Founding of Universidad Francisco Marroquín and Its Antecedents* (Guatemala: UFM, 1992), p. 13.

8. Anthony Daniels, *"Sweet Waist of America": Journeys around Guatemala* (London: Arrow Books, 1990), pp. 43–44.

9. "The Origins of Neoliberalism in Latin America: A Special Issue," Maria Eugenia Romero Sotelo, ed., *PSL Quarterly* 72.289 (2019); Romero Sotelo, *Orígenes del neoliberalismo en México: La Escuela Austriaca* (México: Fondo de Cultura Económica, 2016).

10. Manuel F. Ayau, "The Role of Higher Education in Guatemala," in John C. Goodman and Ramona Marotz-Baden, eds., *Fighting the War of Ideas in Latin America* (Dallas: National Center for Policy Analysis, 1990), p. 138.

11. Interview with Fritz Thomas, professor of economics at Universidad Francisco Marroquín, current president of the sponsoring committee, and dean of the School of Economic Sciences from 1988 to 1996 and again from 2006 to 2015. Interview conducted by the author at the UFM campus, February 15, 2017.

12. CEES, "Guatemala: 50 aniversario del CEES," *HACER Latin American*

News, December 8, 2009, http://www.hacer.org/latam/guatemala-50
-aniversario-del-cees-cees; Ayau, "The Role of Higher Education in Guatemala," pp. 141–42; Ayau, *Memoirs and Comments*, p. 11; interview with
Edgar Ortiz Romero, executive director of CEES, conducted by the author,
February 16, 2017.

13. Margaret Power, "Afterword for Pensar las derechas en América Latina
en el siglo XX," *Nuevo Mundo, Mundos Nuevos*, January 25, 2016, p. 6, http://
journals.openedition.org/nuevomundo/68922 .

14. Sotelo, *Orígenes del neoliberalismo en México*, pp. 200–206.

15. Interview with Julio H. Cole, conducted by the author on the UFM
campus, February 22, 2017.

16. Ibid.

17. Ludwig von Mises, *Economic Freedom and Interventionism: An Anthology
of Articles and Essays* (Indianapolis: Liberty Fund, 1990), pp. 206 and 211;
see also Mises, *Human Action: A Treaties on Economics* (San Francisco: Fox &
Wilkes, 1994), ch. 9, "The Role of Ideas," pp. 177–93.

18. Ayau, *Memoirs and Comment*, p. 12.

19. The Naumann Foundation, associated with the Free Democratic Party,
generously financed CEES from German public tax funds. Between 1965 and
1968, 860,000 deutsche marks (equal to 215,000 U.S. dollars at that time)
were donated to CEES, a fact about which the German embassy was not entirely
happy. In a letter to the Foreign Ministry, the ambassador reported that the
development benefit of these contributions was very low, because CEES
focused predominantly on seminars with scholars that attracted only a small
audience. Moreover, the ambassador quoted from a CEES publication in
which teaching social justice was equated with the promotion of communism,
socialism, and violence. The ambassador criticized the antisocial character
of CEES publications and assumed the founding activities of the Naumann
Foundation detrimental to Germany's foreign policy. Letter from the German
ambassador in Guatemala, Wilhelm Helmuth van Almsick, to the German
Foreign Office, April 8, 1968, pp. 4 and 5, Politisches Archiv des Auswärtigen
Amts, Berlin, B90-600 I(V1) bd. 716.

20. Leonard P. Liggio, "A University with a Future," Foundation for

Economic Education, July 1, 1990, https://fee.org/articles/a-university-with
-a-future, p. 1.

21. Interview with Fritz Thomas, conducted by the author, February 15,
2017.

22. Ayau, *Memoirs and Comments*, p. 13.

23. Private universities had and still have to be approved by the Consejo de
la Enseñanza Privada Superior (Council of Private Higher Education), on which
delegates from the public university and private universities have a seat. The
rectors of the public Universidad San Carlos and of Jesuit Universidad Landívar
opposed a first attempt for political and financial reasons, as Juárez-Paz
states. See Rigoberto Juárez-Paz, *El nacimiento de una universidad* (Guatemala:
Ediciones Papiro), pp. 19–20; see also Ayau, *Memoirs and Comments*, p. 22.

24. Álvaro Velásquez, *Ideología burguesa y democracia: Una aproximación
al Movimiento Libertario en Guatemala y sus discursos* (Guatemala: Serviprensa,
2014), p. 101.

25. According to Goodman and Marotz-Baden, UFM and its School of Theology ran satellite schools in Costa Rica, Honduras, El Salvador, and Nicaragua.
They were mainly dedicated to the cultivation of priests. See Goodman and
Marotz-Baden, editors' introduction to Ayau, "The Role of Higher Education in
Guatemala," in *Fighting the War of Ideas in Latin America*, p. 137. In 1999, the
faculty was transferred to another university. UFM now offers public theologi-
cal studies under the auspices of the Escuela Superior de Ciencias Sociales
and its director, Armando de la Torre; see Universidad Francisco Marroquín,
"Diplomado en Teología," https://escs.ufm.edu/buena-nueva.

26. Ayau, *Memoirs and Comments*, pp. 74 and 24; list of trustees from 1971
to 2006, pp. 96–97.

27. Ayau, *Memoirs and Comments*, pp. 19, 21, 25, 37, and the author's own
investigations. For insights into the interlinked, transnationalized business
groups, see Benedicte Bull, Fulvio Castellacci, and Yuri Kasahara, *Business
Groups and Transnational Capitalism in Central America: Economic and Political
Strategies* (Basingstoke: Palgrave Macmillan, 2014). For a historic perspective
on family ties and economic groups in Guatemala, see Marta Elena Casaús
Arzú, *Guatemala: Linaje y racism* (Guatemala: F&G Editores, 2018).

28. Martín Rodríguez Pellecer, *Los militares y la élite: La alianza que ganó la guerra, 1982/1983* (Guatemala: Plaza Pública, 2013), pp. 15 and 27. See also Ayau, *Memoirs and Comments*, pp. 10, 19, 21, and the list of trustees following p. 96.

29. Ayau, *Memoirs and Comments*, pp. 28–29.

30. Henry Manne (1987), Leonard P. Liggio (1990), James M. Buchanan (2001), Walter Williams (2003), Vernon Smith (2004), Lawrence White (2011), and Peter J. LiBoettke (2012).

31. Ayau writes about "conversations in Germany and with members of certain universities to get support through donations from England and the United States." See Ayau, *Memoirs and Comments*, p. 84.

32. Calzada is founding president of the Juan de Mariana Institute, a think tank dedicated to Austrian economics located in Madrid. He is a high-profile representative of market environmentalism and climate-change skepticism and prides himself on the fact that one of his studies helped to bury a green jobs initiative in the United States.

33. Andrés Marroquín and Fritz Thomas, "Classical Liberalism in Guatemala," *Econ Journal Watch* 12.3 (2015), p. 465.

34. Syllabi of the core courses Ethics of Liberty, Economic Process I and II, and the Philosophy of Hayek and Mises are available at the website of the Centro Henry Hazlitt at https://chh.ufm.edu/mejores-practicas.

35. Universidad Francisco Marroquín, *Philosophy Statement*, p. 29; English and Spanish versions available at https://www.ufm.edu/Ideario. In a meeting with the High Council of San Carlos University in November 1970 that was part of the accreditation process, Ayau defined academic freedom quite differently. He responded to criticism that the teaching orientation of the planned university "might be dogmatically directed" by saying that "a particular point of view will not be defended as it is by the Center for Economic and Social Studies [CEES]. The University should have academic freedom. It should provide all points of view and theories, and they should be presented by persons who believe in them and not by those who criticize them.... We consider socialism to be a very important ideological tendency that has had influence throughout the world and that everyone should learn about it from someone who defends it and not from someone who criticizes it. It would be dishonest on our part to

present a partial perspective to the students." Transcript of the meeting in Ayau, *Memoirs and Comments*, pp. 85–86.

36. Daniels, *"Sweet Waist of America,"* p. 45.

37. Manuel F. Ayau, "La Falacia empobrecedora," *Tópicos de Actualidad* 513 (1985), and *Sobre la desigualdad* (Guatemala: CEES, 2007), quoted in Velásquez, *Ideología burguesa y democracia*, p. 103, my translation.

38. Giancarlo Ibárgüen, "University Francisco Marroquín: A Model for Winning Liberty," in Colleen Dyble, ed., *Taming Leviathan: Waging the War of Ideas around the World* (London: Institute of Economic Affairs, 2008), pp. 85–86.

39. Interview with Hugo Maul and Maria Isabel Bonilla from CIEN, conducted by the author on the UFM campus, February 23, 2017.

40. Ayau, "The Role of Higher Education in Guatemala," p. 140.

41. Marroquín and Thomas, "Classical Liberalism in Guatemala," pp. 469–70.

42. Ibárgüen, "University Francisco Marroquín," pp. 86–87; Carlos Sabino and Wayne Leighton, *Privatization of Telecommunications in Guatemala: A Tale Worth Telling* (Guatemala: UFM, 2013), pp. 25–27; Benedicte Bull, *Globalización, Estado y Privatización: Proceso político de las reformas de telecomunicaciones en Centroamérica* (San José: FLACSO, 2008), pp. 61–63, 85, 103. In El Salvador, Ayau succeeded more quickly. There, the extreme right-wing party Arena came to power in 1989, and Alfredo Mena Lagos, a disciple of Hayek and Mises, was appointed chief of the presidential commission on the modernization of the state. Mena Lagos contracted his fellow, Ayau, and together they initiated a far-reaching privatization program supported by the U.S. Agency for International Development, the World Bank and the Banco Interamericano de Desarrollo, the Inter-American Development Bank. See Bull, *Globalización, Estado y Privatización*, pp. 102–103; José Fernando Valdez, *El gobierno de las élites globales: Cómo se organiza el consentimiento. La experiencia del Triángulo Norte* (Guatemala: Editorial Cara Parens, 2015), pp. 136–37.

43. Manuel F. Ayau, *Algunas consideraciones del impuesto sobre la renta* (Guatemala: Centro de Estudios Económicos y Sociales, 1960), http://www.biblioteca.cees.org.gt/topicos/web/topic-005.html.

44. The World Bank, "Tax Revenue (% of GDP): International Monetary Fund, Government Finance Statistics Yearbook and Data Files, and World Bank and OECD GDP Estimates," https://data.worldbank.org/indicator/GC.TAX .TOTL.GD.ZS.

45. Marroquín and Thomas, "Classical Liberalism in Guatemala," p. 471.

46. See Instituto Fe y Libertad, https://feylibertad.org.

47. Marroquín and Thomas, "Classical Liberalism in Guatemala," p. 472.

48. Ibid., pp. 472–74. See also http://muso.ufm.edu/images/b/bb/Pro _reforma.pdf (Spanish version) and https://muso.ufm.edu/en/wp-content /uploads/2017/11/ProReforma.pdf (English version) for an overview of the project.

49. Former Vice President Villagrán Kramer accused ten to fifteen members of the "Amigos" of being "directly linked with organized terror." See Jonathan Marshall, Peter Dale Scott, and Jane Hunter, *The Iran-Contra Connection: Secret Teams and Covert Operations in the Reagan Era* (Boston: South End Press, 1987), p. 53.

50. They traveled frequently to Miami and Washington to target politicians. Ayau took part in a "public relations mission" to Washington in 1979. It is reported that he and Roberto Alejos Arzú, a Guatemalan sugar industrialist and head of the Amigos, personally met Ronald Reagan. Reagan later described Ayau as "one of the few people...who understands what is going on down there." See Marshall, Scott, and Hunter, *The Iran-Contra Connection*, p. 53, and Peter Dale Scott, "Contragate: Reagan, Foreign Money, and the Contra Deal," *Crime and Social Justice*, no. 27–28 (1987), p. 127, with reference to various sources.

51. Allan Nairn, "Reagan Administration's Links to Guatemala's Terrorist Government," *Covert Action Quarterly*, Summer 1989, http://www.hartford-hwp.com/archives/47/160.html. See also Luis Solano, "La franja transversal del norte: Neocolonización en marcha," *El Observador* 2.7 (2007), p. 14.

52. Avri Beard, "Neoliberalism and Democratization in El Salvador and Guatemala," paper prepared for the twenty-fifth meeting of the Latin American Studies Association, Las Vegas, October 7–9, 2004.

53. Liggio, "A University with a Future," p. 2.

CHAPTER TEN

The Mediterranean Tiger:
How Montenegro Became a Neoliberal Role Model

Mila Jonjić & Nenad Pantelić

The end of the Cold War marked the beginning of an unprecedented socioeconomic transformation of Eastern Europe. In less than two decades, Eastern European countries went from laggards to forerunners of neoliberal policy implementation.[1] Beneath the general trend, we have only few detailed studies of neoliberal individuals and groups in Eastern Europe that shaped the transformation period in their respective countries.[2] This chapter fills part of the gap by exploring the contributions of neoliberals during the transition and state-building period in Montenegro. In concurrence with the goal of this volume, we introduce new actors from the European periphery and their organizations while contextualizing them in the broad international neoliberal movement.[3]

But why focus on Montenegro, a small country on the periphery of the European Union, in the first place? While the countries of former Yugoslavia have seen ebbs and flows of liberal economic thought in their respective histories,[4] Montenegro is particularly interesting for the extensive number of neoliberal policy reforms and institutional transformations that were accomplished between the late 1990s and the first decade of the twenty-first century under the supervision of neoliberal academics. In contrast with other countries such as Romania, where autonomous actors without deep roots in the international neoliberal community were the main figures driving institutional change, or with countries where neoliberal ideas never ventured far beyond the discursive level, the institutional transformation in Montenegro was quite different.

In Montenegro, an influential and effective network of academics centered on Veselin Vukotić, a former government official and university professor, was involved in designing, executing, and supervising neoliberal policy reforms ranging from monetary policy to privatizations and tax policy. Vukotić and his group established ties to foreign neoliberal actors and organizations, profited from their experience and knowledge, and actively participated in the exchange of ideas in the international neoliberal community. For example, we count at least six members of the Mont Pelerin Society (MPS) from Montenegro, all of whom are or were involved in the overall reform process, often in key positions.[5]

The strong neoliberal presence on the ground has had consequences. The influence on the transition process was well documented by Vukotić and his partners,[6] and their work did not escape public scrutiny, either.[7] Perhaps their overall achievement may be best summarized by the fact that between 2005 and 2010, Montenegro improved its position in the Heritage Foundation and *Wall Street Journal* Economic Freedom Index from the ninetieth to the forty-third position.[8] It was hailed as the "Mediterranean Tiger" for achieving rapid reforms.[9] In the area of tax policy, Montenegro even became a neoliberal leader, or as a major local newspaper put it, when it comes to cutting taxes Montenegro is "more Catholic than the pope."[10]

The reform process also happened under very specific background conditions.[11] First, the Democratic Party of Socialists (DPS) has ruled the country since 1991 under its leader, Milo Đukanović, whose functions have alternated between prime minister and president with only short interruptions since the early 1990s.[12] This uninterrupted political dominance meant that neoliberal reforms happened under different political circumstances than in the neighboring states with electoral turnover. Second, Montenegro became independent only in

2006. Though Montenegro did not need to build many institutions from scratch, since it was a federal state in Yugoslavia with substantive rights, the path toward independence did provide an opportunity to shape the long-term trajectory of the country during a time of neoliberal ascendance in Eastern Europe.

In this chapter, the genesis and spread of neoliberalism is examined through the work of individuals, organizations, and networks associated with the Mont Pelerin Society (MPS), the Atlas Network, and related organizations, a methodological approach that has become prominent with the work of Philip Mirowski and Dieter Plehwe.[13] The chapter is focused on the first two decades following the breakup of the Socialist Federative Republic of Yugoslavia and covers the activities of Veselin Vukotić and associates. While necessarily focused on certain persons and aspects, it aims to present a detailed showcase of neoliberal influence in an organized, successful, and well-connected network in the region.

We proceed in three steps. First, we provide an overview of the institution-building process, including the key neoliberal figures and their organizations. Second, we describe the influences on the reform process, specifically highlighting the rationale, controversy, and networks behind it. Third, we examine the private University of Donja Gorica as a special case of neoliberal entrepreneurship and institution building.[14]

AFTER YUGOSLAVIA: BUILDING NEOLIBERAL INSTITUTIONS

The Socialist Federative Republic of Yugoslavia developed a unique market-socialist system in postwar Europe. The country was growing strongly during the first decades, but in the aftermath of the 1970s oil shocks, the macroeconomic situation deteriorated fast. After a disastrous decade of stagflation and debt crisis, the last Yugoslav government, led by Ante Marković, was planning a substantial transformation of the economy, fulfilling all main parts of the Washington Consensus program.[15] An important part of the agenda was the responsibility of the minister for privatization and entrepreneurship. This position was given to Veselin Vukotić,[16] a party member and economics professor who specialized in statistics and labor productivity and who already had accumulated political experience by being part of the regional government of Montenegro under Prime Minister Vuko Vukadinović (1985 to 1988).

Yugoslavia had a decades-long experience with (market-)liberal reforms, its economists had considerable knowledge and exchange with "Western" neoclassical economists,[17] and there were socialist critics and market-liberal exiles such as Ljubo Sirc and Svetozar (Steve) Pejovich (MPS member in the early 2000s) whose work gained some attention. This pointed to favorable conditions for substantial market-liberal reform, but by the time the government agenda was gaining steam, the country was already breaking up politically, the reforms stopped, and the (neo)liberal economists' hour was cut short.[18] Vukotić went back to academia and became a tenured professor of economic statistics, entrepreneurship, and economic philosophy at the University of Montenegro in Podgorica. However, this was by no means the end of his career. Over the next three decades, Vukotić engaged successfully in free-market advocacy, institution building, founding enterprises, and economic consultancy. For his industrious work, he was recognized in the neoliberal community as a "Freedom Champion" and became part of the board of directors of MPS which he had joined in 2002–2003.[19]

When Vukotić was an assistant professor in the 1980s, he was already organizing a group of like-minded students. The project name was "University Tribune," and one of the participants was Milo Đukanović. This was followed by the creation of the postgraduate studies Entrepreneurial Economy program in 1992 at the University of Montenegro. The program was based on the tradition of the Austrian school of economics, and a number of academics with neoliberal roots helped set it up, for example, Leonard P. Liggio (the Atlas Network),

John H. Moore (Grove City College), Enrico Colombatto (University of Turin) and Steve Pejovich (Texas A&M).[20] The aim of the program was to teach and discuss neoliberal ideas, and many of the participating students and organizers/teaching assistants ended up in key political and administrative roles, such as the former ministers Milorad Katnić, Igor Lukšić, Petar Ivanović, and Vladimir Kavarić.[21] Additionally, in 2002, the economic journal *Entrepreneurial Economy* was established by Vukotić's associates and former students.

One of the figures involved in the postgraduate studies program and the journal was Petar Ivanović. Born in Belgrade and educated in the United States, Ivanović is a member of the Mont Pelerin Society and the U.S. domestic libertarian/conservative debating organization, the Philadelphia Society, as well as the more technocratically oriented Global Development Network. He filled multiple roles in government, having served as deputy prime minister for a brief period in 2016, as minister for agriculture and rural development (2012 to 2016), as chief economic adviser to the prime minister (2009 to 2010), and as CEO of the Montenegrin Investment Promotion Agency (2005 to 2012).[22] Before he was active in government, Ivanović became an important partner for Vukotić in building free-market institutions in Montenegro. They cofounded the Institute for Entrepreneurship and Economic Development (IPER) in 1993.[23] The institute has functioned among other things as a facilitator for the exchange of ideas within the neoliberal community in Montenegro. The IPER has received an award (Initiative in Public Relations) from the Atlas Network for organizing the conference "Parallels of Economic Reforms in Slovakia and in Montenegro" with the Slovakia-based Hayek Foundation.[24] Recently, IPER has mainly devoted its energies to entrepreneurship promotion through various projects, targeting young people and other specific audiences.[25]

An even more important collaboration between Ivanović and Vukotić commenced several years later when they founded the Institute for Strategic Studies and Prognoses (ISSP) in 1997–1998, the first and major comprehensive free-market think tank in Montenegro. The

ISSP provided a home for market-liberal intellectuals as researchers and contributors, with staff largely recruited from the Entrepreneurial Economy postgraduate program. The funding came from the United States.[26] In collaboration with other experts, the ISSP prepared and laid out many of the reform programs that became part of the governmental agenda, such as the privatization plan and the monetary reform that replaced the Serbian dinar with the German mark.[27] The influence of the ISSP on policy was far reaching, according to Vukotić. He wrote that "the ISSP coordinated the work on the Agenda of Economic Reforms 2002–2006 and the Agenda of Economic Reforms 2002–2007. We proposed the Agenda of Economic Reforms 2007–2011, which contained the outlook for the Montenegrin economy and society until 2025. After minor changes, these were adopted as official government documents."[28] The institute is still active, and besides publishing books, policy studies, and working papers, it also produces economic outlooks in cooperation with the European Agency for Reconstruction. The research area is wide ranging, including European integration, labor markets, immigration, and environmental policies.[29]

But there were still other attempts at spreading free-market ideas. The "Christmas Talks" invented by Vukotić in the 1990s have provided a yearly round table for scholarly and policy discussions, and the Miločerski Razvojni Forum organized by the Montenegrin Association of Economists and Managers also provides an annual forum for discussions. Apart from Vukotić as the president of the association and other Montenegrin members, there are also foreign neoliberals present on the board and at other meetings: Barbara Kolm from Austria, Jose Pinera from Chile, Eduardo Mayora from Guatemala,[30] and Yoshinori Shimizu from Japan, among others.[31]

THE REFORM PROCESS: (RE)MAKING THE STATE IN MONTENEGRO

The building of neoliberal institutions in Montenegro started in the midst of the civil war in Yugoslavia, when major reforms were halted and the GDP shrank to 39 percent of prewar production. Once the war ended, a split within the ruling socialist party DPS occurred when Milo Đukanović, a student of Vukotić, established himself as the leader of the pro-Western, anti-Milošević group. His wing of the party emerged victorious and initiated a reorientation toward market-liberalization politics in Montenegro as the 1990s ended.[32] The first milestone in the reform process was currency reform. During the 1990s, Yugoslavia experienced a hyperinflation episode, and while prices were eventually stabilized, the reputation of the dinar was damaged, and savings and transactions switched to other, more trustworthy currencies, especially the German mark. Coupled with a growing rift between Montenegro and Serbian elites regarding fiscal and monetary policy, this set the background for reform.

In retrospect, monetary reform would prove a first important step toward an independent Montenegro, but it is also interesting for a different reason, namely, the fact that three different options were discussed: creating a new currency, the "perper," a currency-board solution, and outright "dollarization" by adopting the deutsche mark as the new currency. The first solution was promoted by some domestic bankers; the currency-board solution was initially promoted by Steve H. Hanke; and the third solution, which was eventually adopted, direct adoption of the deutsche mark without a currency board, was promoted by Vukotić and his associates.[33] Hanke, an MPS member and economist at Johns Hopkins University, served as a senior economist on Reagan's Council of Economic Advisers (1981 to 1982) and became an international currency-reform expert advising many countries, including Montenegro (1999 to 2003), Lithuania (1994 to 1996), Bulgaria (1997 to 2002), Venezuela (1995 to 1996), Indonesia (1998), Ecuador, Albania, Kazakhstan, the United Arab Emirates, Bosnia-Herzegovina, and Yugoslavia.[34]

Before he served as a state counselor in Montenegro (1999 to 2003), Hanke was already involved in counseling Yugoslav policy makers in the short-lived Ante Marković regime, where he recommended the currency-board solution to end Yugoslav inflation. His work was published in Serbo-Croatian and became widely known in the region. Before he became an adviser to Đukanović in the late 1990s, he was an adviser on the currency-board solution in Bosnia-Herzegovina. He coauthored a book, *Crnogorska marka* (The Montenegrin Mark, 1999), that laid out the means for transitioning from the Yugoslav dinar to the German mark.[35]

Hanke explained how he envisioned a system of competitive currencies in Montenegro along the lines of Hayek's "denationalization of money." In such a system, the government adopts one currency as a means of payment, but allows other currencies to be used in the domestic market for private contracts.[36] The currency-board solution, which was at least initially part of the plan,[37] was dropped later on, even though it had been implemented in other Balkan countries just a few years before. Vukotić opposed the currency-board solution on two grounds. First, it would still have meant printing some amount of coins and banknotes for which an expensive and time-consuming system of quality control would be necessary, and second, there was still some possibility of government interference, which was anathema to Vukotić.[38] In the end, Montenegro officially adopted the German mark, first as legal tender and later, in 2001, as its sole currency, before it was replaced the following year by the euro. The ISSP, under the supervision of Vukotić, prepared the ground for leaving the Yugoslav dinar and changing to another currency.[39]

Another major reform was privatization, which was restarted with a new law in 1999 and consisted of multiple privatization strategies, including international sale tenders, auctions, and mass voucher privatization. Within a few years, 80 percent of the economy was privatized.[40] Vukotić had already gained some experience in developing a privatization plan during his brief period as minister for privatization in the former Yugoslavia. Some preparations were done with the help of Robert Stone from the British Know How Fund established by the Thatcher administration.[41] In 1998, Vukotić became the vice president of the privatization council and developed and executed the privatization process together with the ISSP.[42]

By 2004, Vukotić declared the process to be mostly finished after the large aluminum combine (KAP) was privatized.[43] Three years later, he argued for further privatization, including strategic (public) goods such as airports, ports, the railway company, and the electric power utility.[44] The privatizations continued, and after a full decade, more than 90 percent of the economy was in private hands and almost all major public companies were sold, including the oil distribution company, the national telecommunications company, and parts of the national electric power utility.[45]

Reflecting on the process of privatization, the former ministers Luksić and Katnić acknowledged that besides intended effects such as generating private-property incentives and foreign direct investment, the process also caused significant problems. Some big companies did not survive the process, and after an initial boom period, the stock prices fell substantially, leading to negative public reactions.[46]

Vukotić was also responsible for the creation of the capital market in Montenegro. In an interview in 2008, he explained how the process of privatization and currency reform was connected to the capital market. Currency reform curbed the power of the central bank to influence monetary policy and thereby intervene in the financial market. Since the functioning of the capital market depends on agents trading capital shares, swift privatization supplied the new capital market with enough "material" to trade. The voucher part of the privatization process was supposed to guarantee popular support by enabling mass participation.[47] Vukotić's involvement in the creation of the capital market had begun in the early 1990s. Later, when he became president of the Council for Capital Market Development, he laid out the strategy of the organization. He helped establish the Central Depository Agency and the Securities Commission, and he worked on the drafts for several accompanying laws, such as foreign investment legislation, company law, and the insolvency law.[48] An especially valuable partner in this part of the reform process was Zoran Đikanović, one of the students of the postgraduate studies program, who had worked in a consulting company with Vukotić in the early 1990s.[49] Đikanović was involved in various groups working on laws for capital markets, investment funds, private pensions, and other projects, and he was the coordinator for the voucher privatization program (1999 to 2000). Immediately after that, he became a board member and then president of the Montenegrin commission for capital markets, a function he has held since 2002. Therefore, he was substantially involved in designing, shaping, and supervising the capital markets in Montenegro since their inception. Đikanović is also an MPS member.[50]

Vukotić and his group were involved in the execution and supervision of other projects, as well. Trade was liberalized and simplified. Integration into the world market became a priority at the time the accession talks with the European Union and the World Trade Organization intensified. Pension reform was started in 2002, and a three-pillar system with mandatory pension funds, mandatory capitalized pension funds, and voluntary capitalized pension funds was introduced. Later, the retirement age was raised to 67 for both sexes, and early retirement was made more difficult. Labor-market legislation was introduced to ease layoffs, and a flat tax was implemented.[51]

During the reform process, important roles were played by Vukotić's three doctoral students, Igor Lukšić, Milorad Katnić, and Vladimir Kavarić. Lukšić became involved in the state apparatus and politics at the end of the 1990s and rose through the ranks to become finance minister (2004 to 2010), prime minister (2010 to 2012), and after that, minister of foreign affairs (2012 to 2016). Katnić, an MPS member, started in the ISSP, working on currency, fiscal, monetary, and pension reform (2002 to 2004), but switched to government as deputy finance minister (2004 to 2010), then finance minister (2010 to 2012) to help Lukšić in introducing and implementing neoliberal reforms. After Lukšić's two-year term as prime minister, Katnić remained as a governmental advisor (2012 to 2014). Together, Lukšić and Katnić were strongly involved in implementing new tax reforms in Montenegro. After the introduction of a value-added tax in 2003, in 2004 the government decided to initiate a reduction of payroll taxes by 10 percent.[52]

The International Monetary Fund was concerned about the announced tax changes, since it meant a loss of revenue, and it thus urged more ambitious cutbacks in spending or postponing some of the planned tax cuts. Despite the concern of the IMF, Lukšić and Katnić did not want to reassess their decision and insisted on going ahead with their announced tax reform.[53] As finance ministers, they later recalled, "we still vividly remember fighting with the IMF on the decision to cut payroll taxes by 10 percent."[54] After the payroll tax cut in 2004, further major tax reforms followed. In 2006, Montenegro's Parliament approved a 9 percent flat tax on corporate income, the lowest rate in Eastern Europe—replacing the previous two-rate system of 15 percent and 20 percent—and a 15 percent flat tax on personal income, replacing the previous system of three rates, effective as of mid-2007. The tax rate on personal income was further reduced to 9 percent in 2010. Besides that, individual long-term capital gains were generally exempt from taxes.[55]

With these tax reforms, Montenegro's tax regime became one of the lowest in Europe. The process of restructuring Montenegro's tax system was supported by Slovak finance minister Ivan Mikloš. Slovakia had already implemented the flat tax in 2004,[56] and Lukšić and Katnić were eager to transfer experience from Slovakia, signing a cooperation agreement with Mikloš in the same year.[57] Since the introduction of the flat tax in 2007, income inequality in Montenegro edged up slightly.[58] The posttax national income share of the top 10 percent increased from 27 percent in 2007 to 27.8 percent in 2015. The posttax national income share of the bottom 50 percent increased from 24.7 percent in 2007 to 24.9 percent in 2015. Although the Gini coefficient, a measure of welth or income inequality, fluctuated substantially during this period, it tended to increase from 2007 to 2015, ending at 39 percent in 2015.[59]

Another fellow from the Entrepreneurial Economy postgraduate studies program, Vladimir Kavarić, worked at the ISSP[60] before becoming secretary to the minister of finance in 2004. After an interlude in the agency tasked with supervising insurance companies, he became minister of the economy from 2010 to 2016. The ministers were active as authors in that period, as well. Together, they published *In Search of Economic Freedom*.[61] Lukšić's postgraduate works include *Spontaneous Order and Transition* and articles on (Austrian) business-cycle theory and the failure of the welfare state.[62] Lukšić and Katnić supervised the reform process, and they have written an insightful insider story about their governmental experience in Montenegro for the *Cato Journal*.[63]

Other members of Vukotić's team also stand out. Maja Drakić-Grgur, an MPS member and postgraduate studies fellow, worked for the ISSP beginning in 2001 and consulted with the government on privatization. Furthermore, she was a visiting scholar at the Mercatus Center of George Mason University in 2005.[64] Milica Vukotić, another MPS member, also worked at the ISSP (2000 to 2009), has served as a council member for the governmental Agency for Electronic Communications and Postal Services (2008 to 2017), and has also been a board member of the Montenegro Stock Exchange (2009 to 2014).[65]

The overall agenda for the neoliberal transformation of Montenegro in the first decade of the twenty-first century was quite ambitious, and members from Vukotić's group were present at every step of the way, from designing to executing and supervising the reforms. There were still some limits on what was possible. The concept of a "Montenegro microstate," which proposed to shrink the size of the state drastically by cutting public consumption in half to about 20 percent of the GDP and organizing the whole administration with only 333 people (not counting security forces), has been rejected, as Vukotić himself acknowledged.[66] Nevertheless, substantial success was achieved and by the time Montenegro became independent, and major reforms were implemented, Vukotić began preparing the ground for his next big project: the founding of the private University of Donja Gorica.

UNIVERSITY OF DONJA GORICA:
EDUCATING THE NEXT FREE-MARKET GENERATION

The roots of the University of Donja Gorica (UDG) can be traced back to 1992, when Vukotić established the postgraduate studies Entrepreneurial Economy program at the University of Montenegro, which continued until the UDG was founded. The establishment of the Faculty for International Economics, Finance, and Business (FIEFB), which continued the mission of the postgraduate studies project, and the Faculty of Law in 2007 marked the inception of the UDG.[67]

There were several founders, both from Montenegro and from foreign countries. Veselin Vukotić and Dragan Vukčević worked as professors at the University of Montenegro and became the deans of the first two faculties. Vukotić advanced to the position of president of the UDG in 2010, while Vukčević is still the dean of the law faculty and, since 2016, also the president of the Montenegrin Academy for Science and Arts.[68] Two more founders coming from academia were foreigners with deep roots in neoliberal organizations: Steve Pejovich and Enrico Colombatto. Pejovich,[69] a Yugoslav emigré born in Belgrade, was an economics professor at the Texas A&M University and became a renowned expert on property rights. As a longtime observer and writer on the peculiarities of the Yugoslav market-socialist economy, he had "extensive communications" with Vukotić during Vukotić's time as government minister[70] and helped Vukotić's educational efforts from the beginning by being a part of the postgraduate studies program. Pejovich is listed as a lecturer at the UDG.

Enrico Colombatto,[71] a former MPS member who worked with Pejovich at the International Centre for Economic Research, an Italian Turin-based think tank, is also a longtime acquaintance of Vukotić. Colombatto was active in Montenegro in different lecturing and consulting roles before Montenegro's independence, and he is still listed among the academic staff of the UDG. The other two founders came from business and politics. Milo Đjukanović has been the leading Montenegrin politician since the 1990s. Tomislav Čelebić leads the family company that is, among other activities, invested in real estate.[72] The company Univerzitats d.o.o., founded by Vukotić, Vukčević, Čelebić, and Đjukanović, owns the University Donja Gorica. Furthermore, the university was built on land owned by Čelebić.[73]

The founding of the university was well received in the neoliberal world and its free-market orientation was worn openly.[74] The rector's introductory words show that in addition to expertise in the subjects taught and IT skills, students also learn an "entrepreneurial approach to life" at the UDG.[75] In an article, Vukotić was even more precise about the overall goal when he stated that the function of the university is to prepare Montenegro as a country and its young people as individuals for the global market: "The cornerstone of the UDG is to integrate Montenegro into the global markets. The essence of this idea is to understand how people from Montenegro can use opportunities from the global marketplace in order to achieve a better quality of life."[76]

In terms of teaching, the FIEFB faculty offers a course on the Austrian and Chicago schools of economics as an elective, while other faculties do not have such a course in the curriculum. The background of many academic staff members, especially in the FIEFB, can be traced to postgraduate studies in economics, neoliberal think tanks, and/or governmental positions.[77] The dean of the FIEFB faculty is Maja Drakić-Grgur, while other lecturers with neoliberal backgrounds include Dragana Radević (ISSP, IPER), Jadranka Kaluđerović (ISSP), Ivana Katnić (ISSP), Barbara Kolm (MPS, the Austrian Economics Center), Jesús Huerta de Soto (MPS), the capital market agency president Đikanović, the former ministers Katnić, Ivanović, Kavarić, and Lukšić, and the already mentioned Colombato, Pejovich, and Liggio. Milica Vukotić is dean of the Faculty for Information Systems and Technology.[78] However, such partisanship should not lead one wholly to dismiss the academic quality of the staff. Lecturers include internationally recognized specialists and scholars who publish in top-ranked academic journals, such as Marija Vukotić.[79]

The University of Donja Gorica has grown steadily over the years. Currently, it has twelve faculties and a total of about three thousand students and three hundred lecturers. It has become an established part of the Montenegrin higher education landscape. There is another private university, Mediteran in Podgorica, that is of comparable size and that opened a year earlier, in 2006. It was founded by Duško Knežević, a businessman with connections to the Clinton Foundation who turned from being a supporter of Đukanović into an opponent in recent years.[80] Another private university, Adriatik, with more than one thousand students, has existed since 2017, and there are several smaller autonomous faculties in Montenegro.

These new competitors notwithstanding, the dominant institution in the higher education system of Montenegro remains the public university of Podgorica, numbering over sixteen thousand students. It is also the dominant institution in terms of university ranking.[81] A general problem that hinders further comparative analysis is the lack of reliable data, the reason being the insufficient transparency of Montenegrin universities, as a study from the NGO Centre for Civic Education / Heinrich Böll Stiftung has shown.[82]

An interesting question relates to the connections of the UDG to other free-market institutions of higher learning. For example, Pejovich, who was a visiting professor at the Francisco Marroquín University in Guatemala in 1977, an experience that was probably helpful in founding the UDG, expressed his opinion in a letter that the UDG is modeled on that institution.[83] (On the Guatemalan university see Karin Fischer's contribution, "Latin America's Neoliberal Seminary: Francisco Marroquín University in Guatemala," in this volume.) Francisco Marroquín University is also listed as a partner university by the UDG. Sponsored by the Atlas Network, Vukotić attended the Thirty-Fourth Annual Meeting of the Association of Private Enterprise

Education in 2009 in Guatemala.[84] In terms of partnerships, the current university web page lists a few striking partnerships (among them Francisco Marroquín University), but the home page of Professor Vukotić shows that the Faculty for International Economics, Finance, and Business has entertained cooperation with universities and institutes such as George Mason University, the Mercatus Center, the Heritage Foundation, the Atlas Economic Research Foundation, the Cato Institute, and the Institute for Humane Studies.[85]

Particularly robust cooperation exists with the neoliberals of Austria. Barbara Kolm has been a leading figure behind the Free Market Road Show in Europe, a yearly event that connects neoliberal thinkers where they present their ideas to (young) audiences with strong participation by the UDG and the ISSP. Vukotić's book *Psycho-Philosophy of Business: Our Mentality through Dialogue* was published by the Austrian Hayek Institute. Some of the connections were established long before the UDG was founded. Particularly interesting is the fact that Vukotić and Ivanović were among the founders of G-17,[86] a group that grew into an important liberal-conservative political party in the 2000s in Serbia. Given that neoliberals were part of both regional governments in the 2000s, it would be interesting to analyze if and how neoliberal ideas influenced the final breakup of the country in 2006, a task beyond the scope of this chapter.

While few observers thus far have noted the peculiar neoliberal character of the UDG, the university's partisan character has not gone entirely unnoticed. The creation of the UDG was controversial from the start. It appears that the university opened before completing the necessary paperwork, and while claiming to be solely financed by the market and by tuition fees, it received public funding later on.[87] In 2010, the government of Montenegro introduced a new law that enabled public funding of private universities for studies that are considered to be in the public interest. The government decides which studies qualify. The introduction of the law was highly criticized by the public and was perceived as a conflict of interest, since the current and previous president, Milo Đukanović, has been one of the owners of the University of Donja Gorica.[88] For the academic year 2012–2013, the government paid around two hundred thousand euros to private universities for studies that are considered in the public interest. Surprisingly, most of the funding went to the UDG.[89] Critics claimed that the introduction of the new law was due to the fact that the University of Donja Gorica had trouble paying back its debt and suspected that the new law was an attempt to solve its financial issues.[90]

Nurtured by the institutions built by the first generation of post-socialist neoliberals, a younger generation of free-market leaders has been emerging in Montenegro. Slobodan Franeta, who finished his master's studies at the UDG in 2019 and was active in the Montenegrin Students for Liberty group, is now the chairman of a new organization with a young team: the Global Communications Network (GCN). This organization was formed in 2019. It is the sole Montenegrin partner of the Atlas Network and was formed as a joint project by members of the Lucha Institute, the Free Society Institute, and members of the Naiad Centre. The GCN describes its mission as "researching and communicating ideas that enhance the performance of the cooperation between the private and public sector." It also produces the *Herald of Freedom,* a bimonthly magazine.[91] Already rich in civil societal infrastructures and positions in the academic and public sectors, organized neoliberalism has no difficulty in strategically replicating and expanding its sphere of influence in the tiny country.

CONCLUSION

Although Montenegro did not commence neoliberal reforms until the late 1990s, it quickly transitioned from a laggard to a leader. The transition was guided and facilitated by Veselin Vukotić and his partners. Vukotić's decades-long work as an educator in free-market thinking paid off when the political orientation of the country changed and his former students came to power. Holding high government positions and playing other key administrative roles, they unleashed a far-reaching agenda, including tax cuts, trade liberalization, pension reform, capital-market expansion, mass privatizations, and labor-market flexibility reforms. They were assisted by foreign experts from different parts of the international neoliberal community. One such instance of idea transmission involved tax reform, when Montenegro took bold steps to advance corporate welfare to become a country with a highly competitive tax system—read: tax haven—in Europe. These efforts showed up in statistics such as the Economic Freedom Index, where Montenegro advanced from the ninetieth to the forty-seventh position from 2005 to 2010. While neoliberal policy was not completely discarded after this period, the transformation years certainly were the most dynamic in terms of market-liberal reform. After 2010, Montenegro's position on the Economic Freedom Index steadily deteriorated for reasons beyond the scope of this chapter.

Our task has been to present a general overview of the rise of neoliberalism in Montenegro. Given the continued strong presence of the neoliberal community in Montenegro, this article should be viewed as offering only a good sketch of the tip of the iceberg, and many more promising directions are open for further research. The revolving door between think tanks, the UDG, and government needs further exploration and analysis. The exchange of ideas and personnel between Montenegro and the international neoliberal community is another promising research path, as is the analysis of the thoughts of the Austrian-Montenegrin school of economics and its original contributions to the neoliberal movement. In general, we still know little about the contributions of Yugoslav intellectuals and émigrés to the neoliberal movement. While the "white migration" to the United States during the Nazi era contributed strongly to the survival of Austrian economics, in particular, the role of émigré scholars in their home countries has not yet received a lot of attention. Montenegro is a great site to document the relevance of reverse transatlantic crossings.

1. Hilary Appel and Mitchell A. Orenstein, "Why Did Neoliberalism Triumph and Endure in the Post-Communist World?," *Comparative Politics* 48.3 (2016), pp. 313–31.

2. For Romania, see Cornel Ban, *Ruling Ideas: How Global Neoliberalism Goes Local* (Oxford: Oxford University Press, 2016); for Russia, see Tobias Rupprecht, "The Road from Snake Hill: The Genesis of Russian Neoliberalism," in this volume. On the "Visegrad" states, see Dorothee Bohle and Béla Greskovits, *Capitalist Diversity on Europe's Periphery* (Ithaca: Cornell University Press, 2012).

3. The roots of the neoliberal movement have been covered by, among others, Jamie Peck, *Constructions of Neoliberal Reason* (Oxford: Oxford University Press, 2010); Philip Mirowski and Dieter Plehwe, eds., *The Road from Mont Pèlerin: The Making of the Neoliberal Thought Collective* (Cambridge, MA: Harvard University Press, 2009); Quinn Slobodian, *Globalists: The End of Empire and the Birth of Neoliberalism* (Cambridge, MA: Harvard University Press, 2018).

4. Miroslav Prokopijević and Slaviša Tasić, "Classical Liberal Economics in the Ex-Yugoslav Nations," *Econ Journal Watch* 12.2 (2015), pp. 260–73.

5. The MPS members are Veselin Vukotić, Milorad Katnić, Petar Ivanović, Milica Vukotić, Zoran Đikanović, and Maja Drakić-Grgur. See also "The Mont Pelerin Society (MPS)," Desmog, https://www.desmogblog.com/mont-pelerin-society.

6. We draw especially on Maja Drakić, Frederic Sautet, and Kyle McKenzie, "Montenegro: The Challenges of a Newborn State," *Mercatus Policy Series, Country Brief* 2 (2007), https://www.mercatus.org/system/files/Montenegro.pdf; Igor Lukšić and Milorad Katnić, "The Making of a State: Transition in Montenegro," *Cato Journal* 36.3 (2016); Jadranka Kaluđerović and Vojin Golubović, "Razvoj ekonomske misli u Crnoj Gori," in Božo Drašković, Jelena Minović, and Aida Hanić, eds., *Ekonomska teorija u periodu, 1958–2018* (Belgrade: Institut ekonomskih nauka, 2018), pp. 350–63; and a number of articles and interviews given by Vukotić.

7. For a recent critical opinion on Vukotić's life and work, see Biljana

Matijašević, "Nevidljiva ruka Veselina Vukotića," *Vijesti Online*, https://
www.vijesti.me/vijesti/ekonomija/431064/nevidljiva-ruka-veselina-vukotica.

8. Fraser Institute, "Economic Freedom of the World: 2019 Annual Report,"
https://www.fraserinstitute.org/resource-file?nid=13069&fid=12710.

9. Drakić, Sautet, and McKenzie, "Montenegro."

10. Tatjana Kuher, "Crnogorski neoliberalizam," *Vijesti Online*, https://
www.vijesti.me/kolumne/313019/crnogorski-neoliberalizam.

11. A general history of modern Montenegro can be found in Kenneth
Morrison, "Montenegro: A Polity in Flux, 1989–2000," in Charles Ingrao and
Thomas A. Emmert, eds., *Confronting the Yugoslav Controversies: A Scholar's
Initiative*, 2nd ed. (West Lafayette: Purdue University Press, 2012), pp. 426–56.

12. The general problem of the DPS's continued rule and its leader Milo
Đukanović has been extensively discussed in the media, for example: "Why
Milo Djukanovic is Europe's Most Durable Ruler, *Economist*, April 13, 2019,
https://www.economist.com/europe/2019/04/11/why-milo-djukanovic-is-
europes-most-durable-ruler, and Marc Santora, "'Balkan Spring' Turns to
Summer and Hopes for Change Dim," *New York Times*, June 1, 2019, https://
www.nytimes.com/2019/06/01/world/europe/balkans-protests-montenegro
-serbia-bosnia-albania.html.

13. Mirowski and Plehwe, eds., *The Road from Mont Pèlerin*.

14. On neoliberal entrepreneurship in general, see Dieter Plehwe, "Schum-
peter Revival?: How Neoliberals Revised the Image of the Entrepreneur,"
in Dieter Plehwe, Quinn Slobodian, and Philip Mirowski, eds., *Nine Lives of
Neoliberalism* (London: Verso, 2020), pp. 120–42.

15. Patrick Mellacher and Nenad Pantelić, "The Ante-Marković Reforms:
Children of the Washington Consensus?," forthcoming.

16. See Veselin Vukotić's home page for an overview of his activities and
connections to other neoliberal projects and institutions: http://vukotic.net
/text.php?what=txt&tag=17. See also Free Market Road Show, "Vukotic,
Veselin," https://freemarket-rs.com/vukotic-veselin, and Vukotić, *Psycho-
philosophy of Business: Our Mentality through a Dialogue* (Vienna: Friedrich
August v. Hayek Institut 2010), p. 43.

17. Johanna Bockman, *Markets in the Name of Socialism: The Left-Wing*

Origins of Neoliberalism (Stanford: Stanford University Press, 2011), ch. 3, pp. 76–104.

18. For a new account of the rise of (free-market) economists, see Binyamin Appelbaum, *The Economists' Hour: False Prophets, Free Markets, and the Fracture of Society* (New York: Hachette, 2019).

19. See Veselin Vukotićs home page for an overview of his activities and connections to other neoliberal projects and institutions: http://vukotic .net/text.php?what=txt&tag=17. See also Free Market Road Show, "Vukotic, Veselin."

20. Veselin Vukotić, "Planting Freedom in the Ashes of a Failed Commu-nist Experiment," in Colleen Dyble, ed., *Freedom Champions: Stories from the Front Lines in the War of Ideas. 30 Case Studies by Intellectual Entrepreneurs Who Champion the Cause of Freedom* (Washington, DC: Atlas Economic Research Foundation, 2011), pp. 219–26, https://www.atlasnetwork.org/assets/uploads/ misc/FreedomChampions.pdf.

21. The Linkedin accounts and University of Donja Gorica biography pages show their connections to Vukotić's Institute for Strategic Studies and Prognoses and/or the university. Milorad Katnić: https://me.linkedin.com/in /milorad-katnic-3aa13a65, and https://fmefb.udg.edu.me/osnovne/predavaci /13; Igor Lukšić: https://fdm.udg.edu.me/predavaci/biografija/39-igor -lukpercentC5percentA1percentC4percent87; Petar Ivanović: https://fmefb.udg .edu.me/osnovne/predavaci/12; Vladimir Kavarić: https://fmefb.udg.edu.me /osnovne/predavaci/14.

22. Members of the Montenegrin Parliament, http://arhiva.skupstina.me /index.php/en/parliament/members-of-parliament/members-of-parliament. See also note 21.

23. Initially named the Centre for Entrepreneurship and Economic Devel-opment (CEED).

24. Atlas Economic Research Foundation, *Highlights: A Quarterly Newsletter for the Atlas Network* (Spring 2006), p. 21.

25. IPER home page, https://iper.org.me/publikacije/page/2.

26. Vukotić, "Planting Freedom in the Ashes," p. 222. Vukotić does not mention what agency was involved, but it was probably the U.S. Agency

for International Development. See U.S. Congress, *Foreign Operations, Export Financing, and Related Programs Appropriations for 2001: Hearings Before a Subcommittee of the Committee on Appropriations*, House of Representatives, One Hundred Sixth Congress, Second Session, Volume 1, Part 2, https://play .google.com/books/reader?id=adkdAAAAMAAJ&pg=GBS.PA1524&hl=en. The USAID is still listed as a partner of the ISSP.

27. See note 26. The strategic role of the ISSP is also mentioned by Vukotić in an earlier interview: Elena Ziebarth, "One-on-One with Veselin Vukotic, President," *Highlights: A Quarterly Newsletter for the Atlas Network* (Summer 2005), pp. 6–7.

28. Vukotić, "Planting Freedom in the Ashes of a Failed Communist Experiment," p. 224.

29. See the home page of the institute, http://issp.me.

30. See the home page of the association, http://www.aemme.me/. For the foreign board members, see http://www.aemme.me/dokumentadrustva/6.pdf. For more information on the influence of neoliberals in Guatemala, see Karin Fischer, "Latin America's Neoliberal Seminary: Francisco Marroquín University in Guatemala," in this volume.

31. There is also another organization, the Centar za aplikativna istraživanja i analize (Center for Applied Research and Analysis), about which we know very little but it also traces its roots to Vukotić and his associates.

32. Lukšić and Katnić, "The Making of a State," pp. 689–709.

33. Kaluđerović and Golubović, "Razvoj ekonomske misli u Crnoj Gori," in Drašković, Minović, and Hanić, eds., *Ekonomska teorija u periodu 1958–2018*, pp. 350–63. For a more detailed discussion of currency boards, see Dieter Plehwe, "Transnational Discourse Coalitions and Monetary Policy: Argentina and the Limited Powers of the 'Washington Consensus,'" *Critical Policy Studies* 5.2 (2011), pp. 127–48.

34. See Johns Hopkins Whiting School of Engineering, "Steve H. Hanke," https://engineering.jhu.edu/ehe/faculty/steve-h-hanke.

35. Steve H. Hanke, "Remembrances of a Currency Reformer: Some Notes and Sketches from the Field," *Studies in Applied Economics* 55 (2016), pp. 1–23.

See also Željko Bogetić and Steve H. Hanke, *Crnogorska marka: Projekat valutnog odbora za Crnu Goru* (Podgorica: Radio Antena M, 1999).

36. See Steve H. Hanke, "Some Reflections on Monetary Institutions and Exchange-Rate Regimes," Cato Institute, January 3, 2000, https://www.cato.org/publications/congressional-testimony/some-reflections-monetary-institutions-exchangerate-regimes.

37. See Bogetić and Hanke, *Crnogorska marka.*

38. Veselin Vukotić, "Deset godina DEM/EURO," http://www.vukotic.net/files/publikacije/1294669427_7865.pdf. Another important reason was probably the security provided to foreign buyers/investors so that they would not face inflation/exchange-rate manipulation if the deutsche mark was adopted directly. See Plehwe, "Transnational Discourse Coalitions and Monetary Policy," p. 142.

39. Vukotić, "Planting Freedom in the Ashes," pp. 223–24.

40. Drakić, Sautet, and McKenzie, "Montenegro," p. 13.

41. See Veselin Vukotić, "Privatization in West Balkans with Special Emphasis on Montenegro," May 2001, http://www.vukotic.net/files/publikacije/1242821339_6869.pdf.

42. Vukotić, "Planting Freedom in the Ashes," pp. 222–23.

43. See Vukotić's interview with *Vijesti*, December 2004, available at Veselin Vukotić, "Interviews," http://www.vukotic.net/publikacije.php?type=4, and http://www.vukotic.net/files/publikacije/1243593431_6238.pdf.

44. See Vukotić's interview with *Vijesti*, December 25, 2007, available at Veselin Vukotić, "Interviews," http://www.vukotic.net/publikacije.php?type=4, and http://www.vukotic.net/files/publikacije/1243593509_1148.pdf.

45. Luksić and Katnić, "The Making of a State," p. 696.

46. Ibid.

47. See Vukotić's interview with the *Economist*, March 2008, available at Veselin Vukotić, "Interviews," http://www.vukotic.net/publikacije.php?type=4, and http://www.vukotic.net/files/publikacije/1243593626_5755.pdf.

48. Veselin Vukotić, "Capitalism," http://www.vukotic.net/text.php?what=txt&tag=17.

49. This and other business dealings by Vukotić led to controversies and

accusations of self-dealing, nepotism, and law-breaking behavior that were covered by the Montenegrin media. See MANS, "Nepotizam i klijentelizam na univerzitetima i fakultetima u Crnoj Gori" August 19, 2009, https://www .mans.co.me/nepotizam-i-klijentelizam-u-viskom-obrazovanju/#, and Monitor, "Predatori iz Donje Gorice," September 18, 2009, https://www.monitor.co.me /predatori-iz-donje-gorice.

50. University of Donja Gorica, "Prof. Dr Zoran Đikanović," https://fmefb .udg.edu.me/osnovne/predavaci/24, and Komisija za tržište kapitala, "Opšte informacije i biografije članova komisije," http://www.scmn.me/me/o-komisiji /opste-informacije-i-biografije.

51. Luksić and Katnić, "The Making of a State," pp. 697–98.

52. Ibid., p. 98.

53. See International Monetary Fund, *Serbia and Montenegro: Fourth Review under the Extended Arrangement (EA), Financing Assurances Review, Request for Waivers, and Modification of an End-December 2004 Performance Criterion,* January 12, 2005, https://www.imf.org/en/Publications/CR/Issues/2016/12/31 /Serbia-and-Montenegro-Fourth-Review-Under-the-Extended-Arrangement-EA -Financing-Assurances-17981, p. 20.

54. Luksić and Katnić, "The Making of a State," p. 698.

55. World Bank Poverty Reduction and Economic Management Unit, Europe and Central Asia Region, *Report No 46660-ME, Montenegro beyond the Peak: Growth Policies and Fiscal Constraints, Public Expenditure, and Institutional Review,* November 24, 2008, http://documents.worldbank.org/curated/ en/190731468053963988/text/466600ESW01ME01eb05020090Box334131B. txt; Daniel J. Mitchell, "Montenegro Joins the Flat Tax Club," Cato at Liberty, April 16, 2007, https://www.cato.org/blog/montenegro-joins-flat-tax-club. See also International Monetary Fund, *Montenegro: 2010 Article IV Consulta-tion — Staff Report; Public Information Notice on the Executive Board Discussion; and Statement by the Executive Director for Montenegro,* May 2010, https://www. imf.org/external/pubs/ft/scr/2010/cr10155.pdf.

56. Hilary Appel and Mitchell A. Orenstein, "Ideas versus Resources: Explain-ing the Flat Tax and Pension Privatization Revolutions in Eastern Europe and the Former Soviet Union," *Comparative Political Studies* 46.2 (2013), pp. 123–52.

57. Luksić and Katnić, "The Making of a State," p. 698.

58. See World Bank Group, *Poverty and Equity Brief, Europe and Central Asia: Montenegro*, April 2019, https://databank.worldbank.org/data/download /poverty/33EF03BB-9722-4AE2-ABC7-AA2972D68AFE/Archives-2019/Global _POVEQ_MNE.pdf.

59. See World Inequality Database, "Montenegro," https://wid.world /country/montenegro, and Knoema World Data Atlas, "Montenegro–GINI Index," 2016, https://knoema.com/atlas/Montenegro/topics/Poverty/Income -Inequality/GINI-index.

60. See University of Donja Gorica, "Doc. Dr Vladimir Kavarić," https:// fmefb.udg.edu.me/osnovne/predavaci/14. Before working for the government, Kavarić also worked in the Centar za aplikativna istraživanja i analize. See note 31 above.

61. Published by the ISSP. See http://issp.me/books/.

62. On Lukšić's academic output, see University of Donja Gorica, Fakultet za Dizajn i Multimediju, "dr Igor Lukšić," https://fdm.udg.edu.me/predavaci /biografija/39-igor-luk%C5%A1i%C4%87.

63. Luksić and Katnić, "The Making of a State," pp. 689–709.

64. See University of Donja Gorica, Postdiplomske studije "Preduzetnička economija," "dr Maja Drakić-Grgur," https://www.udg.edu.me/postdiploma /predavaci.php?pId=6.

65. Milica Vukotić, https://me.linkedin.com/in/milicavukotic?trk=people -guest_people_search-card.

66. For the concept, see Veselin Vukotić, *Montenegro-microstate* (Podgorica: ISSP, 2003). See also PCNEN, "Dr Vukotic: Mikro drzava civilizacijsku buduc-nost Crne Gore," https://www.pcnen.com/portal/2005/01/07/ dr-vukotic-mikro-drzava-civilizacijsku-buducnost-crne-gore.

67. See Veselin Vukotić, "Be the Part of the History of Future!" (*sic*), http:// www.vukotic.net/text.php?what=txt&tag=18.

68. See Crnogorske akademije nauka i umjetnosti, "Dragan K. Vukčević," http://www.canu.me/clanovi/dragan-k-vukcevic.

69. See University of Donja Gorica, "Prof. Dr Steve Pejovich," https:// fmefb.udg.edu.me/osnovne/predavaci/25.

70. Vukotić, "Planting Freedom in the Ashes of a Failed Communist Experiment," p. 221.

71. See Academia, "Enrico Colombatto," http://unito.academia.edu /EColombatto/CurriculumVitae.

72. See Čelebić, "Upoznajte nas bolje," https://celebic.com/o-nama.

73. See b92, "Đukanović osniva univerzitet," https://www.b92.net/biz/ vesti/region.php?yyyy=2006&mm=12&dd=28&nav_id=225251&start=-9.

74. See, for example, Richard W. Rahn, "A Lesson in Free-Market Economics," Cato Institute, May 25, 2010, https://www.cato.org/publications /commentary/lesson-freemarket-economics.

75. See University of Donja Gorica, "Riječ rektora: Dobrodošli na UDG!," https://www.udg.edu.me/o-univerzitetu/rijec-rektora.

76. Vukotić, "Planting Freedom in the Ashes of a Failed Communist Experiment," p. 226.

77. University of Donja Gorica, "Predavači," https://fmefb.udg.edu.me /osnovne/predavaci.

78. See Free Market Road Show, "Vukotic, Milica," https://freemarket-rs .com/vukotic-milica.

79. See University of Warwick, Department of Economics, "Marija Vukotic," https://warwick.ac.uk/fac/soc/economics/staff/mvukotic.

80. Wikipedia, "Duško Knežević," https://en.wikipedia.org/wiki /Du%C5%A1ko_Kne%C5%BEevi%C4%87.

81. See Ranking Web of Universities, "Montenegro," https://www .webometrics.info/en/Europe/Montenegro.

82. See Daliborka Uljarevic, ed., *Univerzitetski zidovi: Analiza stanja u oblasti transparentnosti rada visokoobrazovnih institucija u Crnoj Gori* (Podgorica: Centar za građansko obrazovanje, 2018), http://media.cgo-cce.org/2018/12 /Univerzitetski-zidovi-final.pdf.

83. Wikileaks, "Re: [Analytical & Intelligence Comments] RE: Serbia: A Weimar Republic?," https://wikileaks.org/gifiles/docs/18/1817586 _re-analytical-and-intelligence-comments-re-serbia-a-weimar.html.

84. See University of Donja Gorica, "International Cooperation," https:// www.udg.edu.me/en/international-cooperation.

85. Vukotić, "Be the Part of the History of Future!"

86. For Vukotić, see Veselin Vukotić, "Institutions," http://www.vukotic.net/institucije.php, and also see the CV of Ivanović in note 21 above.

87. Vukotić, "Planting Freedom in the Ashes of a Failed Communist Experiment," p. 226.

88. See Radio Slobodna Evropa, "Novi zakon omogućava finansiranje privatnih univerziteta iz budžeta," https://www.slobodnaevropa.org/a/novi_zakon_omogucava_finansiranje_privatnih_univerziteta_iz_budzeta/2098597.html.

89. See *Vijesti*, "Država će sa 200.000 pomoći privatne fakultete, najviše para za UDG," https://www.vijesti.me/vijesti/drustvo/296398/drzava-ce-sa-200-000-pomoci-privatne-fakultete-najvise-para-za-udg.

90. See *Srbja Danas*, "Tajni krediti, fiktivne transakcije, dugovi: Evo kako posluju Đukanovićeve firme," August 9, 2019, https://www.srbijadanas.com/vesti/region/tajni-krediti-fiktivne-transakcije-dugovi-evo-kako-posluju-du kanoviceve-firme-video-2019-03-09, and "Novi zakon omogućava finansiranje privatnih univerziteta iz budžeta."

91. There is very little public information available about these predecessor organizations. The internet domain of the Lucha Institute has expired, for example. The Free Society Institute is on Facebook: https://www.facebook.com/slobodnodrustvocg, and the Montenegrin Students for Liberty group also has a Facebook page: https://www.facebook.com/studentizasloboducg. The GCN's site is https://www.mgcn.org. There is also another related NGO, Slobodna Misao, or Free Thought, although it is not clear whether this organization is still functional. Information about Slobodan Franeta is taken from his Linkedin account: https://www.linkedin.com/in/slobofraneta/?trk=public-profile-join-page.

CHAPTER ELEVEN

A Hayekian Public Intellectual in Iceland

Lars Mjøset

In January 2004, Hannes Hólmsteinn Gissurarson, an Icelandic polit-ical philosopher and Mont Pelerin Society board member since 1998, published a piece in the *Wall Street Journal*. "Miracle on Iceland" cel-ebrated a period of economic growth and development since Prime Minister David Oddsson took office in 1991.[1] Gissurarson quoted John Stuart Mill to claim that ideas "in human affairs" have efficacy only if they meet with the right circumstances.[2] The ideas of economic lib-eralization, he held, had been just what Iceland needed: "Free-mar-ket economists like Friedrich Hayek, Milton Friedman and James M. Buchanan all visited the country in the 1980s, influencing not only Mr. Oddsson but many of his generation. In the battle of ideas here, the right won."[3] Neoliberal ideas, he claimed, played a critical role in the successful transformation of the Icelandic economy after 1991.

Less than five years later, in a dramatic long weekend between October 2 and 8, 2008, the three largest Icelandic banks all went bust. The Icelandic microstate in the North Atlantic of one hundred thou-sand square kilometers and a population of three hundred and sixty-five thousand, which enjoyed the highest per capita GDP of all very small states, became the first national economy to fall victim to the world financial meltdown. Gissurarson's critics soon turned his rea-soning on its head, arguing that neoliberal ideas were a main cause of the meltdown. For his part, Gissurarson spent much intellectual energy defending Oddsson and his governments from such charges.

In the following chapter, I ask whether the Oddsson government really carried out Gissurarson's "liberal revolution." After a biographical sketch of Gissurarson, Iceland's key Hayekian public intellectual, I investigate the three main institutional complexes—regulating labor, money, and resources—that define the Nordic models of socioeconomic development.[4] I conclude that there was in fact no revolution in Iceland. The Oddsson government adapted their ideas to a set of circumstances defined by the country's twentieth-century history. Oddsson's policies were eclectic and worthy only of the label "neoliberal reformism." Neoliberal ideas were one element in the conjuncture that triggered Iceland's financial meltdown in 2008, but not the most important one.

ICELAND'S FIRST MPS MEMBER

Gissurarson studied philosophy and history (MA) at the University of Iceland, beginning in 1972, participating in a study group of young liberals linked to the youth association of Iceland's liberal-conservative party, the Independence Party (IP).[5] They published the journal *Eimreiðin* (Locomotive) from 1972 to 1975 and various edited volumes afterward. Three of them became prime ministers: Þorsteinn Pálsson (born in 1947), David Oddsson (born in 1948), and Geir H. Haarde (born in 1951). Another, Kjartan Gunnarsson (born in 1951) was the party secretary of the IP for twenty-six years (1980 to 2006).

Gissurarson began his graduate studies in philosophy at Oxford in 1981 and defended his DPhil thesis on Hayek's "conservative liberalism" in 1985. Through the 1980s, he engaged in energetic political entrepreneurship. Together with some of the *Eimreiðin* activists, Gissurarson ran the Libertarian Alliance in Iceland from 1979 to 1989. Inspired by the ascent of Thatcher and Reagan, they formed a libertarian faction of the IP and argued for privatization, deregulation, and restraints on government. The association arranged the visits by the neoliberal founding fathers at that time, including Hayek in 1980,

James M. Buchanan in 1982, and Milton Friedman in 1984. Oddsson was elected mayor of Reykjavik in 1982.

In 1983, the Icelandic alliance of neoliberals founded the Jón Þorláksson Institute, named after the conservative prime minister from 1926 to 1927. Supported by several businessmen, it aimed to spread information about liberalism "in the classical sense."[6] Directed by Gissurarson, it produced small political pamphlets, translations of neoliberal classics, and books by Icelandic liberals. In another notable intervention, Gissurarson established an illegal radio station in Reykjavik with Kjartan Gunnarsson in October 1984. Due to strikes, there were no news broadcasts, and the pirate radio was an act of civil disobedience against the government broadcasting monopoly. It was closed down, and they were fined, but the action was effective, because the monopoly was soon terminated.[7]

Gissurarson became a member of the Mont Pelerin Society in 1984, participating extensively in international neoliberal networks. The book version of his 1985 dissertation gives thanks to both Hayek and other "friends and fellow liberals," including Aaron Director and Karl Popper,[8] and he acknowledges support from various liberal funds. He also contributed to *Economic Affairs*, the Institute of Economic Affairs' (IEA) in-house journal.

Gissurarson became an assistant professor of political science at Iceland University in 1988, and later a full professor. He established himself as a public intellectual, publishing sixteen books in Icelandic from 1989 to 2005.[9] The largest number of titles in his catalog are biographies: a 1989 history of the IP over its first sixty years, on the IP leader Jón Þorláksson (1992), on entrepreneur Pálmi Jónsson (1994), and on liberal economist Benjamín Eiriksson (1996). His magnum opus—a biography of Icelandic author Halldor Laxness—appeared in three volumes, *Halldor* (2003), *Kiljan* (2004), and *Laxness* (2005). Laxness had been a pet topic for Gissurarson for a long time. Laxness had been a Communist Party member and a staunch supporter of Stalin for longer than most other Western intellectuals who admired the

USSR.[10] Gissurarson makes sure to acknowledge that Laxness was a great author, but the brunt of his text is directed at demonizing any left-wing tradition.[11] The Eiriksson biography also revolves around such themes, as does a six-hundred-page book on Icelandic Communists, 1918 to 1998 (2011). Gissurarson also published a "pictorial biography" of his libertarian colleague and later prime minister, David Oddsson, in 2008. Another large portion of Gissurarson's Icelandic catalogue contains essays and introductions to topics in political philosophy, covering Hayek's social theory and the broader tradition of property-rights theory. In English translation, the book titles are: *Libertarianism Is Humanitarianism: A Collection of Essays* (1992); *Where Does Man Belong?: Essays in the History of Political Ideas* (1994); *There Ain't No Such Thing as a Free Lunch* (1997); *Political Philosophy* (1999); and *Twists in the Tales: Essays in Political Philosophy* (2001).

Following splits in the IP, the *Eimreiðin* group raised its profile, making Iceland one of the few countries where a group of explicitly libertarian intellectuals and political activists gained dominance in the main right-wing party. Under their dominance, the party won the 1991 election and ruled in three coalitions from 1991 to 2009. Oddsson was prime minister from 1991 to 2004. Gissurarson recounts that he was an "informal advisor" to Oddsson.[12] He remained nevertheless an intellectual and kept his university job. The Þorláksson Institute was closed down in the mid-1990s. As the institute's website explains, "It was decided to use the University of Iceland, where Gissurarson had become professor of politics in 1988, as a venue for events rather than to organise them separately."[13] One of these events cosponsored by the University of Iceland, on fishing interests, employer groups, and financial interests, among others, was the celebratory regional Mont Pelerin Society meeting in 2005.[14] Until 2012, Gissurarson used his university position as a platform for organizing think-tank type activities.

Gissurarson's doctoral thesis on Hayek remains his most elaborate academic work. If publications in leading journals are any measure of academic success, he remained largely unsuccessful. His main references are to popular works such as Hayek's *The Road to Serfdom* and Friedman's *Capitalism and Freedom* (both of which he translated to Icelandic) and far less often to Hayek's philosophical works. Gissurarson distinguishes between classical liberalism and libertarianism, but seems to regard "neoliberal" as a label imposed only by critics of liberalism.[15] He works with a general framework in which liberalism includes an overall political philosophy incarnated in all works from classics such as Adam Smith's to those by libertarians such as David Friedman. He imposes this timeless, frictionless framework of ideas directly onto circumstances, without concern for subtleties of conceptual development and breaks.

It is impossible to judge the extent to which Gissurarson was an influential advisor to Oddsson. With archives unavailable, one can only rely on his own reporting and the assessments of his critics. What is clear is that he always remained a public intellectual. In this role, he provided ideological legitimation for the politics of the Oddsson government and then after 2008 actively tried to improve its reputation. Gissurarson publishes his interventions with various liberal think tanks, with academic journals linked to liberal networks, and in a recent case, also through a government-financed investigation. His critics mostly consider his interventions in the light of agnotology, the study of how doubt and ignorance is crafted. They note that he rejects alternative views by referring to inaccuracies that actually consist of petty details.[16] Similarly, he discredits opponents by playing up their anti-liberal political sympathies. In his recent synthetic survey on liberalism in Iceland, he subsumes earlier politicians and intellectuals under one grand liberal tradition.[17] Gissurarson portrays Oddsson's rule from 1991 to 2004 as the true fulfillment of the promises of an Icelandic liberalism, one that allegedly was wholly in line with classical, new Hayekian, and property-rights liberalism. To understand if and to what extent such neoliberal ideas influenced and possibly changed the smallest Nordic nation-state, it is necessary to take a closer look at the configuration of Iceland's social, economic, and political institutions.

Iceland shares the Nordic Protestant-Lutheran legacy, which required that the Bible be read in the native language. Consequently, the church promoted education, which led to general literacy by the early nineteenth century, even without a formal school system.[18] When systems of competence-building institutions were established later, Iceland developed the same comprehensive school system as the other Nordic countries. As a result, Nordic political opportunity structures allowed social movements to mobilize extensively. Concerning political and social mobilization, Iceland was roughly in sync with the other Nordic countries. But Iceland was a latecomer by nearly a century in its industrialization. The larger Nordics industrialized throughout the nineteenth century, while industrialization in Iceland was just taking off when it gained home rule from Denmark in 1904, beginning with the motorization of the fishing fleet.

Icelandic investor groups marginalized Danish merchants and investors in the early twentieth century. There was little need for proper capital-market institutions. Instead, specific investor groups organized in personalized networks. These networks were the core of what became the Independence Party (IP) in 1928. A capitalist class based mainly along family lines faced fully organized social movements. In Gissurarson's overviews of Iceland's history, he sees both peasant and labor movements as based on alien collectivist ideas infiltrating from abroad, as if there existed an original individualism rooted back in the free state, from 930 to 1262.[19]

Both peasants and workers formed parties in 1916. The agrarian party (the Progress Party, PP) was closely wedded to the cooperative movement that controlled most of domestic retail trade and distribution networks. The Social Democratic Party (SDP) was originally the political arm of the union movement, but this link was weakened by a Communist splinter party in 1930 that later became the PA (People's Alliance). As reformist competitors to their more radical sister party, the SDP pushed for a combined set of social-protection laws in 1936 and 1946.[20] Although Iceland's welfare state did not become as generous as those in the other Nordics, it is of the same universalist type.[21]

Against the movement-based parties, the IP relied on the legacy of nationalist mobilization: Icelandic elites had pushed for their own nation-state since the mid-nineteenth-century. Unlike the other Nordic conservative parties, the IP was not bothered by liberal or religious splinter parties. It remained a comprehensive liberal-conservative party, uniting business elites, administrative elites, wealthier farmers, and middle-class and even working-class voters (especially in some unions)—an early catch-all party.[22]

Prosperity under U.S. occupation during World War II led to an economic and political system in which closely related elite persons shuttled between positions as politicians, administrators, and businessmen. Until the late 1970s, this state structure led to economic development through devaluation cycles. Devaluation was a policy option, because Iceland is one of the smallest countries in the world to maintain its own currency.

In the classic pattern, the government devalued its currency to improve profitability when the dominant export sector, fisheries, was affected by low catches and/or low prices.[23] With a lag, this led to domestic inflation, which prompted unions to mobilize to defend workers' real wages by indexing wages to consumer prices. The government would then try to counteract this by blocking wage indexing. Unions responded with strikes. Conflicts in the labor market spiraled until good times returned. At the end of the cycle, workers had regained more than they lost. Given the influence of the PP, farmers also gained subsidies. The historical details of successive devaluation cycles need not be recounted here. The system had three main consequences. First, Iceland's labor market was very conflictual. Second, cycles of devaluation implied a peculiar industrial policy that influenced the structure of the fisheries. Third, despite its instabilities and conflicts, the system generated high economic growth.

In all the Nordic countries, systems of repressed finance—dominated by various types of state-imposed regulations—played a major role during the Bretton Woods period. But lacking developed capital-market institutions, Iceland's system was even more state directed. The larger Nordics had fully developed capital markets (banks, central banks, and financial supervision), so even with extensive state intervention, their systems were more "mixed" than the Icelandic system.[24]

Modernization through devaluation cycles led to unintended consequences. When external inflationary pressure began to rise in the 1970s, Iceland—unlike all the other Nordics—recorded persistent double-digit inflation rates, peaking at 83 per cent in 1983. Even more dramatically, just when Iceland had secured a two-hundred-mile zone for its technologically upgraded vessels, signs of resource depletion were looming. There was hardly any institutional protection for the most crucial resource, fish. These were the circumstances in the 1980s that Gissurarson claimed were eminently suitable for the reception of his liberal ideas.

THE LIBERAL INTERPRETATION OF POSTWAR ICELAND

Iceland's various political factions interpreted the devaluation-cycle regime differently. Gissurarson provides a Hayekian account. Iceland, he argued, entered on "the road to serfdom" in the turbulent interwar period under the PP-dominated government.[25] Gissurarson regards its cooperation with the SDP (in 1927, and in coalition, 1934) as the starting point for regulations and interventionist arrangements that responded to the protectionist surge in the world economy. He mostly portrays the IP as defensive, struggling heroically, but unsuccessfully, against such regulations. But this account of the circumstances cannot be generalized for the postwar period. For the whole devaluation cycle period, in fact, it was the IP that was the dominant party.

Iceland's coalition system is an open one.[26] At one point or another, all parties have been in coalition with each other, but the IP was the most frequent coalition participant (thirty-six out of forty-seven years, 1944 to 1991), holding the prime minister post for twenty-seven years. Obviously, the IP was a main player in the devaluation cycles. Mostly, it allied with the PP (with advantages to the farmers/cooperatives complex), but also with the SDP (influenced by fishermen as Iceland's labor aristocracy, due to the sharecropping reward system on the fishing vessels). The PA was the least involved in the coalition system.

Iceland's postwar institutional complementarities were different from those of the other Nordics. There, similar social-protection institutions and systems of competence building were complemented by weak, "non-Nordic" social partnership institutions.[27] Denmark, Norway, and Sweden all lost fewer workdays to strikes by pursuing consensual income policies that kept inflation under control.[28] Iceland's SDP had problems arguing for a reformist political line, because workers repeatedly had to defend their real wages by striking. It is not surprising that the leftist socialists (the PA) continued to capture the largest share of the vote on the Left.

Gissurarson provides a very one-sided history of these Icelandic peculiarities. Discussing the role of labor unions, he chooses to emphasize that some strikes were made possible by financial support from Moscow to unions dominated by Communists.[29] Yet these economic strikes occurred on a recurring basis and constituted what amounted to a labor-market routine. As in other Nordic countries, there were vicious internal struggles in the labor movement, but the alleged risk of a Communist revolution was no more than Cold War rhetoric. Among the many factors woven together in the drama of Iceland's devaluation cycles, external Communist support was a minor one. Iceland's democracy was robust.

More generally, Gissurarson regards the devaluation cycles as proof that government planning led to no good. Such a Hayekian interpretation disregards that most of the decisions in the devaluation cycles were ad hoc crisis solutions deveoped by the networks of politicians, bureaucrats, and investors that dominated the state. The devaluation cycles entailed an unsystematic and wasteful approach to economic development. Political parties were entry points into a system where the main investor groups were linked to the two main parties (IP and PP). Even the SDP was involved in the system, which sustained elements of both cronyism and clientelism.[30] The fisheries sector, other businesses, as well as the farmers could count on generous grants and loans from specialized state funds. Party membership was key to many public-sector jobs. The system led to overinvestments. Rather than planning causing problems, the direct influence of various vested interests undermined planning and attempts at industrial diversification.

Still, the system secured high growth rates, with increased productivity and capacity across the economy. The Icelandic state was a developmental state, escaping problems of economic underdevelopment. It was possible to upgrade both social protection and the educational system. Supplementary pension funds were established in 1963 and extended in 1974, based on the Danish model of funds that were private, but linked to collective bargaining between unions and employer organizations.[31] These circumstances are hardly analyzed at all by Gissurarson. He simply accepts this institutional protection of labor.

Iceland's challenges in the 1980s were graver than those that caused the other Nordics to revise their economic policy models from the 1970s onward. The complementarities that created devaluation cycles had to be changed more radically. With increasing inflation, weak partnership in the labor market made the cycles worse. Furthermore, none of the other Nordics faced the prospect of completely losing their main resource. In this "existential" crisis for Iceland, the IP led by Oddsson took over as the leading government partner. Studying how the Oddsson government tackled the challenges facing Iceland, examine the three institutional complexes that defend labor, resources, and money, respectively. I first deal with institutions of labor and resource protection. I then analyze the internal differentiation of

Iceland's upper middle classes and the importance of these groups for the government's efforts to diversify and upgrade Iceland's economy. That analysis is crucial to the understanding of the problems that affected the institutions defending money, and therefore it precedes my final analysis of these monetary institutions in the run-up to the financial collapse.

INSTITUTIONS PROTECTING LABOR

In his *Wall Street Journal* laudation, Gissurarson praised Oddsson for bringing inflation under control. But unions and employers had already realized the unfortunate consequences of the devaluation cycles by the late 1980s, especially high inflation and ever more generalized indexing, including of interest rates. In 1990, they signed a National Reconciliation agreement. Although there were still a number of internal tensions, both on the union side and on the employer side, this agreement brought Iceland's labor market closer to the kinds of social partnership that prevailed elsewhere in the Nordic region. And that was before Oddsson took over.

In the 2004 article, Gissurarson drew up further plans for his neoliberal revolution. Privatization of the "health and education systems" was first on the list. But the Oddsson government did not launch reforms like those in Sweden. With strong unions, a wholesale privatization effort would have threatened the IP's broad electoral support base. In a recent debate, Gissurarson thus admitted that "Oddsson and his political associates" did not make "the National Pact, but rather that they fulfilled it" by exercising monetary and fiscal restraint.[32]

Ahead of both the 2003 and 2007 elections, Gissurarson, on a mission to defend government policies, issued a fierce critique of the work of his fellow social scientists concerning the development of income inequality (2003) and tax and pension policies (2008) under Oddsson.[33] An interesting feature of this highly polarized debate is how eagerly Gissurarson defended the accomplishments of the welfare state. His main deviation from the mainstream was to honor the IP success in making the Icelandic welfare state more sustainable because they succeeded in making the basic age pension adjusted for income in 1946. Right after the collapse, in 2009, Gissurarson published *The Impact of Tax Raises on Economic Growth and Living Standards* (in Icelandic), a book-length version of his defense of the government, relying on the work of Arthur Laffer, who had visited Iceland in 2007.[34]

Neither classical liberal nor Hayekian neoliberal ideas matched the circumstances of a convergence between labor-market institutions in Iceland and elsewhere in the Nordics. The topic of unions had been discussed within the Mont Pelerin Society in the 1950s, because the ordoliberals disagreed with Hayek on whether unions could be integrated in a market economy.[35] The point of departure for Hayek's ideas were nostalgic dreams of a long-gone situation where business elites did not need to bother about a working class represented by its own parties in parliaments, although as postwar history unfolded, he made concessions to the ordoliberal position. The Icelandic liberals were forced by the presence of a robust democracy with a reformist labor movement to conduct policies that were reformist, since orthodox neoliberal ideas did not match such circumstances.

INSTITUTIONS PROTECTING RESOURCES

While Iceland's population has a long experience preserving their agrarian resources in a cold climate with fragile ecosystems, the challenge of marine resource management was new. This task confronted all coastal states bordering rich fishing grounds. Iceland, the Netherlands, and Canada were the first to adopt quota systems (for certain species of fish) in the late 1970s.

In 1967–1968, the herring stock suddenly collapsed. Iceland's first ITQ (Individually Transferable Quotas) system was legislated in 1979 in the herring fisheries. The 1990 Fisheries Management Act extended ITQs to all commercial fisheries. Quotas were allocated to vessels as a function of their catch history before 1984 ("grandfathering"). When quota systems are implemented in specific contexts, a number of compromises are made, and they seldom end up being legislated in a way that satisfies the basic principles of the original blueprints. The actual quota system resulted from a process involving interested parties, experts (neoclassical economists), politicians, and movements.[36] The 1990 act had several exceptions. It did not apply to smaller boats, and there were restrictions on quota transfers. Total Allowable Catch (TAC) was determined by the state, based on advice from marine biologists at the government-financed Marine and Freshwater Research Institute.

Of all the topics Gissurarson deals with, the quota system is dearest to him. Here he finds circumstances that—nearly—match his ideas perfectly. He recounts how he suggested this solution early on, at a 1980 conference and in a 1983 article for the IEA.[37] However, since the system had emerged in 1975, he states that the system had evolved, thanks to the "Icelandic fishing community," which, "groping for solutions in a process of trial and error," came up with a feasible system that fit liberal ideas. But this was not the emergence of some kind of spontaneous order, since he makes note of "cooperation with government agencies."[38] The strongest forces behind it were the interests of the leading fisheries firms. The Icelandic Association of Fishing Vessels, now Fisheries Iceland, lobbied extensively. Many of the fisheries firms were core supporters of the IP.

Given the importance of the fisheries, debates about the quota system surface regularly in Icelandic politics. The ITQ system generated more efficient fisheries, but also concentrated ownership. During the devaluation cycles, the implicit industrial policy had also been a regional development strategy. A number of coastal villages would have at least one trawler. After the introduction of transferable quotas in 1990, many owners cashed in the value of their quota, selling off to larger fisheries firms with no presence in the village. A liberal party was represented in Parliament for three periods (1999 to 2009), mobilizing in response to these problems.

Whenever debates over the quota system arose, Gissurarson presented books or articles defending the 1990 solution. His conclusions were always the same: although not perfect, the existing system was the best one. He tirelessly rejected alternative schemes, especially proposals of resource rent taxation and state auctions of quotas, and more generally, any scheme he considered contrary to the interests of the fisheries firms.

The 1990s act was a compromise not fully in line with Gissurarson's liberal ideas. He notes that the state still ought to be excluded from the ITQ system. Fisheries firms should themselves determine the TAC, and Fisheries Iceland should be allowed to organize marine research.[39] Already in 1983, he had argued that if fishers/firms became owners, it would be in their self-interest to avoid free riding. The result would be "preservation and…multiplication of the stock."[40] But most experts maintain that management of stocks requires nonpartisan research in marine biology. Because quotas are proportions of the yearly catch, not linked to some geographically fixed plot of land, a state authority must enforce rules to prevent free riding. Furthermore, the state must conduct resource diplomacy with neighboring countries engaged in harvesting the waters through which the fish roam.

CLASS DIFFERENTIATION AND DIVERSIFICATION

Threatened by depletion, Iceland could not remain as dependent on fish as it had been, and Gissurarson contributed his vision of economic diversification. In 2002, he published *How Can Iceland Become the Richest Country in the World?* There, he suggests that Iceland could be turned into an international tax haven and financial center. According to his critics, this view was influential on the right wing.[41] The Oddsson government was happy to celebrate entrepreneurial efforts (such as the biopharmaceutical firm deCODE genetics),[42] but the general industrial policy followed from their Thatcherite/Reaganite model of privatization. The dogma was that diversification of the Icelandic economy would follow automatically if economic actors were given full freedom, and in contrast to the devaluation cycle system, the state should keep its hands off.

Beginning in the 1980s, diversification led to differentiation of Iceland's economic and political elite, which had been tightly knit and uninclusive. Three factions of Iceland's expanding upper-middle classes played roles in this development: financial professionals, the nouveau riche, and white-collar middle-class professionals in Iceland's administrative apparatus, particularly the financial regulators. In order to prepare the ground for an analysis of institutional change in Iceland's financial regulation, we must study how the Oddsson government related to these three groups, especially in the 2000s.

Privatization and financial deregulation opened up more jobs for financial professionals. The brokerage firm Kaupthing (later one of the three big banks) was the pioneer among such private newcomers. Most of the new skilled employees recruited into the various new financial firms (banks, brokerages, and other intermediaries) had business-school degrees in finance (MBAs or lower), mainly from the UK or United States. The leading ones brought with them an aggressive business model adopted from Wall Street investment banks.[43] To reduce its dependence on the fisheries, Iceland needed entrepreneurial talent in a growing onshore business. The nouveau riche were market operators unrelated to any of the earlier tightly knit investor networks. They differed from them in terms of age and class background, as well as individual histories. As for Iceland's administrative apparatus, a higher educational level, more meritocratic forms of recruitment, and increased participation in international agreements had weakened elements of the preexisting clientelism. These white-collar middle-class professionals had made the bureaucracy more accountable by the 1990s/2000s.[44] Of particular interest are the financial regulators, employed mainly in the Ministry of Finance, the Central Bank, and the Financial Supervision Authority.

The Oddsson government should have managed to take advantage of better bureaucracy, more skills, and full-blown financial services. Especially businessmen are the main heroes of MPS intellectuals. Diversification was supposed to follow as privatization created flourishing private firms in a free market, helped by full integration after 1995 into international financial markets. But paradoxically for the liberals, the strengthening of market forces by privatization and deregulation created fractions and conflict along generational lines. Circumstances developed in a way that was inconsistent with liberal ideas, leading to new state interventionism.

For the nouveau riche, a major change unfolded from the 1980s onward. The PP-dominated cooperative retail/distribution complex crumbled. Newcomers in the retail business established a retail chain, Bonus, able to offer consumer goods more cheaply than the cooperative complex, just as inflation peaked. The iconic figure of Iceland's boom and bust, Jón Ásgeir Jóhannesson, ascended from Bonus. He would not buy a toothbrush, it was said, unless he could borrow against it.[45] His activities soon extended globally. At the time of the 2008 collapse, his holding company, Baugur, had pyramid schemes going with all three banks.

In all of Gissurarson's writings, Jóhannesson is the main culprit. From 2002 on, he was a primary concern for the Oddsson government. This is a story of the strong-willed, well-articulated politician, Oddsson, trying to use state power to restrain the activities of one of the nouveau riche. It could have been taken straight out of an Ayn Rand novel, but with Oddsson as the culprit. As with any conflict, the story looks entirely different depending on the side from which one views it.

In 2002, there were police actions against Jóhannesson's business. He obviously claimed that Oddsson was using his position to have the court system clamp down on him.[46] Jóhannesson reacted in 2002 by buying Fréttablaðið, a free newspaper and main competitor to the IP house newspaper Morgunblaðið. He already owned four radio stations, adding a television station in 2003. The units were all parts of

Northern Lights, with Baugur as the main shareholder. These media channels were used against Oddsson, especially in the vicious 2003 election campaign. The Oddsson/Gissurarson side held that Jóhannesson and his media empire were supporting their main political challenger, the Social Democratic Alliance (SDP's new name).

Referring to his 1984 action against the airwaves monopoly, Gissurarson argued in 1990 that with private initiative, any private monopoly would falter under the pressure of market competition.[47] In 2004, however, the Oddsson government suggested state action against dominant ownership in the media market. In May, Parliament passed a media act limiting the extent to which a firm could accumulate market power in terms of radio and TV permits. The opposition held that the law was tailor-made to undermine Jóhannesson's media conglomerate. They were not against the legislation, but objected to Oddsson rushing a law through Parliament as an act of revenge. In the end, for the first time in Icelandic history, President Grimsson used one of the few politically important prerogatives granted an Icelandic president: he referred the act to a referendum.[48] The government withdrew the law and did not submit it again.

This deep, personalized conflict interacted with strategic maneuvering by the new finance professionals. Because repressed finance had been even more driven by the state in Iceland than in other countries, financial deregulation implied privatization of a number of state banks and funds. Oddsson engaged in conflicts with some of the new financial firms. His opposition to Kaupthing related back to an early bank privatization. Kaupthing here—in Oddsson's view—conned the authorities, securing majority ownership for a new investor network, the Orca network, thus undermining his attempts to create financial consumerism on the Thatcher model.[49]

The Oddsson government had tried for some time to convince foreign investors to engage in the Icelandic stock market by buying up formerly state-owned banks.[50] But it failed, despite full external deregulation since 1995. To British financial experts, Iceland's capital market still looked too much like capital markets in less developed economies: immature and overly dependent on local networks. In the end, as the final step in the privatization of financial firms, the two banks were sold (at very favorable terms) to Icelandic investor groups in 2002. Critics claimed that each bank went to "clients" of the two governing parties, the IP and the PP.[51] Gissurarson, in contrast, insists that everything was done according to the book and that the groups that took over the banks did not have strong ties to the parties.

There were other cases in which the governing parties tried to give advantages to other groups of the nouveau riche, hoping that they might balance Jóhannesson, Kaupthing, or other businessmen that the government could not for some reason accept. Since a stock market now existed, such attempts to secure loyalty between the government and selected groups did not last long. In the mid-2000s, economic frenzy and hectic dealmaking cut across any divisions that the government tried to maintain. Thus, if the government wanted to return to the cronyism of the devaluation cycles, it was unsuccessful.

Iceland's generation of nouveau riche investors (most of them born in the late 1960s and early 1970s) are sometimes referred to as "oligarchs." That analogy is not precise. Russia's oligarchs arose from the ruins of the former Soviet Union's socialist planned economy. In contrast, the Icelandic system under the devaluation cycles was not—despite Gissurarson's claims to the contrary—a socialist system. An analogy to present-day Russia might be more apt. Oddsson developed a strong dislike for certain nouveau riche operators that he for some reason defined as outsiders to his project. If we are to believe Boyes's journalistic investigations and at least one of the financial memoirs published after the crash, Oddsson's strategy was reminiscent of Putin's in Russia's state-capitalist system: penalizing "oligarchs" who refused to cooperate with his regime, and rewarding those who supported him.[52] But Oddsson failed where Putin has thus far succeeded.

Iceland's bureaucracy in the 2000s was more accountable than under the devaluation cycles. It was thus not easy for the ministers to use it in politically sensitive cases. At least, the government behaved inconsistently. If Ayn Rand's work is any standard for a government wanting to conduct a liberal revolution, a government that could not keep its hands off business certainly failed.

It now remains to discuss how the Oddsson regime related to the monetary relations of the Icelandic economy. How could it be that the level of financial systemic risk grew so dramatically after the early 2000s?

INSTITUTIONS PROTECTING MONEY

Oddsson left the government in 2005 to become governor of the Central Bank (CBI). This was a political appointment—he had no economics education. Leading the CBI board of governors, he was informed about the growth of systemic risk. The warnings he issued are used for all they are worth in Gissurarson's account of Oddsson's story: success from 1991 to 2004, destabilized by the "media mogul" Jóhannesson, who turned public opinion against Oddsson and brainwashed Icelanders to believe in everlasting prosperity. Gissurarson fails to report that other nouveau riche stock market operators supported Oddsson and the IP.

In the second period, from 2006 to 2009, Gissurarson portrays Oddsson as tirelessly combating the growing financial instability. But Jóhannesson's media exposed his warnings as episodes of "crying wolf." At the time, there were no laws preventing private interests from supporting political parties. Gissurarson holds that Jóhannesson thus also had strong influence in the SDP, the IP's coalition partner beginning in 2006.

It seems unlikely that the frenzied mindset of Iceland's financial mania can be traced back only to Jóhannesson's media campaigns against Oddsson. It must first and foremost be linked to the three new upper-middle-class groups presented above. Since 2009, a growing literature, including a large report from the Special Investigation Commission (SIC) established by the Haarde government in December 2008, has shed light on the processes that interacted to blow up financial risk in Iceland's capital market.[53] The main features of this vicious circle were the "incestuous" relations between banks and holding companies.[54] The investment companies of the *nouveau riche* interacted with the aggressive banks run by the new finance professionals both at home and abroad. Regulators struggled to keep track of what was happening around them, working very hard, but increasingly stymied by undercapacity, loss of skilled personnel to private banks, regulatory capture, and politicians infected by the mania of everlasting financial frenzy. In the end, regulators were unable to control the forces unbound in the stock market bubble.

Although Haarde, another former *Eimreiðin* activist, was prime minister from 2006 to 2009, Gissurarson's defense centers on Oddsson. The question is whether the government and central bank under Oddsson should be seen as a necessary part of the vicious circle that triggered systemic risk. There is no simple answer to this question. Instead, two explanatory strategies can be suggested: one political and one structural.

Several studies—many of them connected to or relying on the SIC—suggest a political explanation. They point to instances where government strategy and decisions played a role: the privatization of the two banks in 2002, its strategy of turning Iceland into an international financial sector,[55] and government fiscal policies. There are also the CBI monetary policies.

However, these sequences may also be related to structural factors, particularly to international monetary integration since the end of the Bretton Woods monetary regime. The turn to flexible exchange rates and EU monetary integration in the Eurozone led to internal and external financial deregulation across Western Europe. In a Nordic comparison, the timing of Iceland's deregulation stands out: it was later and faster than the four others. Only by the early 1990s had Iceland terminated the main internal elements of its peculiar state-directed repressed finance system.[56]

Furthermore, Iceland was on the way to establish fully developed capital market institutions for the first time, much delayed compared with the other Nordic countries. The system was still rudimentary. The Central Bank had been established in 1961, and a separate Financial Supervision Authority was established only in 1999. Bank privatization was in progress until 2002. External financial deregulation—opening up for short-term capital movements—happened four to five years after the larger Nordics and in one stroke, when Iceland joined the European Economic Area, beginning on January 1, 1995. While both Iceland's new bank employees and the regulators were surely skilled, none of them had any experience concerning local bubbles and banking crises: a crucial difference from their Nordic peers, who had experienced early 1990s banking crises.

This structural explanation of the vicious circle necessarily includes the regulators, the newly rich, and the finance professionals. In a formal sense, the government is responsible for the decisions of the financial regulators, but in monetary regulation, politicians depend on the expertise of the regulators. The thorny question here involves a counterfactual: Would any other realistic government coalition in Iceland have managed to prevent the growing systemic financial risk? Given the immature state of capital-market institutions and the lack of experience of the skilled groups of financial sector professionals and regulators, the structural argument is that no political coalition would have been able to stabilize the situation by the mid-2000s. Although Iceland's financial crash is well researched, it is still not clear whether the structural or the political explanation is the best one.

INTERNATIONAL FACTORS IN THE 2008 COLLAPSE

High systemic risk does not automatically lead to a financial meltdown. In 2006, Iceland was already challenged by hedge funds and other speculators using the new financial instruments such as credit default swaps against the banks. This came to be known as the Geyser Crisis, but it was solved by concerted domestic action in April 2006, even involving the union pension funds.[57]

In 2018, Gissurarson's report on the reasons for Iceland's collapse was published.[58] Gissurarson claims that Iceland would have managed its liquidity problems if the U.S. Federal Reserve and/or other central banks (in particular the European Central Bank and the Bank of England) had provided liquidity through swap lines such as those offered to many other central banks, including the other Nordic banks.

Here is another historical irony for the IP as a liberal party. The question of neutrality versus Western alliance and NATO membership was a permanent postwar foreign policy cleavage, with the U.S. Keflavik base as the focal point. The IP was the most pro-U.S. party, playing a key role when Iceland became one of NATO's founding members. Gissurarson always supported this line. However, the IP governments—despite diplomatic efforts—were unable to prevent the United States from pulling out from Keflavik in 2006.

Turning himself into an international relations scholar, Gissurarson has pondered extensively why the Western great powers failed to save Iceland in October 2008. In the end, he provides a "logic of the situation" explanation based on extensive document analysis. In particular, he makes claims about the motives of politicians in the British Labour government.

Most analyses of these matters by economists, however, infer other motives than Gissurarson does, most notably, that leading central bankers and politicians abroad realized that Iceland's banks had both overexpanded and made themselves unpopular in financial centers abroad. Iceland's authorities and regulators, they claim, had failed to regulate the financial sector sufficiently. The topic of the motives of external actors is not as yet extensively researched, but for once, Gissurarson here sketches an analysis that even his left-wing critics may find interesting.

Forced to resign from the Central Bank, Oddsson became editor of *Morgunblaðið* in 2009. The large fisheries firms, at the time the main owners of the newspaper, knew that Oddsson had always been a master of political rhetoric. He could argue against Icelandic EU membership, which they were eager to avoid. In June 2016, Oddsson launched a big campaign to become president of Iceland, but lost to a more neutral and academic candidate. After 2008, Oddsson and Gissurarson lost most of their influence in the IP, which is presently in a coalition government under a left-wing prime minister.

In 2012, Gissurarson again outsourced his think-tank activities to a center outside of the university, possibly because of his loss of influence within the IP. The Research Centre for Innovation and Economic Growth (RNH) took up the legacy of the Þorláksson Institute. It runs a website with miscellaneous information on neoliberal activities.

The RNH accepts donations from individuals and corporations. No information is available on who finances it. It is not clear whether the RNH conducts commissioned research based on funding apart from donations. The RNH has an academic council (including Gissurarson), a board of directors (presently consisting of some hedge fund managers, the owner of *Morgunblaðið*, and the present secretary of the IP), and a managing director. With a Reykjavik publisher, RNH recently launched Icelandic translations of three Ayn Rand novels, *The Fountainhead*, *Atlas Shrugged*, and *We the Living*.

CONCLUSION

With his original reference to John Stuart Mill, Gissurarson suggested that during Oddsson's reign, the "right ideas" met with the "right circumstances." But circumstances and ideas always interact. Circumstances give rise to several sets of ideas that evolve, conflict, or converge. Actors and movements are constantly gathering information on changing circumstances. As knowledge is developed, original ideas are changed, modified, or dropped. Some ideas are revolutionary. They require fundamental social change with reference to normative political philosophies. But exposed to circumstances, revolutionary ideas are mostly converted to reformist ideas, as analysis of context prompts an adjustment of policies to fit the realm of the possible. Circumstances change due to these modified ideas, unintended consequences, and structural forces.

Gissurarson implicitly admits that the Oddsson governments failed to pursue "revolutionary" neoliberal policies. He acknowledges that Iceland's policies converged in the direction of the other Nordics by arguing that the Nordic model is now a liberal one. This has been a common tactic by right-wing think tanks across the Nordic countries since the 2000s, particularly after the four larger Nordics avoided financial meltdown in 2008.[59] In particular, Sweden's austere policies and privatizations since the 1980s incarnate such a model.

Gissurarson's analysis of the Nordic models is eclectic.[60] It combines substantive historical claims with a descriptive history of ideas covering any odd regional contributor to liberal political philosophy. As when he writes Icelandic history, a one-sided individualist stance leads to a bracketing of the role of movements, particularly the labor movement.

Gissurarson's claim to a liberal revolution is unfounded in all the institutional areas discussed above. The IP liberals played along with circumstances. The government relied on existing institutional complexes for the defense of labor and resources. Circumstances forced it to accept the welfare state that Hayek and his first-generation MPS intellectuals viewed with skepticism, however ambivalent. The more important role of means testing was an earlier IP victory, not something that the Oddsson regime introduced. As for social partnership, its income policies respected the framework established by the 1990 National Reconciliation agreement. With regard to resource management, the ITQ system antedated both Gissurarson's own writings and

Oddsson's government. There are indications that Oddsson—working for diversification—used the state against those among the *nouveau riche* whom he considered his enemies. That may have added to the turmoil during Iceland's mania, but not by means of particularly liberal policies.

Learning that circumstances required something different from what liberal ideas implied, the Oddsson governments pursued reformism. They continued to rely on institutional complementarities that made Iceland's political economy more similar to the other Nordic models than ever before. In so doing, they secured relative price stability and avoided extensive labor-market conflicts. In particular, they relied on the complementarities between social-protection institutions, systems of competence building, and social partnership as institutional defenses of labor. In terms of monetary management, different timing compared with the other Nordics was part of the conditions for the 2008 drama. After the collapse, Iceland's monetary management converged toward the present system in the other Nordics. It is only with respect to resource management that a difference from the other Nordics remains. There is no taxation of the resource rent in the fisheries, but that was the case before Oddsson, and it has not been changed after him.[61]

The Oddsson government—hero-worshipped by Gissurarson—achieved little more than tampering with trends and structures that their liberal offensive could not change. Interests and ideas in Iceland converged in ways that left the country ill prepared to deal with the effect of a climate of globalized finance and speculation. The would-be heroes of an Ayn Rand novel were more like victims of circumstance.

1. Hannes H. Gissurarson, "Miracle on Iceland," *Wall Street Journal*, January 29, 2004, https://www.wsj.com/articles/SB107533182153814498; Gissurarson, "Forsendur Frjálshyggjubyltingarinnar" (Premises for the liberal revolution), *Visbending* 24. 49, 2006, pp. 6–11.

2. John Stuart Mill, "The Claims of Labour" (1845), in *Collected Works*, vol. 4, *Essays on Economics and Society, 1824–1879*, John M. Robson, ed. (Toronto: University of Toronto Press, 1967), p. 370. See also Hannes H. Gissurarson "When Ideas Conspire with Circumstances," *Journal des Économistes et des Études Humaines* 10.2 (2000), pp. 285–314; Gissurarson, *Island* (Stockholm: Timbro, 1990), p. 158.

3. Gissurarson, "Miracle on Iceland."

4. Karl Polanyi, in *The Great Transformation: The Political and Economic Origins of Our Time* (1944; Boston: Beacon Press, 1967), regarded institutions as defenses of the three "non-commodities": labor, money, and resources. I turn this into a framework for analysis of institutional complexes. See Lars Mjøset, "A Varieties Approach to the Varieties of Capitalism," in Seán Ó'Riain, Felix Behling, Rossella Ciccia, and Eoin Flaherty, eds., *The Changing Worlds and Workplaces of Capitalism* (London: Palgrave Macmillan, 2015), pp. 15–37. For an application to Nordic varieties of capitalism, see Lars Mjøset, "The Nordic Route to Development," ch. 29 in Erik S. Reinert, Jayati Ghosh & Rainer Kattel, eds., *Handbook of Alternative Theories of Economic Development* (Cheltenham: Edward Elgar, 2016), pp. 533–69.

5. The principal source for what follows is Hannes H. Gissurarson, "Liberalism in Iceland in the Nineteenth and Twentieth Centuries," *Econ Journal Watch* 14.2 (2017), pp. 241–72, https://econjwatch.org/File+download/980/GissurarsonMay2017.pdf?mimetype=pdf.

6. Research Centre for Innovation and Economic Growth, "Jon Thorlaksson Institute," http://www.rnh.is/?page_id=346.

7. Gissurarson, *Island*, p. 159.

8. Hannes H. Gissurarson, *Hayek's Conservative Liberalism* (New York: Garland, 1987), p. 5.

9. Wikipedia, "Hannes Hólmsteinn Gissurarson," https://en.wikipedia

.org/wiki/Hannes_H%C3%B3lmsteinn_Gissurarson; Gissurarson, "Liberalism in Iceland in the Nineteenth and Twentieth Centuries," pp. 258–63.

10. Gissurarson, *Island*, ch. 4; Gissurarson, "Icelandic Liberalism and Its Critics: A Rejoinder to Stefan Olafsson," *Econ Journal Watch* 15.3 (2018), p. 335.

11. Gissurarson, *Island*, p. 108.

12. Gissurarson, "Liberalism in Iceland in the Nineteenth and Twentieth Centuries," pp. 267–68.

13. Research Centre for Economic Growth, "Jon Thorlaksson Institute," http://www.rnh.is/?page_id=346.

14. Research Centre for Innovation and Economic Growth, "Mont Pelerin Society," http://www.rnh.is/?page_id=344.

15. Gissurarson, "Liberalism in Iceland in the Nineteenth and Twentieth Centuries," pp. 241–42.

16. Stefán Ólafsson, "From Political Advocacy to 'Alternative Facts': A Comment on Hannes Gissurarson's Method," *Econ Journal Watch* 14.3 (2017), p. 403. The concept of agnotology was coined by historians of science. See Robert N. Proctor and Londa Schiebinger, eds., *Agnotology: The Making and Unmaking of Ignorance* (Stanford: Stanford University Press, 2008).

17. Gissurarson, "Liberalism in Iceland in the Nineteenth and Twentieth Centuries"; Gissurarson, "Anti-Liberal Narratives about Iceland, 1991–2017," *Econ Journal Watch* 14.3 (2017), pp. 362–98.

18. Gunnar Karlsson, *Iceland's 1100 Years* (Reykjavik: Mál og Menning, 2000), p. 171.

19. Gissurarson, *Island*, p. 42.

20. Gudmundur Jónsson, "The Icelandic Welfare State in the Twentieth Century," *Scandinavian Journal of History* 26.3 (2002), pp. 255–56.

21. Stefán Ólafsson, "From Political Advocacy to 'Alternative Facts,'" p. 418.

22. Ólafur Th Hardarson and Gunnar Helgi Kristinsson, "The Icelandic Parliamentary Election of 1987," *Electoral Studies* 6.3 (1987), p. 220.

23. Birgir B. Sigurjonsson, "National Sovereignty and Economic Policy," *Scandinavian Economic History Review* 33.1 (1985), pp. 51–65. Gudmundur Jónsson, "Iceland and the Nordic Model of Consensus Democracy," *Scandinavian Journal of History* 39.4 (2014), pp. 510–28.

24. See Steffen E. Andersen, *The Evolution of Nordic Finance* (London: Palgrave Macmillan, 2011), p. 9 for the definition of developed capital markets, which include institutions of capital intermediation.

25. Gissurarson, "Liberalism in Iceland in the Nineteenth and Twentieth Centuries," pp. 253–58; Gissurarson, *Island*, ch. 2.

26. Hardarson and Kristinsson, "The Icelandic Parliamentary Election of 1987," p. 219.

27. Systems of competence building refers to capacity institutions such as schools, other skills-related organizations, as well as to technology and innovation policies. Mjøset, "The Nordic Route to Development," p. 536.

28. Ibid., p. 558.

29. Gissurarson, "Anti-Liberal Narratives about Iceland, 1991–2017," pp. 364–65.

30. Gunnar Helgi Kristinsson, "Clientelism in a Cold Climate," in Simona Piattoni, ed., *Clientelism, Interests, and Democratic Representation: The European Experience in Historical and Comparative Perspective* (Cambridge: Cambridge University Press, 2001), pp. 172–92.

31. Jónsson, "The Icelandic Welfare State in the Twentieth Century," p. 260.

32. Gissurarson, "Icelandic Liberalism and Its Critics: A Rejoinder to Stefan Olafsson," p. 335.

33. Summarized in the debate between Gissurarson and Ólafsson in *Econ Journal Watch* in 2017 and 2018.

34. Stefán Ólafsson, "The Political Economy of Iceland's Boom and Bust," in Valur Ingimundarson, Philippe Urfalino, and Irma Erlingsdóttir, eds., *Iceland's Financial Crisis* (London: Routledge, 2016), p. 61.

35. Yves Steiner, "The Neoliberals Confront the Trade Unions," in Philip Mirowski and Dieter Plehwe, eds., *The Road from Mont Pèlerin: The Making of the Neoliberal Thought Collective* (Cambridge, MA: Harvard University Press, 2009), pp. 181–203.

36. For a general framework, see Petter Holm, Jesper Raakjær, Rikke Becker Jacobsen, and Edgar Henriksen, "Contesting the Social Contracts Underpinning Fisheries," *Marine Policy* 55 (2015), pp. 64–72.

37. Hannes H. Gissurarson, "The Fish War: A Lesson from Iceland,"

Economic Affairs 3.3 (1983), pp. 220–23; Gissurarson, "Liberalism in Iceland in the Nineteenth and Twentieth Centuries," p. 23. See also Research Centre for Economic Growth, "Jon Thorlaksson Institute."

38. Gissurarson, "Liberalism in Iceland in the Nineteenth and Twentieth Centuries," p. 264.

39. Gissurarson, "Anti-Liberal Narratives about Iceland, 1991–2017," p. 371.

40. Gissurarson, "The Fish War," p. 222.

41. Gissurarson, *Hvernig getur Ísland orðið ríkasta land í heimi?* (Reykjavik: Nýja bókafélagið, 2002); Ólafsson, "The Political Economy of Iceland's Boom and Bust," p. 74.

42. Armann Thorvaldsson, *Frozen Assets: How I Lived Iceland's Boom and Bust* (New York: Wiley, 2009), p. 51.

43. Ásgeir Jónsson, *Why Iceland?: How One of the World's Smallest Countries Became the Meltdown's Biggest Casualty* (New York: McGraw Hill, 2009), p. 55.

44. Kristinsson, "Clientelism in a Cold Climate," pp. 189–90.

45. Thorvaldsson, *Frozen Assets*, p. 134.

46. Roger Boyes, *Meltdown Iceland: How the Global Financial Crisis Bankrupted an Entire Country* (London: Bloomsbury, 2009), ch. 5; Thorvaldsson, *Frozen Assets*, p. 75 and ch. 4, "The Grand Master Syndrome," pp. 57–86.

47. Gissurarson, *Island*, p. 165.

48. Ólafur Th Hardarson and Gunnar Helgi Kristinsson, "Iceland," *European Journal of Political Research* 44 (2005), p. 1042.

49. Ólafsson, "From Political Advocacy to 'Alternative Facts,'" p. 408; Thorvaldsson, *Frozen Assets*, pp. 54–56.

50. Gudrun Johnsen, *Bringing Down the Banking System: Lessons from Iceland* (London: Palgrave Macmillan, 2014), ch. 5, "Financial Liberalization," pp. 59–74.

51. Thorvaldsson, *Frozen Assets*, pp. 102–14.

52. See Boyes, *Meltdown Iceland*.

53. Jónsson, *Why Iceland?*, ch. 5–6; Johnsen, *Bringing Down the Banking System*, part 3. For the report, see *Report of the Special Investigation Commission* (SIC), http://www.rna.is/eldri-nefndir/addragandi-og-orsakir-falls-islensku-bankanna-2008/skyrsla-nefndarinnar/english. It should be noted that the key

actors in the dominant export sector, the large fisheries firms, were not part of the stock market bubble. With few exceptions, they financed their activities in international financial markets, not in the domestic Icelandic stock market.

54. Jónsson, *Why Iceland?*, pp. 96–97.

55. For the strategy, see Gissurarson, *Hvernig getur Ísland orðið ríkasta land í heimi?* For the Ásgrimsson committee of February 2005, see Jónsson, *Why Iceland*, pp. 109 and 139. For the high interest rate monetary policy since 2001, see Jónsson, *Why Iceland?*, p. 70.

56. Jónsson, *Why Iceland?*, pp. 30–31.

57. Johnsen, *Bringing Down the Banking System*, ch. 7, "The Geyser Crisis," pp. 83–90.

58. Centre for Political and Economic Research at the Social Science Research Institute, University of Iceland, *The 2008 Icelandic Bank Collapse: Foreign Factors*, downloadable from Iceland's Ministry of Finance: https://www. stjornarradid.is/lisalib/getfile.aspx?itemid=29cca5ac-c0c6-11e8-942c-005056bc530c.

59. See Lars Mjøset, "Social Science, Humanities, and 'the Nordic Model,'" in H. Byrkjeflot, K. Petersen, L. Mjøset, and M. Mordhorst, eds., *The Making and Circulation of Nordic Models* (London: Routledge, 2021).

60. Hannes H. Gissurarson, *The Nordic Models* (Brussels: New Direction, 2016).

61. The postcrisis left-wing government, 2009–2013, launched a process of constitutional revision. One of the core issues was whether natural resources not in private ownership should be declared the property of the nation. However, the revision did not pass Parliament and later governments have not revived it. See the chapters in part 3 of Ingimundarson, Urfalino and Erlingsdóttir, eds., *Iceland's Financial Crisis*.

Looking Back to the Future
of Neoliberalism Studies

Dieter Plehwe

This book brings a new conclusion to the Mont Pelerin Society study project that started in 2002 with an initial conference in Berlin. The first English-language statement of the project, *Neoliberal Hegemony: A Global Critique*,[1] opened the quest for research on networks of neo-liberal intellectuals of and around the Mont Pelerin Society (MPS), founded by Friedrich Hayek and others in Switzerland in 1947. The MPS has grown over time to a total of over twelve hundred members distributed unevenly across the world. We set ourselves the task of studying the varieties of neoliberalism across time and space with a particular eye to the transnational networks of intellectuals and their allies in business, media, culture, and politics. The project aimed at intellectual histories of individuals, groups of scholars, and schools of thought, the study of countries and policy fields, the manifestation of neoliberalism in popular culture and overlapping and competing ideologies and worldviews, as well as in neoliberalism's opponents. Neoliberalism, like other worldviews, owes its existence and evolution to collaboration, contestation, and confrontation. The present volume is the fourth in a series of edited volumes that include *The Road from Mont Pèlerin, Nine Lives of Neoliberalism*, and *Neoliberal Hegemony*.[2]

Although global in scope, desire, and practice, a certain Euro-centrism and Anglocentrism still characterizes much of the work published on the MPS-related neoliberalism so far. Most authors come from Western Europe and North America, and most of the intellectuals and countries covered have also been European and American. In this volume, the MPS and Neoliberalism Studies Project left the trodden path. *Market Civilizations* reaches a conclusion by way of delivering on the original promise of an unorthodox approach to the study of ideas and performativity: the authors show how Western stereotypes of diffusion, transfer, and translation do not suffice to explain the instantiation of neoliberalism around the world. We foreground a number of neoliberals in each country hitherto virtually unknown even to those in the field and observe how they were involved in crafting local recombinations of neoliberal ideas and practice. Beyond international diffusion studies, both a local and a transnational social-network perspective is required to make sense of the dynamics in different spaces and arenas of neoliberal reflection and inflection.

At this point, it is worth leaning back a moment to ask where our approach came from in the first place. One book was of particular relevance for the original project: Peter Hall's edited study of Keynesianism in different countries, published in 1989 under the title *The Political Power of Economic Ideas*.[3] Hall asked if the monumental shift from orthodox neoclassical equilibrium economics to the Keynesian understanding of disequilibrium and underemployment was to be explained with an approach focused on economists, states, or coalitions. His answer was that all three perspectives were required, insisting that a new economic approach needs to convince in both academic and political realms, the latter by way of mobilizing support from broad coalitions and demonstrating political viability. Albert O. Hirschman's comments on the chapters of the book at the time already cut across Hall's nation-state-centered comparative approach. Hirschman drew attention to the transnational weight of the United States after World War II, which paradoxically resulted in restraining Keynesianism in occupied Germany and Japan while supporting the new doctrine in the allied countries of France and the United Kingdom due to the role of different wings of the economics profession in the different parts of the foreign-policy establishment of the United States.[4]

Dealing, as we did, with a colossal new shift, from Keynesianism to neoliberalism, there was a lot to learn from Peter Hall's book for our approach in terms of combining intellectual, institutional, and socio-economic levels of analysis in the study of paradigm change. In light of Hirschman's argument, we felt there clearly was an additional need to address international public institutions, international organizations, and international power relations manifest in the ambiguities of European integration, "the Washington Consensus," neoliberalism, and the "Geneva school" of global trade institutions, among others. And there were things apparently different and new when it came to neoliberalism compared with the days of Lord Keynes. Nobody in Peter Hall's volume wrote about networks of intellectuals and organizations, in spite of the pattern set by the Fabian Society or the Vienna Circles,[5] for example, which in certain ways served as templates for the Mont Pelerin Society.

Contrary to the very limited internationalization of the Fabians and the limited international participation in the Vienna Circles, neoliberal networks were transnational at birth, due to war and emigration. They were quite large and growing fast in the postwar constellation of cheaper travel and communications. They were both transdisciplinary and interdisciplinary and not confined to academia, much like the Fabians and the Vienna Circles, only more extensive. Given their regular pattern of work in conferences, publications, elite networks, and (academic) institution building, it was necessary to pay particular attention to them, in addition to the factors previously considered relevant in the study of the prospect of new economic ideas. We needed to study the political and economic power of neoliberal ideas.

We were recently reminded by Rafael Khachaturian that Hall's volume was part of the U.S. Social Science Research Council–funded Committee on States and Social Structures,[6] which also supported the famous book *Bringing the State Back In*,[7] devoted to reintroducing the state to the social-science narratives on class and behaviorism prevailing at the time. The renewed emphasis on the state turned out to be both a blessing and a curse for neoliberalism studies. It ultimately helped to deconstruct neoliberal antistate rhetoric as a strategy to reform and redirect a strong state, but it also restricted necessary attention to class formation and civil society across borders in comparative research programs on topics such as the varieties of capitalism.[8] The parallel attacks on the welfare state and on renewed class struggle driven by strong elements of the bourgeoisie in extractive industries, manufacturing, and finance in conjunction with neoliberal intellectuals suggested the limits to a nation-state-centered comparative approach. For neoliberalism studies, it was time to bring class, civil society, and ideas back in in order to help explain institutional change and neoliberal transformations within and across the borders of nation-states. The many conceptual and organizational links between the chapters of the present volume, for example the Guatemala Marroquín University template for the Montenegro University of Donja Gorica, illustrate the benefit and underline the need for new "open system" comparative studies.

The way in which the focus on international diffusion has come to occupy the mainstream of social science underlines the urgency of a new approach and the need for theoretical development and refinement. Apart from the Stanford sociological "world society" school—focusing on the global diffusion of social norms and standards such as gender equality, human rights, and business practices[9]—the most important approach in political science can be summarized as diffusion and translation, or local adaptation, offering an export/import and adaptation model of international diffusion.

Sprawling *political* diffusion studies were driven to no small degree by the experience of accelerated and intensified market-led globalization, which required the multinational replication of neoliberal policy approaches even if the limits of original policies were well known.[10] Corporation-friendly tax regimes, foreign investment–friendly capital-market regulation, and pension privatization, to name a few, were all policies adopted in many different countries. Diffusion studies observed various mechanisms relevant to the dissemination of new concepts, such as competition, coercion, and learning. In all of the case studies, a policy was exported and imported, already existing in one country and making its way to another. Authors showed how these processes are uneven, depending on conditions in importing countries ready to adopt certain policies because of institutional similarity or political proximity of government orientations. They also showed how they depend on local institutional filters, which modify or translate imported approaches and adapt new knowledge to local circumstances.[11] Unlike the somewhat nebulous sociological focus on the diffusion of norms and standards, the political-science model maintained a traditional interstate perspective and implied a fair amount of functionalism.

We can see some of the empirical and epistemological limits of the diffusion-and-filter approach to neoliberalization clearly in a study on the multicountry phenomenon of privatization of public corporations that employs this approach.[12] Based on the standard model, the authors of "The Decision to Privatize: Economists and the Construction of Ideas and Policies" (2008) account for Chicago-trained economists in relevant government positions outside the United States to explain the global alignment of change in the public sectors. While the network analysis of Chicago-trained economists in key positions in many different countries is certainly interesting, it raises more questions than it answers. To name a few: Why did the authors not add Virginia-trained (public-choice) economists to the group of likely advocates of privatization?[13] Why are German ordoliberals trained in Freiburg, Cologne, or Marburg and the many European public-choice economists trained in different European universities not added to the analysis? The export/import model ultimately fails to account for the multinational and transnational dimensions of groups of economists and other academics in favor of privatization[14] who are involved in neoliberal cross-border networks of intellectuals and organizations such as the Mont Pelerin Society and the closely related think tanks of the Atlas Network.[15]

In contrast to prevailing export-import models related to institutional change and local adaptation, the concepts of transnational communities and private authority widely used in international relations do acknowledge the existence of cross-border agencies and epistemic authority,[16] which leads us to the recent additions to the literature on transnational institutions and professions. The most prominent contributions are epistemic communities and professional communities. Experts and expertise are in fact central in much of the research on transnational governance, with attention to diverse actors ranging from NGOs to professional associations, corporate foundations and corporations, and institutions.[17] Most recently, Ole Jacob Sending,[18] as well as Leonard Seabrooke and Lasse Henriksen,[19] have emphasized the relevance of competing groups of professionals in the quest for issue control and the exercise of power across borders.

The strategic capacities of such actor groups depend to a great degree on the access to and use of organizations, which explains the need for systematic study of the interrelated networks of individuals and organizations.[20] This was of course a staple in the established field of studying professions. In neoliberalism studies, a strong focus emerged on the *economics* profession.[21] Although neoclassical economics and neoliberalism are sometimes treated as synonyms, and the economics profession as a whole has been blamed for neoliberalism, serious scholarship is careful to observe ongoing conflicts within the economics profession and the particular influence that neoliberalism is able to exert. Cornel Ban analyzed struggles between market socialists, structuralists, and neoliberals in Romania in the 1990s and the somewhat surprising victory of neoliberal economics in that country.[22] Important conflicts with regard to regulatory reforms have been found to pit neoliberal economists and legal scholars against each other,[23] while the discipline of law and economics was originally promoted specifically (by MPS member Henry Manne) to align neoliberal economic ideas and legal scholarship.[24] Such efforts demonstrate the need to develop further a keen interest in and explanation of the neoliberalization of quite a number of professions, the transformation of political technocracy, and the cross-cutting dimensions of neoliberal norms and principled beliefs in academic, political, professional, and other fields.[25]

In light of the shortcomings of epistemic and other transnational community approaches[26] and the focus on professions in "diffusion" and transformation studies, the MPS study project has relied on the concepts of "thought collectives" and "thought style," following the work of Karl Mannheim and Ludwik Fleck.[27] Such individual and competing groups of intellectuals rise, connect, interact, institutionalize, and otherwise develop over time in diverse ways. The present collection shows how little a diffusion-and-adaptation model tells us, compared with what we can learn if we look at how and why actors reflect on, negotiate, and renegotiate local challenges and develop neoliberal approaches locally in isolation (in the Soviet Union originally, for example) with partial reliance on the work of neoliberals from other countries, or in close interaction with organized neoliberals from abroad, not always harmoniously.

Worldviews and concepts arise in similar constellations[28] and offer opportunities to connect and guide social forces in conflicts and contestations within and across borders that nevertheless differ greatly across time and space. The labor of both neoliberal convergence and divergence in response to challengers and partners is important to keep thought collectives alive and ideologies thriving. Mont Pelerin provided intellectuals in many countries with resources to advance within and across professions, even if the political orientations of organized neoliberals differed—mosaic neoliberalism, rather than a uniform party.

This finding can make the mapping of neoliberalism challenging, but political and ideological discussions rarely come in neat packages, and neoliberal conversations are no exception. While the equation of neoliberalism by Pierre Bourdieu and others with a *pensée unique*[29] distracts from the diversity within neoliberalism, the neoliberalization of both conservatism and social democracy help explain the exasperation with academic and public debates emerging under the condition of a dominating thought style.[30] Such hegemony creates the conditions for the invisible "third face" of power to come forcefully into play beyond coercion and agenda-setting capacities.[31] While such (neoliberal) hegemony nonetheless can always be only partial and temporary, the lack of relevant opposition and significant contestation explains why certain ways of reasoning (on choice architectures, financial markets, austerity, or rational behavior assumptions, for example) can survive even a great upheaval like the global financial crisis. The accounts of neoliberalism in this collection contribute to a better understanding of both the strengths and weaknesses of contemporary neoliberalism, because they closely follow neoliberals, rather than imagining its universal (non)existence.

Rereading the contributions to this volume, at least three themes emerge that are striking in the ongoing need to deal with the evolution of neoliberal thought over time. First, there is clear evidence from the chapters on Turkey, Japan, India, and Guatemala in support of the ongoing effort of neoliberal intellectuals to realign their worldview with cultural traditions and suitable interpretations of local world religions such as Islam, Hinduism, or Christianity. Brazil and South Africa can be cited to point to the neoliberal opportunities presented by cultural change. Second, the chapters on Montenegro, Iceland, and Guatemala show the expansion of neoliberal partisan think tanks into the realms of academia and vice versa. And third, almost all chapters in this book underline the growing concern about the multifold tensions between neoliberalism and democracy and the sometimes parallel rise of both authoritarian neoliberalism and illiberal democracy.[32]

According to Esra Nartok's chapter, the neoliberal work on Islam in Turkey in the new millennium presents a way out of the traditional opposition of secular and religious approaches in the country and offers Indigenous alternatives to competing interpretations of the world religion from both within and outside Turkey that are less amenable to the neoliberal cause. Reto Hofmann and Aditya Balasubramanian explain how in Japan and India, culture and religion have been embraced in the effort to anchor neoliberalism in local contexts in expressed opposition to the Western spirit of individualism. Karin Fischer explains how in Guatemala and across Latin America, neoliberals helped build an alliance with conservative Catholicism in an effort to fight the progressive alliance of socialists and liberation theology.[33]

Local constellations and struggles in the various world regions necessarily differ, and yet they share the common objective of securing capitalist development and social integration with a particular focus on the preservation and advancement of what is defined as economic freedom. Social and cultural conservatism can be difficult to reconcile with liberal values, but many neoliberals have been keen from the beginning in their emphasis on evolution, rather than radical change, and on reconciliation with cultural and social conservatism.[34] Bruno Leoni's paper delivered at the first MPS meeting in Tokyo in 1966 provides a good example. The acting MPS president interpreted Confucian teaching of restricted (inner) freedom as freedom of actors to perform their own duty and said he "would even go [so] far as to suggest that Confucius could be fully eligible as a member of the Mont Pèlerin Society if he lived in our day."[35]

In a different vein, Antina von Schnitzler's chapter provides an excellent example of neoliberal investment in cultural change, which offered deracinated tools of selective inclusion (of entrepreneurial and self-sufficient Black people) in urban development. Jimmy Casas

Klausen and Paulo Chamon's chapter on Brazil shows the ability of neoliberals to tap into the aesthetics and culture of youth movements. In contrast to the "religious neoliberalism" of the elderly, the authors introduce us to a stunning merger of cultural conservatism and progressive identity concerns arguably most relevant to the younger generations of neoliberals, or what they call "ultraliberals." Both the rapprochement of neoliberalism with cultural tradition and the adaptation of cultural reform document the versatility of neoliberal movements in the pursuit of key objectives. Moving in different cultural directions at the same time produces or reinforces centrifugal forces within the neoliberal movement, no doubt. Certain alliances with religious right-wing or cultural liberals tend to preclude each other or require an improbable culture of tolerance.

NEOLIBERALISM, THINK TANKS, AND ACADEMIA

Closer to policy making, neoliberals are known to invest strongly in the dual relevance of knowledge and expertise, academic and political partisanship. The chapters on Guatemala by Karin Fischer and Montenegro by Mila Jonjić and Nenad Pantelić introduce readers to two universities dedicated as a whole to the neoliberal cause. In stark contrast to the traditional commitment to academic freedom and pluralism, these places have been developed into academic safe havens for a narrow range of neoliberal ideas, orientations, and teaching. While Hayek and the majority of MPS neoliberals still insisted in the earlier days of their community on the formal separation between intellectual deliberation at academic institutions and partisan efforts to exert influence via think tanks, the Marroquín University and the University of Donja Gorica demonstrate seamless upstream and downstream integration of neoliberal partisanship and academia.

Although the neoliberals of the Chicago school of economics, the Virginia school of public choice, the law and economics movement, and Freiburg's ordoliberalism certainly left strong marks in academic disciplines of law, economics, and political science, in particular, most, if not all traditional universities feature neoliberal scholarship next to varieties of competing theoretical and normative orientations. Neoliberals and their funding partners from corporations and corporate philanthropies felt the need to fight a certain amount of Marxism at public universities in the 1960s and 1970s, and it is unclear how academic pluralism will fare if much, if not most of academic life comes under the increasing influence of corporate interest groups and neoliberal agendas without counterweight. What alternative models of academic institutions that cease to commit to academic pluralism look like can be observed at "the Marro" in Guatemala, in particular.

Lars Mjøset's chapter on Icelandic neoliberalism adds another angle to the discussion. He shows how the university and think tanks can be substitutes for each other. Iceland's leading neoliberal intellectual, Hannes Gissurarson, first organized a think tank. The institute was discontinued when his university position offered equivalent space and resources during the heyday of Icelandic neoliberalism. But Gissurarson once again organized a think tank after the collapse of the Icelandic financial house of cards. The interplay of academic institutions and partisan think tanks and the expansion of each on the turf of the other still deserves a lot more attention. Prominent among the places still needing attention are the ESEADE Business School in Buenos Aires, Grove City College in Pennsylvania, and the University of Buckingham in the UK, for example, in addition to centers of neoliberal academic gravitas hitherto unknown. Even Germany's renowned Walter Eucken Institute in Freiburg, which counts Germany's Bundesbank among its long-standing financial supporters, still waits for a critical history. Apart from examinations of individual academic institutions, a lot of work remains to be done on academic associations such as the European Public Choice Society or the International Society for Institutional and Organizational Economics (SIOE, formerly known as the International Society for New Institutional Economics, ISNIE). While individual academic institutions provide harbors and hubs of neoliberal ideas, studying academic networks allows observing the broader institutionalization of neoliberal ideas within and across academic disciplines. While a lot of work has already been done on the discipline of economics,[36] the work on the important field of legal studies is still in the fledgling stages, for example.[37]

NEOLIBERALISM, AUTHORITARIANISM, AND DEMOCRACY

Since authoritarian forms of government have been almost synonymous with early neoliberalism in Latin America, in particular, a third theme of this collection is all but new. Since many neoliberals were outspoken about the need to constrain democracy, tensions between democracy and neoliberalism should come to nobody's surprise. The original liberal concern with majority rule resulted in the institutional protection of minorities. When economic freedom became the primary concern, however, minority protection has been turned into systematically constrained majority rule more generally, if not into upper-class minority rule: neoliberals subordinated questions of democratic sovereignty to the protection of economic liberty, which means that property rights, freedom of contract, and protections from government interference in commercial affairs are to be imposed on the people regardless of election results.

Three ways of obtaining this end in the framework of parliamentarian democracies have been observed by students of neoliberal regimes. "One is the reduction and blockade of the power resources of those actors that could challenge neoliberalism with alternatives; the second is the increase of the power resources of businesses interested in the continuity of neoliberalism; and the third is the institutionalization of neoliberal policies in a way that made them more difficult to reverse."[38] The widely celebrated honeymoon of democracy and capitalism following the end of dictatorships in Latin America and the transition from socialism to capitalism in the 1980s and 1990s[39] turned out to be fleeting. Following the rapid proliferation of neoliberal TINA politics ("There Is No Alternative") and the rise of the new economic constitutionalism, scholars observed the hollowing out of parliamentarian democracy[40] and democratic backsliding.[41]

While some of the most recent infringements of democratic rules by right-wing populist governments have been a response to the politics of cosmopolitan neoliberalism, the political aims pursued were mainly in the realm of culture and minorities. Central pillars of market-conforming democracy have remained unchallenged by the rise of cultural and social conservatism, no matter if we look at Brexit in the UK or Hungary under Viktor Orban. Still, neoliberals, much like those with competing worldviews, can, but do not have to support antidemocratic varieties of political rule. In Turkey, the group of organized neoliberals examined by Nartok split in the new millennium because some of the members did not want to go along with the authoritarian tendencies in the ruling Justice and Development Party they had previously supported. While the Russian neoliberals embraced authoritarianism as a prerequisite of neoliberal reforms and even looked favorably at Pinochet's Chile, according to Tobias Rupprecht, they bemoaned Putin's regime of repressed neoliberal opposition. Isabella Weber shows how willing and malleable neoliberals have been to advise Communist leaders in China. India's road to neoliberalism was paved by authoritarian rule back in the 1970s, as Aditya Balasubramanian shows, and has been advanced to the extent it has in conjunction with the present democratic backsliding of the Modi government. How the Modi regime will respond to the current wave of opposition to neoliberal reforms of agriculture will be an important indicator of the direction the country will go, in terms of both neoliberalism and democracy.

Even a more settled democratic regime such as Australia's is not immune to the antidemocratic challenge of neoliberalism. Jeremy Walker shows how fossil-fuel interest groups and the Murdoch press have taken the country hostage, leaving it ill prepared to respond to the key challenge of global warming and marked by the pathologies of the petrostate. In Australia and Brazil, the massive manipulation of the media, old and new, has arguably been most important in supporting ultraliberal political perspectives that incapacitate government planning—as in the United States. To be sure, neoliberalism does not have to coincide with illiberal democracy or authoritarian rule, and authoritarianism does not have to entail neoliberalism. We know enough about the varieties of neoliberalism and authoritarianism to reject such claims. But we also know the common origins and overlapping histories of neoliberalism and illiberal democracy.[42] And the propensity of neoliberalism to skepticism of democracy and to "thin" democracy have frequently made neoliberalism complicit with illiberal governments, and suggest shared responsibility for the outcome of the "low level equilibrium" of incomplete democracy and imperfect market economy in many countries.[43]

Both the priority of economic freedom and the ambivalent attitude toward democracy seem to cripple neoliberals and raise serious doubts about the capacity of neoliberalism to deal productively with problems such as global warming, migration, and human rights, as well as other effects of escalating social inequality. Even in countries in which neoliberal ambitions have been dethroned in dramatic fashion, such as Iceland (see Lars Mjøset in this volume) or Argentina, the legacy of neoliberal transformations remains strong in the shape of severe economic constraints.

GLOBAL NEOLIBERALISM TODAY AND TO COME

The history of neoliberalism is not over. Economic constitutionalism is difficult to remove, and the opposition to neoliberalism must still be considered highly fragmented. Neoliberal think-tank capacities, on the other hand, have been growing around the globe since the global financial crisis, both those of the "mainstream" mosaic neoliberalism camp of the Mont Pelerin Society related to the Atlas Network and those of the paleolibertarian network of the Mises Institutes. Atlas added about one hundred and fifty think tanks, many of them in the

Global South.[44] The Mises-Rothbard (paleolibertarian) split from the mainstream,[45] in the meantime, expanded under the umbrella of the Property and Freedom Society, founded by Hans-Hermann Hoppe in 2006. Under this umbrella, about thirty Mises Institutes have been set up around the world, albeit some were short-lived. Others, though, are quite agile, as documented in our chapter on Brazil. Support for the varieties of neoliberal think tanks may be subject to increasing competition, but cannot be considered to be in decline.

The contemporary challenges for neoliberalism result from the multiple crises of global capitalism, adding global warming and public health to the growing concern over financialization, stagnation, and the resulting increase in social inequality.[46] Socialism and industry-based trade unions are no longer the greatest domestic foe of neoliberalism in many countries, but new activism driven by social and labor movements united in opposition to it sometimes emerges in surprising strength, as demonstrated in India and Chile in 2020. How liberal or illiberal and how democratic neoliberalism will become or remain in response to contestations will be the subject of future studies. Within the neoliberal worldview, we will continue to find future-oriented[47] and reactionary[48] wings and instincts, and both are likely to continue playing important roles. The neoliberal core will have to offer more than economic freedom, "market-conforming" democracy (if any), communitarian individualism, and exclusionary solidarity when it comes to tackling increasingly urgent challenges related to global warming, species extinction, and resource depletion. If we take cues from the chapters in this volume, we can still expect more volatility and ambiguity from neoliberalism, not less.

1. Dieter Plehwe, Bernhard Walpen, and Gisela Neunhöffer, eds., *Neoliberal Hegemony: A Global Critique* (London: Routledge, 2006).

2. Philip Mirowski and Dieter Plehwe, eds., *The Road from Mont Pèlerin: The Making of the Neoliberal Thought Collective* (Cambridge, MA: Harvard University Press, 2009); Dieter Plehwe, Quinn Slobodian, and Philip Mirowski, eds., *Nine Lives of Neoliberalism* (London: Verso, 2020). Additional monographs, journal articles, and book chapters are cited in the Introduction.

3. Peter A. Hall, ed., *The Political Power of Economic Ideas: Keynesianism across Nations* (Princeton: Princeton University Press, 1989).

4. Albert O. Hirschman, "How the Keynesian Revolution Was Exported from the United States, and Other Comments," in Hall, ed., *The Political Power of Economic Ideas*, pp. 347–60.

5. Friedrich Stadler, *Studien zum Wiener Kreis: Ursprung, Entwicklung und Wirkung des Logischen Empirismus im Kontext* (Frankfurt am Main: Suhrkamp, 1997).

6. Rafael Khachaturian, "Studying the State: The Legacy of the Committee on States and Social Structures," *Items*, SSRC, September 22, 2020, https://items.ssrc.org/insights/studying-the-state-the-legacy-of-the-committee-on-states-and-social-structures.

7. Peter Evans, Dietrich Rueschemeyer, and Theda Skocpol, eds., *Bringing the State Back In* (Cambridge: Cambridge University Press, 1985).

8. Peter Hall and David Soskice, *Varieties of Capitalism: The Institutional Foundations of Comparative Advantage* (Oxford: Oxford University Press, 2001).

9. John Wilfred Meyer, Gili S. Drori, and Hokyu Hwang, *Globalization and Organizations* (Oxford: Oxford University Press, 2006).

10. Jacqueline Best, "The Quiet Failures of Early Neoliberalism: From Rational Expectations to Keynesianism in Reverse." *Review of International Studies* 46.5 (2020), pp. 594–612.

11. Beth A. Simmons, Frank Dobbin, and Geoffrey Garrett, eds., *The Global Diffusion of Markets and Democracy* (Cambridge: Cambridge University Press, 2008).

12. Bruce Kogut and J. Muir Macpherson, "The Decision to Privatize: Economists and the Construction of Ideas and Policies," in ibid., pp. 104–40.

13. Sonja Amadae, *Prisoners of Reason: Game Theory and Neoliberal Political Economy* (Cambridge, UK: Cambridge University Press, 2016); Nancy MacLean, Nancy, *Democracy in Chains: The Deep History of the Radical Right's Stealth Plan for America* (New York: Penguin, 2017).

14. Furthermore, the link between university affiliation and ideological orientation is tenuous. Chicago training may be a good proxy for neoliberal orientation in general, but the university's economics department also counts the Marxist development economist André Gunder Frank among its graduates.

15. Marie-Laure Djelic and Reza Mousavi, "How the Neoliberal Think Tank Went Global: The Atlas Network, 1981 to the Present," in Plehwe, Slobodian, and Mirowski, eds., *Nine Lives of Neoliberalism*, pp. 257–82.

16. Michael Zürn, "From Constitutional Rule to Loosely Coupled Spheres of Liquid Authority: A Reflexive Approach," *International Theory* 9.2 (2017), pp. 261–85.

17. Marie-Laure Djelic and Sigrid Quack, eds., *Transnational Communities: Shaping Global Economic Governance* (Cambridge: Cambridge University Press, 2010).

18. Ole Jacob Sending, *The Politics of Expertise: Competing for Authority in Global Governance* (Ann Arbor: University of Michigan Press, 2015).

19. Leonard Seabrooke and Lasse Folke Henriksen, eds., *Professional Networks in Transnational Governance* (Cambridge: Cambridge University Press, 2017).

20. Lasse Folke Henriksen and Leonard Seabrooke, "Transnational Organizing: Issue Professionals in Environmental Sustainability Networks," *Organization* 23.5 (2016), pp. 722–41, https://doi.org/10.1177/1350508415609140.

21. Cornel Ban, *Ruling Ideas: How Global Neoliberalism Goes Local* (Oxford: Oxford University Press, 2016); Marion Fourcade-Gourinchas and Sarah L. Babb, "The Rebirth of the Liberal Creed: Paths to Neoliberalism in Four Countries," *American Journal of Sociology* 108.3 (2002), pp. 533–79, https://doi.org/10.1086/367922.

22. Ban, *Ruling Ideas*, ch. 7, "Romania: Recurrent Coercion and Fast-Track Socialization," pp. 149–82.

23. Cornel Ban, Leonard Seabrooke, and Sarah Freitas, "Grey Matter in Shadow Banking: International Organizations and Expert Strategies in Global Financial Governance," *Review of International Political Economy* 23.6 (2016), pp. 1001–33.

24. John J. Miller, *A Gift of Freedom: How the John M. Olin Foundation Changed America* (San Francisco: Encounter, 2005).

25. Still the best statement of the postpositivist argumentative turn is in Frank Fischer and John Forrester, eds., *The Argumentative Turn in Policy Analysis and Planning* (Durham: Duke University Press, 1993).

26. For a full discussion, see Dieter Plehwe, "The Making of a Comprehensive Transnational Discourse Community," in Djelic and Quack, eds., *Transnational Communities*, pp. 305–26.

27. Dieter Plehwe, "Neoliberal Thought Collectives: Integrating Social Science and Intellectual History," in Damien Cahill, Melinda Cooper, Martijn Konings, and David Primrose, eds., *The SAGE Handbook of Neoliberalism* (London: Sage, 2018), pp. 85–97.

28. Samuel Moyn and Andrew Sartori, eds., *Global Intellectual History* (New York: Columbia University Press, 2013).

29. Geoffrey Geuens, "Les médiamorphoses du (néo)libéralisme: Propagande, idéologie dominante, pensée unique," *Quaderni* 72 (2010), pp. 47–48, http://journals.openedition.org/quaderni/484.

30. Stephanie L. Mudge, *Leftism Reinvented: Western Parties from Socialism to Neoliberalism* (Cambridge, MA: Harvard University Press, 2018); Elizabeth Humphrys, *How Labour Built Neoliberalism: Australia's Accord, the Labour Movement and the Neoliberal Project* (Leiden: Brill, 2019).

31. Steven Lukes, *Power: A Radical View* (London: Macmillan, 1974).

32. Aldo Madariaga, *Neoliberal Resilience: Lessons in Democracy and Development from Latin America and Eastern Europe* (Princeton: Princeton University Press, 2020).

33. Bethany Moreton, "Our Lady of Mont Pelerin: The 'Navarra School' of Catholic Neoliberalism," *Capitalism: A Journal of History and Economics* 2.1 (2021), pp. 88–153.

34. Ronald M. Hartwell, *A History of the Mont Pelerin Society* (Indianapolis:

Liberty Fund, 1995), p. 38. Karl Popper and Frank Knight's attack on the illiberalism of the clerics in the founding meeting's discussion of liberalism and religion at the same time shows that MPS neoliberalism was all but homogeneous.

35. Bruno Leoni, "Two Views of Liberty, Occidental and Oriental (?)," *Mises Institute Libertarian Papers* 1.5 (2009), https://mises.org/library/two-views-liberty-occidental-and-oriental.

36. Notably, Philip Mirowski, *Never Let a Serious Crisis Go to Waste: How Neoliberalism Survived the Financial Meltdown* (London: Verso, 2013), and Philip Mirowski and Edward Nik-Khah, *The Knowledge We Have Lost in Information: The History of Information in Modern Economics* (Oxford: Oxford University Press, 2017).

37. Honor Brabazon, ed., *Neoliberal Legality: Understanding the Role of Law in the Neoliberal Project* (London: Routledge, 2018).

38. Madariaga, *Neoliberal Resilience*, pp. 12–13.

39. Francis Fukuyama, *The End of History and the Last Man* (New York: Free Press, 1992).

40. Peter Mair, *Ruling the Void: The Hollowing of Western Democracy* (London: Verso, 2013).

41. Béla Greskovits, "The Hollowing and Backsliding of Democracy in East Central Europe," *Global Policy* 6.1 (2015), pp. 28–27.

42. Ray Kiely, "Assessing Conservative Populism: A New Double Movement or Neoliberal Populism?," *Development and Change* 51.2 (2020), pp. 398–417; Reijer Hendrikse, "Neo-illiberalism," *Geoforum* 95 (2018), pp. 169–72.

43. Béla Greskovits, *The Political Economy of Protest and Patience: East European and Latin American Transformations Compared* (Budapest: CEU Press, 1998).

44. Djelic and Mousavi, "How the Neoliberal Think Tank Went Global," p. 260.

45. Janek Wasserman, *The Marginal Revolutionaries: How Austrian Economists Fought the War of Ideas* (New Haven: Yale University Press, 2019).

46. Thomas Piketty, *Capital in the Twenty-First Century* (Cambridge, MA: Harvard University Press, 2014).

47. Karen Horn, Stefan Kolev, David M. Levy, and Sandra J. Peart,

"Liberalism in the 21st Century: Lessons from the Colloque Walter Lippmann," *Journal of Contextual Economics* 139 (2019), p. 181.

48. Wasserman, *Marginal Revolutionaries*, pp. 278–83.

Index

energy privatization, 208–209; fire-storms of 2019, 211; fossil assets, devaluation of, 212; fossil fuel export, 190, 198–99; fossil-neoliberal coali-tion, 207–208, 212; greenhouse emissions, 190; Greens, 207; infra-structure privatization, 206, 209; "Loans Affair," 200–201; national coal strike (1949), 197; neoliberal economic policy, 207; North West Shelf, 203, 207, 210; resource nation-alism, 199, 201, 202–203, 207; and zero-emissions economy, 212.

Australian, 193.

Australian Broadcasting Commission, 194.

Australian Broadcasting Corporation, 206, 209, 211.

Australian Heritage Commission Act, 199.

Australian Industry Greenhouse Net-work, 209.

Australian Institute for Progress, 213 n.10.

Australian Institute of Directors, 202.

Australian Labor Party, 196, 203, 207, 209.

Australian Mining Industry Council, 200, 205.

"Australian Settlement," 190–91.

Australian Taxpayers Alliance, 213 n.10.

Austria, 290.

Austrian School, 18, 112, 231, 235–36, 261, 278.

Authoritarianism, 123, 137 n.68, 252, 267, 344–46.

Aven, Petr, 117.

Ayau, Inés, 265.

Ayau, Manuel, 8, 18, 251, 252–53, 255–57, 259–60, 262, 264–68.

BALASUBRAMANIAN, ADITYA, 13, 80, 341, 345.

Ballieu, William, 193.

Ban, Cornel, 54, 338.

Band Baaja Baaraat, 58–59.

Bank of England, 195, 324.

Bank of New South Wales, 197, 204.

Bao, Tong, 123.

Barry, Norman, 91, 92, 93, 98.

Barwick, Garfield, 216 n.40.

"Basic Economic Policy" (Shenoy), 13, 62.

Bauer, Peter, 13, 62.

Baugur, 318.

Bayly, C. A., 55.

Bebbington, Anthony, 190.

Becker, Gary, 102 n.19.

Bedford, A. C., 192.

Belotserkovskij, Vadim, 120.

Beltrão, Helio, 9–10, 17, 228, 230, 231–33, 235, 242.

Benegas Lynch, Alberto, Jr., 259–60.

Bennelong Society, 208.

Berger, Óscar, 264, 265.

Berlin, Isaiah, 84.

Bernart, Cris, 241.

Berzeg, Kazım, 87.

Bhagwati, Jagdish, 66–67.

Bharatiya Janata Party, 59, 69–70.

BHP, *see* Broken Hill Proprietary.

Biden, Joe, 211.

BJP, *see* Bharatiya Janata Party.

Black Lives Matter, 240, 242.

Blair Athol, 204.

Block, Walter, 235, 242–43.

Bloomington school, 261.

Boettke, Peter J., 265.

Bogomolov, Oleg, 116.

Boletim da Liberdade, 223.

Bolsonaro, Jair, 9, 223, 226, 229, 230, 238.

Bonython, John, 205.

Economics, Finance, and Business (UDG).

Financial crisis of 2008, 19, 53, 109, 303–304, 323–24, 326.

Financial Supervision Authority (Iceland), 317, 322.

Fiscal constitutionalism, 345, 346.

Fischer, Karin, 341, 342.

Fisher, Antony, 79, 205.

Fisher, Malcolm, 205.

Fisheries Iceland, 315, 316.

Fisheries Management Act (1990), 314–16.

Fitzgerald, Thomas Michael, 201.

Fitzgerald Report, 204.

Fleck, Ludwik, 339.

Foreign Trade Regimes and Economic Development: India (Srinivasan), 67.

Fórum da Liberdade, 226, 233.

Forum of Free Enterprise, 69.

Fossil capital, vs climate science, 189, 193, 206, 209.

Foundation for Economic Education, 18, 61, 204, 226, 256, 262.

Foundation Francisco Marroquín, 260.

Fox Television, 193.

Fracking, 212.

Fraga, Armínio, 229.

Francisco Marroquín University, 18, 19, 251, 260, 268, 289–90, 336, 342, 343; and academic freedom, 261–62; campus, 253–54; curriculum, 261–62; faculty, in politics, 265–66; founding of, 253; funding, 258, 260; institutional affiliations, 260–61; Instituto Fe y Libertad, 265; internal organization, 258; Liberty Fund colloquia, 263; programs, 260.

Franeta, Slobodan, 291.

Frank, André Gunder, 349 n.12.

Frankel, Francine, 63.

Frankfurt Institute, 147.

Fraser, Malcolm, 203, 206–207.

Free Democratic Party, 15.

Free Democratic Party (Germany), 270 n.19.

Free Economic Review, 61.

Freeman (magazine), 61.

Free Market Road Show, 290.

Freiburg school, 142, 154.

Fréttablaðið, 318.

Friedman, David, 307.

Friedman, Milton, 20, 43, 53, 62, 87, 114, 154, 224, 303, 305; in Australia, 200, 208; and Brazil, 226; *Capitalism and Freedom*, 307; and China, 141, 151–52, 155; on German price reform of 1948, 143–44; and Guatemala, 265; and Japan, 40, 44; monetarism, 39, 151, 152; and radical price reform, 140; in Soviet context, 121, 125, 131.

Friedman, Rose, 151.

Friedrich Naumann Foundation, 91, 102 n.19, 257.

Friends of Universidad Francisco Marroquín, 260.

Fudan University, 145.

Fukuzawa, Yūkichi, 32.

G-17, 290.

G-77, 198.

Gaidar, Yegor, 14, 114, 115, 116, 120, 124, 126, 127–28.

Game, Phillip, 196.

Gandhi, Indira, 64.

Gazeta do Povo, 233.

GCN, *see* Global Communications Network.

Gelb, Stephen, 169.

General Electric, 192, 204.

George Mason University, 260, 286, 290.

Georgia, Republic of, 253.
German Democratic Republic, 131.
Geyser Crisis, 323–24.
Giersch, Herbert, 155.
Gill, Stephen, 10.
Gillard, Julia, 210.
Gissurarson, Hannes Hólmsteinn, 20, 21, 303–307, 308, 310, 311, 312, 313–14, 315–16, 318–21, 343; academic work, 304, 305–307; on financial crisis, 324; *How Can Iceland Become the Richest Country in the World?*, 316; *The Impact of Tax Raises on Economic Growth and Living Standards*, 313; and Independence Party, 324; *Libertarianism Is Humanitarianism*, 306; "Miracle on Iceland," 303, 313; on Nordic models, 326; and Oddsson, 306, 307, 321, 325–26; *Political Philosophy*, 306; *There Ain't No Such Thing as a Free Lunch*, 306; *Twists in the Tales*, 306; *Where Does Man Belong?*, 306.
Glasnost, 111, 115, 120.
Glazkov, Grigorij, 115.
Global Communications Network, 291.
Global Development Network, 279.
Global warming, 198, 206, 209, 346.
Global Warming Policy Foundation, 203.
Gomes, Ciro, 239.
Goodrich, Pierre, 256; *Education in a Free Society*, 256.
Gorbachev, Mikhail, 115, 116, 118, 119, 120, 126.
Gordon, Andrew, 34.
Gosplan, 113, 117, 119.
Graduate Institute for International Studies, Geneva, 192.
Gramsci, Antonio, 268.
Granai, Mario, 259.
Great Depression, 195–97.
Great Society, 166.

Green, Marshall, 202.
Greenhouse effect, 207.
Gregg, Samuel, 265.
Greiner, Nick, 208.
Grímsson, Ólafur, 319.
Grove City College, 343.
Grupo Abril, 229.
Gu, Mu, 146, 148.
Guatemala, 18; Catholic Church in, 252; central bank reform, 263–64; CIA intervention (1954), 252; constitution, 266; death squads, 266; "dirty war," 252; Fatherland League, 266; Law of Free Negotiation of Currencies, 264; military aid to, 267; privatization, 264; ProReforma movement, 266; taxation, 264–65.
Guatemala Freedom Foundation, 267.
Guedes, Paulo, 9, 229.
Guevara, Che, 237.
Gujarat University, 61.
Gunnarsson, Kjartan, 20, 304, 305.
Gutiérrez, Luis Canella, 259.
Gutowski, Armin, 141, 149–51, 152, 154.

H. R. NICHOLLS SOCIETY, 208.
Haarde, Geir H., 20, 304, 321–22.
Haberler, Gottfried, 192, 257.
Hall, Peter, 53, 334–35.
Halldor (Gissurarson), 305.
Hancock, Lang, 204.
Hanke, Steve H., 281–82; *Crnogorska marka*, 282.
Hardt, Michael, 10.
Hartwell, Ronald, 205.
Hartwich, Oliver, 191–92.
Hawke, Robert, 207.
Hayek, F. A., 7, 8, 18, 20, 53, 62, 191, 303, 304, 333; academic vs partisan activity, 342; Australia tour, 200, 205, 206; in Brazil, 226, 235; on central

planning, 122, 142; and chain of liberal institutes, 79; "Council of Elders," 266; critique of "unlimited democracy," 206; on culture, 165–66, 171; denationalization of money, 282; and early history of MPS, 192; fiscal constitutionalism, 266; in Guatemala, 257; IPA speech (1976), 206; and Japan, 30, 35–36, 38, 40; and morals of the market, 31; Nobel speech (1974), 206; on pretense of knowledge, 122; *Prices and Production*, 61; and rationalism, 164–65; "The Rebirth of Liberalism," 61; *The Road to Serfdom*, 86, 123, 142, 307; on socialism, 146; in South Africa, 165, 171, 175–76; and Soviet thinkers, 114, 121, 125, 131; "spontaneous order," 41, 43, 166, 176, 315; on tradition, 166, 171; and Turkey, 84, 86, 88; and Unification Church, 46; on welfare state, 326; writings of (course syllabi), 261.
Hayek Foundation (Slovakia), 279.
Hayek Institute, 290.
Hayek Society, Moscow, 126.
Hazlitt, Henry, 256, 257, 261.
Heartland Institute, 206.
Heinrich Böll Stiftung, 289.
Henriksen, Lasse, 338.
Henry Hazlitt Center, 261.
Herald and Weekly Times newsgroup, 194.
Herald of Freedom, 291.
Heritage Foundation, 8, 260, 276, 290.
Heritage Society, 126.
Hindu Equilibrium, The (Lal), 9.
Hindu religion, 9, 59, 80.
Hirschman, Albert O., 334–35.
Hitler, Adolf, 45, 147.
Hobsbawm, Eric, 251.
Hocking, Douglas, 205.

Hoernlé, Alfred, 167–69.
Hofmann, Reto, 12, 341.
Holiday, Fernando, 239–40, 241.
Hoppe, Hans-Hermann, 235, 347.
Howard, John, 203, 209.
Huerta de Soto, Jesús, 288.
Human Science Research Council, South Africa, 181.
Humphrys, Elizabeth, 190.
Hungarian Academy of Sciences, 117.
Hungary, 116.
Hutt, William H., 170, 257.
Hydrocarbon fuels, 189, 190, 191, 198–99, 201, 203, 212.
Hytten, Torleiv, 16, 195–97, 204.

IBÁRGÜEN, GIANCARLO, 263, 264.
ICC, *see* International Chamber of Commerce.
Iceland, 346; banking sector, 319–20, 322, 323; currency devaluation, 309–10, 311–12, 313, 317, 320; deregulation, 304, 317, 319, 322; economic diversification, 316–17, 318; educational system, 308; government broadcasting monopoly, 305; industrialization, 308; inflation, 310, 311, 313; labor, 308, 309, 311, 312–13, 327; marine resource management, 309, 312, 314–16; National Reconciliation (1990), 313; pensions, 312, 313, 324; privatization, 304, 313, 316–17, 318, 320, 322, 323; religion, 308; stock market, 319, 320, 321, 322, 332 n.53.
Icelandic Association of Fishing Vessels, 315.
IEA, *see* Institute of Economic Affairs.
Independence Party (Iceland), 20, 21, 304, 305, 308, 309, 310–11, 312, 313, 320, 321, 324, 325, 326.
India, 347; agricultural reform, 345; and

Near Futures series design by Julie Fry

Typesetting by Meighan Gale

Printed and bound by Maple Press